The Palgrave Macmillan Transnational History Series

Series Editors: **Akira Iriye**, Professor of History at Harvard University, and **Rana Mitter**, Professor of the History and Politics of Modern China at the University of Oxford

This distinguished series seeks to: develop scholarship on the transnational connections of societies and peoples in the nineteenth and twentieth centuries; provide a forum in which work on transnational history from different periods, subjects, and regions of the world can be brought together in fruitful connection; and explore the theoretical and methodological links between transnational and other related approaches such as comparative history and world history.

Editorial Board: **Thomas Bender**, University Professor of the Humanities, Professor of History, and Director of the International Center for Advanced Studies, New York University; **Jane Carruthers**, Professor of History, University of South Africa; **Mariano Plotkin**, Professor, Universidad Nacional de Tres de Febrero, Buenos Aires, and member of the National Council of Scientific and Technological Research, Argentina; **Pierre-Yves Saunier**, Researcher at the Centre National de la Recherche Scientifique, France and Visiting Professor at the University of Montreal; **Ian Tyrrell**, Professor of History, University of New South Wales

Titles include:

Gregor Benton and Edmund Terence Gomez
THE CHINESE IN BRITAIN, 1800–PRESENT
Economy, Transnationalism and Identity

Manu Bhagavan
INDIA AND THE QUEST FOR ONE WORLD
The Peacemakers

Sugata Bose and Kris Manjapra (*editors*)
COSMOPOLITAN THOUGHT ZONES
South Asia and the Global Circulation of Ideas

Sebastian Conrad and Dominic Sachsenmaier (*editors*)
COMPETING VISIONS OF WORLD ORDER
Global Moments and Movements, 1880s–1930s

Martin Conway and Kiran Klaus Patel (*editors*)
EUROPEANIZATION IN THE TWENTIETH CENTURY
Historical Approaches

Joy Damousi, Mariano Ben Plotkin (*editors*)
THE TRANSNATIONAL UNCONSCIOUS
Essays in the History of Psychoanalysis and Transnationalism

Desley Deacon, Penny Russell and Angela Woollacott (*editors*)
TRANSNATIONAL LIVES
Biographies of Global Modernity, 1700–present

Jonathan Gantt
IRISH TERRORISM IN THE ATLANTIC COMMUNITY, 1865–1922

Abigail Green and Vincent Viaene (*editors*)
RELIGIOUS INTERNATIONALS IN THE MODERN WORLD

Pawel Goral
COLD WAR RIVALRY AND THE PERCEPTION OF THE AMERICAN WEST

Per Högselius
RED GAS
Russia and the Origins of European Energy Dependence

Eric Hotta
PAN-ASIANISM AND JAPAN'S WAR, 1931–45

Robert David Johnson (*editor*)
ASIA PACIFIC IN THE AGE OF GLOBALIZATION

Martin Klimbe and Joachim Scharloth (*editors*)
1968 IN EUROPE
A History of Protest and Activism, 1956–77

Erika Kuhlman
RECONSTRUCTING PATRIARCHY AFTER THE GREAT WAR
Women, Gender and Postwar Reconciliation between Nations

Deep Kanta Lahiri Choudhury
TELEGRAPHIC IMPERIALISM
Crisis and Panic n the Indian Empire, c. 1830–1920

Per Lundin and Thomas Kaiserfeld (*editors*)
THE MAKING OF EUROPEAN CONSUMPTION
Facing the American Challenge

Bruce Mazlish
THE IDEA OF HUMANITY IN THE GLOBAL ERA

Nicola Pizzolato
CHALLENGING GLOBAL CAPITALISM
Labor Migration, Radical Struggle, and Urban Change in Detroit and Turin

Glenda Sluga
THE NATION, PSYCHOLOGY, AND INTERNATIONAL POLITICS, 1870–1919

Giles Scott-Smith
WESTERN ANTI-COMMUNISM AND THE INTERDOC NETWORK
Cold War Internationale

Mark Tilse
TRANSNATIONALISM IN THE PRUSSIAN EAST
From National Conflict to Synthesis, 1871–1914

Luc van Dongen, Stéphanie Roulin, and Giles Scott-Smith (*editors*)
TRANSNATIONAL ANTI-COMMUNISM AND THE COLD WAR
Agents, Activities, and Networks

**The Palgrave Macmillan Transnational History Series
Series Standing Order ISBN 978–0–230–50746–3 Hardback
978–0–230–50747–0 Paperback**
(*outside North America only*)

You can receive future titles in this series as they are published by placing a standing order. Please contact your bookseller or, in case of difficulty, write to us at the address below with your name and address, the title of the series and the ISBN quoted above.

Customer Services Department, Macmillan Distribution Ltd, Houndmills, Basingstoke, Hampshire RG21 6XS, England

The Making of European Consumption
Facing the American Challenge

Edited by

Per Lundin
Associate Professor, Uppsala University, Sweden

and

Thomas Kaiserfeld
Professor, Lund University, Sweden

Editorial matter and selection © Per Lundin and Thomas Kaiserfeld 2015
Remaining chapters © Contributors 2015
Softcover reprint of the hardcover 1st edition 2015 978-1-137-37403-5

All rights reserved. No reproduction, copy or transmission of this publication may be made without written permission.

No portion of this publication may be reproduced, copied or transmitted save with written permission or in accordance with the provisions of the Copyright, Designs and Patents Act 1988, or under the terms of any licence permitting limited copying issued by the Copyright Licensing Agency, Saffron House, 6–10 Kirby Street, London EC1N 8TS.

Any person who does any unauthorized act in relation to this publication may be liable to criminal prosecution and civil claims for damages.

The authors have asserted their rights to be identified as the authors of this work in accordance with the Copyright, Designs and Patents Act 1988.

First published 2015 by
PALGRAVE MACMILLAN

Palgrave Macmillan in the UK is an imprint of Macmillan Publishers Limited, registered in England, company number 785998, of Houndsmills, Basingstoke, Hampshire, RG21 6XS

Palgrave Macmillan in the US is a division of St Martin's Press LLC, 175 Fifth Avenue, New York, NY 10010.

Palgrave is the global academic imprint of the above companies and has companies and representatives throughout the world.

Palgrave® and Macmillan® are registered trademarks in the United States, the United Kingdom, Europe and other countries.

ISBN 978-1-349-47680-0   ISBN 978-1-137-37404-2 (eBook)
DOI 10.1057/9781137374042

This book is printed on paper suitable for recycling and made from fully managed and sustained forest sources. Logging, pulping and manufacturing processes are expected to conform to the environmental regulations of the country of origin.

A catalogue record for this book is available from the British Library.

Library of Congress Cataloging-in-Publication Data
The making of European consumption : facing the American challenge / [edited by] Per Lundin, Thomas Kaiserfeld.

  pages cm. — (Palgrave Macmillan transnational history series)
Includes bibliographical references.

  1. Consumption (Economics)—Europe—20th century. 2. Consumers—Europe—History—20th century. 3. New products—Europe—History—20th century. 4. Manufactures—Europe—History—20th century. 5. United States—Foreign public opinion, European. 6. United States—Relations—Europe. 7. Europe—Relations—United States. I. Lundin, Per, 1971–   II. Kaiserfeld, Thomas, 1964–
 HC240.9.C6M35 2015
 339.4'7094—dc23   2014038802

Typeset by MPS Limited, Chennai, India.

Transferred to Digital Printing in 2015

Contents

List of Figures	vi
Series Editors' Preface	x
Acknowledgements	xii
Notes on Contributors	xiv

Introduction 1
Per Lundin

1 Negotiating American Modernity in Twentieth-Century Europe 17
   Mary Nolan

2 Americanization as Creolized Imaginary: The Statue
   of Liberty During the Cold War 45
   David Nye

3 Forging Europe's Foodways: The American Challenge 65
   Karin Zachmann

4 Tackling Norwegian Cold: The Breakthrough of Home Freezing 89
   Terje Finstad, Stig Kvaal, and Per Østby

5 Americanization and Authenticity: Italian Food Products and
   Practices in the 1950s and 1960s 111
   Emanuela Scarpellini

6 Love and Hate in Industrial Design: Europe's
   Design Professionals and America in the 1950s 134
   Kjetil Fallan

7 Confronting the Lure of American Tourism: Modern
   Accommodation in the Netherlands 157
   Adri A. Albert de la Bruhèze

8 Exploring European Travel: The Swedish Package Tour 178
   Thomas Kaiserfeld

9 Coping with Cars, Families, and Foreigners:
   Swedish Postwar Tourism 200
   Per Lundin

Select Bibliography 229

Index 247

List of Figures

2.1 As part of the 1876 Centennial Exposition in Philadelphia, the Statue of Liberty's arm and torch were erected as a special exhibit. The intention was to help raise funds for erecting the statue as a whole. (Courtesy of Library of Congress, Prints & Photographs Division.)   53

2.2 This cartoon, entitled "Playing with Fire," depicts South Africa's prime minister as toying with the torch, which represents equality. Note that this use of the Statue of Liberty has little to do with the United States. (Source: London *Daily Telegraph*, 1967.)   56

2.3 Artist Joseph Pennell's 1918 poster advertised bonds. "That Liberty Shall Not Perish" references the last line of the Gettysburg Address: "…that government of the people, by the people, for the people, shall not perish from the earth." (Courtesy of Library of Congress, Prints & Photographs Division.)   59

3.1 The U.S. Food for Peace Program promised to deliver world peace through the provision of food. This chart shows the global distribution of Food for Peace shipments from 1955 to 1963. (Source: George S. McGovern, *War against Want: America's Food for Peace Program* [New York, 1964], 134.)   73

3.2 Via the European Productivity Agency, American experts worked with Europeans to standardize food-related processes from production to marketing to packaging. This photo represents a scene from the European Exhibition on Prepacking of Fresh Fruits and Vegetables of 1958. (Source: EPA, Project no. 372: *Pre-Packaging for Fruit and Vegetables. Report of the European Conference and Exhibition held in London* [Paris 1958], 107.)   77

3.3 To some experts, irradiated food appeared to be on the verge of entering the market in the 1950s. Featured here: an irradiation canal containing spent fuel elements from the reactor at the Nuclear Energy Study Center in Mol, Belgium. (Source: European Productivity Agency,

Project No. 396: *Report of Working Conference*
[Paris, 1959], 128.)   81

4.1 In this photo, two women place food in their freezer-lockers. The plain, non-branded packaging suggests that they have prepared the food themselves. (Source: Tröndelag Folk Museum, The Schröder archive.)   91

4.2 In this advertisement for the manufacturer Aanonsen, the headline reads: "Aanonsen Home Freezer: The Modern Storehouse"—a portrayal of the home freezer as a continuation of traditional storage practices. (Source: Aanonsen Fabrikker, "Aanonsen hjemmefryser: Det modern stabbur," *Husmorbladet*, October 24, 1959.)   100

4.3 In this ad, the home freezer contains mostly industrially produced frozen foods. For Europeans, this was not the norm: freezers were used primarily to store home-produced foods. (Source: "På kjøkkenveien" [Mandal RadioElektro, 1964].)   104

5.1 In the case of refrigerators, large companies in Italy did not invest significantly in the new sector. For for several years, Fiat produced refrigerators under the Westinghouse license before ceasing production. The victors in the Italian market were small players. (Source: *La Cucina Italiana*, July 1957, 598.)   118

5.2 Featured here: one version of the modern "American" kitchen within an ideal home. Italian women approached the American kitchen with caution. In fact, the women of Italy domesticated American elements, absorbing them into the traditional Italian vision of the kitchen. (Source: *La Cucina Italiana*, July 1957, 603.)   125

5.3 Despite the efforts of manufacturers and advertisers, consumers responded in different ways to newfangled American products. Italian consumers happened to be enthusiastic about margarine—and adopted it as part of their traditional meals. (Source: *La Cucina Italiana*, October 1958, 950.)   129

6.1 Norwegian designers understood both mass production and plastics technology—despite the controversy surrounding them. Pictured here: allegedly the world's first telephone made entirely from thermoplastics. Designed by Arne E. Holm and Johan Christian Bjerknes, manufactured by Elektrisk

	Bureau (1953). Photo: Cato Normann. Courtesy of the Norwegian Telecom Museum.)	140
6.2	In 1953, the official U.S. design-propaganda machine made landfall in Scandinavia. Pictured here: the *American Design for Home and Decorative Use* exhibit, on the first leg of its tour, in Oslo. (Photo: Karl Teigen. Courtesy of the Norwegian Museum of Science and Technology.)	145
6.3	In the 1950s, fiberglass leisure boats emerged as a market for the Norwegian plastics industry. In this photo, a Skibsplast Seamaster 15' (1958), inspired by American boat magazines, skims the waters of a fjord. (Courtesy of the Norwegian Museum of Science and Technology.)	147
6.4	The Nordic countries promoted their design internationally. Perhaps the most celebrated event: *Design in Scandinavia— An Exhibition of Objects for the Home*, which toured the U.S. and Canada from 1954 to 1957. Featured here: the illustration of a Norwegian interior included in the introduction to the exhibit catalog.	151
7.1	Dutch tourist organizations frowned on the "American leisure activities" sponsored by British-run Butlins holiday camps, featured in this photo. The Dutch feared these activities would encourage "irresponsible and disorderly behavior" on the part of working-class tourists. (Courtesy of Butlins Archives.)	162
7.2	The American hotel represented a decidedly modernist blueprint, which became controversial in Europe: each country had its own hotel traditions, standards, and architecture. Pictured here: a quintessentially American Statler Hotel room of the 1930s, complete with studio bed. (Courtesy of Hospitality Industry Archives, University of Houston.)	164
8.1	This graph shows the flow of non-scheduled civil air traffic between European countries in 1965. The numbers relate to units of 100,000 passengers; only volumes of 100,000 passengers appear on the chart. (Source: Arne Rosenberg, Air *Travel within Europe*, The National Swedish Consumer Council [Stockholm: Norstedts, 1970], 22.)	185
9.1	The hostel offered low-cost, communal accommodation with minimal amenities. Originally, hostels served	

List of Figures   ix

	biking tourists, especially youth. Often, these simple accommodations were located in rural settings—in this case, a farm building. (Source: Nordiska museet, Swedish Tourist Association's Archive.)	202
9.2	The Swedish Tourist Association's chairman, Arthur Lindhagen (in the middle), with the association's managing director, Carl-Julius Anrick, and his wife, Calla Anrick. Taken at the inauguration of the first Swedish hostel in the town of Gränna: May, 1933. (Source: Nordiska museet, Swedish Tourist Association's Archive.)	210
9.3	These two maps compare the number of "bed nights"—occupancies—at hostels in Europe and the U.S. in 1949. The figures reinforce the idea of the hostel as a primarily European phenomenon. (Source: Uppsala University Library's Manuscript Collections, Calla Anrick's Archive, box 7.)	212–13
9.4	In the postwar period, the hostel's "family room" replaced the hostel dormitory, which had accommodated men and women in separate rooms. Aside from being updated in various ways, hostels remained simple accommodations. (Source: *Svenska Turistföreningens årsbok* (2004), 27.)	221

Series Editors' Preface

Historians have been paying increasing attention to such phenomena as cross-border movements, encounters, and interactions. In doing so, they have made use of analytical terms like interconnectedness, blending, and hybridity. These are all concepts that emphasize movement and transformation and are in sharp contrast to more traditional ideas such as identity, authenticity, order, and system maintenance, all of which assume most societies and nations are basically unique and stable entities.

The essays in this volume exemplify the current scholarly emphasis on movement and transformation rather than stability and order. The chapters describe post-1945 European societies that transformed themselves as they interacted with American people, goods, and ideas—and in the process making American society "creolized" or hybrid. The key here is to recognize that neither "Europe" nor "America" is a fixed and static entity. Each keeps changing at all times, so the important question is how both Europe and the United States transformed themselves through their mutual contact. Of course, this is not a simple question and must be understood at various levels: geopolitical, economic, cultural, and social. The conventional literature tends to focus on the Cold War as the overarching framework for the age, but the recent scholarship has helped bring into the picture various other themes, for instance economic globalization. In retrospect, we may note that globalization was a far more extensive historical development that changed the way people everywhere lived, whereas the Cold War was a more traditional geopolitical drama, part of the story of "the rise and fall of the great powers."

Globalization, of course, was not limited to the economic sphere. It involved social and cultural interactions across borders, eventually leading to the building of a more and more transnational world. Nations, national identities, and nationalistic emotions remain, and some even argue that the twenty-first century is, if anything, even more driven by parochial, nation-centric forces that are now far more widespread than ever before. But it must be noted that nationalism is never a static phenomenon; just like everything else, it keeps changing, and change today is driven as much by global forces as by local conditions. In fact, these two are closely interconnected.

The essays in this volume focus on European–U.S. transnational linkages and show how these linkages "hybridized" both Europe and America. The contributors write about "hybrid solutions," "hybrid forms of domestic consumption," "Americanization as creolization," "hybrid consumption regimes," and the like as European societies sought to define their postwar economic and social affairs by turning to the American example. These affairs ranged from production to consumption, and from architecture to tourism. But there was never a wholesale Americanization of Europe but rather "hybrid solutions," resulting from the constant engagement between Americans and Europeans. In the process, it is not surprising that "authenticity" steadily gave way to a broader definition of self-identity. What a contributor calls "pan-European identity" became Euro-American or Atlantic identity. But ultimately, such identities would come to matter less than hybridity. What is frequently referred to as Americanization, therefore, is better understood as hybridization. Of course, hybridization occurred as much within Europe as between Europe and the United States, as some of the chapters point out. We may add that hybridization is really a global process, a key aspect of transnationalization. In the end, therefore, we reach the phenomenon of global transformation. The globe has been undergoing the process of hybridization for centuries, and to understand European–American interactions in that framework makes an important contribution to transnational history.

Akira Iriye
Rana Mitter

Acknowledgements

This book was written under the auspices of the EUROCORES research program, "Technology and the Making of Europe, 1850 to the Present" and its collaborative research project, "European 'Ways of Life' in the American Century" (EUWOL), funded by the European Science Foundation (ESF). Since 2006, we have worked together in an international network supported by the ESF as well as by several national research councils.

Two colleagues have been particularly supportive of this book project. Throughout the process, Ruth Oldenziel and Mikael Hård have commented on various sections and chapters as well discussed with us the content in general—never complaining about the barrage of questions and queries. Early in the process, Milena Veenis was pivotal in getting this book off the ground. Adri Albert de la Bruhèze contributed generously throughout the book's evolution. At a decisive stage, Phil Scranton provided us with invaluable comments. The book was conceived at several workshops and conferences (in Tours, Lisbon, Amsterdam, Stockholm, and Sofia) organized by participants of the EUROCORES research program. We are grateful to have benefitted from the support of Marc Ferrière le Vayer and Dobrinka Parusheva, among others.

We would also like to thank Esra Akçan, Liesbeth Bervoets, Silvia Cassamagnaghi, Els De Vos, Florence Hachez-Leroy, Emiliya Karaboeva, Iliyana Marcheva-Atanasova, Giovanni Moretto, Elitsa Stoilova, Michael Wagner, Jean-Pierre Williot, and Meglena Zlatkova for their contributions and their support at various stages in the process of writing this book. Excerpts have been presented at seminars at the Division of History of Science, Technology and Environment at The Royal Institute of Technology in Stockholm, as well as at Uppsala Science and Technology Studies Center at Uppsala University. These occasions yielded valuable comments on many aspects of the manuscript.

Later in the process, anonymous reviewers at Palgrave provided important feedback and offered alternative approaches, which have strengthened our arguments considerably. Lisa Friedman did a superb job of making the manuscript cogent and consistent, and giving the prose both clarity and eloquence. Finally, the editors at Palgrave, Jenny McCall and Holly Tyler, have helped us through the complex and lengthy process of gathering the disparate parts of the book into a unified, well-aligned volume. With the help of all of you, the texts in this book have improved considerably, as individual chapters and as a whole. We, the editors, are nevertheless responsible for any remaining errors and inconsistencies.

The editors, contributing authors, and publishers wish to thank the following organizations for permission to reproduce copyrighted material: the Library of Congress, Prints & Photographs Division; Aanonsen A/S; Alcatel-Lucent Norway A/S; Sverresborg folkemuseum, the Schrøder Collection; La Cucina Italiana; Telemuseet and Cato Normann; Norsk Teknisk Museum and Teigens Fotoatelier; the National Library of Norway; Norstedts förlagsgrupp and Statens konsumentråd; Nordiska Museet, Uppsala University Library, and Svenska turistföreningen.

Every effort has been made to find rights' holders; if any have been inadvertently overlooked, the publishers will gladly make the necessary arrangements.

Notes on Contributors

Adri A. Albert de la Bruhèze is Assistant Professor of History of Technology at the University of Twente (the Netherlands), from which he received his PhD in 1992. From 1993 to 2002, he was the editorial secretary of the Dutch national research program Technology in the Netherlands in the Twentieth Century (TIN-20). He coedited the seven-volume book series *Techniek in Nederland in de Twintigste Eeuw* (Technology in the Netherlands in the Twentieth Century) (1998–2003), and *Manufacturing Technology, Manufacturing Consumers* (2009).

Kjetil Fallan is Professor of Design History at the University of Oslo. He is the author of *Design History: Understanding Theory and Method* (2010). He edited *Scandinavian Design: Alternative Histories* (2012), and co-edited (with Grace Lees-Maffei) *Made in Italy: Rethinking a Century of Italian Design* (2013). His numerous journal articles have appeared in the *Journal of Design History*, *Design Issues*, *Design and Culture*, *History and Technology*, *Enterprise and Society*, *Architectural Theory Review*, and *Modern Italy*, among other publications. Professor Fallan is an editor of the *Journal of Design History*.

Terje Finstad is a researcher and lecturer in Science and Technology Studies at the Norwegian University of Science and Technology. Previously, he worked on the history of genetic engineering in Norway, the salmon-farming industry, the evolution of the frozen-food chain in Norway, and the history of vermin. Currently, he is researching the history of food safety.

Thomas Kaiserfeld was Professor of History of Science and Technology at the Royal Institute of Technology in Stockholm from 2007 to 2010. Since then, he has held the position of Professor of History of Ideas and Sciences at Lund University, Sweden. Apart from the history of tourism and consumption studies, his academic interests include the history of science and technology in the eighteenth century. His most recent book is *Legitimizing ESS: Big Science as a Collaboration Across Boundaries* (2013, co-edited with Tom O'Dell). He has published articles in *Technology and Culture*, *Eighteenth-Century Studies*, and the *Journal of Tourism History*, among other journals. Since 2009, he has been a member of the executive committee of the International Committee for the History of Technology.

Stig Kvaal is Associate Professor of Technology and Science Studies at the Norwegian University of Science and Technology, Centre for Technology and Society. He received his PhD in Science Policy from the same university. His research areas include the history of food and kitchen technologies, consumption and science policy. His most recent published work focuses on the Norwegian chocolate industry. Co-written with Per Østby, the chapter, "Something Old, Something New, Something Stolen, Something Blue: Designing a Chocolate Bar," appeared in *Scandinavian Design: Alternative Histories* (2012).

Per Lundin is Associate Professor of Economic History at Uppsala University. He received his PhD in History of Technology from the Royal Institute of Technology in Stockholm. His published dissertation, *Bilsamhället* (The Car Society, 2008), was awarded the Johan Nordström and Sten Lindroth Prize for outstanding scholarly work in the history of ideas. Publications in English include *Science for Welfare and Warfare: Technology and State Initiative in Cold War Sweden* (2010, co-edited with Niklas Stenlås and Johan Gribbe), and *Computers in Swedish Society: Documenting Early Use and Trends* (2012). Currently, he is researching the history of tourism.

Mary Nolan was trained as a Modern German historian and has written on German social and labor history and on the politics of Holocaust and Second World War memory in Germany. Her recent research focused on twentieth-century European–American relations, economic, political, and cultural; on anti-Americanism and Americanization in Europe; as well as on American anti-Europeanism. Her new project involves the entanglements of human rights and market fundamentalism from the 1970s to the 1990s. She teaches classes on the Cold War in Europe and America, Women and Gender in Modern Europe, Human Rights and Humanitarian Interventions, and Consumption and Consumer Culture. She is on the editorial boards of *International Labor and Working-Class History* and *Politics and Society*. Her books include *Visions of Modernity: American Business and the Modernization of Germany* (1994), and *The Transatlantic Century: Europe and America, 1890–2010* (2012).

David Nye received his PhD from the University of Minnesota. He has taught American Studies in the United States, Spain, Britain, the Netherlands, and Denmark. He is the author of 200 publications and reviews; his books with MIT Press include *Electrifying America* (1990, Dexter Prize and the Abel Wolman Award), *American Technological Sublime* (1994), *Consuming Power* (1997), *America as Second Creation* (2003),

Technology Matters (2006, Sally Hacker Prize), *When the Lights Went Out* (2010), and *America's Assembly Line* (2013). He has been a visiting scholar at Harvard University, MIT, the Netherlands Institute for Advanced Study, and the Universities of Leeds, Cambridge, Notre Dame, and Warwick. He is a by-fellow of Churchill College, Cambridge. He received the Leonardo da Vinci Medal from the Society for the History of Technology (2005), and he was knighted by the Queen of Denmark in 2014.

Per Østby is Professor of History of Technology at the Norwegian University of Science and Technology, Centre for Technology and Society. He has been head of both the Department of Historical Studies and the Centre for Technology and Society. His main research interest is in the field of the cultural integration of science and technology: medical science and technology, biotechnology, environmental science and technology, the cultural implications of design and innovation, environmental history, and mass motorization and transport. He has participated in and led several Norwegian and international projects.

Emanuela Scarpellini is Full Professor of Modern History at the University of Milan. She has been a visiting scholar at Stanford University and the University of Cambridge; she has also been a visiting professor at both Stanford and Georgetown universities. She is Founding Director of the research center MIC—Moda Immagine Consumi (Fashion Image and Consumer Culture)—at the University of Milan. Her current interests are the economic and cultural aspects of consumer society in Europe and America; the spread of mass culture from the United States; and the role of consumers. Her books include *Material Nation: A Consumer's History of Modern Italy* (2011) and *A tavola! Gli italiani in sette pranzi* (2012).

Karin Zachmann is Professor of History of Technology at the Central Institute for the History of Technology and the Technical University of Munich. She is known internationally for her scholarship on engineering professions and technical education; history of consumption; gender history; and technologies of the Cold War. Her current research focuses on the industrialization of food and foodways. Her book *Mobilisierung der Frauen: Technik, Geschlecht und Kalter Krieg in der DDR* (Mobilization of Women: Technology, Gender, and the Cold War in the German Democratic Republic, 2004) received the Deutsches Museum's Award for Best Book. Karin Zachmann's recent books include *Cold War Kitchen: Americanization, Technology, and European Users* (2009, co-edited with Ruth Oldenziel), and *Past and Present Energy Societies: How Energy Connects Politics, Technologies and Cultures* (2012, co-edited with Nina Moellers).

Introduction

Per Lundin

American ideals and models feature prominently in the master narrative of postwar European consumer societies. To wit: in her influential book *Irresistible Empire: America's Advance through Twentieth-Century Europe* (2005), the American historian Victoria de Grazia maintains that a U.S.-style "Market Empire" marched across Europe and swept away the old economic order. By focusing on ideals and models that originated in the United States, de Grazia demonstrates how myriad American interests and actors contributed to the "unique formation of the Market Empire"—and to America's status as the world's first regime of mass consumption.[1]

Indeed, after the Second World War, the United States emerged as the world's greatest power. During the initial postwar decades, Europe was flooded with consumer experts, marketing professionals, and Marshall Plan administrators. Accordingly, the "Old World" was flooded with American products, from refrigerators to cars; blue jeans to chewing gum; movies to music; magazines to radio shows. American exhibits abounded in Europe, and these, too, promoted U.S. images and attitudes, American norms and values. The widespread circulation of American elements notwithstanding, a crucial dimension is missing in the claim that the American way of life ultimately gained hegemony in Europe.

In recent years, several scholars have disputed the claim of American hegemony in Europe.[2] America's political, economic, and military dominance during the twentieth century has, of course, been acknowledged. So has U.S. policymakers' intention of doing business with the European countries: according to scholar John Krige, U.S. policymakers, in the arena of science, at the very least, stated clearly their opinion that Europe needed to be "Americanized." But, beyond the realities of American power were the realities of European power, the often-complex actions taken by Europeans. U.S. policymakers, while zealous in their pursuit of U.S. interests in Europe, did not prevent Europeans from leaving "their own imprint on the hegemonic regime."[3]

In this book, we maintain that it is necessary to go beyond the contested thesis of American hegemony in order to further our knowledge of how postwar European consumer societies were made. After all, as Mary Nolan has succinctly observed, "Americanization is only part of a much more complex story."[4] Our approach to the making of European consumer societies and the re-examining of the U.S. challenge is to focus on technology: from the freezer locker and the refrigerator to the package tour by bus and air, from the prefabrication of homes to the use of franchising protocols. We employ the useful concept of consumption regimes, coined by Victoria de Grazia, as a way of relating consumption technologies to broader processes in society.[5] But we imbue the term "consumption regime" with a somewhat different meaning. While de Grazia uses the concept primarily to refer to major historical shifts—from an aristocratic to a bourgeois consumption mode, for example; or a Fordist to a post-Fordist mode—we define a consumption regime as a dynamic set of institutions, ideologies, and technologies. De Grazia implies that one American regime of mass consumption replaced one bourgeois European consumption regime. In contrast, we identify multiple, co-existing consumption regimes in Europe.[6]

We examine how technologies of consumption interacted with ideologies and institutions in different regional, national, and transnational settings to form the consumption regimes of postwar European consumer societies. Our empirical research, presented in these chapters, encompasses technologies related to food, housing, and tourism. The studies in this volume indicate that Europeans did not import the allegedly irresistible American mode of mass consumption as a single, self-contained package. Instead, Europeans appropriated American products and processes selectively, and, usually, with great deliberation. Appropriation often took place in the context of extensive negotiation—negotiation between actors on both sides of the Atlantic, as well as debate among Europeans themselves.

In this volume, overviews as well as case studies from different European countries demonstrate that Europeans maintained myriad views of America; Europeans did not appropriate a homogenous notion of America. Specifically, the chapters illustrate how distinguishing between product and process innovations enables us to discern patterns of appropriation. To this end, the distinction is made between introducing a new product (or simply a new version of that product) on the one hand, and introducing a new method of production or a new way of managing a commodity, on the other hand.[7] Further, the authors demonstrate the wisdom of describing postwar European consumption in terms of selective appropriation—rather than the wholesale acceptance or rejection—of American ideals and models.

The contributors to this volume identify the main promoters of the emerging European consumption regimes. The first decades of the postwar period were a time of continuous making and remaking of European consumption regimes. Many played key roles in this: experts and planners, government agencies and special-interest groups, cooperatives and trade unions, journalists and the media, among many others. These actors shaped consumption regimes by engaging with producers and consumers who did not necessarily share their views of how societies should be modernized. The processes took place in close connection with powerful economic, military, and political actors: the defense industries, financial industries, and social democratic governments, for example. These intermediary actors, as we refer to them, functioned as spokespeople between consumer groups, sometimes even intervening between individual consumers. Roles for these intermediary actors included negotiating, directing, and creating scripts for consumer behavior.[8] In the negotiation processes that took place, rarely did intermediary actors function as neutral partners: rather, they were proactive advocates of particular interests, ideals, and norms. Consciously or not, intermediary actors promoted middle-class values. Accordingly, these actors tended to exclude groups that did not share their norms: blue-collar workers, immigrants, and rural dwellers; children, the elderly, and women, for that matter. They competed—and cooperated—with each other in order to attain the pivotal position of mediator between producers and consumers. They pursued various programs of modernity and, consequently, represented various ideologies, institutions, and technologies of consumption.

How did intermediary actors in the European context perceive the American model of mass consumption? How did they selectively appropriate American elements and ideas? The contributing authors' conclusions take the form of two main themes. First and foremost, intermediary actors in Europe used images and representations of America to evoke feelings of national identity; to strengthen national bonds; and to advance national projects (and eventually pan-European ones) during the postwar period. Second, the contributors to this volume demonstrate that American elements—from models to practices to technologies—were more prominent in European process innovations than in product innovations.

The Many Images of America

In the America of the 1940s and 1950s, a concerted effort was made to invent and project the image of a nation whose values and virtues were an exemplar to the world. The promoters of this thinking included U.S. policymakers; business and labor leaders; intellectuals, academics, and writers.[9] This effort notwithstanding, multiple Americas—rather than a single, consolidated, exemplary version of America—developed in the minds of Europeans. In conjunction with the Marshall Plan, many American agencies participated in promoting the U.S. in Europe: the United States Information Agency (USIA), the Department of Commerce, and the State Department, among them. These organizations launched cultural programs; staged exhibits; and promoted—in close collaboration with large corporations, such as IBM, the Walt Disney Company, and General Mills—participation in numerous trade and world fairs during the first postwar decades. These programs and events certainly reached a large audience: U.S. government officials boasted that nearly 14 million people visited American pavilions at fairs in 1960 alone.[10]

However elaborate, the U.S.-government-led initiatives to promote America as part of the Cold War were only part of a much longer, even more elaborate history: the selective appropriation of American mass culture in Europe had begun far earlier.[11] Since the 1920s, if not earlier, Europeans had been exposed to a range of American elements, from advertising campaigns to Hollywood films, music to photography to popular culture. This enormous quantity of cultural elements came from a variety of sources and circulated throughout Europe. And these American elements, in the European context, contributed to a rich, powerful, and all-embracing discourse between the two continents in which multiple images of America emerged.

Indeed, the abundant American elements circulating throughout Europe created a dialogue between the U.S. and Europe; this circulation of goods and ideologies was anything but a one-way process. As Mary Nolan narrates in her chapter in this volume: "ideas, techniques, and products did not flow only from the United States to Europe—not even in the classic 'American Century' from the 1940s to the mid-1970s, when American economic might and political influence were greatest." Nolan goes on to describe how "Europeans debated, negotiated with, and altered the economic and cultural forms and norms that the United States established—and often sought to impose."

In his chapter, David Nye elaborates on this theme of Europeans interacting extensively with American elements—rather than engaging in submissive appropriation. Nye underscores the concept of cultural icons as malleable when introduced into new systems of meanings. Specifically, he examines the ways in which the Statue of Liberty as an icon was re-visualized and re-contextualized during the postwar period. The non-exceptional, diverse, and heterogeneous nature of America, Nye reminds us, provided a rich cache of images, sounds, and texts from which Europeans borrowed, selected, and interpreted, giving these American elements new meanings, in the process.

A key example of "multiple Americas" can be observed in the American design scene of the 1950s. America was experiencing a newly technology-based consumer economy and a huge rise in consumption. The design, advertising, and marketing sectors were coming to the fore. In this context, American production of consumer durables diversified—and distinct versions of American design emerged. One extreme was the commercial, populist, streamlining aesthetic: the 1950s Oldsmobile with fins, for example. At the other extreme was the elitist "good design" movement, led by New York's Museum of Modern Art, design schools, and a handful of high-end manufacturers. Between these two extremes existed a multitude of other movements in American design.[12] In 1953, the U.S. chose representative products for its exhibit, *American Design for Home and Decorative Use*, which was to tour selected European countries. Of the many possible versions of the American design scene to project, the exhibit portrayed only one: the elitist, carefully curated, Museum of Modern Art image of American design.

In his chapter on postwar design in this volume, Kjetil Fallan demonstrates how European designers used the repertoire of American design to deploy various images of America on both sides of the Atlantic. For example, Norwegian proponents of Scandinavia's applied-art tradition denounced the U.S. avant-garde culture represented by the Museum of Modern Art by linking it to the U.S. ideals of mass-scale production. This rather surprising connection between these two opposing scenarios in American design was made in order to portray the domestic artisans and craft-based production systems as democratic and socially responsible.

Europeans continually repositioned and reinterpreted America's cultural messages to suit their own needs and agendas; Europeans re-purposed messages. A prime example of this pattern is the debate surrounding the "American kitchen"—one of the more prominent symbols of American-style consumerism during the early postwar period. In this case, a constellation of government agencies and corporations promoted the American kitchen at fairs and exhibits: General Motors' traveling *Kitchen of Tomorrow* exhibit toured major European cities in 1957. And General Electric's lemon-yellow kitchen at the American National Exhibit at the Moscow fair in 1959 has attracted considerable attention from historians: this was the setting for the famous "Kitchen Debate" between U.S. vice president Richard M. Nixon and Soviet premier Nikita S. Khrushchev. The debate has been inscribed in American historiography as a fundamental clash between East and West, and between two ideologically opposed systems, superpowers, and spheres of influence. Both claimed to represent radically different modes of production and consumption. On the American side was a model based on individual consumption; on the Soviet side was a model based on collective and cooperative consumption. If there had been any doubt, the exhibit confirmed to parties on both sides of the Atlantic that the realm of consumer durables had become a Cold War battleground of equal importance to those of nuclear and space technologies.[13]

In her contribution to this volume, Emanuela Scarpellini examines these Cold War conflicts in the context of the kitchen. She concludes that the American kitchen, with its conflation of working and living spaces, challenged one of the core values of modern European domesticity: the separation between the "male" and "female" spheres. The masculine realm was external and social, linked to work and money; the "female" domestic interior was based on feelings such as love, solidarity, and sacrifice. Scarpellini's case study illustrates how, in Italy and other European countries, the American kitchen clashed with the prevailing image of women and the family in the 1950s and 1960s. Scarpellini also demonstrates how, in her words, "by selectively appropriating new 'American' foods, appliances, and kitchens, Italian society emerged from the postwar period with a dynamic balance of traditional and modern food products and processes."

Indeed, far from taking the consumer-oriented American way of life at face value, Europeans used America and its representations as cultural shorthand for ideas about modernity. America provided the framework in which Europeans interpreted and debated modernity. A case in point is the contested reception of the motel in Europe, which symbolized an American-style form of leisure. The motel represented automobility, individual freedom, open-road vacations; motels were synonymous with open frontiers and borders. The first American motel opened in

1926; the motel trend in America skyrocketed in the following decades. The motel became a vital part of the American service infrastructure, ensuring travel mobility for middle-class families in particular.[14] With the rise of mass motorization in Europe, the motel quickly gained status as an icon of American automobile-minded modernity. Notably, Europe's national automobile associations celebrated the American motel as a symbol of a new, mobile, modern lifestyle. This promised rationally organized comfort, freedom, and solitude for the stressed-out, overworked "modern man and his family."[15]

These promises notwithstanding, the motel did not gain a foothold in Europe. Intermediary actors in Europe—national tourist associations, hotel associations, cooperative travel and holiday organizations, and trade unions—launched and promoted other forms of accommodation, particularly for the working classes. For example, as I show in my contribution to this volume, the Swedish Tourist Association, with its ambition to shape national identity through tourism, organized and ran domestic hostels—a low-price, collective form of accommodation planned with biking tourists in mind. The motel challenge prompted the Swedish Tourist Association to modernize its hostel movement, but it modernized along another path.

The Many Meanings of Modernity

These examples underscore Europeans' increasingly diversified understanding of modernity. This contrasts sharply with the homogenous, hegemonic vision of American modernity orchestrated by U.S. programs during the first decades of the Cold War. These examples also illustrate that, as early as the 1950s—the very decade in which U.S. military, political, and economic power reached its zenith—it is indeed possible to discern alternative visions of modernity.

In the Netherlands, intermediary actors such as the Dutch Hotel Association evoked images of America to tease out and develop the alleged "Dutch character" of tourist accommodation. In the 1950s and 1960s, the Netherlands was purportedly one of the most Americanized countries in Europe; it was also one of the top recipients of financial aid from the Marshall Plan (measured per capita). In contrast with the practicality and modern conveniences offered by U.S. hotels, the association maintained that Dutch accommodations represented the country's architectural heritage and tradition.[16]

Early in the postwar period, other alternative visions of modernity were promoted in the Scandinavian countries as well as in Britain by government agencies and municipal authorities, cooperatives and trade unions, planners and social reformers. One point of departure for these visionaries was the American model of mass consumption, which was commercially oriented, technologically attuned, and focused on the expanding middle class. In the Scandinavian countries, the majority argued for communal facilities and collective, rather than individual, solutions. The consumption regimes that emerged were tied to allegedly egalitarian Scandinavian values and social democratic traditions. Food, housing, and tourism technologies were incorporated in the great social democratic modernization project.[17] Europeans accepted modernity as a goal, but they interpreted "modern" in a flexible way.

The case studies in this book demonstrate that, to Europeans, America was not a geographic place so much as a metaphor for otherness evoked by intermediary actors as a way to establish and strengthen collective identities.[18] Indeed, the perception and attribution of "American" was more important than the fact of whether or not the element in question originated in America. For example, the Royal Dutch Touring Club dismissed the British Butlins holiday camps not only as "un-Dutch" and the result of "shameless exploitation," but as "American forms of amusement." Likewise, some Italian consumers frowned upon—if not raged against—ready-to-eat soups, which they considered to be American, regardless of the soup's German (Knorr) or U.S. (Campbell) origins. By the same token, for young Italians, "Brooklyn" chewing gum, an Italian brand manufactured outside Milan, represented a quintessentially American experience.[19]

Images of America were deployed in debates and challenges on both sides of the Atlantic. In Europe, American elements served primarily as a tool for strengthening existing national identities. For example, against the backdrop of American motel and hotel culture, the Swedish hostel defined its Swedish-ness; likewise, the Dutch hotel defined its Dutch-ness. The American way of life served only in a secondary way to spur a new transnational, pan-European identity.

Appropriating Processes Over Products

To Europeans, America comprised not only dreams, images, and representations, but a set of exemplars, models, and practices, which intermediary actors selectively appropriated. The research results described in this volume indicate that, indeed, Europeans more readily appropriated process innovations—U.S. models, practices, and technologies—than product innovations. In many cases, Europe's intermediary actors appropriated key elements of the American consumption regime as a system: marketing, managerial practices, and organizational methods; research and development approaches as well as standardization, for example. Europeans often rejected the aesthetic design (bulkiness, streamlining), scale, quality, and content of U.S. consumer durables. In this way, the most threatening aspects of Americanism—rampant commercialism and the encroachment of the American way of life—could be avoided. In the making and remaking of consumption regimes, the replacement of European process-related elements with American ones was done on a case-by-case basis. This proved less controversial in the postwar reconstruction of national identities in Europe.

The contributing authors provide various case histories to illustrate this phenomenon. For example, as Adri A. Albert de la Bruhèze narrates in his chapter on tourism and accommodation in the Netherlands, Dutch intermediary actors, hotel managers, professionals, and policymakers, for example, were most impressed by American business processes: marketing and consumer research, public relations, and the vocational training of personnel. The Dutch intermediary actors also admired the apparently professional American managerial practices and the allegedly rational and scientific design and planning of hotels. At the same time, Dutch intermediary actors summarily dismissed U.S. hotel architecture, furnishing, and "gadgets" such as ice-cube machines and air-conditioning.

British, Italian, and Scandinavian designers displayed overtly positive attitudes toward U.S. production methods. Designers in these countries were particularly aware of trends, marketing, and consumer behavior among U.S. industrial designers. At the same time, European design professionals ridiculed American stylistic devices, the formalism of American design, and choice of material that dominated mainstream U.S. industrial design—all of which was considered to represent "dishonesty," "shallowness," and "irrelevance." As Kjetil Fallan aptly phrases it, "mainstream American industrial design had become a Janus-faced figure: alluring and inspirational when showing its organizational side, ridiculous and appalling when showing its aesthetic side."[20]

A similar pattern can be seen in the response of French architects to one American model of housing: single-family suburban homes. When visiting Levittown, visiting French architects admired American rationalization, standardization, the use of prefabricated elements, and streamlined management systems—all processes that the French later adopted, to a large extent. But, when it came to question of design, the French rejected the iconic American wood-frame tract house designed for the suburbs. Instead, the architects sought inspiration from a multitude of European homes.²¹

In the arena of food, postwar European governments welcomed the American fertilizers, the vegetable seeds, the farming equipment, and the expert knowledge of agriculture and the food industry. The European Productivity Agency mediated the processes of standardization, packaging, distribution, and marketing. Europeans reacted harshly, however, to U.S. attempts to fully transform the European foodways into a full-fledged American consumption regime: this transformation would have jeopardized the socially oriented European agricultural policies. As Karin Zachmann so succinctly frames it in her contribution to this volume, "Europeans wanted modernity too, but without sacrificing the romance of farming as a way of life."²²

Why, exactly, did process-oriented American technologies of consumption appeal more to Europeans than product-oriented innovations? The contributors provide an explanation consisting of four closely interrelated elements. First, this pattern of selective appropriation reflects an ambivalence towards the United States that was shared by many Europeans. As part of the comprehensive U.S. Technical Assistance and Productivity Program, which was initiated under the Marshall Plan, several thousand European observers went overseas between 1948 and 1958; more often than not, these observers expressed ambivalence toward the New World.²³ These visitors to the U.S. were political visionaries; industrial leaders; labor union delegates; and, above all, professionals in the state system, in business, in industry, as well as in civil-society organizations. The travelers were profoundly conflicted about the United States. On one hand, the travelers were naïvely optimistic, inspired by the country's stunning economic and technical progress. On the other hand, the travelers were dismayed by what they perceived as America's too-competitive, relentlessly capitalistic society. Many also objected to the American aesthetic. While they themselves experienced conflicting emotions about America, visitors consistently reported feeling that the American way of life would inevitably spread, they believed that their (European) ways of life was being subject to "Americanization."²⁴ Interestingly, proponents of Americanization tended to emphasize process innovations in their rhetoric, while opponents vehemently attacked product innovations.

Second, in the eyes of the consumer, products conveyed meaning in a way that process innovations rarely did. Products could represent authenticity and tradition. But they could also represent modernity and novelty. Process innovations, by contrast, were often perceived as neutral tools; only rarely were they seen as a threat to prevailing conditions. Paradoxically, U.S.-style process innovations were used frequently by intermediary actors to promote alternatives to American modernity. For instance, the first organization in Sweden to introduce American franchising methods was the leftist cooperative movement, and the second was the Swedish Tourist Association, a conservative civil-society organization. On the other hand, product innovations symbolized American modernity in a palpably sensuous way. American products circulating in Europe at the time included American-style cars; motels; wood-frame suburban tract houses; bulky freezers and refrigerators; ice-cube machines; ready-made soups; and materials, like plastic. These products and the like were more susceptible to being rejected outright or to being perceived as a threat by the norm-setting middle class. (Significantly, the working class and unruly youth cultures appropriated the products *and* aesthetics of American modernity as a way of challenging middle-class European norms.)

Consider the twentieth century's quintessential icon of American modernity: the car. Western Europe was packed with cars, although few of them were of U.S. origin. While the total number of new cars sold in Sweden—the country that boasted Europe's greatest number of cars per capita—rose from 62,503 to 169,014 between 1951 and 1959, the number of American-made cars *dropped* from 5,217 to 2,676 during the same period.[25] This signals to us that the sensuous curves, voluptuous forms, and decorative details that characterized the American streamlining aesthetic did not appeal to middle-class European consumers. For similar reasons, only a small fraction of the bulky American-style refrigerators and home freezers ever entered the Italian and the Norwegian markets.

Arguably, the third element that shaped product versus process appropriation was the contrasting economic contexts of America and Europe. In the early 1950s, U.S. citizens consumed three-quarters of the world's appliances. In 1956, the average U.S. consumers had approximately twice as much income at their disposal than their Western European counterparts. And, at the peak of their power, U.S. corporations attracted approximately half of all of the world's foreign investment.[26] Gradually, the gap between the U.S. and European economies diminished. But that gap had a decisive impact during the critical phase of development for Europe's postwar consumption regimes. It was simply impossible to replicate the resource-intensive U.S. consumer economy on European soil. In the immediate postwar period, piecemeal improvement of consumption regimes was often the only viable alternative in many European countries; in the nations ravaged by war, citizens' everyday lives were shaped by austerity and shortages.[27] Thus, a refrigerator scaled to the traditional Italian kitchen was not only less threatening to the existing social order than the American kitchen—it was also a more realistic economic alternative.

In fact, economic conditions—import restrictions, rationing, and political reforms, for example—contributed to the promotion and use of collective consumption technologies, such as freezer-locker plants, hostels and package-tours, and large-scale social housing.[28] Although the Western European economies soon recovered and the economic gap diminished, the consumption regimes often continued along the chosen trajectories.

Admittedly, in some cases, technological solutions imposed by economic necessity proved to be only temporary. For example, as Terje Finstad, Stig Kvaal, and Per Østby demonstrate in their chapter on the breakthrough of frozen food and freezing technology in Norway, the collective freezer-locker plants were soon followed by home freezers. In other cases, however, the resulting solutions endure today. Hostels and package tours still enjoy popularity, for example, as do the social-housing developments that accommodate large numbers of Europe's urban dwellers. Arguably, in many countries the proactive state has continuously promoted alternative solutions for policy reasons. A case in point is the collective laundries in Sweden, which have come to serve as a physical manifestation of the social democratic welfare state.[29]

The fourth contributing factor to favoring process innovation was technical: implementing product innovations required infrastructure. Many of the U.S. gadgets depended on a technological environment that simply did not yet exist in Europe. For example, in an attempt to introduce an industrial model of food production and distribution in Yugoslavia, the U.S. Department of Commerce launched the *Supermarket USA* exhibit in 1957. Given that agriculture and food distribution were not yet industrialized—and that core supermarket technologies like refrigeration were not available in 1950s Yugoslavia—the initiative was doomed.[30] The dependence on infrastructure also came into play when Norwegian intermediary actors promoted collective solutions, such as the freezer-locker plants, instead of the individual home freezer. In addition to rationing and import restrictions, electricity-supply problems and a lack of construction materials made it difficult to implement an American-style cold chain.

In some cases, the necessary infrastructure did exist in Europe, although it had been built for other purposes. The Swedish package-tour industry exemplifies how infrastructure set up by the United States during and after the Second World War was harnessed for new and distinctive European consumption regimes. In his contribution to this book, Thomas Kaiserfeld shows that the air-package tours set up for mass consumption in Sweden relied on American-built infrastructure. Specifically, Swedes could conceivably take off in American-built jetliners and, inspired by originally American advertising, find themselves flying to the Mediterranean—under NATO-ratified regulations negotiated by civil and military aviation authorities. But, after all, infrastructure was only one of the prerequisites for a new consumption regime to be formed. Other factors proved as important to Swedish tour operators. For example, European labor laws, which included a minimum paid vacation, contributed mightily to crystallizing the package-tour regime.

In short, selective appropriation enabled Europeans to incorporate elements of U.S.-style modernity into their evolving new collective identities. At the same time, Europeans were not required to give up the products and processes that characterized their traditional identities. For example, Norwegians could continue their traditional hunter-gatherer regime of picking berries—with the help of freezers. Similarly, Italians could continue to prepare their traditional three-course meals—with the help of process-oriented products like bouillon cubes and margarine. On the other hand, mass-produced frozen food, TV dinners, and ready-made soups signaled a radical break with social and cultural traditions and habits. But, few middle-class Europeans were actually willing or prepared to make this radical break. In the turbulent postwar world, Europeans looked for technological solutions that would secure—not threaten—the social order. Traditional values and existing power relationships offered this security. The examples in this volume show that the appropriated technologies of consumption were tethered to—and reinforced by—existing norms rather than by new norms.

Notes

1. Victoria de Grazia, *Irresistible Empire: America's Advance through Twentieth-Century Europe* (Cambridge, MA: Belknap Press of Harvard University Press, 2005), 4–10. The hegemony thesis has recently been reiterated by historian Howard Le Roy Malchow in *Special Relations: The Americanization of Britain?* (Stanford, CA: Stanford University Press, 2011).
2. See, for instance, Adrian Horn, *Juke Box Britain: Americanisation and Youth Culture, 1945–60* (Manchester: Manchester University Press, 2009); Matthias Kipping and Nick Tiratsoo, eds., *Americanisation in 20th Century Europe: Business, Culture, Politics*, vol. 2 (Lille: Centre d'Histoire de l'Europe du Nord-Ouest, 2001); John Krige, *American Hegemony and the Postwar Reconstruction of Science in Europe* (Cambridge, MA: MIT Press, 2006); Richard F. Kuisel,

The French Way: How France Embraced and Rejected American Values and Power (Princeton, NJ: Princeton University Press, 2012); Daniel T. Rodgers, *Atlantic Crossings: Social Politics in a Progressive Age* (Cambridge, MA: Belknap Press of Harvard University Press, 2000); Robert W. Rydell and Rob Kroes, *Buffalo Bill in Bologna: The Americanization of the World, 1869–1922* (Chicago: University of Chicago Press, 2005); Harm G. Schröter, "Economic Culture and Its Transfer: An Overview of the Americanisation of the European Economy, 1900–2005," *European Review of History* 15 (2008): 331–44; Alexander Stephan, ed., *The Americanization of Europe: Culture, Diplomacy, and Anti-Americanism after 1945* (New York: Berghahn Books, 2006); Jonathan Zeitlin and Gary Herrigel, eds., *Americanization and Its Limits: Reworking US Technology and Management in Post-War Europe and Japan* (Oxford: Oxford University Press, 2000).
3. Krige, *American Hegemony and the Postwar Reconstruction of Science in Europe*, 6, 265–9.
4. Mary Nolan, "Consuming America, Producing Gender," in *The American Century in Europe*, ed. R. Laurence Moore and Maurizio Vaudagna (Ithaca, NY: Cornell University Press, 2003), 243–61. See also Jan Logemann, *Trams or Tailfins? Public and Private Property in Postwar West Germany and the United States* (Chicago: University of Chicago Press, 2012); Klaus Nathaus, ed., "Europop: The Production of Popular Culture in Twentieth Century Western Europe," special issue, *European Review of History: Revue europeenne d'histoire* 20, no. 5 (2013).
5. Victoria de Grazia, "Changing Consumption Regimes in Europe, 1930–1970: Comparative Perspectives on the Distribution Problem," in *Getting and Spending: European and American Consumer Societies in the Twentieth Century*, ed. Susan Strasser, Charles McGovern, and Matthias Judt (Cambridge: Cambridge University Press, 1998), 59–83; Victoria de Grazia and Ellen Furlough, eds., *The Sex of Things: Gender and Consumption in Historical Perspective* (Berkeley: University of California Press, 1996).
6. Cf. Shmuel N. Eisenstadt,"Multiple Modernities," in *Multiple Modernities*, ed. Shmuel N. Eisenstadt (New Brunswick: Transaction Publishers, 2002), 1–29. See also Björn Wittrock, "Modernity: One, None, or Many? European Origins and Modernity as a Global Condition," in ibid., 31–60.
7. The Austrian-American economist Joseph A. Schumpeter introduced the distinction in *The Theory of Economic Development: An Inquiry into Profits, Capital, Credit, Interest, and the Business Cycle* (Cambridge, MA: Transaction Publishers, 1934), see especially p. 66. See also James M. Utterback and William J. Abernathy, "A Dynamic Model of Product and Process Innovation," *Omega* (1975): 639–56. For discussions in the vast literature that has appeared on the subject the last decades, see Richard A. Wolfe, "Organizational Innovation: Review, Critique and Suggested Research Directions," *Journal of Management Studies* 31 (1994): 405–31; Rosanna Garcia and Roger Calantone, "A Critical Look at Technological Innovation Typology and Innovativeness Terminology: A Literature Review," *The Journal of Product Innovation Management* 19 (2002): 110–32.
8. Cf. Johan Schot and Adri Albert de la Bruhèze, "The Mediated Design of Products, Consumption, and Consumers in the Twentieth Century," in *How Users Matter: The Co-Construction of Users and Technology*, ed. Nelly

Oudshoorn and Trevor Pinch (Cambridge, MA: MIT Press, 2003), 229–45; Ruth Oldenziel and Adri Albert de la Bruhèze, "Theorizing the Mediation Junction for Technology and Consumption," in *Manufacturing Technology, Manufacturing Consumers: The Making of Dutch Consumer Society*, ed. Adri Albert de la Bruhèze and Ruth Oldenziel (Amsterdam: Aksant, 2009), 9–39.
9. Alan Brinkley, "The Concept of an American Century," in *The American Century in Europe*, ed. R. Laurence Moore and Maurizio Vaudagna (Ithaca, NY: Cornell University Press, 2003), 7–24. For a recent critical discussion of the "American Century," see Andrew J. Bacevich, ed., *The Short American Century: A Postmortem* (Cambridge, MA: Harvard University Press, 2012).
10. Robert H. Haddow, *Pavilions of Plenty: Exhibiting American Culture Abroad in the 1950s* (Washington, DC: Smithsonian Institution Press, 1997), 15.
11. David W. Ellwood, *The Shock of America: Europe and the Challenge of the Century* (Oxford: Oxford University Press, 2012); Mary Nolan, *The Transatlantic Century: Europe and America, 1890–2010* (Cambridge: Cambridge University Press, 2012); Rydell and Kroes, *Buffalo Bill in Bologna*.
12. Jeffrey L. Meikle, *Design in the USA* (Oxford: Oxford University Press, 2005), chap. 4.
13. Ruth Oldenziel and Karin Zachmann, eds., *Cold War Kitchen: Americanization, Technology, and European Users* (Cambridge, MA: MIT Press, 2009).
14. Warren James Belasco, *Americans on the Road: From Autocamp to Motel, 1910–1945*, new ed. (Baltimore, MD: Johns Hopkins University Press, 1997); Christopher Endy, *Cold War Holidays: American Tourism in France* (Chapel Hill: University of North Carolina Press, 2004); John A. Jakle, Keith A. Sculle, and Jefferson S. Rogers, *The Motel in America* (Baltimore, MD: Johns Hopkins University Press, 1996).
15. Per Lundin, "Confronting Class: The American Motel in Early Post-war Sweden," *Journal of Tourism History* 5 (2013): 305–24.
16. Adri A. de la Bruhèze, chapter 7 in this volume. Hans Ibelings, *Americanism: Nederlandse architectuur en het transatlantische voorbeeld: Dutch Architecture and the Transatlantic Model* (Rotterdam: NAi, 1997); Alan S. Milward, *The Reconstruction of Western Europe, 1945–51* (London: Routledge, 1992), 95–7.
17. See the contributions of Terje Finstad, Stig Kvaal, and Per Østby (chapter 4) and Thomas Kaiserfeld (chapter 8) in this volume. See also Mikael Hård, "The Good Apartment: The Social (Democratic) Construction of Swedish Homes," *Home Cultures* 7 (2010): 117–34. For the Social Democratic modernization project, see Sheri Berman, *The Primacy of Politics: Social Democracy and the Making of Europe's Twentieth Century* (Cambridge: Cambridge University Press, 2006); Francis Sejersted, *The Age of Social Democracy: Norway and Sweden in the Twentieth Century*, trans. Richard Daly (Princeton, NJ: Princeton University Press, 2011).
18. Cf. Richard Pells, *Not Like Us: How Europeans Have Loved, Hated, and Transformed American Culture since World War II* (New York: Basic Books, 1997); Emily S. Rosenberg, "Consuming Women: Images of Americanization in the 'American Century,'" *Diplomatic History* 23 (1999): 479–97.
19. See the contributions of Adri A. de la Bruhèze (chapter 7) and Emanuela Scarpellini (chapter 5) in this volume.
20. Kjetil Fallan, chapter 6 in this volume.
21. Mary Nolan, chapter 1 in this volume.

22. Karin Zachmann, chapter 3 in this volume.
23. Matthias Kipping and Ove Bjarnar, eds., *The Americanisation of European Business: The Marshall Plan and the Transfer of US Management Models* (London: Routledge, 1998); Jacqueline McGlade, "Americanization: Ideology or Process? The Case of the United States Technical Assistance and Productivity Programme," in *Americanization and Its Limits: Reworking US Technology and Management in Post-War Europe and Japan*, ed. Jonathan Zeitlin and Gary Herrigel (Oxford: Oxford University Press, 2000), 53–75.
24. Per Lundin, "Mediators of Modernity: Planning Experts and the Making of the 'Car-Friendly' City in Europe," in *Urban Machinery: Inside Modern European Cities*, ed. Mikael Hård and Thomas J. Misa (Cambridge, MA: MIT Press, 2008), 257–80.
25. Tom O'Dell, *Culture Unbound: Americanization and Everyday Life in Sweden*, new ed. (Lund: Nordic Academic Press, 2012), 137.
26. Philipp Gassert, "The Spectre of Americanization: Western Europe in the American Century," in *The Oxford Handbook of Postwar European History*, ed. Dan Stone (Oxford: Oxford University Press, 2012), 191; Nolan, in this volume.
27. Konrad H. Jarausch and Michael Geyer, *Shattered Past: Reconstructing German Histories* (Princeton, NJ: Princeton University Press, 2002); Ina Zweiniger-Bargielowska, *Austerity in Britain: Rationing, Controls, and Consumption, 1939–1955* (Oxford: Oxford University Press, 2000).
28. See the contributions of Scarpellini, and Finstad, Kvaal, and Østby in this volume.
29. Ulla Rosén, "'A Rational Solution to the Laundry Issue': Policy and Research for Day-to-Day Life in the Welfare State," in *Science for Welfare and Warfare: Technology and State Initiative in Cold War Sweden*, ed. Per Lundin, Niklas Stenlås, and Johan Gribbe (Sagamore Beach, MA: Science History Publications, 2010), 213–32.
30. Shane Hamilton, "Supermarket USA Confronts State Socialism: Airlifting the Technopolitics of Industrial Food Distribution into Cold War Yugoslavia," in *Cold War Kitchen*, 137–60.

1
Negotiating American Modernity in Twentieth-Century Europe

Mary Nolan

Throughout the twentieth century, America presented itself to the world as the model of economic modernity. Europeans—from Britain to Russia, from Sweden to Italy—contended with America's ideological claims and material goods. America represented stunning economic prowess (the Great Depression notwithstanding); pioneering models of capitalism (from Fordism to the IT economy to the most recent model, financialization); and innovative technology and managerial practices. For Europeans, this aroused both admiration and anxiety, often simultaneously. Initially, Europeans regarded the mass consumption of cars, appliances, and televisions as economically impossible and culturally undesirable. But these commodities spread rapidly after the Second World War, first in Western Europe and later and more partially in the East. So, too, did computers, cell phones, and iPods later in the century. American mass culture—from Hollywood movies and TV programs to jazz, rock, and rap, as well as Coca-Cola and McDonald's—was embraced by many Europeans, especially the young. Others in Europe condemned American mass culture as morally corrosive, politically dangerous, and threatening to their national identity.

Europeans were contending with elements of the American consumption regime, with Fordist mass production, and with ideologies of productivism and consumer choice. But did Europeans' attraction to, aversion to, and appropriation of American elements create a recognizably Americanized Europe? And what, indeed, do we mean by that elusive term? Americanization refers to the adoption of American forms of production and consumption. It also refers to technology and techniques of management, political ideas, and social policies; high- and mass-cultural goods and institutions, gender roles, and leisure practices. Americanization encompasses how such borrowings were selectively appropriated and negotiated—how they functioned and acquired particular meanings. Americanization was (and is), in turn, shaped by the images and discourses that present America as a—if not *the*—sterling example of economic, social, and cultural modernity. Americanization, whether real or imagined, anticipated or dreaded, was central to European–American relations in the twentieth century. It was what American business and government sought to export; it fostered concrete images and practices that Europeans used to debate modernity. Many narratives have analyzed the penetration of American capital, goods, ideas, and practices in Europe. Some of these narratives are celebratory, others critical of America; some posit an empire by invitation while others emphasize cultural imperialism. But virtually all narratives assume the one-way movement of consumer technologies from west to east and measure Europe in terms of its proximity to American practices and values.[1] This is one assumption that the authors of this volume seek to revise.

In fact, ideas, techniques, and products did not flow only from the United States to Europe—not even in the classic "American Century" from the 1940s to the mid-1970s, when American economic might and political influence were greatest. Europeans drew on both rich national traditions and shared European discourses when discussing economy, culture, design, and domesticity. America was neither the only referent nor always the most important, and European commodities and cultural goods moved around the continent along multiple east–west and north–south trajectories. Rather than either enthusiastically receiving or sullenly resisting American elements, the European stance was far more nuanced. Specifically, Europeans debated, negotiated with, and altered the economic and cultural forms and norms that the United States established—and often sought to impose.

This was a complex circulation of cultural norms, economic models, goods, and people. The spread of these elements took place across national borders, the Atlantic, and the Iron Curtain. This created hybrid values, products, and processes rather than simply reproducing America in Western Europe and creating envy of it in Southern Europe and the communist east. American economic and cultural influence was always partial and contested; Americanization and anti-Americanism accompanied and constructed one another in ever-changing ways. Becoming modern—and European economies and ways of life became dramatically more modern after 1945—did not mean becoming Americanized. Various components of modern life—mass production; a Fordist consumption regime; mass culture; and commoditized, technology-based domesticity—emerged at varied rates across Europe. But these components were shaped as much, if not more, by national traditions, distinctive economic conditions, political systems, and emerging shared European values than by America. The United States offered inspiring visions of affluence but it was Europeans who constructed the specific forms of mass production and consumption, the meanings assigned to them, and the contexts in which they were embedded. Different European countries developed hybrid models of modernity and ways of living over the twentieth century. And these models came to look more like one another than like the American model, which so many Americans regarded as superior and destined to triumph.

Americanization and alternative modernities can be studied through many products and processes, ranging from motorization and management to mass media. Domestic consumption, to borrow Gary Cross's term, or consumer domesticity—the label preferred by others—is my entry point in this chapter. It refers to both the household consumption of foods, appliances, radios, and televisions, which America pioneered, and to models of domesticity, with their underlying assumptions about family, gender, and sexuality.[2] Architecture and housing policy will also be considered, for they significantly shaped the kinds of domestic consumption that evolved in Europe and America.

Domestic consumption loomed large in the economic exchanges, cultural competition, and political conflicts between the United States and Europe from the early twentieth century. This was the time when modern, rationalized, appliance-filled homes emerged as a middle-class privilege in America; the pattern persisted through the post-Second World War household modernization and the kitchen debates. The single-family apartment or house—and the technologically modern kitchen—were seen as the creator, the experiential center, and the symbol of prosperous, efficient, hygienic, and commoditized living that would transform women, promote new forms of family life, and legitimate very different social orders. They were integral parts of the political project of social democratic, conservative, and communist states. Modernity found its everyday habitus in the home and domestic consumption.[3]

Yet modern homes, appliances, and design choices took distinctive forms in Europe and America. European products, practices, and ideologies drew on national traditions of architecture and design; on the input of national professional groups; on women's associations; as well as on international influences. American influences were significant but not hegemonic. Domestic consumption was shaped by different social policy regimes and gender norms. In Western Europe, the production and consumption of washing machines, refrigerators, electric stoves, vacuum cleaners, and TVs fueled economic growth while transforming family life, expectations, and identities. In the communist east, the pursuit of consumer domesticity proved a source of unending, intractable problems. Europe's domestic consumption regimes, whether successful or failed, were not simply robust or pale imitations of America. In terms of the timing and scale of domestic consumption, the design choices, and the role of the state, European countries, both east and west, shared more with one another than with the United States.

Before the First World War: Domestic Consumption and Images of Modernity

Factories, skyscrapers, railroads, steamships, and automobiles symbolized modern production and ways of living before the First World War; the home was neither a key site nor an alluring symbol of modernity. Of equal importance, most Europeans did not regard American domesticity as worthy of emulation, even though they purchased American products, such as Singer sewing machines, Heinz ketchup, and Kodak cameras.[4] Anxious middle-class British observers feared that American products were invading everyday life. In 1902, Fred McKenzie lamented that:

> The average citizen wakes in the morning at the sound of an American alarm clock; rises from his New England sheets, and shaves with his New York soap, and a Yankee safety razor. He pulls on a pair of Boston boots over his socks from West Carolina, fastens his Connecticut braces, slips his Waterbury watch into his pocket and sits down to breakfast. Then he congratulates his wife on the way her Illinois straight-front corset sets off her Massachusetts blouse, and begins his breakfast at which he eats bread made from prairie flour,...tinned oysters from Baltimore, and a little Kansas City bacon...The children are given Quaker Oats.[5]

Consumer durables were notably absent from his list. William Stead, who coined the phrase "Americanization of the world" at the turn of the century, worried more about American market competition and imperial aspirations than new models of domestic consumption.[6] The Germans and the French were not troubled by similar concerns about American economic products and processes.

There were several reasons for this. Quantitatively and qualitatively, the gap between European and American consumption was not as great before the First World War as it became thereafter. Industrialization, urbanization, rising real incomes, and expanded trade transformed consumption in similar ways on both sides of the Atlantic. Europeans and Americans purchased an increasing amount of food and clothing on the market, and people moved around by mechanized public transportation or bicycle. Working-class women prepared dinners on gas cookers, and they and their middle-class counterparts could choose from a growing array of canned goods. Tea, cocoa, and coffee; sugar and bananas; rubber and cotton; and a variety of tropical oils were widely consumed on both sides of the Atlantic. The sewing machine, used both for family needs and earning income, spread across America and Europe. Americans consumed more of many types of goods than did Europeans and certainly prided themselves unequivocally about so doing, yet the industrialized parts of Europe did not live in a radically different consumption regime.[7]

To be sure, Americans did excel at motorization. In 1913, Great Britain had 106,000 cars; France, 91,000; Germany, 61,000; and Italy, 22,000. By contrast, the United States had 1,190,000 cars.[8] Automobiles were a harbinger of the new form of American mass production that would catapult America far ahead of Europe after the First World War and put household consumer durables at the center of a new consumer economy. This new economy would encompass rural as well as urban households; all classes, but not all races, would participate.

Before 1914, however, class and geography exerted the strongest influence on consumption. Bourgeois consumption on both sides of the Atlantic bore many resemblances, for the middle classes traveled, read about other countries, and emulated the styles, cuisines, and furniture they encountered.[9] Working-class consumption was very sensitive to income, but everywhere mixed a large dose of necessities with as much fashion and entertainment as possible. Everywhere men had more access to discretionary income and consumption possibilities than women. Rural areas, especially in Eastern and Southern Europe and the American South, were largely excluded from this new consumption regime, although sewing machines were purchased surprisingly widely.

Goods produced in America or sold by American firms were not necessarily coded as American. Mona Domosh notes that in Imperial Russia the Singer man on horseback, selling sewing machines and collecting installment payments, was "a common, everyday sight," and there were Singer shops in towns, large and small. Yet, "in many cases, the fact that the product was American—whatever that meant—was not part of the conversation. Many of the machines were produced in Russia at Singer's factory in Podolsk, just outside Moscow. Although decorated with the Singer logo, these machines were stamped with the Kompaniya Singer mark and were sold by Russian agents." The agents, in turn, were supervised by Germans, Englishmen, or ethnic minorities from Russia.[10] Even when goods were identified as American, they were often used in distinctive ways and carried different cultural meanings. American goods did not create homogeneous consumers and consumer cultures in Europe any more than they did at home.

Goods were sold in similar ways on both sides of the Atlantic. The late nineteenth century saw the development of department stores, with European ones modeling themselves on the pioneering Parisian Bon Marché rather than on those in New York or Boston. These "cathedrals of consumption," however, accounted for only a small proportion of sales. Mail-order sales were more popular. Sears and Roebuck was the largest and most famous catalogue company, but the French Bon Marché sent out 1.5 million catalogues in 1894 and even Moscow's Muir and Mirrielees department store had a mail-order business. Although new forms of marketing garnered the most attention, the traditional small store, where goods were displayed behind the counter and purchases negotiated with the owner or employee, continued to predominate. What Victoria de Grazia labeled the Fordist mode of distribution, with mass-produced and widely advertised goods sold in self-service stores, was emerging but not yet triumphant in America and scarcely present in Europe.[11]

European domestic consumption was not Americanized, although American domestic consumption was becoming globalized. In 1914, the United States exported $2.4 billion in goods, but imported $1.9 billion, and many of these imports reshaped everyday life. Women decorated their homes with orientalist motifs; immigrants brought their own foods with them; and cookbooks and women's magazines introduced middle-class housewives to such exotic foods as Hungarian goulash, Spanish Olla Podrida, Dutch cheese, and "rice as the Chinese prepare it." Through this new bourgeois "cosmopolitan domesticity," American middle-class women imagined themselves as both integrally related to the European and global order, and as different from—and superior to—those from whom they borrowed.[12]

European visitors frequently remarked on the peculiarities of the modern American woman, who was seen as free, independent, and enjoying more opportunities for education and cultural influence than her European counterparts. Yet, she was also cold and inaccessible, dominated her husband, and failed to educate her children properly. Interestingly, she was not intimately linked to consumption nor seen as a threat to European gender relations. That changed in the 1920s.

America's Emerging Model: European Responses

The exigencies of the First World War and the postwar recovery sparked intense interest in restructuring the home and reforming housework. Home economics and efficiency were the watchwords in America; rationalization was the preferred term in Germany and elsewhere on the continent. At national and international congresses on housework, women's organizations, politicians, and educators analyzed housework as a profession or vocation and the home as a business enterprise. Exhibits, lectures, and school courses taught women how better to perform household tasks and thereby stimulate the national economy and promote family stability and prosperity. American experts played a prominent role in the new international discourse, for Christine Frederick's pioneering book, *The New Housekeeping*, was immediately translated into several European languages, and many German women traveled to the United States.[13]

In the American model of consumerist domesticity, the housewife (always imagined as middle class) would move rationally through her functionally laid-out home, employing Taylorist techniques and hygienic practices. She was aided by appliances of all sorts—stoves, electric irons, vacuum cleaners, washing machines—and by such conveniences as store-bought canned goods. The powerful combination of efficiency and new household-centered consumption would free the American woman for educational, cultural, and leisure pursuits outside the home—although not necessarily in the labor force.[14]

Interwar Europeans neither imitated this version of consumerist domesticity nor looked to America as a political or aesthetic model for housing. The United States relied almost exclusively on the market to build homes, rejecting state subsidies and social housing, and preferring single-family units to apartment blocks. Neither approach suited postwar European conditions. Americans created modern skyscrapers and grain elevators; Europeans pioneered modern housing complexes. But how did they imagine domestic consumption?

Germans, who debated housing and housework with particular intensity, developed two alternative models of modern domesticity. Left-wing architects, such as Ernst May, Martin Wagner, and Bruno Taut, created functional housing complexes in order to engineer hygienic living, eliminate kitsch, and promote both household and industrial rationalization. Appliances might appear in middle-class versions of modern homes, but Margarete Schütte-Lihotzky's working-class Frankfurt kitchen—the most important model for modern mass housing in interwar Europe—had no refrigerator. Its austere functionalism was embodied in built-in cabinets; the ergonomic arrangement of sink, stove, and countertops; and the separation of the kitchen from other household activities, including eating. The Karl Marx Hof, a key symbol of Vienna's municipal socialism, looked similar. Many workers viewed such housing as an assault on working-class traditions and sociability. Those more receptive could afford apartments in developments, such as Berlin's Hufeisensiedlung, only if they were skilled and well paid.[15]

Most Germans adopted the more austere variant of domesticity promoted by home economics experts, social democratic reformers, and conservative housewives organizations. This version of domesticity recognized that most women lived in old housing and lacked electricity and decent incomes; they could only rationalize housework by Taylorizing their motions, minimally rearranging old furniture, and purchasing a few standardized utensils and dishes and perhaps a linoleum floor. To be sure, spurred by American success, firms like Siemens produced electric irons, vacuum cleaners, hot plates, and refrigerators, and advertised their merits widely. As many acknowledged, however, such appliances were far too expensive for defeated Germany. The interwar Dutch agreed that household technology did not fit a "regime of restricted consumption." Some who had electricity and could afford the new technology dismissed appliances like vacuum cleaners as unnecessary, for the efficient household would not accumulate dust. German home economists and women's organizations criticized store-bought canned goods as a bad American invention. As an alternative, women were encouraged to preserve their own vegetables and jams, store their own apples and potatoes, and eat only national foods rather than "southern fruits" and other foreign products.[16]

Germans opposed American domestic consumption on both economic and cultural grounds. Business circles and right-wing politicians rejected a high-wage, mass-production strategy that could have made appliances affordable; the political Left, which favored it, did not imagine household technology as the goal of Fordism. (Exactly what was to be produced and consumed in their vision of mass production was less than clear.) Many Germans associated mass consumption with homogeneity, inferior quality, and crass materialism that threatened both German "quality work" and *Kultur*.[17]

In America, women came to be defined as the quintessential consumer, whether represented as the daring but dangerous "consuming woman" of automobile and cosmetic ads or the more benign "Mrs. Consumer" to whom marketers of all sorts appealed. German visitors argued that the modern American home, filled with appliances and prepared foods, was the prerequisite for the American New Woman, who destabilized traditional gender relations and lacked the proper domestic and maternal spirit. By borrowing elements of the American economic model, such as Taylorism and rational layouts, but not consumer durables, Germans hoped to avoid the most threatening aspects of Americanism.[18]

Little changed in the 1930s. The Nazis' nationalized variant of mass culture did not seek to satisfy individual needs, as the American model did; rather, it sought to incorporate the individual into a racialized, hierarchical collective. Hitler was fascinated by Henry Ford and mass motorization, but despite the prevalence of the "people's radio" and the promise of the "Strength-Through-Joy (*Kraft durch Freude*) Car" (later renamed the Volkswagen), Americanized mass consumption remained a hope, to be realized only in racialized forms after Germany's anticipated military victory. Whether consumerist domesticity would have been part of that remains unclear. Nazi women's organizations endorsed the efficient, but non-mechanized, home, presided over by a non-working housewife/mother, who purchased national foods and rationalized domestic practices. To it they added racism, pro-natalism, and motherhood education, but not consumerism. Insofar as new goods flowed into German homes in the Third Reich, they came primarily from plundering the property of the deported and exterminated Jews of Europe.[19]

The Soviet Union was no more open to domestic consumption. Although "mass culture generally had a positive meaning in both the United States and the Soviet Union that it lacked in the ethnically constructed imaginaries of Western European nations,"[20] mass consumption proved more problematic. In the 1930s, Stalin asserted the need for more cultured consumption. Accordingly, the Soviets produced canned foods, sausages, and chocolate, along with a few luxury items like perfume and champagne. They also manufactured some consumer durables, such as bicycles and gramophones. But the state prioritized heavy industry, and the earlier promise of collectivized household services had not completely faded. When Schütte-Lihotzky worked in the Soviet Union in the early 1930s, she did not design any modern kitchens: in the superblocks intended for cities like the new iron and steel center Magnitogorsk, all services were to be communal.[21]

Alternative European Models in the American Century

After the Second World War, European and American housing, consumption regimes, and conceptions of domesticity changed dramatically. Initially, America had the world's largest economy; produced and purchased the vast majority of the world's consumer durables; and exported its products, people, and prescriptions for living across Western Europe. As American politicians and pundits proudly proclaimed the American Century, they promised Europeans, "You can be like us." When Europeans embarked on recovery and modernization, however, they not only borrowed from the United States, but also drew on their own products, practices, and traditions—and on new postwar social commitments. By the 1970s, Western Europeans achieved levels of prosperity comparable to those in the United States, but neither their homes nor their domestic consumption regimes replicated America's. And Eastern Europeans looked more to Western Europe than to the United States as they sought to build an alternative socialist modernity.[22]

Consider housing, the site of new forms of domestic consumption. The United States endorsed international modernism, especially the glass-wall skyscraper, as the architecture of freedom, but it did not advocate high-rise apartments. Rather, Marshall Plan officials and the United States Information Agency (USIA) promoted single-family homes like those in suburban Levittown. Western European office and government architecture balanced American influences and national traditions and concerns. But housing in Western Europe was less susceptible to American influences, for national and European models carried more weight; funding and ownership patterns differed; and suburbanization was limited. To be sure, Europeans flocked to the 1949 *How America Lives* exhibit in Stuttgart, the 1950 *America at Home* exhibit in West Berlin, and numerous smaller trade shows across Europe that had products, model homes, and even American actors performing "the American way of life." Many European architects visited Levittown, but the response of French ones was typical. The French admired American rationalization, standardization, and streamlined management systems; they adopted many of these processes—but did not build the iconic, postwar American wood-frame suburban tract houses.[23]

The French Ministry of Reconstruction and Urbanism, which was committed to building nearly a quarter of a million housing units per year, looked to mass production and prefabrication, and designed similar housing for the working and middle classes. Its first experimental project at Noisy-le-See in Paris contained models from Britain, Canada, France, Finland, Sweden, Switzerland, and the United States. The functionally designed interiors drew more on interwar French and German influences than on American ones. Although some single-family homes were built, grand ensembles—vast apartment blocks with 800 to 3,500 units—were preferred. Le Corbusier's Unite d'Habitation in Marseilles had extensive communal facilities as well. Like many Frenchmen, he regarded suburbs as "[t]he Great American Waste."[24]

Postwar British planners criticized American housing as chaotic and sprawling, preferring denser new towns and housing projects. The 1951 Festival of Britain built modern housing in London's bombed-out East End that looked to the models displayed at the 1930 Stockholm Exhibition. Likewise, postwar reconstruction in Warsaw, Belgrade, and Sweden drew more on interwar models than on postwar American ones. In the Netherlands, which received the most Marshall Plan aid per capita, new housing adapted Dutch and European traditions of austere modernism. The much-praised Lijnbaan in Rotterdam reflected Dutch modernism; pioneered Europe's first pedestrian zone; and combined housing density with mixed-use zoning in distinctively European ways. West German conservatives criticized American homes as too high-tech and expensive. When single-family homes were built, their layout and appearance remained traditional.[25]

After Stalin's death in 1953, the Soviets turned away from socialist realism and superfluous ornamentation. Instead, they adopted standardized construction techniques to meet the acute housing shortage. Premier Nikita Khrushchev sent study trips to Scandinavia and West Germany and made the single-family apartment with its own kitchen the goal. Between 1956 and 1970, 34 million housing units were built, and more than half of the population moved into these dwellings. In the mid-1950s, the *khrushcheby*, squat five-story brick apartment buildings with plain facades and functionally designed interiors predominated. Thereafter, larger prefabricated buildings with modern, standardized, interiors were favored. Across Eastern Europe, governments followed suit, building thousands of prefab apartment blocks that looked like their counterparts in Western and Northern Europe and employed American methods of industrial-housing construction much more fully than America itself.[26]

The millions of homes built across postwar Europe differed not merely in style and location but also in ownership, funding, and pedagogical intent. In most European countries, renting was the norm, and American efforts to promote ownership, such as in the Ruhr, met with opposition.[27] Belgium did have high rates of private ownership, but little else about homes resembled American ones. State-funded social housing was the dominant form in postwar Europe, due to both the severity of the housing crisis and to the social democratic commitments of governments in countries such as Britain, France, the Netherlands, and Sweden. In the Soviet Union, individuals and cooperatives did much of the construction in the 1950s but then the state took over. Across Europe, housing was defined as a social right, and broad sectors of the population benefitted from publicly subsidized apartments. In the United States, housing was thoroughly commodified, and only the poor lived in public housing.

The massive, European modernist housing programs aimed to transform inhabitants as well as to improve material conditions. Soviet politicians, planners, and architects hoped that living in a functional apartment with modern furniture and no clutter would improve everyday practices and wean people from the petty bourgeois attitudes that the high-Stalinist preference for overstuffed furniture and lampshades with fringe ostensibly promoted. British architects and urbanists embraced a social democratic vision of rational, productive living and leisure in modern, functional apartments. French planners wanted to rationalize everyday life and to discipline consumption so as to encourage families to have more children. In Germany, new housing was to foster rational and restrained consumption, vital to national recovery.[28] Everywhere architects, designers, and government planners condescendingly dismissed the tastes of the intended inhabitants. The discourse surrounding American homes, in contrast, emphasized affluence as well as rising expectations and desires. Homes were sites of individual choice and mobility—not places of pedagogical projects and societal transformation.

The European focus on housing had practical, political, and ideological roots. It was a response to not only wartime devastation but to the failure to build homes in the crisis-ridden interwar years. In early postwar West Germany, 2.3 million dwellings were destroyed or uninhabitable. Across Europe, many homes lacked basic amenities; in France, for example, 75 percent of homes lacked running water.[29] Housing was central to a broad political commitment to break with interwar poverty and insecurity by vastly expanding social programs. In America, private housing was viewed as a key engine of private production and consumption.

Across Europe and in the United States, there was a postwar retreat into the home and away from problematic national pasts and threatening, postwar presents. For example, Americans sought solace from Cold

War anxieties by pursuing domestic as well as international containment; West Germans wanted to escape from the material and emotional damage of Nazism; and East Germans and Soviets tried to bolster their legitimacy and compete economically against the West. Common to all efforts to build new homes and valorize domesticity was a desire to stabilize families and normalize traditional domestic gender relations—whether or not women were in the workforce.[30]

This diversity of motives converged on a similar form—apartments or houses occupied by a single, usually small, nuclear family. A central element was the small working kitchen, which might be sealed off from the adjacent dining area or might include—or open out to—it. (This was a highly contentious issue, with architects preferring the former and most inhabitants the latter.) A family-centered living room was to be used on a daily basis rather than being reserved for special occasions and guests, and parents and children had their own bedrooms.[31] The clear separation of functions within was paralleled by a sharp division between the private home and the public street. What made these dwellings modern was not the rational layout alone; it was the infrastructure and accouterments—plumbing; electricity; central heating; modern furniture; and, most important, consumer durables.

American government and business imagined the modern kitchen as a distinctly American invention, embodying the essence of what the USIA called "People's Capitalism": choice, abundance, and free enterprise. They promoted this heavily commodified domesticity in home exhibits; through the Caravan of Modern Food Service, a model supermarket that toured Western Europe; and in lavish displays of ultra-modern, appliance-filled kitchens at the 1958 Brussels World's Fair as well as in Moscow a year later. They predicted that Western Europe would adopt what West German critics called the American "Fat Kitchen."[32]

Both assumptions represented misleading simplifications of complex processes of transatlantic exchange and negotiated appropriation. The American modern kitchen, like modern architecture, was only partially American, for U.S. architects drew on interwar modernist traditions that were Dutch, French, and German. Many postwar Europeans found it easier to acknowledge European influences coded as American than to recognize the German roots of so much domestic modernism, but the design traditions of other European countries remained usable. Dutch, French, and Finnish postwar architects and planners certainly knew about American kitchens, but many found them too affluent and style-conscious for European conditions. National design councils in every European country sought to develop recognizably modern but distinctively national domestic cultures. Women's organizations in Belgium and the Netherlands judged America's large, gadget-filled kitchens to be excessive, even decadent, preferring more austere forms of modernism. A 1944 poll of British women's organizations revealed modest desires for postwar kitchens: a rational layout and built-in cabinets; a stove and hot running water; a refrigerator that would supplement the traditional larder, not replace it; and a good copper pot for clothes washing with a wringer rather than a washing machine. Similarly, West German women were urged to acquire new consumer durables but in a cautious manner that would not endanger family finances.[33]

Americans claimed that average workers enjoyed the modern amenities displayed in the exhibits and movies seen across Europe. While this ignored rural poverty and poverty among Blacks, Americans did consume three-quarters of the world's appliances in the early 1950s. No European country had anything comparable to the commoditized prosperity enjoyed by White Americans of all classes. Consumerist domesticity was realized at uneven rates across Europe, arriving first as image and promise. In the mid-1950s, electric stoves and vacuum cleaners were ceasing to be luxury items in West Germany and many families purchased new furniture, although only one in twenty West German households had a refrigerator. In contrast, half of all households in the United States and in Switzerland had refrigerators. By 1963, nearly two-thirds of Belgian and Dutch households had washing machines, while nearly half of British and Swiss households and roughly one-third of Austrian, French, and West German ones did. Only 8 percent of Italian households had one, illustrating the delayed onset of consumer culture in Southern Europe. The Dutch had the highest percentage of vacuum cleaners, exceeding the 79 percent U.S. level, while Britain and West Germany came close to it. West Germany led in refrigerators, with 58 percent of households owning one. While only one-third of West German households had a phone by decade's end, over 60 percent had a washing machine and nearly three-quarters owned a television.[34] The spread of kitchen appliances, TVs, and cars in new housing with indoor plumbing and central heating meant that "for the first time in history, ease and comfort were now within the reach of most people in [Western] Europe."[35]

The purchase of new consumer durables marked a familization rather than an individualization of consumption. The purpose of household technology was not only to lighten women's workload, but to create a healthier, happier, and more modern life for the rest of the family.

Consumer durables were to be used by the family, within the home. The iconic image was of the family gathered around the TV in a living room with modern, functional furniture, the husband/father relaxing, surrounded by his children while the wife/mother prepared food with her modern appliances. The kitchen was indisputably women's domain, but the home became increasingly that of husbands and children as well, for there was a new emphasis on the family-centered consumption of leisure. Everyday life became privatized to an unprecedented degree.

Although America offered an inspiring image of prosperity, Western Europeans did not emulate its large, gadget-filled kitchens. They instead developed hybrid forms of domestic modernity that differed visibly from the American model. Initially, Europeans had less stuff in their homes; kept what they had longer; and moved less frequently. This was by necessity, and, later, by choice. The French grand ensembles of the late 1950s, for example, had heating, indoor plumbing, and electricity; they did not, however, come equipped with appliances, which had to be acquired over time. Every apartment in London's upper-middle-class Barbican housing development of the 1960s had the same small, prefabricated, functional kitchen, with basic appliances and few electrical outlets. The kitchen was not an arena for displaying and constantly updating affluence.[36] Spacious American kitchens with large, often-streamlined appliances required suburbs and cars; the former came only partially to Europe, the latter belatedly.

As household technology spread in Europe, appliances did not become larger and more energy consuming. Notably, Europeans refrained from buying two items that were increasingly popular in American homes: air conditioners and clothes dryers. The American "high-energy home," which paid little attention to climate and conservation, had no European counterpart.[37] The obsessive, never-satisfied, wasteful nature of American consumerist domesticity, criticized so strongly by John Kenneth Galbraith, Betty Friedan, and Vance Packard, did not cross the Atlantic. Europeans preferred a more austere modernism, emphasizing functionality, rationality, ergonomics, and basic yet durable appliances. This was in contrast to the American emphasis on technological abundance, space, and constant change. The reasons were economic and political as well as cultural. European incomes were lower, taxes higher, credit purchasing limited, and the division between private and public spending very different.

Marketing differed as well. Although European self-service stores multiplied, American-style supermarkets spread more slowly. In 1971, Americans spent 70 percent of their food money in supermarkets, while the French spent only 32 percent; Germans, 14 percent; and Italians a meager 2 percent. American firms opened supermarkets in Belgium and Italy, but Germans built their own. The U.S. Department of Commerce and the National Association of Food Chains built an American-style supermarket in Zagreb, but Yugoslav agriculture was not equipped to produce standardized goods to stock it. Subsequent Yugoslav imitations were small and combined self-service and more-personal forms of retailing.[38] Although print advertising was influenced by American methods, American-style TV ads found no place on Europe's state-owned, highly regulated networks. In short, substantial elements of the bourgeois consumption regime persisted in Europe. Emphasized there were quality, durability, and personal interactions between buyers and sellers.

Women in Europe, as in America, were assigned a key role in domestic consumption, whether or not they in fact made major purchasing decisions. Women's magazines and advertising conveyed detailed information about specific appliances and purveyed broad definitions of modernity and women's place in it. These media depicted "a way of life characterized by comfort, hygiene, time-saving, and a both practical and charming way of tackling everyday tasks," to quote one Swedish ad. The housewife took her responsibilities seriously, but she was equally dedicated to making her work—and thus her family's life—easier by a judicious choice of products. With the right technology, another Swedish ad for refrigerators promised, "you will be able to take care of household tasks as easily and elegantly as the American wife." Frequently, the modern housewife, easily recognizable by her youth, fashionable clothing, modish haircut, and excessive cheerfulness, was contrasted with the shabbily dressed and harried interwar housewife. Whether depicted alone in her modern home, with women friends, showing off her whiter-than-white laundry, or with the male expert or helpful husband, the modern housewife was relentlessly optimistic and proud of her domestic accomplishments. She embodied a carefree modernity, one in which technology was benign and progressive.[39]

But did image reflect reality? Did women buy into this new version of domesticity? Elaine Tyler May suggests that white, middle-class, American women found the new gender traditionalism of the commodified home appealing; even if it failed to satisfy them as promised, few regretted their life choices or imagined alternatives. In Western Europe, the image of the stay-at-home wife and mother, which, to be sure, did not reflect the varied conditions found in the United States, was much less threatening than the 1920s New Woman had been. But from economic necessity, political ideology, or cultural preference, she was not wholeheartedly imitated. In Britain and West Germany, the legal and social pressures on women to stay home were enormous and the social policy supports for alternative choices meager. On the contrary, in France and Sweden, women were encouraged to work. The possibility of actually being a consuming modern housewife arrived only slowly, and, even today, European women do not seem to have embraced the new domesticity with the same genuine or desperate enthusiasm Americans did. For example, German ads historically encouraged consumption but equally emphasized women's duties to husbands and children and to family stabilization and national economic recovery. The modern West German housewife was never as carefree as her American counterpart.[40]

By the 1970s, Western European domestic consumption certainly resembled that in America in relation to the types of goods purchased; the mechanisms by which they were marketed; and the images of rational, carefree modernity that proliferated. But similar products and processes took on distinctive characteristics in different national settings, and Europeans came to associate their new kitchens and homes with national or other European models more than with American ones. One can trace this appropriation and nationalization through several West German publications. In 1951, the Rationalization Curatorium for the German Economy (Rationalisierungs-Kuratorium der Deutschen Wirtschaft or RKW) published *Housewife, Make Your Housework Easy!* (*Hausfrau: mach dir die Arbeit leicht!*). This pamphlet, a virtual reprint of the 1920s publication with a similar title, told housewives how to arrange kitchens ergonomically and Taylorize their movements, but never mentioned appliances. The German home bore no resemblance to the widely exhibited American models. A pamphlet on household rationalization, published the same year, lauded the promise of electrification and household technology, but noted that only 4 percent of West Germans could afford a refrigerator. Five years later, the RKW's publication on washing clothes at home discussed both machine washing and hand washing, suggesting the growing presence of the former.[41]

In 1958, Constanze-Verlag published *The Ideal Household*, a 200-page compendium of ads and articles advising how to purchase the appropriate stove, refrigerator, washing machine, and vacuum cleaner for one's particular household. By this time, household technology was no longer viewed as a luxury but as something both desirable and affordable for people at many different income levels. It promised to lighten women's work and help them be "healthy, well groomed, and in a good mood" so that they could make their well-run home "a quiet island in our tumultuous times." America was not the only model cited; a comparison of efficient kitchen-floor plans, for example, discussed both U.S. and Swedish layouts. The vast majority of ads featured a wide array of German appliances, cabinets, furniture, and flooring made by firms like Bosch, Siemens, AEG, and smaller furniture manufacturers. Frigidaire was among the few American companies represented.[42]

These publications suggest that household technology, once the preserve of privileged America, moved rapidly into depictions of the modern German home, while losing its explicit association with the United States. Similarly, hybrid forms of domestic consumption developed in other European countries, as the Germans and the Dutch exported appliances to Western Europe; Scandinavian design circulated widely; and Italian low-cost refrigerators were sold all over Western Europe (and in limited quantities in the East). Even in Sweden, "labeled the most Americanized nation in Europe...visiting Americans found that the American styles, goods and rituals mostly had been Swedified beyond recognition." The use of appliances, the preferred color schemes of homes, the shape of brooms, even the smell of multinational disinfectant—in short, everyday modernity—were at once American, European, and profoundly, if often elusively, national.[43]

Socialist Consumer Modernity

Communist Eastern Europe, usually presented as the antithesis of capitalism, developed forms of domestic consumption bearing a family resemblance to those in Western Europe. In an attempt to catch up and overtake the United States, Khrushchev called for single-family apartments to have plumbing, electricity, and a modern kitchen with a stove and a refrigerator. Households were also to have TVs but not cars. Khrushchev and his successors both feared that such domestic consumption would inculcate petty bourgeois attitudes and hoped that a modern, rationalized home, replete with appliances, would introduce women to the "technological scientific revolution" and make them model Soviet citizens. The 1959 Moscow kitchen debate between Nixon and Khrushchev, held in front of a canary-yellow, General Electric-made, all-electric kitchen, showed that the Cold War rivals agreed that the modern home was a measure of civilization. Soviet officials and some visitors, however, criticized the American model of affluence and planned obsolescence, favoring instead kitchens that were lean, less gadget-filled, and similar to those in Western Europe. The ultimate winner of the kitchen debate may well have been Sweden, widely admired on both sides of the Iron Curtain, or either the Netherlands or Germany—and not Nixon, as Americans widely assume.[44]

The minimalist Soviet interiors resembled the Nordic modernism popular in Western Europe. In 1957, the yearbook of the *Great Soviet Encyclopedia* displayed model interiors for prefabricated apartment blocks that "would hardly have looked out of place in household magazines in the West at the time," even though affinities with Western modernism were not explicitly discussed.[45] Most Soviets assumed the new style was indigenous, while those in the design community looked for inspiration to the Baltic States, Czechoslovakia, East Germany, Poland, not America. Other Eastern bloc modernists were influenced by Scandinavian design and West Germany's Ulm Institute for Design, just as Western Europeans were. Europeans across the continent used plastic, "a modern material *par excellence*," for furniture and dishware, but in the West, the market controlled production, while in the East, the Soviets sent oil to East Germany, which supplied the entire bloc with plastic goods.[46]

Members of the German Communist Party turned toward domestic consumption more grudgingly, for they viewed production as the privileged site of social transformation. Nonetheless, the 1953 uprising; constant pressure from women trying to negotiate the double burden of waged work and housework; and, above all, competition with West Germany forced the regime to turn attention to consumer durables as well as "the 1000 little things" from sewing needles to shoelaces that were essential to everyday life. East Germany looked abroad to Czechoslovakia, Denmark, Sweden, the United States, and the Soviet Union for model household goods, which slowly entered East German homes. In 1960, only 6 percent of homes had washers and refrigerators, but by 1970, over half did and two-thirds had TVs; thereafter, domestic consumption rose steadily.[47] Under communism as under capitalism, household technology would help women master modern domesticity and fulfill other economic and social functions without disrupting the traditional domestic division of labor.

East German consumer domesticity shared much with that of Western Europe. East Germany drew on both prewar German traditions and contemporary Swedish and West German examples, given that their functional designs, smaller appliances, and more modest consumption regimes proved closer to what was economically possible and politically desirable than more distant American models. East Germany assumed that the consuming housewife would also be a woman worker. In the provision of public housing, childcare, and social services, East

Germany and other socialist states looked more like Northern Europe or France than the United States. East Germany also tried to develop an alternative consumer culture that would distribute goods more equitably; to find non-market mechanisms to regulate supply and demand; and to allocate public and private spending differently.[48] The very longevity of this socialist, modern experiment suggests that these efforts met with some success. Yet, in three crucial ways, the experiment failed. First, the state remained suspicious of the potentially subversive consequences of private consumption; consequently, the state sought to teach people what they should want and combined the provision of more goods with more surveillance by the Stasi.[49] Second, East Germany, like other socialist states, failed to develop an alternative to the individual family, surrounded by the commodified accouterments of modern life—ovens and refrigerators, electric mixers and vacuum cleaners, washing machines and dishwashers, Tupperware and TVs. Gone were earlier visions of radically transforming gender, sexuality, and domesticity. East as well as West, the basic unit remained the consumerist domestic space with the modern woman as consuming housewife, responsible for all domestic labor. The ideologically promiscuous modern kitchen could be instrumentalized by communist, Christian democratic, social democratic, and liberal regimes. But domestic consumption, which brought prosperity to Western capitalist economies, contributed significantly to the failure of socialist ones. Unable to produce enough goods, East Germany borrowed heavily to import them. It stimulated consumerist desires that it could not satisfy and thereby undermined its own legitimacy. This was "the revenge of the domestic."[50]

Domestic Consumption, Social Policy, and Consumer Citizenship

Europeans and Americans experienced everyday life differently not only because of what was in kitchens and homes, but also because of the sociopolitical context in which they were embedded. Americans prioritized the individual, the private, and the market. They created a "consumers' republic" in which family-centered mass consumption and consumer choice were expected to produce optimal economic outcomes and individual happiness—and legitimize the state.[51] By comparison, across Europe public authorities built more homes and provided extensive and inclusive social programs. There were more public goods and decommodified services, and the modern home and family were less isolated from the public sphere.

The relationship of consumption and citizenship varied. Collective movements to regulate the production of consumer goods emerged on both sides of the Atlantic in the first decades of the twentieth century. After the Second World War, however, Americans defined consumer citizenship as the individual's exercise of free choice in the market. This conflicted with European conceptions of social citizenship, existing class hierarchies, and more ideological political parties. In East Germany, France, and Sweden, for example, the state provided extensive childcare and generous maternity benefits. Across Europe, health care was a right, not a commodity. [52] "The European *citizen-consumers*... were hybrids...for they turned uneasily between state and market, between the security promised by the European welfare state and the freedoms promised by American consumer culture."[53]

These differences increased when the United States embraced neoliberalism in the wake of the collapse of Bretton Woods, the oil shocks, and the crises of Fordism and Keynesianism. After 1945, America stood for an appealing mixture of Fordist economic prowess and Keynesianism; New Deal social policies, international law, and multilateralism. Since the 1980s, America has represented a more problematic mixture of market fundamentalism, unilateralism, and extreme individualism. In the last decades of the twentieth century, mass consumption and the modern kitchen have continued to transform everyday European life. As Spain, Greece, and Portugal joined the European Community and intra-European circuits of exchange, these countries' domestic consumption regimes came to resemble those in Northern and Western Europe. In the American South, by contrast, sunbelt capitalism not only promoted suburban sprawl, fat kitchens, large houses, and over-the-top consumerism—it also pioneered neo-liberalism. While most European nations have liberalized finance and trade, they have neither abandoned their social programs nor embraced hyper-consumption. Those that did—Britain from the 1980s on, Russia in the 1990s, and Iceland after 2000, for example—met with mixed results at best, catastrophic ones at worst.

The influence of the American model of consumer capitalism, always more limited than imagined, diminished well before the 2008 global economic crisis, one distinctly "Made in America." In the wake of the global economic crisis, what is the likely future of domestic consumption? Consumer domesticity in hybrid forms has outlived the crisis and demise of Fordist mass production in the United States and its weakening in Europe. But whereas the manufacturing of most goods—all the traditional ones, plus computers, mobile phones, and entertainment-related electronics—that go into American domestic consumption has been outsourced, mainly to China, more manufacturing remains in Europe. The de-linking of production and consumption structurally weakened the U.S. economy. The 2008 crisis discredited the American model of financialization with its subprime loans, byzantine financial instruments, and extraordinary leveraging, and called into question the feasibility of the ever-expanding domestic consumption via unprecedented individual and national indebtedness. But no clear alternative has emerged.

Domestic consumption on an American scale has created enormous ecological problems in the United States as well as in poorer countries that consume much less but suffer the consequences of producing for America and Europe. While Western Europe is attentive to environmental issues related to consumption, much of Eastern Europe is not. Socially, the American neo-liberal model has created pronounced inequality. After the Second World War, America offered a vision of prosperity and increased equality, built on greater productivity, new homes, and a new consumption regime. Now, America stands for greater income inequality, reduced social protection, and poorer health. European nations have developed alternative models of capitalism and domestic consumption that show how to live as well as, or even better than, the average American with less income and higher taxes, but better benefits, higher-quality goods, and practices that are more environmentally sustainable.[54] If the nineteenth century was British and the twentieth American, perhaps the twenty-first will be European and Chinese?

Notes

1. For an introduction to the vast literature on Americanization, see David Ellwood, *The Shock of America: Europe and the Challenge of the Century* (Oxford: Oxford University Press, 2012); Victoria de Grazia, *Irresistible Empire: America's Advance through 20th-Century Europe* (Cambridge, MA: Belknap Press of Harvard University Press, 2005); Rob Kroes, *If You've Seen One, You've Seen the Mall: Europeans and American Mass Culture* (Urbana: University of Illinois Press, 1996); Geir Lundestad, "Empire by Invitation? The United States and Western Europe, 1945–1952," *Journal of Peace Research* 23 (1986): 263–77; Mary Nolan, *The Transatlantic Century: Europe and America, 1890–2010* (Cambridge: Cambridge University Press, 2012); Daniel T. Rodgers, *Atlantic Crossings: Social Politics in the Atlantic Age* (Cambridge, MA: Belknap Press of Harvard University Press, 2000); Alexander Stephan, ed., *The Americanization of Europe: Culture, Diplomacy and Anti-Americanism after 1945* (New York: Berghahn Books, 2006); Mel van Elteren, *Americanism and Americanization: A Critical History of Domestic and Global Influence* (Jefferson, NC: McFarland & Co., 2006).

2. Gary Cross, *An All-Consuming Century: Why Commercialism Won in Modern America* (New York: Columbia University Press, 2000), 67.
3. Paul Betts and David Crowley, "Introduction," in "Domestic Dreamworlds: Notions of Home in Post-1945 Europe," special issue, *Journal of Contemporary History* 40 (2005): 213–35; Ruth Oldenziel and Karin Zachmann, "Kitchens as Technology and Politics: An Introduction," in *Cold War Kitchen: Americanization, Technology, and European Users*, ed. Ruth Oldenziel and Karin Zachmann (Cambridge, MA: MIT Press, 2009), 3, 7.
4. Mona Domosh, *American Commodities in an Age of Empire* (New York: Routledge, 2006), 7, 41–2, 98, 114.
5. Fred McKenzie, *The American Invaders* (New York: Arno Press, 1976), 142–3.
6. W. T. Stead, *The Americanization of the World* (New York: Horace Markley, 1901).
7. Eric Hobsbawm, *The Age of Empire, 1875–1914* (New York: Vintage, 1989), 53; Geoffrey Barraclough, *Introduction to Contemporary History* (Baltimore, MD: Penguin, 1967), 45–9, 346–8; Charles F. McGovern, *Sold American: Consumption and Citizenship, 1890–1945* (Chapel Hill: University of North Carolina Press, 2006).
8. Angus Maddison, *Monitoring the World Economy, 1829–1992* (Paris: OECD, 1995), 72.
9. Kristin Hoganson, *Consumers' Imperium: The Global Production of American Domesticity, 1865–1920* (Chapel Hill: University of North Carolina Press, 2007), 105–51.
10. Domosh, *American Commodities*, 7, 41–2, 98, 114, quote on 42.
11. Geoffrey Crossick and Serge Jaumain, eds., *Cathedrals of Consumption: The European Department Store, 1850–1939* (Aldershot: Ashgate, 1999), 2–29, 117–22; Victoria de Grazia, "Changing Consumption Regimes in Europe, 1930–1979: Comparative Perspectives on the Distribution Problem," in *Getting and Spending: European and American Consumer Societies in the Twentieth Century*, ed. Susan Strasser, Charles McGovern, and Matthias Judt (Cambridge: Cambridge University Press, 1998), 59.
12. Kristin Hoganson, "Stuff It: Domestic Consumption and the Americanization of the World Paradigm," *Diplomatic History* 30 (2006): 571–94; Hoganson, *Consumers' Imperium*, 13, 105–51.
13. Mary Nolan, "'Housework Made Easy': The Taylorized Housewife in Weimar Germany's Rationalized Economy," *Feminist Studies* 16 (1990): 549–78; Liesbeth Bervoets, "'Consultation Required!' Women Coproducing the Modern Kitchen in the Netherlands, 1920–1970," in *Cold War Kitchen*, 211–20.
14. Nolan, "'Housework Made Easy.'"
15. Martina Hessler, "The Frankfurt Kitchen: The Model of Modernity and the 'Madness' of Traditional Users, 1926–1933," in *Cold War Kitchen*, 169–71; Helmut Gruber, *Red Vienna: Experiment in Working-Class Culture, 1918–1934* (New York: Oxford University Press, 1991); Mary Nolan, *Visions of Modernity: American Business and the Modernization of Germany* (Oxford: Oxford University Press, 1994), 226.
16. Nolan, *Visions of Modernity*, 216–17; Bervoets, "'Consultation Required!'" 215; Martina Hessler, "Die Einführung elektrischer Haushaltsgeräte in der Zwischenkriegszeit: Der Angebotspush der Produzenten und die Reaktion

der Konsumentinnen," *Technikgeschichte* 65 (1998): 297–312; Nancy Reagin, *Sweeping the German Nation: Domesticity and National Identity, 1870–1945* (New York: Cambridge University Press, 2008), 95.
17. Nolan, *Visions of Modernity*, 58–119.
18. Uta Poiger, "The Modern Girl Around the World: Cosmetics Advertising and the Politics of Race and Style," in *The Modern Girl Around the World: Consumption, Modernity, and Globalization*, ed. Alys Eve Weinbaum et al. (Durham, NC: Duke University Press, 2008); Emily S. Rosenberg, "Consuming Women: Images of Americanization in the 'American Century,'" *Diplomatic History* 23 (1999): 479–97; McGovern, *Sold American*, 36; Nolan, *Visions of Modernity*, 120–7, 211–17, 225.
19. Adam Tooze, *The Wages of Destruction: The Making and Breaking of the Nazi Economy* (New York: Penguin, 2007), xxiv–xxvi; Reagin, *Sweeping the German Nation*, 110–81; Carola Sachse, *Siemens, der Nationalsozialismus und die moderne Familie: Eine Untersuchung zur sozialen Rationalisierung in Deutschland im 20. Jahrhundert* (Hamburg: Rasch und Röhring, 1990); Götz Aly, *Hitler's Beneficiaries: Plunder, Racial War, and the Nazi Welfare State*, trans. Jefferson Chase (New York: Metropolitan Books, 2006).
20. Susan Buck-Morss, *Dreamworld and Catastrophe: The Passing of Mass Utopia in East and West* (Cambridge, MA: MIT Press, 2000), 148.
21. Jukka Gronow, *Caviar with Champagne: Common Luxury and the Ideals of the Good Life in Stalin's Russia* (Oxford: Berg, 2003); Amy E. Randall, *The Soviet Dream World of Retail Trade and Consumption in the 1930s* (Basingstoke: Palgrave Macmillan, 2008), 17–43; Esra Akcan, "Civilizing Housewives versus Participatory Users: Margarete Schütte-Lihotzky in the Employ of the Turkish Nation State," in *Cold War Kitchen*, 194; Stephen Kotkin, *Magnetic Mountain: Stalinism as Civilization* (Berkeley: University of California Press, 1995), 109–23.
22. Jan Logemann, *Trams or Tailfins? Public and Private Property in Postwar West Germany and the United States* (Chicago: University of Chicago Press, 2012).
23. Greg Castillo, "Domesticating the Cold War: Household Consumption as Propaganda in Marshall Plan Germany," *Journal of Contemporary History* 40 (2005): 261–88; Greg Castillo, "The American 'Fat Kitchen' in Europe: Postwar Domestic Modernity and Marshall Plan Strategies of Enhancement," in *Cold War Kitchen*, 38–40, 47–50.
24. Nicole Rudolph, "Who Should Be the Author of a Dwelling: Architects versus Housewives in 1950s France," *Gender and History* 21 (2009): 541–59; Nicole Rudolph, "Domestic Politics: The Cité expérimentale at Noisy-le-See in Greater Pairs," *Modern and Contemporary France* 12 (2004): 483–95; David Crowley, "Europe Reconstructed, Europe Divided," in *Cold War Modern: Design, 1945–1970*, ed. David Crowley and Jane Pavitt (London: V&A Publishing, 2008), 54; Jean-Louis Cohen, *Scenes of the World to Come: European Architecture and the American Challenge, 1893–1960* (Paris: Flammarion, 1995), 175–6.
25. Cohen, *Scenes of the World to Come*, 197; George H. Marcus, *Design in the Fifties: When Everyone Went Modern* (Munich: Prestel Verlag, 1998), 74–7; Becky E. Conekin, *"The Autobiography of a Nation": The 1951 Festival of Britain* (Manchester: Manchester University Press, 2003), 9–10, 17, 26, 47;

Crowley and Pavitt, "Introduction," 17; Liesbeth Bervoets, "The Marshall Plan and the Promise of Industrial Housing: The Appropriation of a 'Failed' Revolution in Post-War Holland" (paper presented at the European Ways of Living in the American Century Conference, Stockholm, January 16–17, 2010); Werner Durth, "Architecture as a Political Medium," in *The United States and Germany in the Era of the Cold War, 1945–1968: A Handbook*, ed. Detlef Junker (New York: Cambridge University Press, 2004), 482–3.

26. Steven E. Harris, "In Search of 'Ordinary' Russia: Everyday Life in the NEP, the Thaw and the Communal Apartment," *Kritika* 6 (2005): 596–7, 607–8; Christine Varga-Harris, "Homemaking and the Aesthetic and Moral Perimeters of the Soviet Home during the Khrushchev Era," *Journal of Social History* 41 (2008): 565; Mark B. Smith, "Khrushchev's Promise to Eliminate the Urban Housing Shortage: Rights, Rationality and the Communist Future," in *Soviet State and Society under Nikita Khrushchev*, ed. Melanie Ilic and Jeremy Smith (London: Routledge, 2009), 26, 31; Henry W. Morton, "What Have Soviet Leaders Done about the Housing Crisis?" in *Soviet Politics and Society in the 1970s*, ed. Henry Morton and Rudolf L. Tökés (New York: Free Press, 1974), 163; Blair A. Ruble, "From *khrushcheby* to *korobki*," in *Russian Housing in the Modern Age: Design and Social History*, ed. William Craft Brumfield and Blair A. Ruble (Cambridge: Cambridge University Press, 1993), 233, 238–40; David Crowley, "Thaw Modern: Design in Eastern Europe after 1956," in *Cold War Modern*, 130–2; David Crowley, "Paris or Moscow: Warsaw Architects and the Image of the Modern City in the 1950s," *Kritika* 9 (2008): 786.

27. Rebecca Boehling, "U.S. Cultural Policy and German Culture during the American Occupation," in *The United States and Germany in the Era of the Cold War*, 392.

28. Varga-Harris, "Homemaking and the Aesthetic and Moral Perimeters," 564–6, 570; Victor Buchli, "Khrushchev, Modernism, and the Fight against Petit-bourgeois Consciousness in the Soviet Home," *Journal of Design History* 10 (1997): 168; Susan E. Reid, "Destalinization and Taste, 1953–1963," *Journal of Design History* 10 (1997): 178; Conekin, *"The Autobiography of a Nation,"* 212–13; Rudolph, "Domestic Politics," 493; Erica Carter, *How German Is She? Postwar German Reconstruction and the Consuming Woman* (Ann Arbor: University of Michigan Press, 1996), 45–71.

29. Robert G. Wertheimer, "The Miracle of German Housing in the Postwar Period," *Land Economics* 34 (1958): 338; de Grazia, *Irresistible Empire*, 361.

30. Betts and Crowley, "Introduction," 215–17, 224–5; Becky Conekin, "'Here Is the Modern World Itself': The Festival of Britain's Representations of the Future," in *Moments of Modernity: Reconstructing Britain, 1945–1964*, ed. Becky Conekin, Frank Mort, and Chris Waters (London: Rivers Oram Press, 1999), 228–33; Elaine Tyler May, *Homeward Bound: American Families in the Cold War Era* (New York: Basic Books, 1988), 10–15; Mary Nolan, "Consuming America, Producing Gender," in *The American Century in Europe*, ed. R. Laurence Moore and Maurizio Vaudagna (Ithaca, NY: Cornell University Press, 2003), 243–6; Kristin Ross, *Fast Cars, Clean Bodies: Decolonization and Reordering of French Culture* (Cambridge, MA: MIT Press, 1996), 4–10, 71–8.

31. Nicole Rudolph, "At Home in Postwar France: The Design and Construction of Domestic Space, 1945–1975" (PhD diss., New York University, 2005); Kirsi

Saarikangas, "What's New? Women Pioneers and the Finnish State Meet the American Kitchen," in *Cold War Kitchen*, 298–9.

32. Walter L. Hixson, *Parting the Curtain: Propaganda, Culture, and the Cold War, 1945–1961* (New York: St. Martin's Press, 1998), 133–4; Greg Castillo, "Domesticating the Cold War: Household Consumption as Propaganda in Marshall Plan Germany," *Journal of Contemporary History* 40 (2005): 265–77; Castillo, "The American 'Fat Kitchen' in Europe," 32–3, 38–40, 47–50; Robert H. Haddow, *Pavilions of Plenty: Exhibiting American Culture Abroad in the 1950s* (Washington, DC: Smithsonian Institution Press, 1997), 106–11, 201–29; Karel Ann Marling, *As Seen on TV: The Visual Culture of Everyday Life in the 1950s* (Cambridge, MA: Harvard University Press, 1994), 242–83; Cristina Carbone, 'Staging the Kitchen Debate: How Splitnik Got Normalized in the United States," in *Cold War Kitchens*, 63–75.

33. Gwendolyn Wright, "Good Design and 'The Good Life': Cultural Exchange in Post-World War II American Domestic Architecture," in *Across the Atlantic: Cultural Exchanges between Europe and the United States*, ed. Luisa Passerini (Brussels: P.I.E.-Peter Lang, 2000), 269–78; Julien Holder, "The Nation State or the United States? The Irresistible Kitchen of the British Ministry of Works, 1944–1951," in *Cold War Kitchen*, 235; Bervoets, "'Consultation Required!'"; Rudolph, "At Home in Postwar France"; Saarikangas, "What's New?" in *Cold War Kitchen*; Betts and Crowley, "Introduction," 220; M. Pleydell-Bouverie, *Daily Mail Book of Post-War Homes* (London: Daily Mail, 1944), 48–54; Oldenziel and Zachmann, "Kitchens as Technology and Politics," 20; Els De Vos, "The American Kitchen in Belgium: A Story of Countering, Reversing, Selective Appropriation and Sidelining" (paper presented at the European Ways of Living in the American Century Conference, Stockholm, January 16–17, 2010).

34. Michael Wildt, *Am Beginn der 'Konsumgesellschaft': Mangelerfahrung, Lebenshaltung, Wohlstandshoffnung in Westdeutschland in den fünfziger Jahren* (Hamburg: Ergebnisse-Verlag, 1994); Sue Bowden and Avner Offer, "Household Appliances and the Use of Time: The United States and Britain since the 1920s," *Economic History Review* 47 (1994): 725–48; Carter, *How German Is She?* 4–9, 45–59; Marling, *As Seen on TV*, 255; Arne Andersen, "Das 50er-Jahre-Syndrom: Umweltfragen in der Demokratisierung des Technikkonsums," *Technikgeschichte* 65 (1998): 334.

35. Tony Judt, *Postwar: A History of Europe since 1945* (New York: Penguin, 2005), 353.

36. Oldenziel and Zachmann, "Kitchens as Technology and Politics," 20; Nicole Rudolph, "Living Small: The *Cellule d'habitation* and the Democratization of Comfort in 1950s France" (paper presented at the Western Society for French History, Thirty-Third Annual Conference, Colorado Springs, October 27–29, 2005); David Heathcote, *Barbican Penthouse Over the City* (Chichester: Wiley, 2004), 138–46.

37. Adam Rome, *Bulldozer in the Countryside: Suburban Sprawl and the Rise of American Environmentalism* (New York: Cambridge University Press, 2001), 45–86.

38. de Grazia, *Irresistible Empire*, 398, 403; Shane Hamilton, "Supermarket USA Confronts State Socialism: Airlifting the Technopolitics of Industrial Food Distribution into Cold War Yugoslavia," in *Cold War Kitchen*, 145–53.

39. Orvar Löfgren, "Consuming Interests," *Culture and History* 7 (1990): 25; May, *Homeward Bound*, 23.
40. Elisabeth Heineman, *What Difference Does a Husband Make? Women and Marital Status in Nazi and Postwar Germany* (Berkeley: University of California Press, 1999), 75–137; May, *Homeward Bound*, 183–207; Joanne Meyerowitz, ed., *Not June Cleaver: Women and Gender in Postwar America, 1945–1960* (Philadelphia: Temple University Press, 1994. Carter, *How German Is She?*; Jennifer Ann Loehlin, *From Rugs to Riches: Housework, Consumption and Modernity in Germany* (Oxford: Berg, 1999), 62, 64, 86, 117, 120.
41. Eleonore Saur-Jaumann, *Hausfrau: mach dir die Arbeit leicht*, Heft 1 (Munich: Rationalisierungs-Kuratorium der Deutschen Wirtschaft, 1951).
42. *Der ideale Haushalt: ein Sonderheft der Constanze-Verlag* (Hamburg: Constanze-Verlag, 1958), quotes on 188, 198.
43. Emanuela Scarpellini, chapter 5 in this volume; Orvar Löfgren, "Materializing the Nation in Sweden and America," *Ethnos* 58 (1993): 190.
44. Susan E. Reid, "The Khrushchev Kitchen: Domesticating the Scientific-Technological Revolution," *Journal of Contemporary History* 40 (2005): 289–316; Susan E. Reid, "'Our Kitchen Is Just as Good': Soviet Responses to the American Kitchen," in *Cold War Kitchen*, 89–104; Oldenziel and Zachmann, "Kitchens as Technology and Politics," 8.
45. Reid, "Destalinization and Taste," 189.
46. Buchli, "Khrushchev, Modernism, and the Fight," 163; Crowley, "Thaw Modern," 139–42, 148–9; Raymond G. Stokes, "Plastics and the New Society: The German Democratic Republic in the 1950s and 1960s," in *Style and Socialism: Modernity and Material Culture in Post-War Eastern Europe*, ed. Susan E. Reid and David Crowley (Oxford: Berg, 2000), 65–80.
47. Donna Harsch, *Revenge of the Domestic: Women, the Family, and Communism in the German Democratic Republic* (Princeton, NJ: Princeton University Press, 2007), 165–97; Judt, *Postwar*, 445; Karin Zachmann, "Managing Choice: Constructing the Socialist Consumption Junction in the German Democratic Republic," in *Cold War Kitchen*, 261–7.
48. Ina Merkel, *Utopie und Bedürfnis: Die Geschichte der Konsumkultur in der DDR* (Cologne: Böhlau, 1999).
49. Paul Betts, "Building Socialism at Home: The Case of East German Interiors," in *Socialist Modern: East German Everyday Culture and Politics*, ed. Katherine Pence and Paul Betts (Ann Arbor: University of Michigan Press, 2008), 118–24.
50. Ibid.; Merkel, *Utopie und Bedürfnis*; Harsch, *Revenge of the Domestic*, 312–19.
51. Lizabeth Cohen, *A Consumers' Republic: The Politics of Mass Consumption in Postwar America* (New York: Knopf, 2003).
52. Frank Trentmann, "Bread, Milk and Democracy: Consumption and Citizenship in Twentieth-Century Britain," in *The Politics of Consumption: Material Culture and Citizenship in Europe and America*, ed. Martin Daunton and Matthew Hilton (Oxford: Berg, 2001), 129–63; Katherine Pence, "Domestic Consumption in the Two New German States," in *Gender Relations in German History: Power, Agency, and Experience from the Sixteenth to the Twentieth Century*, ed. Lynn Abrams and Elizabeth Harvey (Durham, NC: Duke University Press, 1997), 232–4.

53. de Grazia, *Irresistible Empire*, 343.
54. Peter Dauvergne, *The Shadows of Consumption: Consequences for the Global Environment* (Cambridge, MA: MIT Press, 2008); Godfrey Hodgson, *The Myth of American Exceptionalism* (New Haven, CT: Yale University Press, 2009), 129–59. See also Stephen Hill, *Europe's Promise: Why the European Way Is the Best Hope in an Insecure Age* (Berkeley: University of California Press, 2010); Tony Judt, *Ill Fares the Land* (New York: Penguin, 2010).

2
Americanization as Creolized Imaginary: The Statue of Liberty During the Cold War

David Nye

In 1991 and 1992, a team of six scholars spent a year together at the Netherlands Institute for Advanced Study, researching the phenomenon known in the *lingua franca* as "Americanization." The project, which focused on Europe, was the brainchild of historian Rob Kroes, and the result was several individual books and six volumes of essays.[1] One of these, *American Photographs in Europe*, is a collection of essays (edited by myself and Mick Gidley) that focuses on the transatlantic movement of images during the twentieth century.[2] This chapter reconsiders this theme. Notably, the scholarly vocabulary has changed since the 1990s: while the term "Americanization" endures, it continues to be redefined, expanded, and contested. This chapter recasts the concept of Americanization as creolization. This is a process in which senders and receivers of cultural messages continually reposition and reinterpret cultural icons to suit their needs. The term "creolization" references how American images were changed and adapted, tinkered with and selectively appropriated—in Europe and elsewhere. This chapter examines this often playful reconception of American images outside the United States during the Cold War period and the forms of creolization these images represent. To exemplify this process, the Statue of Liberty provides a case study of an American icon that acquired many new meanings.

Centrality of the Image in the Twentieth Century

The Cold War coincided with the period when images per se had achieved a central place in international communication systems; until roughly 1920, communication systems were based on the printed word. During the Cold War, Americans built on a photographic presence they achieved before 1945. By around 1960, American photography had achieved a dominant position for a variety of interlinked reasons. Most obviously, corporations based in the United States owned two of the largest press agencies, United Press International and the Associated Press. They hired many photographers to cover what they deemed significant events and then selected and distributed the resulting images worldwide. Even when the photographers themselves were Europeans, American editors chose what stories to cover and which images to use. Early in the Cold War, a good many American photographers achieved international recognition. In Europe, these photographers' work was often first seen in issues of *Fortune*, *Look*, or *Life Magazine*. Indeed, the American newspaper and magazine press in general had embraced photography more than Europeans, providing many men and women with careers. These included Edward Steichen, Margaret Bourke White, Gordon Parks, John Vachon, and Eugene Smith. At the end of the Second World War, there was a powerful press apparatus to broadcast the work of American image makers to the rest of the world, at a time when the European press was struggling to recover from the war.

Just as important, American museums began to treat photography as an art form earlier than their counterparts in most other nations. Even leading European photographers often saw their work featured in major New York exhibitions before that was possible in Paris or Berlin. For example, the first major retrospective of Henri Cartier-Bresson's work was held at the Museum of Modern Art (MoMA) in 1947. The early involvement of museums also meant that American curators had an expertise that the United States Information Agency (USIA) appreciated. When Edward Steichen put together the *Family of Man* exhibit in 1955 to celebrate the first quarter century of MoMA, the power and popularity of the exhibit led the USIA to adopt it for worldwide distribution. Five traveling sets of the 503 *Family of Man* images were sent on the road, where more than 9 million people saw the show over a period of seven years.[3] In addition, the book version of *The Family of Man* was translated into many languages and sold more than 4 million copies. When the show reached Hamburg, for example, 43,308 people visited in one month, making it the most popular event the USIA had staged there in many years. In Amsterdam, more than 100,000 people came to see it, including the queen.

In many nations, that exhibit decisively shifted the orientation of the photographic community toward the United States, which suddenly emerged as a leader in photography. In both the Netherlands and Denmark, for example, the leading amateur photographic magazines scarcely contained any images from the United States before *The Family of Man* exhibit, but frequently showcased American work afterward.[4] Reinforcing the interest created by the exhibition were advertisements for the latest in Kodak photographic papers and films which, during the 1950s, were available in most parts of the world. One measure of the powerful appeal of American images is that the semiotician Roland Barthes referred to them frequently in his writings. A surprising number of the images in Barthes' *Mythologies* were American, and of twenty-five images reproduced in *Camera Lucida*, twelve were American, including some from the nineteenth century. The American photographers whom Barthes discusses had become canonical in Europe, including Alexander Gardner, Alfred Stieglitz, Lewis Hine, Richard Avedon, and Robert Mapplethorpe.

If the United States dominated the Cold War image economy, the reach of this visual discourse was even more powerful because of the advertising campaigns of American corporations. This visual discourse was a central element of the mass consumption regime that emerged first in the United States in the late nineteenth century, culminating in the development of the assembly line in 1913. European manufacturers immediately took an interest in mass production and regularly visited US factories during the 1910s and 1920s, though they were only able to adopt some aspects of American production for use in manufacturing for their smaller markets.[5] After the First World War, some American companies situated factories in Europe and many increased their exports. The large American advertisers had followed their clients to Europe in the 1920s; and well before the Second World War, they had gone through a process of adapting to European conditions. One should not exaggerate the degree to which Europeans were willing or able to embrace American patterns of mass consumption, however. In 1925, for example, there was one car for every American family, but only one for every hundred Germans. Moreover, there was a conflicted ideological response to the very idea of mass consumption, which was often rejected as antithetical to European values. The full tide of this change would not reach Europe until after 1945.

Likewise, the visual discourse that accompanied mass consumption became noticeable in Europe in the 1920s, planting the seeds for full development after the Second World War. American advertisers used a good deal of photography, especially staged fashion photography, but the leading agencies also had a strong tradition of using detailed drawings in color illustrations. Indeed, by the 1930s, American advertisers emphasized imagery over text, because they had concluded that viewers could absorb it more quickly and because drawings aroused less psychological resistance than sales text.[6] Advertisers also realized the power of "before-and-after" stories, which were particularly powerful in the wake of the Second World War. After 1945, American advertisers were ready not only to sell products but to do public relations work for NATO.[7] Finally, Hollywood films, already quite popular in Europe during the 1920s, completed the powerful American visual discourse. In short, from before the Cold War, American images reached Europeans from multiple sources, in large numbers, at the service of many different agencies, creating a complex visualization of the world of mass consumption.

American Images in the European Context

What is one to make of this powerful visual discourse? The essays in *American Photographs in Europe* were part of a larger argument that the cultural products of the United States—whether styles, foods, and images; songs, texts, or films—were not simply transmitted across the Atlantic but also selected and interpreted by Europeans. When the same cultural products were received in different national contexts, their meanings were inflected, simplified, exaggerated, satirized, or, in some cases, even reversed. The term to describe this complex process of cultural transmission was "creolization." Kroes developed this concept in several influential essays and in his book *If You've Seen One, You've Seen the Mall*.[8] He argues that the process of creolization began not with the transmission of popular American culture to Europe but within America itself. The United States, long at the periphery of European culture, amalgamated a wide range of its cultural traditions. During the nineteenth century, Americans developed an irreverent "way" with culture, a "picaresque tradition of creolization" marked by "its freedom from genteel control, its freedom to borrow, to cut up and hybridize."[9] They took apart European cultural forms and combined them in new ways, starting with the very American language itself. When these combinations were re-exported back to Europe, they were already half familiar. Kroes thus sees creolization as a process that is hardly mechanical but rather endlessly mutable. Nor has this American form of culture-making necessarily been at the service of hegemonic capitalists. Quite the reverse: those on the margins often invent new dances, new foods, new musical idioms, new slang words, new clothing styles, or, in short, they invent many of the fads that Europeans adapt from U.S. mass culture.

Creolization is, however, just one of the possible theoretical positions one might adopt in thinking about Americanization. Many scholars have adopted some form of the hegemonic argument, which, in its most assertive form, argues that after 1945, U.S. culture rolled like a mighty wave over the rest of the world. George Ritzer presents this view in *The McDonaldization of Society: An Investigation into the Changing Character of Contemporary Social Life*.[10] As referenced in the introduction to this volume, Victoria de Grazia later developed a more nuanced version of this position in *Irresistible Empire*.[11] The hegemonic argument emphasizes the sender's intention, pointing to State Department cultural programs and the marketing campaigns of U.S. corporations. It is not difficult to document these efforts. The USIA set up libraries, offered courses, and sent lecturers to European universities. It also sent thousands of selected Europeans on tours of the United States. Furthermore, the USIA constantly wrote reports to chronicle its activities and to ask for more money based on its claims of success. Both advertisers and government agencies tended to overstate the effectiveness of their efforts, however, in order to convince clients that funds had been well spent. Some Europeans sent by the USIA to tour the United States later became outspoken critics of American foreign policy, and many who attended and enjoyed American-sponsored jazz performances nevertheless viewed the United States as a deeply racist nation. Those who borrowed books from the USIA library did not thereby necessarily become pro-American. The thousands of Fulbright scholars who went abroad were not doctrinaire government appointees but rather professionals chiefly interested in their academic specialties. Few saw themselves as government spokespersons, and some were critics of the Vietnam War. Moreover, the hegemonic argument must take account of the fact that since the 1980s, U.S. government public relations efforts have been scaled back. Most USIA libraries have closed, fewer Fulbright grants are available, and the USIA sends out fewer lecturers compared to earlier years. To the extent that the hegemonic argument is correct about the primary importance of the U.S. government as a sender, Americanization should have begun to wane a decade before the Cold War was over. Yet this seems not to be the case.

Beyond Hegemony

Does one really need to argue for intentional, government-sponsored hegemony? A more straightforward economic explanation is worth consideration. The export of U.S. popular culture might also be seen as the result of four interlinked factors. First, consider the origins of American music, film, and popular culture in a multicultural society during the late nineteenth and early twentieth centuries. These cultural products early appealed to a wide spectrum of consumers with many cultural backgrounds, notably the immigrants to the United States who had crowded into American cities. A song or a film that sold well to such an audience might be equally appealing to their kinsmen back in Europe.

Second, early on, the United States had a large internal market, compared to a still-fragmented European market. This meant that, early on, Americans learned to mass-produce consumer goods at a modest price. The United States had 150 million people at the end of the Second World War, a far larger and more affluent single market than could then be found in Europe. To cater to these consumers, Americans had developed volume production that was still uncommon in Europe.[12] American exporters of popular culture could offer products of proven appeal at low prices. A film, television show, or popular song usually had already turned a tidy profit even before it was exported. As a result, Americans could sell cultural goods abroad for less than Europeans could afford to make competing products at a comparable price. This became particularly obvious in the case of films and television programs.

Third, the world market was prepared linguistically for Americanization, because the British Empire had spread the English language across the globe. Millions of people everywhere were able to understand U.S. cultural productions. During the 1950s, the collapse of the British and the French imperial networks left a vacuum to be filled. Who could have filled that vacuum more easily than the United States? This is a central part of Geir Lundestad's influential argument that particularly in the immediate aftermath of the Second World War, the United States was "an empire by invitation."[13]

Fourth and finally, while most nations lay in ruins at the end of the Second World War, the United States had only been bombed at Pearl Harbor. Its manufacturing infrastructure was completely intact, and it had a large mercantile fleet demobilized from the war effort. De Grazia's argument, to her credit, does take account of these commercial factors, and sees hegemony not merely in political terms or even in terms of the export of particular goods, but also in terms of the export of American advertising and commercial culture.

Taking these four factors together, it seems indisputable that American popular culture was well positioned for dissemination to all parts of the world after 1945. Its products were already tested on a multicultural audience. For two generations or more, Americans had developed the capacity to manufacture for mass markets.[14] The English language was already widely understood, which fostered comprehension. Europe's potential competing firms often lay in ruins. How much help did

American business really need from the State Department? A French or German studio had to struggle to finance a small number of new films, while Americans could simply add subtitles or dub high-budget films that were already paid for by U.S. domestic ticket sales. To reach Europeans, American companies needed only to pay the costs of marketing and distribution, as production costs were already covered.

Creolization in Context

With these arguments in mind, let us return to the concept of creolization. In *Buffalo Bill in Bologna*, Kroes and Robert Rydell demonstrated that the transmission and creolized reception of American mass culture in Europe had begun by the middle of the nineteenth century.[15] Long before McDonald's existed, U.S. cultural exports were being modified to suit European audiences, who imposed their own interpretive frameworks on the Wild West Show or early American films. Moreover, American companies learned to adapt. Even a McDonald's menu is not the same everywhere. In Spain, they sell wine to go with the hamburger; in Scandinavia, they do not. In India, they do not serve beef; in the Arab world, they omit pork. Even the emblematic McDonald's, in short, has learned to accommodate national and religious tastes.

In a refinement of the creolization argument, Americanization can be regarded as less a matter of content than one of context. American images, styles, and cultural products do not simply have certain meanings; rather, they saturate the environment. This position offers a way out of the contradictions between the theories already outlined. Rather than think of Americanization as hegemonic cause and effect or as the result of historical circumstances or as the product of active consumers making selections, one might think of Americanization as an encompassing context or environment, in which images play an important role. Americanization is not simply a matter of cause and effect; nor a historical outcome caused by various factors; nor a process of consumer selection. Rather, what is called Americanization involves a cavalcade of images, sounds, and texts that together have become a *lingua franca* in the meaning systems of other societies.

Fundamental to this idea of Americanization as context is the realization that during the Cold War, U.S. culture often offered neither one position nor one product, but variant positions, doubling and redoubling its presence. Considering popular music alone, the United States offered Europeans not just Rock and Roll, but also Blues, Motown, Acid Rock, Disco, and much more, including Country and Folk music. A whole universe of sounds became available, with something for every taste or political persuasion. Similarly, during the Cold War, there was not a single image of the United States, but rather multiple iconic presences. In most areas of cultural controversy, one could find American alternatives, surrogates, or reverse images. Europeans protesting the Vietnam War were often clad in jeans and knew the lyrics of Bob Dylan by heart. American iconic images were parodied, reversed, re-conceptualized, and translated into new forms, in a process that accelerated and intensified during the Cold War.

Case Study: The Statue of Liberty as Creolized Image

The Statue of Liberty is among the small number of images that are instantly recognizable and need no caption. In every culture, literally millions of images are produced each year, most of which quickly seem so anonymous that few recall who or what is depicted without help from a caption. When people recall an iconic figure, such as Ronald Reagan, Marilyn Monroe, or the Statue of Liberty, what comes to mind is often not a specific image, but a generalized one. The icon is a recognizable site or person even when presented as a distortion or parody. Indeed, one good test of whether an image has been fully internalized is to see if people can recognize that a drawing, painting, editorial cartoon, or album cover is playing with it.

The universal iconicity of the Statue of Liberty does not date from its assemblage in New York in 1886. Even within the United States, it was not at first understood as a national symbol; rather, it emerged as one over four decades. After the United States received it as a gift from France, Americans had to raise money to pay for its pedestal, and for several years the money was not forthcoming. In 1876, the arm and the torch of the statue were erected at the Philadelphia Centennial Exposition, and people paid admission to climb the stairway inside its forearm to look out at the fairgrounds from the rim beneath its flame.

This display was meant to encourage contributions (in addition to the small admission fee) to finance the erection of the statue as a whole. Although more than 9 million people visited the exposition, little money was raised in this way. The City of New York, the State of New York, or the national government in Washington might also have paid for it, but all declined. It fell to the ordinary citizens to raise the money, in many small contributions, spurred on by a newspaper campaign. Only in 1886 was the statue dedicated, and it required another generation before it began to compete with the image of Columbia—the female personification of the

Americanization as Creolized Imaginary 53

Figure 2.1 As part of the 1876 Centennial Exposition in Philadelphia, the Statue of Liberty's arm and torch were erected as a special exhibit. The intention was to help raise funds for erecting the statue as a whole.

U.S.—as the representative of the nation. It seems to have become fully iconic by the First World War, when it was frequently used on posters for war bonds.

As the Statue of Liberty came to represent the United States, however, its meaning was in transition.[16] Originally, it was given to the United

States to represent the shared Franco-American commitment to democracy and liberty. Nothing in the original conception of the statue had to do with immigrants. In fact, as Werner Sollors has emphasized, some early writers, such as Thomas Bailey Aldrich, saw the statue as a "white goddess," that would "guard freedom against the menace of the rather beastly invaders."[17] Once erected in New York's harbor, in near proximity to the point where millions of immigrants arrived seeking admission to the United States, the statue began to be associated with what Emma Lazarus called the "huddled masses," tired, poor, and yearning to be free. Yet her famous poem was not read at the dedication of the Statue of Liberty. Only in 1903 were her stanzas inscribed on a plaque and installed on the second floor. As late as 1936, on the statue's fiftieth anniversary celebrations, immigration was still not a major theme. As John Higham emphasizes, the national celebrations "clung to the traditional motifs—Franco-American friendship and liberty as an abstract idea."[18] These motifs proved useful during the Second World War, but during the Cold War, the French connection faded somewhat from the public imagination. The statue became the quintessential American symbol and became more widespread than the older national images, Columbia and Uncle Sam. The association with immigration also became stronger, particularly as refugees from Communist regimes came to the United States. The statue came to stand for the liberty and democracy that immigrants found in America, in contrast to the totalitarian regimes of Hitler, Stalin, and Mao.

The Statue of Liberty was highly visible throughout the Cold War, standing for the values of liberty and democracy. Unlike such commercial figures as Kentucky Fried Chicken's Colonel Sanders, Walt Disney's Donald Duck, or Ronald McDonald, no one controlled its copyright. Any agency, institution, or artist who felt the urge to produce a parody, satire, cartoon, or reinterpretation of the Statue of Liberty could do so, including the Chinese students protesting in Tiananmen Square, Beijing, in 1989. Even the briefest Internet search reveals literally millions of representations of the statue. These images provide a rich array of examples, but they are incomplete unless supplemented by books published at the time of its centennial.[19] Analysis of these materials discloses at least five types of iconic creolization, ranging from celebration to complete rejection of the United States.

In the first form of creolization, which is quite widespread, the iconic image is playfully embraced. For example, Lego sells a boxed set of 2,882 plastic blocks that can be assembled into a model of the Statue of Liberty. At the Danish Legoland, another American icon, Mt. Rushmore, is similarly reconstructed in plastic. Another famous example is the cover of the British rock group's Supertramp album, *Breakfast in America* (1979), which takes considerable liberties with the Statue of Liberty. She has been replaced by a towering waitress, who holds not a torch but a glass of orange juice, with a menu in her other hand. In the background, the New York City skyline has become boxes of cereal, salt-and-pepper shakers, and condiments suitable to a diner. While this cover might be read as a satirical critique of the culture of consumption, there is little in the music of the album to support that reading. It seems more appropriate to put this cover into the same class of images as a cartoon showing Miss Liberty eating an ice cream cone or one where she is using a mobile phone. Such images play with the Statue of Liberty but they do not criticize American values or move her to a new cultural setting.

Moreover, this embrace of the Statue of Liberty is often blatantly commercial. Many advertising images in the United States put a product in the upraised hand of the Statue of Liberty. She has held bottles of vodka, worn sunglasses, modeled dresses, and been used to sell airline tickets and much else. Advertisers around the world followed suit. For example, in 1979, Toshiba had her grasp an early model of a cell phone. The entire text was in Japanese, and the advertisement was clearly directed at home consumers. The values associated with the statue seem to be entirely secondary, and the use of the statue is primarily meant to be eye-catching.[20] Almost from its dedication in 1886, the Statue of Liberty has been used to sell a huge range of products, including breakfast cereal and hot dogs. Advertisers do not use the statue to make a political or social comment, but simply identify their products with a popular icon. In the process, there is a conflation of political liberty and democratic choice with the liberty to consume and choices in the marketplace. In such cases, advertisers are intermediate actors who both celebrate the Statue of Liberty and shift its meaning.

A second form of creolization appropriates an American cultural icon and inserts it in a new context while maintaining the underlying values associated with it. Such creolization assumes that the viewers know the original so well that what it stands for can be separated from its cultural location. In other words, the values signified do not change, but the signifier undergoes considerable transformation at the hands of intermediate actors. For example, during the apartheid regime in South Africa, the London *Daily Telegraph* published in 1967 a cartoon where the Statue of Liberty figure, with crown, robe, pedestal, and appropriate gestures, has become the South African prime minister B.J. Vorster. He holds a flameless torch in one hand while the other clutches a lighted match. The cartoon's caption, "Playing with Fire," refers to the words,

Figure 2.2 This cartoon, entitled "Playing with Fire," depicts South Africa's prime minister as toying with the torch, which represents equality. Note that this use of the Statue of Liberty has little to do with the United States.

Vorster's own, carved on the pedestal, "If it should happen that South Africa has to compete in the finals against a coloured country, we shall do so." He is promising that the all-white South African sports teams are willing to play against non-white teams in international competition. The cartoon suggests that if South Africa begins to play with the fire of equality, it may be hard to avoid lighting the torch of liberty. This use of the Statue of Liberty has little to do with the United States. A British newspaper serves a cultural intermediary that transforms an American icon into an international symbol for racial equality and liberty, in order to comment on the policies of a third nation.

A third form of creolization is closely related to the second. It displaces the image, typically taking the Statue of Liberty off her pedestal, usually with satiric intent. In it, an icon's location changes in order to suggest inconsistencies between the values it represents and historical realities. The statue may be placed along the Berlin Wall or juxtaposed with a major icon of another nation. This form of creolization is about ironic juxtaposition and may have considerable satiric force, directed either at the United States or another nation that has hypocritically said one thing while doing another. In such cases, the intermediary actor has not been content to change the cultural reference of the icon (as in the second form), but has also changed its physical location and thereby moved it into a new context.

A fourth form of creolization makes a stronger critique that is directed against the United States. It occurs when an image becomes part of a jeremiad, which can be defined as a sermon, speech, or other text that bitterly laments the loss of national values. A jeremiad may sound like a prophecy of doom, but usually it is a call for a return to former virtues.[21] The Statue of Liberty has often been used as a convenient shorthand visualization of values that have been violated. For example, during the Vietnam War, in what became known as the My Lai Massacre, a large number of Vietnamese civilians were killed during a raid on a village. A British newspaper cartoon showed the Statue of Liberty, her torch raised high, illuminating newspapers before her on the ground that recount this terrible story. In her other hand, she holds two books that are labeled "Inquiry" and "Court Martial."[22] In this instance, the statue was being used to call attention to the violation of fundamental rights that are guaranteed by democracies but which were violated in the massacre of the My Lai civilians. This critique of the United States Army's behavior does not challenge or in any way deny the values of the Statue of Liberty. Rather, as in any jeremiad, the denunciation is particularly powerful because the nation is seen to be violating its own moral codes. The jeremiad typically comes not from an enemy but a severely disappointed ally or friend. The intermediary actor has used an American icon to criticize the behavior but not the values of the United States. Editorial cartoonists inside the country regularly do the same thing.

In contrast, the final category of creolization is a form of anti-Americanization. Here, the meanings attached to an icon have shifted so radically that the reconfigured image undermines the form and mocks the values of the original. This kind of creolization is more commonly produced inside nations that consider themselves enemies of the United States. Therefore, Cold War examples of anti-American creolization were less common in the Western European countries than they were in Latin America, Africa, Asia, and the Soviet Union. For example, a Cuban artist, Alberto Blanco, produced a poster calling for Puerto Rican independence.[23] In it, the Statue of Liberty is draped in the American flag and holds in her upraised hand not a torch but a Puerto Rican flag. The substitution of the flag is an erasure. It undermines American claims to represent liberty by reminding viewers that the United States seized Puerto Rico during the Spanish-American War. From the Cuban perspective, the United States seemed an imperialist power bent on domination in the Caribbean. The poster suggests Puerto Rico's liberation by depicting newly broken chains that had forcibly linked the Puerto Rican flag to Liberty's arm.

Anti-American creolization often lacks subtlety, and at times may be difficult to distinguish from parody. What first looks to be a socialist-inspired cartoon from the height of the Cold War depicts a capitalist raping the Statue of Liberty. However, it appeared a decade after the Cold War ended, in *Our Dumb Century*, published by a satiric magazine, *The Onion*.[24] More serious anti-American creolization has been particularly visible in the Middle East. For example, in September of 1984, *Arabia: The Islamic World Review* had the Statue of Liberty on its cover, holding aloft a pistol instead of a torch, while behind her were missiles instead of New York skyscrapers.[25] More recently, a Palestinian newspaper, *Al Quds*, represented Condoleezza Rice as a Zionist Statue of Liberty. Or again, on the wall of the former American embassy in Tehran is painted a grisly Statue of Liberty as a shrouded, grinning corpse, an image later reproduced in Germany's *Der Spiegel*.[26]

In some cases, the purpose is simply to be offensive, notably an image of a small boy standing on the Statue of Liberty's shoulder and urinating on the tablet she holds.[27] Such images seem to express a complete rejection of the United States. Yet even this iconography is only meaningful within the orbit of American culture. One has to know where the Statue of Liberty is and what she usually represents before such anti-American creolization has any force.

The most powerful rejection of the United States would be to imagine its destruction. Curiously, the Statue of Liberty has persistently been used to suggest this scenario. In *Planet of the Apes* (1968), a remnant of the statue pokes out of the sand on an empty beach. All other traces of American society have disappeared. But visions of Liberty being destroyed are much older.[28] In 1887, the year after the statue's dedication, a short

Americanization as Creolized Imaginary 59

Figure 2.3 Artist Joseph Pennell's 1918 poster advertised bonds. "That Liberty Shall Not Perish" references the last line of the Gettysburg Address: "...that government of the people, by the people, for the people, shall not perish from the earth."

story described, and an illustration in *Life* showed, the statue in ruins, after an attack on New York City by a "hostile fleet."[29] In 1918, Joseph Pennell produced a lurid red and black poster for the fourth Liberty Loan campaign that showed New York City in flames.[30] In the left foreground stands the dark silhouette of a damaged Statue of Liberty, her arm broken, her torch lost. The caption alludes to Lincoln's *Gettysburg Address*, "That Liberty Shall Not Perish from the Earth—Buy Liberty Bonds." Since 1918, the Statue of Liberty has been frequently damaged or destroyed in both art and film. She has been destroyed by aliens from Mars, submerged under the sea by global warming, and forced to drink so much alcohol that she collapses into the sea.[31]

As these final examples suggest, some of the most negative versions of the Statue of Liberty have been produced within the United States. This is in keeping with Kroes' definition of creolization, as a cutting and pasting of familiar elements to create something new, which is a fundamental process in American popular culture.

The re-envisionings of the Statue of Liberty in Europe may run the gamut from celebration and playful embrace to hatred and rejection, but this very playfulness with the image is the hallmark of Americanization. In billions of images disseminated through film, advertising, public relations, tourism, and government programs, the myriad forms of American popular culture have spread, not as single images, each with a clear meaning, but rather as a cloud of imagery, at once serious and humorous, patriotic and irreverent, commercial and idealistic, utopian and apocalyptic, and all in a process of continual re-contextualization. This image environment was a crucial part of Cold War Americanization, offering not merely specific ideas or images but multiple, even self-contradictory, icons. This image environment accompanied the export of mass consumption, and it was in place by the time of the *Family of Man* Exhibition and had saturated European culture to such a degree that Barthes could assume his readers knew the many American images he discussed in his writings on photography. In most contexts, American images became essential not only to appreciating the culture and politics of the United States, but also to expressing rejections of American culture. Americanization thus became more than a cluster of messages; it became a context, indeed an entire visual discourse. A theory of visual creolization can explain the pervasiveness of American images in the Cold War era, and at the same time offer ways to distinguish between five different forms of engagement with the popular culture of the United States. While the extended example used here has been the Statue of Liberty, the method developed could also be applied to other icons that are universally recognized, such as Mt. Rushmore, the Alamo, the flag raising at Iwo Jima, the Grant Wood painting "American Gothic," the Chrysler Building, and many others. In each case, a survey of the reception and re-conception of these icons would range from (1) an uncritical embrace of the image, especially its playful use in advertising; (2) the de-contextualization and reuse of the icon in a different cultural setting with little or no reference to the United States; (3) the visual transformation of the icon in order to make a satiric point through its juxtaposition with a specific historical situation, often a current event; (4) the use of the icon to deliver a jeremiad against the United States for failing to live up to its values; and (5) an anti-American attack on U.S. foreign policy and/or culture. These five forms of creolization come from foreign intermediary actors who, no matter how critical they become, remain inside an American system of images. During the Cold War, allies, critics, and sworn enemies of the United States all found themselves using an iconography that was indisputably American. The older discussions of Americanization are not entirely eliminated or replaced by this analysis. Rather, they are enfolded within this American visual discourse, with its endless play of signifiers. As the variants of American icons multiplied during the twentieth century, it became difficult for Europeans to find any cultural location outside this new system of meanings.

The new mass-consumption regime was intertwined with this discursive system at many levels. Most obviously, the images themselves were mass-produced and appeared in newspapers, magazines, billboards, and theaters. This inundation of images promoted both consumption and a conflation of economic freedom with democracy. Yet even this conflation was only the simplest of the five forms of creolization, which, together, expanded the range of possible meanings and values in the image system. Just as the Statue of Liberty could be endlessly re-contextualized and reinterpreted, cultural intermediaries learned the irreverent American way with icons, including playful irony, satire, and even virulent anti-Americanism. If Walter Benjamin early on declaimed against the emerging image empire because it seemed to empty the meaning out of all that it copied,[32] by the last years of the Cold War, Jean Baudrillard and Umberto Eco had come to view the visual discourse that accompanied mass consumption quite differently, as an endless semiosis of signifiers without referents, of copies with no original, all within a permanently de-stabilized image empire.[33] This re-conception coincided not only with the waning of the Cold War but also with the emergence of digital culture and its unceasing flows of images and information, as well as its erosion of mass markets in favor of more differentiated production and marketing. But that is another story, beyond the concerns of this chapter and this volume.

Through every revision and reinterpretation, the Statue of Liberty's iconic status grew. It had become one of the small number of icons instantly recognized by people in all parts of the world. In 2013, the National Park System created a virtual tour of the Statue, designed to provide "a global audience with equal and unprecedented access to one of the world's best known, beloved and inspiring symbols."[34] The creolized feelings it arouses are more complex than this statement suggests, however. The Statue needs extensive security and suffers occasional closures due to fears of terrorism.[35] Its possible destruction, imagined for at least a century, remains a central part of its system of meanings.

Notes

1. On photography, see also Rob Kroes, *Photographic Memories: Private Pictures, Public Images, and American History* (Lebanon, NH: University Press of New England, 2007).
2. David E. Nye and Mick Gidley, eds., *American Photographs in Europe* (Amsterdam: VU University Press, 1994).
3. Eric J. Sandeen, "The Family of Man on the Road to Moscow," in ibid., 255–69.
4. See David E. Nye, "Transnational Photographic Communication," in ibid., 31–2.
5. Patrick Fridenson, "Ford as a Model for French Car Makers, 1911–1939," in *Ford: The European History, 1903–2003*, ed. Hubert Bonin, Jannick Lung and Steven Tolliday (Paris: Éditions P.L.A.G.E. 2003), 126–7. On Fiat and Italian adoption of the assembly line, see Duccio Bigazzi, "Gli operai della catena di montaggio: la Fiat 1922–1943," in *Annali della Fondazione Giangiacomo Feltrinelli* (1979–1980) (Milan: Feltrinelli, 1981), 895–949; Wayne Lewchuk, "Fordist Technology and Britain: The Diffusion of Labour Speed-up," in The *Transfer of International Technology: Europe, Japan and the USA in the Twentieth Century*, ed. David J. Jeremy (Aldershot: Edward Elgar, 1992), 19; J. Ronald Shearer, "The Reichskuratorium für Wirtschaftlichkeit: Fordism and Organized Capitalism in Germany, 1918–1945," *The Business History Review* 71 (1997): 569–602.
6. Roland Marchand, *Advertising the American Dream: Making Way for Modernity, 1920–1940* (Berkeley: University of California Press, 1985), 154.
7. See Victoria de Grazia, *Irresistible Empire: America's Advance through 20th-Century Europe* (Cambridge, MA: Belknap Press of Harvard University Press, 2005), 226–83.
8. Rob Kroes, *If You've Seen One, You've Seen the Mall: Europeans and American Mass Culture* (Urbana: University of Illinois Press, 1996).
9. Ibid., 169.

10. George Ritzer, *The McDonaldization of Society: An Investigation into the Changing Character of Contemporary Social Life* (Thousand Oaks, CA: Pine Forge, 1993).
11. de Grazia, *Irresistible Empire*.
12. David E. Nye, *America's Assembly Line* (Cambridge, MA: MIT Press, 2013), 73–95.
13. Geir Lundestad, "'Empire by Invitation' in the American Century," *Diplomatic History* 23 (1999): 189–217.
14. Nye, *America's Assembly Line*, 41–53.
15. Robert W. Rydell and Rob Kroes, *Buffalo Bill in Bologna: The Americanization of the World, 1869–1922* (Chicago: University of Chicago Press, 2005).
16. Pascual De Ruvo, The Statue of Liberty, Copyright released to the public domain, Wikipedia Commons.
17. Werner Sollors, "Of Plymouth Rock and Jamestown and Ellis Island – Or Ethnic Literature and Some Redefinitions of 'America,'" in *Multiculturalism and the Canon of American Culture*, ed. Hans Bak (Amsterdam: VU University Press, 1993), 270–81.
18. John Higham, *Send These to Me: Jews and Other Immigrants in Urban America* (New York: Atheneum, 1975), 76.
19. Pierre Provoyeur and June Hargrove, Liberty: *The French-American Statue in Art and History* (New York: Perennial Library, 1986); Michael Grumet, *Images of Liberty* (New York: Arbor House, 1986).
20. Reproduced in Grumet, *Images of Liberty*, 68.
21. Sacvan Bercovitch, *The American Jeremiad* (Madison: University of Wisconsin Press, 1978).
22. "Concerning the My Lai Massacre," *Daily Telegraph*, November 26, 1969. Can be seen at British Cartoon Archive, http://www.cartoons.ac.uk/record/NG0522.
23. Reproduced in Grumet, *Images of Liberty*, plate 21.
24. The Onion, *Our Dumb Century: The Onion Presents 100 Years of Headlines from America's Finest News Source* (New York: Three Rivers Press, 1999).
25. Reproduced in Grumet, *Images of Liberty*, 55.
26. Spiegel Online International, accessed June 3, 2010, http://www.spiegel.de/international/world/0,1518,473932,00.html.
27. Hamas weekly newspaper, *Al-Risala*, July 10, 2006. For a reproduction of the image, see Little Green Footballs, accessed June 13, 2014, http://littlegreenfootballs.com/article/20846_Palestinians_Denigrate_Statue_of_Liberty.
28. *Planet of the Apes*, directed by Franklin J. Schaffner (Los Angeles, 1968).
29. "The Next Morning," *Life*, February 26, 1877.
30. Joseph Pennell, "That Liberty Shall Not Perish," Library of Congress, Prints & Photographs Division, LC-DIG-ppmsca-18343 (digital file from original print). Copyright free.
31. Max Page, *The City's End: Two Centuries of Fantasies, Fears, and Premonitions of New York's Destruction* (New Haven, CT: Yale University Press, 2008), 120–1.
32. Walter Benjamin, "The Work of Art in the Age of Mechanical Reproduction," in *Illuminations: Essays and Reflections*, ed. Hannah Arendt, trans. Harry Zohn (New York: Schocken Books, 1969).

33. Jean Baudrillard, *The Consumer Society: Myths and Structures* (Thousand Oaks, CA: Sage, 1998); Umberto Eco, *Travels in Hyperreality: Essays* (New York: Harcourt Brace Jovanovich, 1986).
34. National Park Service, "Statue of Liberty: Virtual Tour," accessed May 24, 2013, http://www.nps.gov/stli/photosmultimedia/virtualtour.htm.
35. Corey Kilgannon, "Cameras to Seek Faces of Terror In Visitors to the Statue of Liberty," *New York Times*, May 25, 2002.

3
Forging Europe's Foodways: The American Challenge

Karin Zachmann

The simple yearning for enough food, and the freedom to choose what tastes best: these were among people's most fervent wishes in war-ravaged Europe. The inhabitants of Nazi-occupied countries—and eventually the Germans themselves—had been forced to adopt the Nazi austerity food regime's poor diet: cereals, potatoes, and vegetables instead of animal products such as pork, beef, and mutton. Indeed, Europeans' hope for peace was inseparable from their longing for more—and for better—food.[1] Of the two superpowers that emerged from the Second World War, only the United States possessed the capacity to provide food aid for easing the transition towards peace. In fact, it was during the Second World War that the United States began planning Europe's food provisions to be made after the projected Allied victory.[2] The connection between food and peace was complex for the United States. The European need for food aid opened a channel for distributing American agricultural surpluses, a result of the postwar spike in agricultural productivity.[3] The American government also responded to European food requirements as a means of shaping Europe's postwar reconstruction process.[4] To the United States, this meant much more than exporting surplus agricultural products. U.S. government officials strove to modernize European food chains—the processes by which food was grown and produced, sold, and eventually consumed. Moreover, the U.S. sought to remake European food chains in America's own image.

American government officials believed that the U.S. food chain, based as it was on a liberal-capitalist model, was superior, that the American model could sustainably provide freedom from want, and that it offered freedom of choice to Europeans. Adopting the American model would also transform European food chains into viable commercial markets for U.S. industrial-agricultural products and services, such as fertilizers and farm machines, vegetable seeds and expert knowledge. So, the United States pressured European countries into following its pioneering path, which fostered newly organized food chains—and, eventually, new consumption regimes. Europe's food chains were to be extended, increasing the distance between the field and the fork. This new organization featured American knowledge and information as critical to the success of all involved—including farmers, agricultural suppliers, food industrialists, retailers, and consumers. The new model also increased the importance and influence of food processing and distribution as connecting nodes in the food chain. This, in turn, promoted food marketing to a major commercial activity within the system.[5]

The American government's push to modernize European food chains can be understood as the push to shift European nation-states to the Fordist mode of consumption: that is, consumption based on standardized, industrialized production. Achieving Fordist consumption entailed forming a new social contract, one that treated citizens as consumers. And, according to this Fordist logic, it was these citizen-consumers' capacity to consume that would determine European potential for economic growth and thus European political stability.

As noted in the introduction to this book, the analysis of America's allegedly forceful role in shaping Europe has provoked considerable protest. What critics object to, apparently, is the idea that, given an imposed consumption regime, we can assume a straightforward appropriation of that regime. In this volume, we make no such assumption. The appropriation of products and processes—foods, in this case—is anything but a straightforward process. Deciding whether to accept or reject, integrate or adopt a food is one of the most basic cultural activities. It is a fundamental way of giving meaning to the world.[6] In doing so, people rely on their cultural experiences and traditions. It is the materiality of the food that people digest that mediates the meanings derived from the mundane practices around eating. Anthropologist Marshall Sahlins has proposed that one hallmark of Western culture is that it ascribes symbolic meaning to products—and institutionalizes that meaning in the realm of production.[7] And so, in this chapter, to more fully understand what European lifestyles meant to European individuals, we address in-depth the ways in which foods were produced and used. This will contribute to the understanding of how European lifestyles were transformed in the so-called American century.

The idea of consumption regimes takes on special importance with regard to food. As a specific aspect of lifestyle, foodways are considered "a culture's primary form of nutritional sustenance."[8] Foodways "constitute a part of a cultural heritage of the group and are taught to each succeeding generation."[9] Thus, "foodways create cultural eating practices that dictate what to eat, when to eat, and how to eat. Each foodway relies upon one particular food source as the foundation for one's meal. For the Japanese it is rice, for the Mexicans it is corn, for large parts of Africa it is yam, and for the Americans it is meat."[10] For Europeans of all regions, the foodway during preindustrial times was grains such as wheat, rye, or barley. In Southern Europe, it was also rice and corn. Potatoes, too, became part of Central Europe's foodway starting in the nineteenth century.

For centuries, the world's food chains were organized on a predominantly regional basis: local geography and climate—as well as the regional culture—determined foodways. Food products imported from the Far East and from overseas—including spices and sugar cane, coffee and cocoa—remained luxury goods until the eve of the Industrial Revolution. These food products from afar did not challenge regional foodways—as long as the foreign product did not become a domestic variety.

Foodways have been molded into local cuisines. A cuisine works as a means of transformation and classification. Namely, through the selection, preparation, and cooking of food, a cuisine transforms nutritional raw materials from a natural to a cultural state. We classify the world as we divide the universe into what is edible and what is not. And, whereas the forms of cuisine are many, the aim of cuisine is clear-cut: cuisine labels, stamps, and defines, thus identifying the food as well as the eater. Cuisine, as part of the language of food, creates a sense of belonging.[11] Sharing a meal forms a community whose identity derives from the very food that is shared. Moreover, food chains, foodways, and cuisines are closely connected. Each represents particular facets of humans' relationship to food; exploring food chains, foodways, and cuisines contributes to our essential understanding of consumption regimes.

Starting in the mid-nineteenth century—and more intensely after the First World War and onwards—European food chains were extended as part of the move towards industrialization and urbanization. This gave rise to a growing distance between the field and the fork. As the regional organization of food chains and foodways was erased, so, too, was the material and symbolic foundation of cuisines.[12] In addition, the increasing number of actors and institutions that began to mediate between the field and the fork helped to change the process of securing trustworthy and reliable food. In favoring mass production and scientific knowledge, for example, government agencies, big business, and the scientific community spurred the departure from regional cultural traditions. Indeed, scientific knowledge, which was supposed universal, and efficient methods of mass production, became the norms. This transition became obvious in the apparently contradictory strategy used by American meat packers: while their advertisements extolled the homemade taste of canned meat, the meat packers organized factory tours—à la Upton Sinclair's scenario in *The Jungle*—for visitors, to whom they boasted a streamlined manufacturing process. The industrialization of food chains gained further momentum with the emergence of modern agribusiness, the blossoming of home economics and nutritional science, and the euphoria surrounding rationalization and efficiency. These realms offered up ideals for the future of food production. And from roughly 1920 to 1960, these ideals held for food consumption, as well.[13] One ideal—if not fantasy—of rationalizing food consumption emerged as the notion of replacing daily meals with a daily pill. Indeed, this was one attraction at the food and farm exhibit of the 1939 World's Fair in New York, the theme of which was "Building the World of Tomorrow."[14]

All of this accelerated the process of adapting the farm to the industrial model. This shift toward the industrial model certainly gained traction on both sides of the Atlantic; but given the retarding influence of the two world wars on Europe, the United States led the process of industrialized farming.[15] In contrast, the food chains in several European countries, including France, Germany, Sweden, and Italy, became increasingly constrained by the national ideology of self-sufficiency regarding food. This was pursued most vigorously by Germany in the form of food autarky.[16] A bizarre "blood-and-soil" mystique prevailed, in which the individual's lineage (blood) and connection to the land (soil) were emphasized in an extreme expression of nationalism. This ideology fostered a widespread agrarian romanticism that prolonged the viability of small farms, out-of-date agrarian structures, as well as local cuisines.[17]

To recap: the Nazi regime had re-ordered European food chains, and diets had deteriorated; the Second World War had had devastating effects. This provided a strong incentive for all of the countries liberated from the Nazi regime and the Nazi occupation to restructure and modernize their food chains. The United States government was eager to guide this process, given the advantages it presented—from serving as an effective means to secure political stability in a war-ravaged Europe to gaining ground on the battlefields of the Cold War. But the American re-ordering of European foodways also served to open up

Toward "Fordist" Food Consumption

The American government's provision of food aid constituted the first case that challenged existing foodways: the food provided as aid clashed with the foodways and cuisines of the recipients. This became evident as early as the years after the First World War, when Belgians rejected U.S.-relief corn, because they did not consider corn to be food for humans.[18] During and after the Second World War, those in starving Allied countries also became recipients of U.S. farm surplus. This time, to ensure the success of the surplus-food redistribution, economists called for an investigation of relief recipients' food habits.

Economists' efforts received institutional support only during the Second World War, when the National Research Council agreed to establish not one but two nutrition-related committees: the Food and Nutrition Committee (later the Food and Nutrition Board) in the Division of Biology and Agriculture, and the Committee on Food Habits in the Division of Anthropology and Psychology. The key proponent of this dual-committee approach was M.L. Wilson, an agricultural economist from the University of Montana, who described the need for two committees as follows:

> Science has brought about almost a revolution in nutrition and has given us a new base for diet, which is founded on the science of biochemistry. We have a very decided cultural lag between this new science of nutrition and our food habits and our ideas about food and diet as they exist in our present patterns of culture. I therefore feel that when it comes to getting actual results in bringing the diet up to a biological minimum, the lag is on the side of human behaviour.[19]

This reads like a version of William Ogburn's famous concept of cultural lag, which has been a point of reference in many social science textbooks published since the 1930s.[20] But in contrast to Ogburn, who took a neo-positivist stance and had no interest in social engineering, Wilson aimed to not only explore but to overcome the "cultural lag." And by tackling the food problem from two points of view—the biochemical and the behavioral—Wilson's primary goal was to shape human behavior according to the principles of biochemistry. The implicit subordination of consumers notwithstanding, this dual approach took foodways seriously and encompassed the cultural aspects of food.

The task for the Committee on Food Habits was to evaluate systematically ways of exploring—and gradually changing—consumers' food habits: to encourage people to desire to eat the foods that were available to them. Founded in 1941, the committee was led by some of the best-known figures in American anthropology of the time, including a past president of the American Anthropological Association, Carl Guthe, and Margaret Mead, who served as executive secretary. The anthropologists presented their results in the form of attitude surveys and monographs. The attitude studies explored domestic food habits in relation to new or more abundant, available foodstuffs; problems of rationing and scarcity were also analyzed. To help facilitate the most efficient distribution of food aid, the monographs provided knowledge about food habits and foodways in several European countries, including Czechoslovakia, Great Britain, Hungary, Italy, the Netherlands, Poland.[21] Even after the end of the war and the postwar crisis, this knowledge was still used to guide American projects in modernizing European food chains.

The Committee on Food Habits did not survive the immediate postwar era, despite the fact that its proponents saw the committee as a permanent, "applied anthropological" government adviser. The committee's explicit task was to provide empirical data that could help bridge the gap between production and consumption. Other institutions and actors—including marketing experts, corporate advertisers, and various consumer-research agencies—helped to link the different parts of the food chain. And so it was the Committee on Food Habits that helped to forge new food chains; that placed consumers center stage; and that emphasized food's cultural importance to other actors in the chain.

Food for Peace

In contrast with the state-founded Committee on Food Habits, which was rather short-lived and superseded by numerous private actors, U.S. food aid programs—also state-financed—were re-launched nearly ten years after the war ended. This was due to the same, persistent problem that had prompted former food aid programs: farm surpluses. Another reason for re-starting food aid was the opportunity to use it as a diplomatic weapon and as a means of restructuring existing food chains during the Cold War.

In July of 1954, approximately half a year after U.S. President Dwight Eisenhower's "Atoms for Peace" speech to the General Assembly of the United Nations, the U.S. Congress passed the Agricultural Trade Development and Assistance Act (Public Law 480). This law established a framework for American food diplomacy and became known as the Food for Peace Program.[22] Just as the Atoms for Peace Program promised to secure world peace through research on peaceful uses of atomic power, Food for Peace promised to deliver world peace through the provision of food. George S. McGovern, the liberal senator from South Dakota who headed Food for Peace under the John F. Kennedy administration, published a report to mark the tenth anniversary of Food for Peace. In the report, he stated bluntly the domestic benefits of the program: "Public Law 480, on which our Food for Peace Program is based, was originally conceived in 1954, largely as a means of disposing of the mounting agricultural surpluses for foreign currencies when their sale abroad for dollars proved impossible."[23] The U.S. government bought domestic farm products with U.S. dollars and sold them either government-to-government (for local currencies, on credit terms of up to thirty years) or donated the food to countries in need. From 1954 to 1964 the United States distributed 27 percent of its agricultural exports via the Food for Peace Program's channels.[24] The local money obtained from sales made under Public Law 480 was reinvested in the purchasing country and reserved for development projects, cultural exchange, and U.S. propaganda.

McGovern's report describes the success of the program. Not only were more than one-quarter of U.S. agricultural exports during this period financed through Food for Peace, but for wheat, the figure was even higher, accounting for two-thirds of U.S. exports.[25] Hence, Food for Peace provided tremendous subsidies for U.S. agriculture and, via commercial coupling effects (farm machinery, fertilizers, seeds, insecticides, and consumer goods), for the U.S. economy as a whole. Paradoxically, Food for Peace represented strict Keynesian thinking in reference to agriculture at a time when the United States claimed to be the model of a liberal market economy.

Noting a second major contribution to the national interest, McGovern highlighted the new commercial marketing opportunities available through Food for Peace: "A substantial part of the proceeds of foreign currency sales has been used to advertise and promote American farm products. Many of our private commercial organizations have cooperated with the government in sponsoring trade fairs and other market promotional activities abroad."[26] McGovern also stressed the effect of the Food for Peace Program on food habits in the recipient countries. "The great food markets of the future are the very areas where vast numbers of people are learning through Food for Peace to eat American produce. The people we assist today will become our customers tomorrow. Our best markets are in those nations with the most developed agricultural and industrial economies."[27] McGovern singled out Italy, Spain, and Japan, which had indeed transitioned from being Food for Peace recipients to strong buyers of American food products.

Finally, McGovern's report also reveals the importance of Food for Peace in the context of American foreign policy during the Cold War. From 1957 to 1964, the United States accepted local currencies from Food for Peace recipients and gave cheap export credits based on Public Law 480 to Poland ($671 million) and Yugoslavia ($906 million). McGovern described this new phase of the Cold War:

> An interesting by-product of our food shipments to Poland and Yugoslavia is that both countries have discarded the Communist technique of trying to raise farm products through government collectives. They have moved back toward private family farms.... Our surpluses may be helping those two nations to show not only their people but also the Russians that independent family farming is superior to collectivism.[28]

American food diplomacy succeeded roundly in both Poland and Yugoslavia: neither country made the transition to collective farming. Also noteworthy is McGovern's frankly positive appraisal of family farms, which, at the time of his report, were more an ideology than a reality in the United States. This idealized view of the family farm dates to Thomas Jefferson's homage to the "yeoman farmer," the ideal citizen for the newly established state of Virginia, according to Jefferson.[29] Indeed, McGovern clung to the Jeffersonian ideal, whereas the U.S. farm structure was perceived differently by Europeans: in their view, American agriculture was dominated by corporate farms with large estates and complex machinery. In contrast to this rejected model, Europeans proffered their version of the family farm as an alternative—despite that model being outdated for Europe.[30]

The Food for Peace prepared the European market for the appropriation of American foodstuffs. One case in point is the approximately three million pounds of frozen and canned chicken and turkey that was shipped to West Germany after an agreement under the Food for Peace Program was signed on December 23, 1955.[31] These shipments helped to re-launch frozen food in West Germany, and they encouraged the development of a domestic chicken industry.[32]

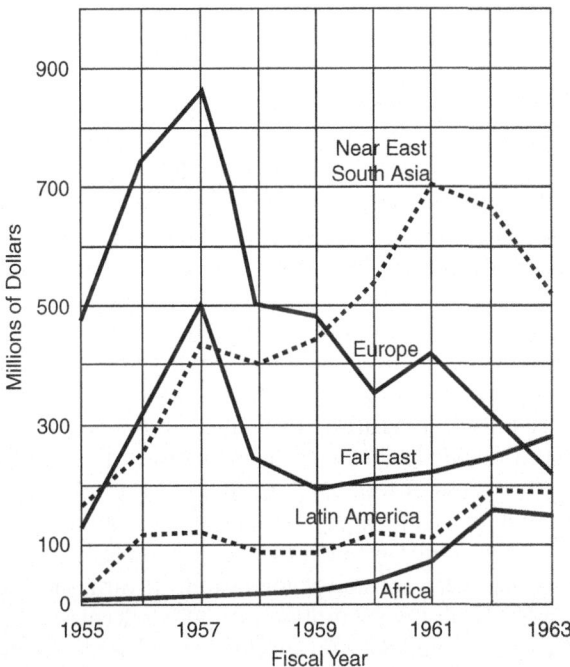

Figure 3.1 The U.S. Food for Peace Program promised to deliver world peace through the provision of food. This chart shows the global distribution of Food for Peace shipments from 1955 to 1963.

By the end of the 1950s, the Food for Peace Program's focus had shifted from Europe to the East, the Far East, and to Africa. And, while the program now had less of an impact on Europe, it remained extremely influential: Food for Peace went on to restructure the international postwar food order. As far as European foodways were concerned, however, other U.S. programs, institutions, and actors carried on the challenge. In terms of achieving longer range and far deeper effects, it was the European Recovery Program (ERP)—also known as the Marshall Plan—and its productivity mission that spurred European appropriation, selective though it was, of the American model. This program fostered knowledge and technology transfer, which facilitated the emulation of main elements of the American-style food chains in many countries participating in the Organisation for European Economic Cooperation (OEEC) countries.

The European Recovery Program: Changing European Foodways

The European Recovery Program served as a cornerstone for building the American century: the many initiatives and programs, which it both fostered and financed, helped to introduce U.S. technology and management methods to Western Europe. How did this transfer work? And, to what extent was the American model adapted, renegotiated, or abandoned? This has been the subject of a range of studies in which the role of industry, for the most part, has been analyzed.[33] But the productivity policy of corporate America also targeted the agriculture and food sectors, which influenced the OEEC's strong interest in these areas as well. Food scarcity in war-ravaged Europe sparked a major concern for political stability. Modernizing food chains was a priority—not only because of the urgent need for more food in most of the European countries, but because of food and agriculture's key role in stabilizing national economies. Achieving affordable production and distribution of inexpensive foodstuffs would increase disposable income, thereby raising the demand for consumer goods and, in turn, facilitating the transition to the Fordist consumption regime. Modernizing agriculture would also create new markets for machinery and seeds, fertilizers and pesticides, breeding animals, feeds, and antibiotics. Markets would also expand for transport services and refrigeration technologies as well as for ancillary products and services. Restructuring the West European food chain by adapting it to the American model was, indeed, a core element of the United States' productivity mission, which hinged on the conviction that efficiency was the solution to all societal ills.[34]

A main mediator of American technology and business practices was the European Productivity Agency, founded in 1953. It grew out of the U.S. Technical Assistance and Productivity Program, which was launched as one of the first Marshall Plan initiatives in 1948.[35] As a semi-autonomous organization within the framework of the OEEC, the European Productivity Agency existed from 1953 to 1961; during that entire period, it received two-thirds of its total budget from the United States.[36] According to the allocation of money, two areas received priority: business management as well as food and agriculture.[37] The European Productivity Agency was originally designed as an institution to direct knowledge and technology transfer from the United States to Western Europe. Later, the agency was transformed into a structure providing European solutions to reconstruction problems.[38] Unquestionably, the European Productivity Agency enforced the

Forging Europe's Foodways 75

American productivity mission in Europe; at the same time, it strongly encouraged West European cooperation and integration. A range of those within the agency—both Americans and Europeans—perceived the technology and knowledge transfer taking place to be a mutual exchange in both directions, not a one-way street from the United States to Europe. Given that the United States was the European Productivity Agency's primary funder, however, American officials would not have allowed the agency to undertake projects that conflicted with U.S. priorities. For example, American officials sought to initiate projects that institutionalized management education; that involved non-communist trade unions in recovery plans; and that condemned restrictive business practices. But European actors openly voiced their criticism when they perceived that U.S.-driven projects contradicted European expectations. In 1953, this occurred in reference to an American attempt to demonstrate the advantages of refrigeration equipment for the modernization of food distribution. The case sparked the following protest:

> The Americans have no inhibitions about trying to sell their goods: for example the Technical Assistance mission no. 142—a team of Americans employed travelling round Europe training retailers in modern methods of food distribution—is accompanied by a large caravan full of [the] latest types of American refrigerating [sic] equipment, and since last June they have been doing it at the agency's expense.[39]

The agency financed projects that were proposed by either a member country, the secretariat of the European Productivity Agency, or an OEEC committee. In the case of food and agriculture, the project agenda was prepared not within but outside of the European Productivity Agency, by the OEEC's Committee of Deputies of the Ministerial Committee of Agriculture and Food.[40] Reviewing the project areas and specific approaches provides insights into the European Productivity Agency's role in restructuring West European food chains—and the degree to which the American model was appropriated.

One of the European Productivity Agency's reports from 1960 lists all activities in the realm of food and agriculture since the program's founding in 1953.[41] These activities covered five main areas: agricultural production, marketing, education, technological developments, and communication. A large series of projects was devoted to the field of agricultural production, with projects on improvements in the uses of agricultural resources, on farm management, and on advisory work. The OEEC administrators, along with their U.S. advisers, organized missions to the United States to explore farm management, accounting methods, and agricultural advisory work. Several projects dealt with land consolidation and the creation of economically viable farm units. One report, titled *The Small Family Farm: A European Problem* and published in 1959, estimated the total number of small, non-viable family farms to be 50 percent or higher for countries like France, West Germany, Greece, Ireland, Italy, the Netherlands, Norway, Sweden, and Portugal. These small farms cultivated one-fourth of the agricultural acreage in France and Italy.[42] The report stated clearly that small, non-viable farm holdings posed a serious problem for the economy as a whole. The recommended solutions were to extend land-lease systems and to require the peasants to abandon their "mystical relationship" with land ownership. The report did not openly criticize family farms as an outdated institution, though it clearly established the American corporate farm as a model.

Other European Productivity Agency projects dealt with productivity measurement on farms and methods for measuring cost-return ratios as a basis for pricing and income policies. These few examples alone provide evidence of the OEEC's strategy: to impose the logic of industry on farms using yield increase—a main concern of farm management—as a pretext. Thus, running a farm was no longer to be a way of life, but a method of earning profits and accumulating cash.

A clear majority of the agency's activities involved the marketing of foodstuffs. These projects included workshops on up-to-date methods of preparing and selling meat (with the incentive of providing butchers with more knowledge of foreign consumer tastes and habits). Also included were meetings with experts on ways to promote milk and the consumption of other dairy products, ways to standardize vegetable produce and other foods as well as packaging, and experiments with pre-packing fruits and vegetables. This area of work also entailed surveys on the marketing and distribution of frozen fish. And, last but not least, a range of activities aimed at developing a cold chain that would reach from the north to the south of Europe: this would help to distribute frozen fish from Iceland and Norway to the southern regions and facilitate exports from Italy, Greece, and Turkey to the northern areas. In 1959, European Productivity Agency Project No. 6/13 established so-called demonstration regions in France (Lyon) and Italy (Milan and Rome) in order to promote the production, distribution, and consumption of frozen food.[43] A mission of sixteen European experts studied the application of market and consumer research methods to livestock products, including milk and milk products, in the United States.[44]

Figure 3.2 Via the European Productivity Agency, American experts worked with Europeans to standardize food-related processes from production to marketing to packaging. This photo represents a scene from the European Exhibition on Prepacking of Fresh Fruits and Vegetables of 1958.

In the category of dairy products, a Canadian consultant visited twelve member countries and gave a series of talks and demonstrations of the various merchandizing techniques.[45] These are few but representative examples of the extensive work done in this area.

The array of marketing projects was to supplement the rationalization of production with the rationalization of distribution. The projects explored the need for introducing new actors and institutions in the food chain in order to manage the problem of the increasing distance between the field and the fork. In the future, this would reduce the farm's share of the profits and increase the cost of marketing food—which accounted for two-thirds of food-sector expenditures in the United States. In fact, this had been the case since the late 1950s.[46] All of these activities were designed to increase consumption capacities. Accordingly, these activities strengthened not only the links between all parts of European food chains, but enabled food chains to be adaptable to American food surpluses such as chicken.[47] Even more importantly, European food chains were now primed to appropriate the American ingredients of an industrialized food chain, such as seeds, fertilizers, antibiotics, feedstuff, breeding materials, and freezing technologies. Therefore, we can see the European Productivity Agency's food and agriculture program as a driving force behind the transformation of traditional foodways and consumption regimes.

The agency's educational activities focused on developing vocational training. Further, they included advanced training—lasting ten months, on average—for specialists from OEEC member countries. The training took place in the United States and covered topics like marketing of agricultural products, advanced statistics, farm management, agricultural communication, and applied nuclear science in food and agriculture. The educational projects were intended to promote cooperation between agricultural faculties of universities and comparable research institutes.[48] Closely related to these educational projects were initiatives for improved communication. For example, a food and agricultural technical information service (FATIS) was established by the OEEC and operated through permanent FATIS liaison centers in the member countries of Canada and the United States. Parallel to a multilingual review and films, a seminar on "Television in Agricultural Advisory Work" aimed to introduce new media for improved communication. All of these projects put knowledge and information at the forefront of action in the area of food and agriculture. In doing so, they worked toward replacing locally available knowledge and information with supposedly universal expertise.

Nearly all of the European Productivity Agency's activities were tied in some way to technological developments, though the OEEC also initiated a range of projects devoted specifically to process innovations in European food chains. In a summary of its activities, the European Productivity Agency administration highlighted three of these process innovations: the application of atomic science in agriculture and food; international cooperation in agricultural aviation; and the improvement of farm buildings.[49] One of these projects will be analyzed in greater detail: this case provides evidence of the enormous hope (and hype) that science and technology could help restructure post-Second World War food chains. It also reveals the complexities of the transatlantic knowledge and technology transfer.

Atomic Science in Food and Agriculture

At the time of the first Geneva Conference in August of 1955, the atom was seen as a powerful resource, promising to yield quantum improvements in food and agriculture. Many actors and institutions took this promise seriously and promoted activities to employ the peaceful atom for restructuring food chains.[50] The OEEC's Committee of Deputies of the Ministerial Committee for Agriculture and Food also intervened and tasked the European Productivity Agency with organizing Project No. 396, entitled "Application of Atomic Science in Agriculture and Food." This entailed a spectrum of activities covering the entire field of nuclear research and development in food and agriculture. Project No. 396 included, for example, the actual and potential application of atomic tools (isotopes and irradiation) in research work connected with soil and plant problems, animal science, radiation biology, and food preservation. Also included was the development of techniques for inducing mutations to speed up breeding and to preserve crops and food.

The European Productivity Agency project started in the spring of 1957, when a delegation consisting of twenty experts from nine OEEC member countries visited the United States from March to June.[51] The delegation's program encompassed visits to a number of research and education institutions, ranging from institutions of higher education such as MIT and Iowa State College, to the research laboratories of food-technology companies, like Swift & Co. Also on the agenda were visits to trade associations such as the American Meat Institute Foundation and the U.S. Army Quartermaster's Food and Container Institute in Chicago, an important military research institution in the food sector. During the last four weeks of the mission, the participants attended a training course at the Oak Ridge National Institute of Nuclear Studies in Tennessee, which introduced them to the use of radioisotopes as research tools. As part of Eisenhower's Atoms for Peace Program, the institute's Special Training Division offered courses for foreign nationals. The trip allowed the visiting Europeans to inspect the American facilities designed for developing atomic cooking: in this way, it helped to establish the United States as "head chef" in the envisioned atomic kitchen. Subsequent to the trip, and following up on recommendations received there, four American consultants began working with the agency to advise OEEC member countries on planning and executing research programs.[52]

Another part of European Productivity Agency Project No. 396 was a study trip to Great Britain from May 19 to June 2, 1958. It included visits to fifteen establishments—all university institutes and government research laboratories active in nuclear research and development in food and agriculture. At first glance, this trip appears to be a facsimile of the previous one, to the U.S. But, on closer examination, it appears to be a display of British rather than American achievements in the food sector. The delegations' conclusions emphasized the need for better training of graduates in agricultural science, including elementary courses in atomic science. Great Britain had already established a training center in Harwell that was to be comparable to the American facility in Oak Ridge.[53]

As the final part of Project No. 396, a "working conference" was organized in consultation with the European Nuclear Energy Agency and held at the OEEC headquarters in Paris, in July of 1958. Here, the U.S. consultants presented the results of their surveys. The outcome of the conference was remarkable in several respects. Unlike the second Atoms for Peace conference in Geneva earlier that year—a conference dominated by a pessimistic view of nuclear energy's potential—the Paris conference was overly optimistic. Its recommendations called for more investment and more activities to close the gap between research and "application on the farm and the plant level." Another recommendation read: "In the irradiation field it seems clear that within a decade or so the application of gamma radiation or the use of such machines as linear accelerators might well prove to be economic."[54]

The last and most detailed recommendations dealt with "International Co-operation." The European Productivity Agency was thought to be the most appropriate body to organize a supply chain for irradiated food at the European level. This meant "maintain[ing] a very close connection on the international level between associations representing producers, marketing organizations, the food industry and wholesale and retail distribution associations as well as associations for consumers."[55] Linking all actors in the irradiated-foods supply chain throughout Western Europe would result in an "irradiation chain" that resembled the cold chain—another series of European Productivity Agency projects initiated in the early 1950s.[56]

A related project was proposed to the agency for inter-European cooperation: Norman W. Desrosier suggested that the EUROCHEMIC Company's plant for reprocessing irradiated fuel in Mol, Belgium, become "a pilot plant for testing the food irradiation processes and for training industrial research workers." Desrosier was a U.S. consultant

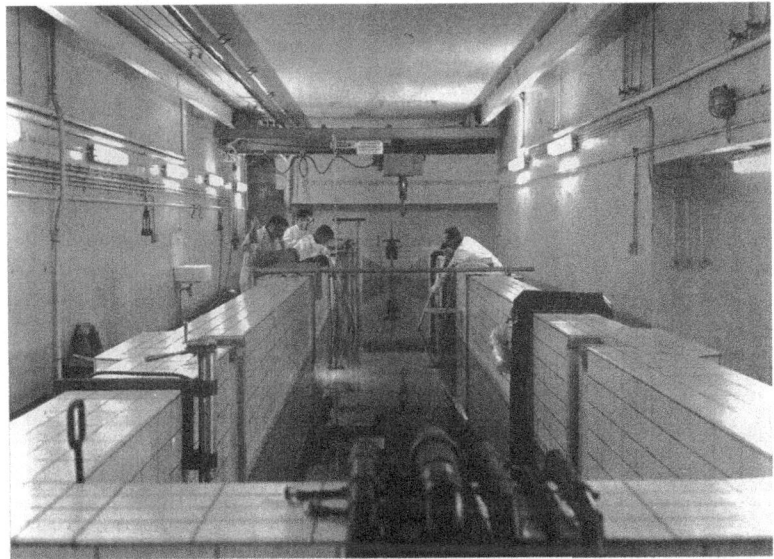

Figure 3.3 To some experts, irradiated food appeared to be on the verge of entering the market in the 1950s. Featured here: an irradiation canal containing spent fuel elements from the reactor at the Nuclear Energy Study Center in Mol, Belgium.

and director of the Food Radiation Preservation Division at the Chicago-based Quartermaster Food and Container Institute for the Armed Forces. Desrosier envisioned the Mol pilot plant as a promising complement to the U.S. Army's pilot-plant project in Stockton, California. The experience gained from both pilot plants, he stipulated, would enable food-processing organizations in OEEC countries "to formulate plans for the integration of radio-stabilised foods into the current channels of food distribution."[57]

Thus, for Desrosier, just as for his co-workers at the European Productivity Agency, irradiated food appeared to be on the verge of entering the market. They suggested developing alliances in order to help parlay research results into industrial applications. They also called for joint research projects and better regional cooperation, in Scandinavia and the Mediterranean region, for example. Although the agency's assumption about the short-term future of irradiated food soon proved to be far too optimistic, Project No. 396 was vital: it opened the door for developing close inter-European cooperation on the application of atomic science in agriculture and food. The project worked as a lever of both Americanization—given that Eisenhower's Atoms for Peace initiative propelled atomic agriculture and food—and Europeanization, given how the project facilitated the emergence of a research and development network in food and agriculture. This network fostered European collaboration in an array of follow-up activities, such as the inauguration of a European Society of Nuclear Agriculture, formed at a conference at the Agricultural University in Wageningen, the Netherlands, in 1969.[58] Nuclear agriculture did not meet the high expectations that many had invested in the "radiant food" idea. Nuclear agriculture did, however, prove to be a significant step in the transition toward science-based food chains—food chains free of traditional constraints such as the geography and climate determined by the local region.

Cooperation and Conflict

The modernization of food chains ranked high among the U.S. recovery and stabilization projects for war-ravaged Europe. Modernizing food chains was also a priority of European governments; it was part of rebuilding their countries. The Soviet Union—the other superpower emerging from the battlefields of the Second World War—was not able to provide food aid for its bloc partners plagued by food shortages; the Soviet Union itself depended on help from the United States. Thus, relying on its highly productive food chains, the U.S. could provide food aid and serve as a model for the reconstruction process within its sphere of influence west of the Iron Curtain. America's dual interest was to stabilize Western Europe politically and to develop it as a market for American foods—not to mention as a market for agricultural and industrial consumer goods. And these interests meshed with the need of Western European governments to secure food and other goods for their populations after years of shortages and privation.

This common interest, however, did not instantly erase the different experiences and attitudes toward agriculture and food that had developed on both sides of the Atlantic during the first half of the twentieth century. For example, the European resistance to accepting de-population of the countryside persisted after the Second World War. The U.S. agricultural economist Paul Lamartine Yates, who worked for the Food and Agriculture Organization of the United Nations (FAO) as the regional representative for Europe until the late 1960s, criticized the majority of European governments for opposing "any diminution in farm numbers, thereby retarding industrial growth and adding to the inflation danger."[59]

Many reasons contributed to this attitude, including: national security concerns, the wish to maintain a healthy balance of payments through import substitution, the imperfections of the labor market, conscription requirements in case of a new war (the farming population was perceived as able to supply the majority of soldiers), the desire to help disadvantaged regions, as well as an idealization of farming as the most socially healthy way of life. Thus, European agricultural lobby groups had successfully pushed for agricultural policies to be categorized not as food policies but as social policies. This decision favored the farmers and operated to the detriment of consumers.

With these pro-farmer policies in place, the majority of European governments—with the exception of Denmark and, to some extent, the Netherlands—set up farm income support programs.[60] Now, even small farms with limited potential for increased efficiency could survive: this hampered farm modernization projects. It also decelerated the transition to the Fordist consumption regime: for the consumer, the percentage of the household budget spent on food was still relatively high; this failure of food prices to drop quickly also hindered consumers' capacity to buy more non-food products and services. Food expenditures in OECD countries fell from 18.1 percent of gross national product in 1956 to 15.5 percent in 1966. Food expenditures were lowest in the United States, with a percentage of 12.2 in 1966 and highest in Greece, with a percentage of 28.4 during the same year, followed by Italy (23.9 percent), Ireland (22.5 percent), West Germany (19.4 percent), and France (18.5 percent).[61] Yates, the FAO regional representative for Europe, urged the agricultural establishment not to use subsidies to keep small farms alive. Instead, he advocated production of marketable products in fewer but much bigger farms. In this constellation, electrical energy, irrigated plots, and scientifically bred livestock could be used more efficiently, based, as they were, on economies of scale.[62] In fact, the feasibility of many of these suggestions had already been explored in projects conducted by the European Productivity Agency. In essence, Europeans too, wanted modernity—but without sacrificing the romance of farming as a way of life.

The social-policy approach to farming gained traction when a common Western European agricultural policy was established as part of the European Economic Union.[63] It proved a difficult process, however, and the agreements leading to an agricultural union were attained only gradually and partially. Ironically for the United States, the European discontent with the U.S. Food for Peace Program became a driving force behind forging the new agreements: it was Food for Peace that had brought highly subsidized food products to the European market in the first place.[64]

Thus, the American Food for Peace Program did not impart freedom to its European allies; rather, the program conveyed an experience of American hegemony. As collaboration via the European Productivity Agency and transatlantic communications illustrate, European counterparts were more likely to accept help with process innovations along the food chain than with product innovations. By selectively appropriating the American model, Western European countries modernized and extended their food chains. Accordingly, science and technology became ever more important facets of food, and food supplies became abundant. Western Europe gradually transitioned to the Fordist consumption regime, although foodways and cuisines remained distinctively European, given that ways of cooking and eating continued to differ, not just nationally, but regionally. But the meaning of foodways and cuisines did change: they lost their old function of conveying trust in food[65] and became essential ingredients of cultural lifestyles, which consumers could, indeed, choose at will.

Notes

1. *Food Consumption Levels in OEEC Countries: Report of the Working Group on Food Consumption Levels* (Paris: OEEC, 1950). For more detail on diets in Europe as well as wartime and postwar nutrition programs, see Paul Lamartine Yates, *Food, Land and Manpower in Western Europe* (London: Macmillan, 1960), chaps 2–3.
2. *Food for Europe after Victory* (Washington: National Planning Association, 1944).
3. Whereas a single farmer provided food for ten people in 1930 and for eleven people in 1940, a farmer could feed fifteen people in 1950. Wayne D. Rasmussen, "The Impact of Technological Change on American Agriculture, 1862–1962," *The Journal of Economic History* 22 (1962): 583.
4. Working within the framework of the Marshall Plan, American farmers shipped huge amounts of food to Europe. The U.S. Department of Agriculture expected food exports to become a booming business for American farmers. Wayne D. Rasmussen and Jane M. Porter, "Strategies for Dealing with World Hunger: Post-World War II Policies," *American Journal of Agricultural Economics* 63 (1981): 810–18.
5. Jean D. Kinsey, "The New Food Economy: Consumers, Farms, Pharms, and Science," *American Journal of Agricultural Economics* 83 (2001): 1113–30.
6. See one of the most influential books in the vast literature on consumer culture: Mary Douglas and Baron C. Isherwood, *The World of Goods* (New York: Basic Books, 1979).
7. Marshall Sahlins, *Kultur und praktische Vernunft* (Frankfurt am Main: Suhrkamp, 1999), 296.

8. Barbara E. Willard, "The American Story of Meat: Discursive Influences on Cultural Eating Practice," *Journal of Popular Culture* 36 (2002): 116.
9. Helen H. Gifft, Marjorie B. Washbon, and Gail G. Harrison, *Nutrition, Behavior, and Change* (Englewood Cliffs, NJ: Prentice-Hall, 1972), 27.
10. Willard, "The American Story," 116.
11. Claude Lévi-Strauss, "Das kulinarische Dreieck," in *Strukturalismus als interpretatives Verfahren*, ed. Helga Gallas (Darmstadt: Luchterhand, 1972).
12. One of the first—and still one of the best—explorations of the mechanization of food and of cultural tastes in food: Giedion Sigfried, *Mechanization Takes Command: A Contribution to Anonymous History* (New York: Oxford University Press, 1948). Since this book's publication, a range of dissertations have tackled this subcategory of the history of technology. For more detail on the United States, see Mark W. Wilde, "Industrialization of Food Processing in the United States, 1860–1960" (PhD diss., University of Delaware, 1988); Gabriella Petrick, "The Arbiters of Taste: Producers, Consumers, and the Industrialization of Taste in America, 1900–1960" (PhD diss., University of Delaware, 2006); Shane Hamilton, *Trucking Country: The Road to America's Wal-Mart Economy* (Princeton, NJ: Princeton University Press, 2008).
13. Warren James Belasco, *Meals to Come: A History of the Future of Food* (Berkeley: University of California Press, 2006), 174.
14. Ibid.
15. Vaclav Smil, *Transforming the Twentieth Century: Technical Innovations and Their Consequences* (Oxford: Oxford University Press, 2006), 141.
16. Yates, *Food, Land and Manpower*, 6.
17. For more on Nazi-German food politics—especially in relation to Nazi ideology—see Gustavo Corni and Horst Gies, *Brot – Butter – Kanonen: Die Ernährungswirtschaft in Deutschland unter der Diktatur Hitlers* (Berlin: Akademie-Verlag, 1997).
18. Rebecca L. Spang, "The Cultural Habits of a Food Committee," *Food and Foodways* 2 (1988): 378.
19. Ibid.
20. William Fielding Ogburn, *Social Change with Respect to Culture and Original Nature* (New York: B.W. Huebsch, 1922); Rudi Volti, "William F. Ogburn, Social Change with Respect to Culture and Original Nature," *Technology and Culture* 45 (2004): 396–405.
21. "The Problem of Changing Food Habits," in *NAS-NRC Pub. 108* (Washington, DC: National Research Council, 1943); "Manual for the Study of Food Habits: Report of the Committee on Food Habits," in *NAS-NRC Pub. 111* (Washington, DC: National Research Council, 1945); *Translating Science into Living Habits: Liaison Session of the Committee, May 19, 1945* (Washington, DC: National Research Council, 1945).
22. Harriet Friedmann, "The Political Economy of Food: The Rise and the Fall of the Postwar International Food Order," in "Marxist Inquiries: Studies of Labor, Class, and States," supplement, *American Journal of Sociology* 88 (1982): 248–86.
23. George S. McGovern, *War against Want: America's Food for Peace Program* (New York: Walker, 1964), 45.
24. Ibid., 22.
25. Ibid., 21.

26. Ibid., 24.
27. Ibid., 25.
28. Ibid., 24. McGovern's figures are slightly higher than those from other sources. On food aid to Poland, see also Stephen S. Kaplan, "United States Aid to Poland, 1957–1964: Concerns, Objectives and Obstacles," *The Western Political Quarterly* 28 (1975): 147–66.
29. Thomas Jefferson, *Notes on the State of Virginia* (London: J. Stockdale, 1787).
30. Lorraine Bluche and Kiran Klaus Patel, "Der Europäer als Bauer: Das Motiv des bäuerlichen Familienbetriebes in Westeuropa nach 1945," in *Der Europäer – Ein Konstrukt: Wissensbestände, Diskurse, Praktiken*, ed. Lorraine Bluche, Veronika Lipphardt, and Kiran Klaus Patel (Göttingen: Wallstein, 2009).
31. *Quick Frozen Food* 18 (1956): 159–60. The shipment of frozen poultry to West Germany marked the opening of new export markets.
32. Erwin Hilck and Rudolf Hövel, *Jenseits von minus Null: Die Geschichte der deutschen Tiefkühlwirtschaft* (Cologne: Deutsches Tiefkühlinstitut, 1979); Hans Jürgen Teuteberg, "Zur Geschichte der Kühlkost und des Tiefgefrierens," *Zeitschrift für Unternehmensgeschichte* 36 (1991): 139–55.
33. Jonathan Zeitlin and Gary Herrigel, eds., *Americanization and Its Limits: Reworking US Technology and Management in Postwar Europe and Japan* (Oxford: Oxford University Press, 2000); Matthias Kipping and Ove Bjarnar, *The Americanisation of European Business: The Marshall Plan and the Transfer of US Management Models* (London: Routledge, 1998).
34. On productivity policy, see Charles S. Maier, *In Search of Stability: Explorations in Historical Political Economy* (Cambridge: Cambridge University Press, 1987), chap. 3.
35. Jacqueline McGlade, "Americanization: Ideology or Process? The Case of the United States Technical Assistance and Productivity Programme," in *Americanization and Its Limits*, 53–75; Bent Boel, *The European Productivity Agency and Transatlantic Relations, 1953–1961* (Copenhagen: Museum Tusculanum Press, 2003).
36. Boel, *The European Productivity Agency*, 119.
37. Ibid.
38. This finding by Bent Boel, who analyzed the European Productivity Agency as an institution that shaped transatlantic relations in the early Cold War, has been confirmed regarding the agency's activities in the field of food and agriculture. Bent Boel, "The European Productivity Agency: A Faithful Prophet of the American Model?" in *The Americanisation of European Business*, 37–54.
39. Ellis-Ries to Strath, February 2, 1954, cited in ibid., 50. This remark obviously challenged a supposedly boastful American claim of superiority in areas such as refrigeration.
40. Boel, *The European Productivity Agency*, 224.
41. *Agriculture and Food: Summary Report on Activities Undertaken by EPA since Its Establishment in 1953* (Paris: EPA, 1960).
42. *The Small Family Farm: A European Problem: Methods for Creating Economically Viable Units: Project No. 199/2* (Paris: EPA, 1959).

43. A report was published by two European Productivity Agency consultants on the subjects of results achieved and difficulties encountered. See *Agriculture and Food*, 43. On efforts to set up a cold chain in Norway and to introduce frozen food into the Norwegian diet, see the contribution by Terje Finstad, Stig Kvaal, and Per Østby (Chapter 4) in this volume.
44. *Agriculture and Food*, 24, 27.
45. Ibid., 26.
46. *Food Marketing and Economic Growth* (Paris: OECD, 1970), 51.
47. In the summer of 1956, U.S. private traders started selling frozen poultry to West German importers for West German currency under the Agricultural Trade Development and Assistance Act of 1954. A U.S.–West German agreement was signed on December 23, 1955. Under this agreement, the United States sent to West Germany approximately $1.2 million worth (about 3 million pounds) of high-quality frozen and canned chickens and turkeys. See *Quick Frozen Food* 18 (1956): 159–60.
48. *Agriculture and Food*, 47–9.
49. Ibid., 50–2.
50. See also Karin Zachmann, "Atoms for Peace and Radiation for Safety – How to Build Trust in Irradiated Foods in Cold War Europe and Beyond," *History and Technology* 27 (2011): 65–90; Zachmann, *Risky Rays for an Improved Food Supply? Transnational Food Irradiation Research as a Cold War Recipe*, Preprint 7 (München: Deutsches Museum, 2013).
51. *Application of Atomic Science in Agriculture and Food: Report of Mission to the United States Sponsored by the European Productivity Agency under Project No. 396* (Paris: EPA, 1958).
52. *Applications of Atomic Science in Agriculture and Food: Present Positions, Future Trends and Techniques: Report of the Working Conference, Project No. 396* (Paris: EPA, 1959), 246. See also *Agriculture and Food*, 50–1.
53. Victor Middleboe, "Report of the EPA/OEEC Mission to the United Kingdom," in *Project No. 396*, 32–44.
54. *Project No. 396*, 11.
55. Ibid.
56. In 1950—before the European Productivity Agency's founding (1953)—an OEEC-organized delegation visited the United States to study the cold chain. *The Cold Chain in the U. S. A.: Report of a Group of European Experts* (Paris: OEEC, 1951). It was followed by European Productivity Agency Project No. 239 in 1955, which entailed analyzing refrigeration research and its applications in industry via a mission to Western European countries. See *European Refrigeration Research and Its Practical Applications: Project No. 239* (Paris: EPA, 1959).
57. *Project No. 396*, 148.
58. Zachmann, *Risky Rays*, 40–7.
59. Yates, *Food, Land and Manpower*, 13.
60. Ibid., 264–5. On the Western European trend of pursuing agricultural policies as social policies, see also Guido Thiemeyer, *Vom "Pool Vert" zur Europäischen Wirtschaftsgemeinschaft: Europäische Integration, Kalter Krieg und die Anfänge der Gemeinsamen Europäischen Agrarpolitik, 1950–1957* (Munich: Oldenbourg, 1999), 25–50.

61. *Food Marketing*, 25.
62. Yates, *Food, Land and Manpower*, 282.
63. Ann-Christina L. Knudsen, "Ideas, Welfare, and Values: Framing the Common Agricultural Policy in the 1960s," in *Fertile Ground for Europe? The History of European Integration and the Common Agricultural Policy since 1945*, ed. Patel Kiran Klaus (Baden-Baden: Nomos, 2009).
64. Thiemeyer, *Vom "Pool Vert" zur Europäischen Wirtschaftsgemeinschaft*, 158.
65. Karin Zachmann and Per Østby, "Food, Technology, and Trust: An Introduction," in "Food, Technology, and Trust," special issue, *History and Technology* 27 (2011): 1–10.

4
Tackling Norwegian Cold: The Breakthrough of Home Freezing

Terje Finstad, Stig Kvaal, and Per Østby

During the 1950s and 1960s, Norwegian life changed socially, economically, culturally—comprehensively. One manifestation of this change was the new products that found their way into daily life. The car, the TV, and the home freezer, for example, became embedded in Norwegian lifestyles—and pivotal to the country's transformation. Modern technologies signaled that Norwegian society was advancing; the car, TV, and home freezer were powerful symbols of progress and the modern way of life. Indeed, the significance of the home freezer surpassed its practical use: the freezer's introduction and its growth spurred new lifestyles and new consumption regimes.[1]

As many sociologists and historians of technology have shown, however, the choices of users and consumers are usually anything but self-evident. Often, during the early stages of a diffusion process, many different technological solutions remain available; only as the process advances do selected solutions emerge as dominant. For example, in the early days of household refrigeration, gas refrigerators existed alongside electric models, scholar Ruth Schwartz Cowan has shown. The battle for market dominance between the gas and electric industries resulted in a victory for the electric refrigerator.[2] Cowan's example emphasizes the importance of challenging the reductive assumption that consumers and users simply choose the "best" technology. Instead, she urges, it is canny to ask how a particular technology became part of everyday life.

In this chapter, we reference Cowan's argument about technology's pivotal role in forming and transforming societies. We argue that the choice of one technological alternative over another can reveal information about a society's values. Technological choices are linked to ideology, after all. So, it is important to investigate the actors who promote a particular technology and to explore their interests in doing so.[3]

During the 1950s and 1960s, American technology—along with American consumer products, movies, literature, and advertising, for example—became increasingly important to Norwegian mass culture. Traditionally, Norway had taken its cultural and technological cues from other parts of Europe, including Germany, Great Britain, and even the Soviet Union. After the Second World War, however, the United States became the main source of technology, of ideas, and of visions for Norway and, indeed, much of Europe.

The United States also featured in creating Norway's mass-consumer society. The "American" model—namely the Fordist model, in which everyone has access to an enormous variety of mass-produced consumer products—apparently became a standard of comparison in the development of postwar Norwegian society.[4] Undoubtedly, the United States was a technological role model for many in Norway after the war—and perhaps even more importantly, the American dream was a rhetorical resource (see also David Nye's chapter in this volume). And so we explore the technologies, the products, and the dreams that came from the United States, in terms of who, in Norway, imported, transformed, and mediated these elements.[5] Indeed, in this chapter we explore how home-freezing technologies were imported and further appropriated by Norwegian society. By looking at the mediators promoting these technologies to the Norwegian public, we analyze the freezer as a catalyst to the formation of new food-consumption regimes, new foodways.[6]

Importing Technology and Knowledge

During the Second World War, the Norwegian government's exiled officials busily made plans. From their temporary base in London, they plotted the liberation of Norway as well as the country's postwar reconstruction and modernization. Industry committees were set up to study the latest technological developments in the fields of particular interest to Norwegian industry; the countries of interest were Great Britain and the United States.[7] In compiling this information, the committee cast its net wide, reporting, for example, that the Americans had constructed so-called freezer-locker plants, where people could rent a locker and store their foodstuffs. In many ways, the lockers themselves were similar visually to the lockers found in many schools today. The freezer-locker plants consisted of a large, refrigerated room containing small lockers of about a hundred liters each. The size of the plants varied; they often contained approximately 500 or more lockers.[8]

Figure 4.1 In this photo, two women place food in their freezer-lockers. The plain, non-branded packaging suggests that they have prepared the food themselves.

Construction of these plants had begun in the 1930s. By 1946, more than 11,000 freezer-locker plants in the United States serviced some 3.3 million families: 13 million individuals. Most of the freezing facilities were owned by private companies, which were often engaged in commercial activities beyond the freezer plants.[9] This category of freezing solution was an important service in rural parts of the United States for some twenty years; but, by 1950, the American heyday of freezer-locker plants was over. For Northern Europe, however, this same period marked the freezer-locker's popularity.[10]

We view the spread of freezer-locker plants as the outcome of initiatives taken during and after the Second World War. This link between Cold War politics and consumption technologies may not be obvious.

But the connection is evident: it was during the Cold War that new international organizations—primarily the United Nations (UN) and the Organisation for European Economic Cooperation (OEEC)—were created to generate growth and development. So-called "productivity missions" to promote the exchange of knowledge and technology were established by the UN, the Marshall Plan's Technical Assistance Program, and the Norwegian government. The U.S. was not the only inspiration, however. During the interwar period, a Norwegian socialist movement, Towards Dawn (Mot Dag), and later the Social Democratic Party, developed an affinity for the economic and social experiments in the Soviet Union. In the years following the end of German occupation, this effort was to a certain degree continued even if the Social Democrats had broken their ties to the Comintern during the 1920s and followed a reformist line.[11] The planned-economy experiments were part of the quest for efficiency and technological development promoted by the Marshall Plan. Norwegian political leaders, labor union delegates, and industrial leaders visited the United States to learn about industrial development and consumer behavior. But the delegation returned with far more than the lessons of efficiency and innovation: the visitors brought home new ideas about how to build a "good" society—a process that was largely synonymous with promoting consumer happiness.

A course on food freezing arranged by the Food and Agriculture Organization of the UN in Copenhagen in 1948 is one example of these efforts. The participants included key figures in European agriculture, domestic-science institutions, and technical and scientific circles. The stated purpose of these efforts was to improve European productivity. The freezer-locker plant was among the technologies that Norwegian delegates encountered through the course. One of these delegates, Bergliot Qviller Werenskiold, headed the State Research Institute of Home Economics (Statens forsøksvirksomhet i husstell or SRIHE), which had been established in 1936 to modernize Norwegian households. Werenskiold encouraged building such plants in Norway.[12] Further, Werenskiold became an important mediator between industrialists, technocrats, and Norwegian housewives.

Technology for Better Nutrition

In the years after the Second World War, the construction of freezer-locker plants took off in Norway. By 1951, there were approximately 200 collective freezer facilities nationwide.[13] Five years later, the number of such units had doubled, and the number of individual rental lockers had grown to 70,000.[14] By the end of the 1950s, Norway had more than a thousand freezer-locker plants containing in excess of 150,000 lockers. This meant that more than 15 percent of households were renting a locker or in any case had access to a locker.[15] What, exactly, was behind the freezer locker's popularity in Norway?

Norway suffered a shortage of many foodstuffs in the aftermath of the war. The country's foreign currency reserves were limited, and reconstruction was prioritized over consumption. In the years between 1945 and 1960, all types of imported goods were restricted due to a lack of foreign currency. Foods that were not perceived as essential were strictly rationed in an effort to secure enough food for the whole population while at the same time keeping imports low. Sugar was one of the products rationed until 1951, leading to a shortage. This complicated the preservation of fruits and berries by making jam or juice, prompting the Norwegian National Nutritional Council (Statens Ernæringsråd) to research the prospect of freezing as an efficient food-preservation method.[16] So, the appropriation of American agricultural solutions was linked to the Norwegian shortage of consumer goods.

At this time, Norway was a rural country with low levels of urbanization. With food-store shelves stocked only sparsely, the ideal of self-sufficiency held great appeal. For example, people fished, foraged for berries, and grew their own crops to obtain enough food for themselves and their families. It was important to preserve the food that one managed to procure, given the food shortage; this, combined with the short supply of sugar, made frozen food a promising alternative. At the same time, the SRIHE pointed out that, as the storage method with the lowest impact on nutritional value, freezing technology could provide great nutritional benefits.[17]

The freezer-locker was understood as a technology that not only extended the life of raw materials, but it helped to improve the Norwegian diet—as well as national public health.[18] In essence, the freezer-locker facilities constituted a health technology. Why, though, did Norwegian government officials choose to promote collective freezer units rather than home freezers? After all, the home freezer was a known breakthrough in the United States at the time, and access to home freezers clearly spared housewives from having to leave their homes to freeze food. Surely the home freezer would have been a more labor-saving solution to the problem of food conservation?

Norway's Collective Ways of Life

Norwegian import restrictions on freezing machinery presented an important reason for favoring collective freezer facilities over home freezers.[19] The Norwegian ban on importing compressors for the construction of home freezers was in effect until 1956.[20] Centralized freezer-locker units reduced the need for imported parts; offering freezer-locker plants for private use could be coordinated with building facilities for the refrigeration and freezing of dairy products and more. Another contributing factor was the country's electricity supply, which was rather unstable during this period.[21] Generators could be used to protect collective freezer units against the effects of power cuts; obtaining the same protection for private households would have been difficult and costly.

The solution that would have best served the individual housewife, then, was not necessarily a sustainable solution for society at large. Indeed, a free flow of ideas across borders influenced the visions that guided postwar reconstruction, but the infrastructure for bringing the actual goods into the country was less straightforward. The appropriation process was therefore guided by clear-cut necessities as well as by political ideology. The Norwegian move to build collective freezer units represented aligning American industrial models with the planned-economy thinking that swayed Norwegian political ideology at the time. This becomes obvious when examining who built the food-freezing facilities.

In some areas of Norway, the municipal authorities took responsibility for the construction of collective freezer facilities.[22] In other parts of the country, the construction was organized by individuals who formed cooperative societies dedicated to building small freezer-locker units.[23] This cooperative effort coexisted with another cooperative approach to the construction of freezer plants. Oddvar Lund, head of the Ministry of Agriculture's office for horticulture, was convinced that the freezer-locker facilities should be operated on a cooperative basis and that the local dairies were fully qualified for the task.[24] In many small towns, the Norwegian Dairy Cooperative was a central actor in the development of freezer-locker facilities.[25]

Unions and cooperatives—rather than a privately owned food-freezing industry—were usually responsible for the construction of freezer-locker plants. The plants were expensive to build, and the unions had the great advantage of receiving government subsidies for the purpose. In its 1953 election manifesto, the Labor Party stated that efforts of this kind should be encouraged: "An important prerequisite for rational and profitable agriculture is close cooperation between production and sales. All efforts aimed at achieving such cooperation must continue to receive state subsidies. This concerns dairy cooperatives; silage plants; refrigeration and freezer plants."[26]

Unlike in the United States, in Norway it was the state that subsidized cooperatives.[27] For example, Norwegian cooperatives were allowed to keep 40 percent of the sales tax for investment in a construction fund. In addition, they were given interest-free government loans. In contrast, private providers received no help in the form of interest-free loans or grants.[28] The construction of freezer plants was organized in a more collectively oriented manner than in the U.S. Norway's social democratic government wanted state-controlled communal facilities and collectives rather than private solutions.

It is clear that the initial inspiration for developing a system of freezing food in collective freezer plants came from the United States; and, as in America, this system was also used to regulate the prices of meat and vegetables to a certain extent. The differences between the two countries are more striking than the similarities, however. In Norway, freezer lockers were used primarily to preserve self-produced foods. The freezer-locker plants were well suited to the Norwegian reality of the early postwar period, which was characterized by a scarcity of goods. Norway's food-freezing facilities were seen as a component part of the effort to build a modern society, for which social democracy formed the backdrop. As such, these facilities were regarded as social technologies rather than technologies of consumption; from their inception, they were linked to what can be called a collectivist consumption regime.

The Emergence of the "Norwegian" Home Freezer

The first home freezers made their way into American homes in the late 1930s; only after the Second World War did freezer sales take off. In 1946, approximately 200,000 freezers were produced in the U.S. By 1949, American households owned some 1.2 million home freezers.[29] During the same period, there was no production of home freezers in Norway due to the import restrictions on essential components.[30] Meanwhile, Norwegian industrialists were convinced that the production of home freezers would be permitted sooner or later: they saw that refrigerators with small freezer compartments gradually entered the Norwegian market—making it possible for individual households to store industrially produced frozen food for home use. Indeed, the home freezer atttracted the industry's interest.

Among those committed to the future of freezers was the Aanonsen Company, whose products included refrigerator display cases in grocery stores.[31] In 1956, the company built a new factory outside Oslo. That same year, the import restrictions were eased on refrigeration machinery for the production of home freezers.[32] This was also the year of a visit to the United States by Aanonsen's construction manager, R.F. Hermansen. The purpose of the trip was to study home-freezer manufacturing—and to build contacts with American firms.[33] Aanonsen embarked on a joint venture with the American Motors Corporation's Leonard Division. This gave Aanonsen access to freezing-technology expertise. Aanonsen designed the home-freezer cabinet, but American Motors retained the right to conduct the quality testing.[34] Thus, the so-called domestically produced home freezers were not "completely Norwegian" as advertised, but hybrids, created via the encounter between American and Norwegian industry.

Approximately a thousand home freezers were sold in Norway during that first year of "domestic production."[35] Paradoxically, the figures dropped the following year.[36] By 1959, a total of some 6,500 home freezers had been sold nationwide.[37] It was only in 1962 that the sale of home freezers took hold, with a turnover that year of between 20,000 and 25,000 freezers.[38] Three years later, the turnover had increased to some 70,000. This translated to approximately 250,000 Norwegian households—or 22 percent of the total—owning a home freezer.[39] Freezer lockers were the technology of the 1950s; by the 1960s, the future apparently belonged to the home freezer. Undoubtedly, it was large-scale changes in the Norwegian economy that spurred the purchase of home freezers. Norwegians, like most Europeans, became more affluent in the 1960s, and that enabled more household appliances.[40]

In Line with New Lifestyles?

The journal of the Norwegian frozen-food industry, *Norsk Fryserinæring*, predicted that the collective freezer plants would run into problems due to Norwegian consumers' access to home freezers. This prognosis was based on U.S. developments: the number of customers per plant had dropped from 414 in 1946 to 343 in 1950.[41] Meanwhile, in Norway, the SRIHE promoted food-freezer facilities as a time- and labor-saving technology, consistent with a carefully planned and rational lifestyle. The reality, though, was that collective facilities placed considerable demands on one's lifestyle—if proper use was to be made of the freezers. One problem was that many customers had to travel far to reach the nearest unit. Another problem was the difficulty of planning meals far in advance. In short, it was not the remote freezer locker but the home freezer that adapted better to unplanned events. So, when the shortages of money, materials, and electricity disappeared, so, too did the advantages of the collective freezer.

In many ways, the SRIHE was an extension of the state-initiated campaign to improve the health of the Norwegian population; by linking scientific knowledge of food with the political message of the Labor Party, the SRIHE became a mediator in that campaign. The organization translated the message of a modern welfare state into household routines that could be communicated to housewives. Given this focus on the greater good, it is hardly surprising that the SRIHE promoted collective solutions such as freezer plants. For years after collective solutions—and, indeed, the larger planned-economy approach—declined, the SRIHE retained its emphasis on nutrition and a healthy lifestyle.[42]

In light of the anticipated competition, many freezer plants adopted new practices. For example, in 1952, the Norwegian food industry's journal reported that freezer-plant operators had introduced a service to help customers wrap their food, and, more importantly, introduced a system of ordering so that customers could buy food in volume and receive a discount. This yielded lower prices than the local supermarket could offer.[43] In principle, this reform of collective consumption could have fended off the challenge of the home freezer; but apparently, the days of collective living were drawing to a close. A 1956 article in *The Housewife's Magazine* (*Husmorbladet*) claimed that individualism was on the rise: "These days, there is a conflict between collective solutions and the individual. In the 1930s, people were looking forward to all kinds of collective solutions, but most people have turned out to be more and more individually minded."[44]

Housewives abandoned the freezer-locker unit, a technology tied to a discourse of not only better nutrition, but to shortages of sugar and other foods; electrical-power problems; the importance of communal solutions; lack of construction materials; rationing; and import restrictions. One by one, each of these factors lost its significance: the conditions that once contributed to the collective freezer-locker as a good solution had all but disappeared.

At the same time, home economics teachers were apparently influenced by a new narrative, which featured the home freezer as a time- and labor-saving technology. Like the freezer-locker plants, the home freezer helped improve general health—but it also eased the burden of housework.[45] And this, indeed, became the focus: making housewives' domestic work more efficient. This was, in fact, good advertising for the manufacturers of home-freezing technology, as Aanonsen's branding of home freezers will demonstrate.

The Home Freezer: A Technology for All

Aanonsen's marketing materials can provide us with an idea of how "ideological" elements were constructed around the home freezer. In what ways was the public made aware of the existence of the home freezer and how was it presented? Aanonsen used the magazine *All about Cold* (*Alt om Kaldt*) to advertise its goods.[46] In an article about its first home freezer, the company claimed that, to date, housewives had relied on freezer-locker facilities to preserve their food. But, the article claimed, "[A]ny housewife would, of course, prefer to keep her frozen foodstuffs in her own home. Here, the home freezer marks a new phase in the rationalization of food preparation, saving work, time, and money."[47] Aanonsen tapped into the rationalization discourse, emphasizing that the home freezer represented a more rational technology than the freezer-locker plants. With the help of the home freezer, the housewife could be spared time-consuming trips to the collective freezer-locker unit.

The freezer was also linked to the ideal of self-sufficiency. The advertisements presented the home freezer as a technological appliance that made it easy for the housewife to preserve ingredients she had cultivated or harvested herself; the technology also allowed her to buy ingredients when they were at their cheapest. Ads featured this message, accompanied by a photograph of a mother and daughter removing food from a freezer. A traditional storehouse can be seen in the background. In addition to the photograph and text, there are two drawings. One shows a housewife standing by her home freezer; she gazes out the window while waving to a woman carrying bundles who is struggling to get home from the supermarket in a downpour. The message is that a housewife who owns a home freezer will be spared from having to venture out in bad weather, loaded down by heavy bags of groceries: owning a home freezer is like having an at-home supermarket. The second drawing shows a couple welcoming surprise visitors. They accommodate easily—thanks to their home freezer, which contains cakes and other foods suitable for entertaining.[48]

The advertisements created a multi-layered narrative about the merits of the home freezer. The freezer was primarily a rationalization tool that made it easy to preserve the fruits of the soil. At the same time, it was a means by which the household could save on grocery purchases—both financially and via the efficiencies of buying food in bulk. The advertising presented the freezer, both visually and textually, as a technology suited to modern life. Clearly, these ads did not equate the freezer's introduction with a total break from the past. Linking the home freezer and the storehouse created continuity between traditional food-storage practices and the innovation of home freezing. In essence, freezer manufacturers cast the home freezer as a modern storehouse.

Presenting people with home freezers as role models to be emulated was a common strategy in Aanonsen's marketing. *All about Cold* published several articles about families who had acquired the home freezer.[49] The articles took readers on a tour of Norway's social strata. This parade of families from different classes—all posed beside their freezers—contained a targeted message. Aanonsen signaled that the freezer was not only a technology for the affluent and for those with special needs: it was a practical appliance that satisfied everyone's needs. Displaying the range of families—from humble to wealthy—was part of a concerted effort to turn the freezer into a must-have technology.

The fact that Aanonsen marketed the home freezer as a technology for everyone did not mean that freezers were necessarily inexpensive or even universally available. In 1956, the cost of a small (100-liter) freezer corresponded approximately with the average blue-collar workers wages for two months. Larger freezers cost about double that, if not more.[50] The price of freezers remained relatively stable throughout the 1950s and 1960s.[51] Clearly, the purchase of a home freezer represented a considerable investment.[52] So, in purely economic terms, there is little evidence that the freezer, in its early years, comprised a technology for all—despite Aanonsen's advertising messaging. Nevertheless, approximately 250,000 Norwegian households— about one-third—owned a home freezer by 1965.[53]

Why did so many households purchase home freezers despite the hefty investment? Freezer manufacturers offered favorable financing: a mere 25 percent of the full sum was required in cash at the point of purchase; the rest could be paid in installments during the following eighteen months. Some manufacturers even offered a three-year deal.[54] The rhetoric that positioned the freezer as a must-have, combined with the easy access to credit, soon made the home freezer a standard feature of practically every home.

Mediating Consumption?

Books on deep freezing were an important part of the freezing industry's marketing of the home freezer. These were often included when

Figure 4.2 In this advertisement for the manufacturer Aanonsen, the headline reads: "Aanonsen Home Freezer: The Modern Storehouse"—a portrayal of the home freezer as a continuation of traditional storage practices.

people bought a home freezer. Home freezing was by no means an exclusively Norwegian phenomenon. American housewives had long enjoyed access to books on home freezing and many of the "Norwegian" books were actually translations of Swedish books.[55] The fact that Swedish rather than American role models were used links to the closer kinship Norwegians felt with Swedish food traditions and culture. Combining books with advertising was not unique to the Norwegian context: it was part of an international trend led by American corporations. The field of home economics inspired the creation of the SRIHE, but, at the same time, those trained in this field were often hired by companies to "enlighten" the public about different products. This information was often linked directly to the promotion of specific goods. In Norway, too, information about home freezers came from sources close to the home-freezing industry.[56]

Not only did the home freezer become vital to family households, but it became vital to the food-processing industry as a catalyst for industrial production, distribution, and consumption of fish and vegetables. The significance of the centralized freezer facilities is much less evident in this context. In 1959, a number of companies jointly established the Deep-Freezing Office (Dypfrysningskontoret or DFO). The participating companies were Norwegian Frozen Fish (Norsk Frossenfisk), Findus, Aanonsen, Lehmkuhl, and Strømmen Værksted. The DFO was formed to promote "sound development [of frozen foods] with respect to the correct use and increased consumption of frozen foods." At the same time, the DFO was to "promote the acquisition and proper use of freezing equipment."[57] The DFO was headed by one of Norway's leading celebrities, the radio star Rolf Kirkvaag. Compared to the SRIHE—which had, until that point been the information hub—the DFO was an altogether different kind of institution. While the SRIHE had tried to promote "neutral" information independent of commercial connections, the DFO was owned and run by large industrial actors. By combining education, advertising, and entertainment, the DFO acted as a mediator between housewives and commercial interests.

A closer look at the 1965 book written by the DFO's Bjørg Eliassen reveals that it contains much the same information as the booklet *The Freezing of Food* (*Frysing av Matvarer*), published by the SRIHE. *We Are Deep-Freezing* (*Vi Dypfryser*) is considerably more extensive, however, and includes information about the freezing of everything from meats to desserts and baked goods. Eliassen was clear about the primacy of home freezers: "There is no doubt that, in the long run, it pays to have your own home freezer." Her arguments in favor of buying a home freezer mirrored those of SRIHE researchers: the freezer was practical because it was easily accessible, and, in the long run, it would make financial sense to own one. Eliassen's book went beyond the idea of freezing self-produced and self-procured food, however: the book also promoted "manufactured frozen food."[58]

According to Eliassen, commercially produced frozen food represented a solution to many of the housewife's problems:

> The housewife is spared time-consuming work, such as peeling, cleaning, and rinsing. This way, she saves time and avoids the boring tasks involved in preparing food. At the same time, she can rest assured that the family is fed nutritious food. If you have a home freezer in your house or a freezer chest in your basement, you can purchase ingredients for several days' dinners in one go. You can save a great deal of time by not having to do the shopping every day. By supplementing your own home freezing with [commercially] manufactured frozen food, you also achieve more variation in your "modern storehouse."[59]

Here, the home freezer, that modern storehouse, is linked directly to commercially manufactured frozen food. Thus, the DFO's book on freezing was more than a publication aimed at enlightening the population: the book was a means of achieving the dual goals of compelling Norwegians to buy both a home freezer and frozen foods. Just as the SRIHE had done previously, Eliassen appealed to the housewife's conscience and showed her the prospect of an easier everyday life; but this time, it was advertising dressed up as "factual information."

A community of stakeholders evolved around the home freezer. Some portrayed the freezer as a vehicle for self-sufficiency and inexpensive purchases. Others saw it as a storage unit for mass-produced frozen foods. These were complementary rather than opposing interests. The SRIHE was eager to link the home freezer to the frozen food produced by people in their own homes, while SRIHE members also viewed mass-produced frozen food in a positive light. After analyzing the frozen pollock produced by the companies Norwegian Frozen Fish and Freia, the SRIHE made a declaration that illustrates their position: "If frozen pollock can be purchased as a product as fine as this, it is an excellent and convenient food."[60]

Industry's Highway to the Home

The DFO's dual promotion of home freezers and mass-produced frozen foods warrants a closer look at frozen-food producers' interests in the home freezer. In 1949, Nils L.S. Jacobsen of the Association of Norwegian Cold-Storage Plants (Norske Fryseriers Forening) commented that many people in the freezing industry mistakenly feared that home freezing would compete with that industry. After all, home freezing enabled housewives to produce their own frozen food rather than buying their food from the industry. Referring to experiences that Niels W. Pettersen-Hagh, among others, had brought home from a study trip to the United States, Jacobsen asserted that this was not the case:

> Perhaps more than any other factor [in the making of a Norwegian market for frozen foods], home freezing helps break down traditional resistance to a new form of [food] preservation, giving housewives first-hand experience of the advantages of preservation by freezing. So let us hope that it won't be too long before it is also possible to purchase these freezers in our country at an affordable price.[61]

Nils W. Pettersen-Hagh was one of the founders of the DFO and an assistant manager at the East Norwegian Cold-Storage Plants (Østlandske Fryserier). He took the same position as Jacobsen, and during a study trip to the United States in 1955, he identified the home freezer as the missing link in the cold chain: "The home freezers constitute the basis for the great success of frozen foods in the United States because they bring the last link of the cold chain out to the consumers." According to Pettersen-Hagh, sales of frozen foods in Norway matched those in America before home freezers boomed in Norway; he considered it likely that "the lifting of restrictions on the manufacturing and sale of home freezers [would] give a significant boost to the sale of frozen products and create the conditions required for continued expansion." He went so far as to say that the lack of home-freezer manufacturing in Norway prevented a "natural development of these products in [our country]."[62]

Such ideas also resonated on a European level. In 1960, Otto Hanssen, director of Norwegian Frozen Fish, submitted a report to the European Productivity Agency of the OEEC. Addressing the marketing and use of frozen fish in Europe, the report was later presented to a joint meeting of the European freezing industry and marketing experts. Hanssen claimed that the failure of the frozen-food industry to grow in Europe was attributable to the general lack of home freezers—consumers were not sufficiently "frozen-food minded." Only when they had their own home freezers could housewives discover that potential of frozen foods to help make their housekeeping more efficient:

Figure 4.3 In this ad, the home freezer contains mostly industrially produced frozen foods. For Europeans, this was not the norm: freezers were used primarily to store home-produced foods.

> However eager to buy frozen foods the housewife may be, the quantity of each purchase must be restricted to the amount used for one meal, unless she has the facilities to preserve that food for longer periods.[63]

What Hanssen was saying was not that the frozen-food industry depended on the home freezer, but that it could be instrumental in changing people's attitudes toward frozen foods. Enabling the housewife to make large purchases of the products manufactured by the food industry, the home freezer would alert women to the advantages of frozen foodstuffs. Apparently, the rise of the home freezer and increased consumption of commercially frozen foods were seen as interconnected phenomena. Hanssen's report shows that Norway was not the only country in which the home freezer was understood in this way: the association between the home freezer and the frozen-food industry was a European phenomenon.

Kirkvaag summarized the home freezer's significance for the frozen-food market in a talk given at the 1960 refrigeration conference in Oslo. According to Kirkvaag, the Americans had a saying: "Home freezing is to the deep-freezing industry as the highway is to the automobile."[64] At a meeting of the Norwegian Refrigeration Organization two years later, Kirkvaag explained that home freezers would eventually become "a storage unit for mass-produced frozen foods."[65] Thus, the home freezer had a double identity. On one hand, it served a commercial consumption regime of must-have home appliances and frozen foods. On the other hand, the freezer supported a consumption regime based on self-made foods.[66]

Conclusion

The first Norwegian experiments with freezing had taken place immediately after the Second World War; within just over a decade, freezing technologies were fully adopted in Norway. It was a remarkably painless process, particularly given the high economic costs, the need for various infrastructures, as well as the knowledge and change of habits required. What, exactly, propelled the triumph of the home freezer in Norway—and how "American" was this triumph?

The reliance on collective solutions differentiates the Norwegian approach from American developments of the same era. Throughout the 1950s, the cooperative spirit affected the politics of housing and the consumption of technology and food in Norway as well as other Scandinavian countries. Many of the cooperative freezer facilities built in this period and shaped by its cooperative spirit remained in use well into the 1970s. This was fully in line with the government's preference for communal provisions. Through grants and regulations, the government sought to support ventures that satisfied the social democratic ideals of large-scale operations and collective facilities. The centralized plants harmonized with the great modernization project. At the same time, deep freezing became an important part of the discourse on nutrition and the government's efforts to improve public health: freezer technology contributed mightily to a sound diet and adequate nutrition for all segments of the population. The collective freezing facilities, however, proved to be a transitional technology—just as in the United States.

As Norwegian families started to use the new centralized facilities, the home freezer was about to assume market dominance in the United States. Norway followed the same course, but with a considerable delay. This time lag can be attributed to domestic circumstances such as limited access to the necessary freezing technology. The central plants thus represented a way of distributing scarce resources among a large number of people. This availability of freezing technology to the many aligned with the policy objectives of the Labor government. In this sense, the central facilities can be understood as a consequence of negotiating the local Norwegian context. Although home freezers had already been made available in the United States, they did not fit the Norwegian lifestyle at that particular time.

American role models and visions of the future were also important spurs to the Norwegian freezing industry; after all, it was in America that the freezer functioned as the frozen-food industry's "extended arm" into people's homes. This is what Norwegian industry sought to emulate.

During the 1960s, the Norwegian economy improved considerably; with more money to spend, people were increasingly able to buy what they wanted rather than what was essential. The growth of real wages and widespread optimism about the future were only two of the factors in the quick conversion from central-locker facilities to home freezers. Installment plans became common; fractional down payments could be made at the point of purchase and the balance in installments over a period of three years. This catalyzed purchases of home freezers.

Another important factor in the breakthrough of the Norwegian home freezer was the storehouse approach. In Norway, the freezer was promoted as a natural component of traditional food-gathering: one picked berries, caught fish, hunted wildlife—then stored one's natural bounty in the freezer. The promotional material for home freezers played on associations with the rural farming communities' traditional storehouse for food.

Clearly, economic growth facilitated the breakthrough of the home freezer, although economic growth alone cannot explain the freezer's near-omnipresence in Norwegian homes. The fact that Norwegians *could* acquire home freezers does not suffice as an explanation; Norwegians also had to *want* to acquire home freezers. Indeed, for the average Norwegian, the "Norwegian Dream" was one of the most important contributing factors to the freezer's widespread appropriation. The home freezer and the Norwegian Dream alike conveyed the image of an affluent society in times to come—an image of progress and positive associations. Many of the same aspirations were reflected in the governing Labor Party's slogan of "growth and prosperity." This vision was not identical to the American Dream, although it did contain many of the same elements.

In Norway, an interesting discrepancy existed between hypothetical freezer use as promoted by the industry and the practices of actual users.

The frozen-food industry advocated an "Americanized" freezer—an appliance used for storing frozen foods that were mass produced by the industry. To the contrary, most Norwegians used their freezers to store the food that they had produced at home or collected from their natural surroundings—in the same way that food had been stored for centuries, albeit using other preservation methods. The "freezer for processed foods" and the "storehouse freezer" coexisted—and still do—in a single, dual-purpose, technological appliance. The resulting consumption regime became a blend of old and new. And so we see the home freezer as a technology that has promoted hybrid consumption regimes: a nuanced contrast to straightforward, Americanized mass consumption.

Notes

1. Victoria de Grazia, "Changing Consumption Regimes in Europe, 1930–1970," in *Getting and Spending: European and American Consumer Societies in the Twentieth Century*, ed. Susan Strasser, Charles McGovern and Matthias Judt (Cambridge: Cambridge University Press, 1998), 59–83; Victoria de Grazia and Ellen Furlough, eds., *The Sex of Things: Gender and Consumption in Historical Perspective* (Berkeley: University of California Press, 1996).
2. Ruth Schwartz Cowan, *More Work for Mother: The Ironies of Household Technology from the Open Hearth to the Microwave* (New York: Basic Books, 1983).
3. Wiebe Bijker and John Law, eds., *Shaping Technology/Building Society: Studies in Sociotechnical Change* (Cambridge, MA: MIT Press, 1992).
4. Christine Myrvang, Sissel Mykleburst, and Brita Brenna, *Temmet eller uhemmet: Historiske perspektiver på konsum, kultur og dannelse* (Oslo: Pax, 2004); Christine Myrvang, *Forbruksagentene: Slik vekket de kjøpelysten* (Oslo: Pax, 2009); de Grazia, "Changing Consumption Regimes in Europe, 1930–1970."
5. Johan Schot and Adri Albert de la Bruhèze, "The Mediated Design of Products, Consumption, and Consumers in the Twentieth Century," in *How Users Matter: The Co-Construction of Users and Technology*, ed. Nelly Oudshoorn and Trevor Pinch (Cambridge, MA: MIT Press, 2003).
6. Terje Finstad, "Varme visjoner og frosne fremskritt. Om fryseteknologi i Norge, ca. 1920–1965" (PhD diss., Norwegian University of Science and Technology, 2011); For further investigations of this in other realms than the domestic, see: Terje Finstad, "Cool alliances: Freezers, frozen fish and the shaping of industry-retail relations in Norway, 1950–1960," in *Transformations of Retailing in Europe after 1945*, ed. Ralph Jessen and Lydia Langer (Farnham: Ashgate, 2012), 195–210; Terje Finstad, "The means of modernization. Freezing technologies and the cultural politics of artificial cold, Norway 1940–1965," in *History of Artificial Cold. Scientific, Technological and Cultural Issues*, ed. Kostas Gavroglu (London: Springer, 2014).
7. "Instruks for Industrikomiteen oppnevnt ved Kgl. Res. av juli 1943," Industrikomitéene i London og New York, box 5, file: Industrikomitéen i London: Oppnevnelse av medlemmer etc. The National Archives of Norway.

See, for example, Stig Kvaal, "Janus med tre ansikter: Om organiseringen av den industrielt rettede forskningen i spennet mellom stat, vitenskap og industri i Norge, 1916–1956" (PhD diss., Norwegian University of Science and Technology, 1997).
8. *Frysning* (New York: Norwegian Ministry of Provisioning and Reconstruction, 1945).
9. Oscar Edward Anderson Jr., *Refrigeration in America: A History of a New Technology and Its Impact* (Princeton, NJ: Princeton University Press, 1953).
10. Roger Thévenot, *A History of Refrigeration throughout the World* (Paris: International Institute of Refrigeration, 1979), 348.
11. This blend of Soviet-inspired planning ideals and an American-inspired industrial ethos functionally ended in 1952, when parliamentary discussions on price legislation thwarted the ambitions of even the most optimistic supporters of the planned economy. Francis Sejersted, *The Age of Social Democracy: Norway and Sweden in the Twentieth Century*, trans. Richard Daly (Princeton, NJ: Princeton University Press, 2011).
12. "Rivende utvikling av fryseteknikken," *Verdens Gang*, October 19, 1948.
13. "Lang ventetid for kjøle- og fryseskap," *Verdens Gang*, August 26, 1950, 10; "Rapport fra møte i utvalget for husstell, Statens Ernæringsråd," November 13, 1951, box 2: Div frysesaken, National Institute for Consumer Research (SIFO).
14. Ellen Offergaard, "Lønner det seg å fryse matvarer selv?" *Husmorbladet*, June 7, 1956, 12.
15. "Marketing and Consumption of Frozen Fish in OEEC Countries," Report presented at a meeting of experts on deep-frozen foods held in Verona from October 6 to 12, 1959 (Verona: European Productivity Agency of the Organisation for European Economic Cooperation, 1959).
16. "Rapport fra møte i utvalget for husstell, Statens Ernæringsråd," October 19, 1951, box 2: Div frysesaken.
17. Ibid.
18. Anna Jorunn Avdem and Kari Melby, *Oppe først og sist i seng: Husarbeid i Norge fra 1850 til i dag* (Oslo: Universitetsforlaget, 1985); Anna Jorunn Avdem, *Husmorparadiset* (Oslo: Samlaget, 2001). For an insightful (and ironic) look at the intervention of science in private homes, see the movie *Salmer fra kjøkkene*, directed by Bent Hamer (Sandefjord, 2003).
19. Arthur Saunes, "Kommersiell Kjøling," in *Glimt fra norsk kjøleteknisk historie*, ed. Nils W. Pettersen-Hagh and Sæbjørn Røsvik (Oslo: Norsk kjøleteknisk forening, 1986), 212–30.
20. Nils W. Pettersen-Hagh, *Frysing og fryselagring i USA*, Rapport fra studietur 48-23-p2-1-50004 15. april til 15. juni 1955 (Oslo: Norsk Fryseriforening, 1956), 43; Nils W. Pettersen-Hagh, "Refleksjoner omkring stagnasjonen i salget av dypfrosne matvarer i Norge," *Norsk Fryserinæring* 3 (1957): 1–5.
21. See, for example, Stig Kvaal and Astrid Wale, *En spenningshistorie: Trondheim Energiverk gjennom et århundre* (Trondheim: Trondheim Energiverk, 2000).
22. "Moderne frysemetoder: Glimt fra fryserier rundt om i landet" (NRK, November 22, 1947).
23. Bjørn Austigard, "Frå stabbur til frysar: omkring konservering og lagring av mat i Romsdal," in *Årbok Romsdalsmuseet* (Molde: Romsdalsmuseet, 2006), 182–99.
24. "Sett maten i banken," *Verdens Gang*, July 21, 1948.

25. "Meieriene bygger fryserier i fellesskap," Norsk Fryserinæring 4 (1950): 69–73.
26. See also "Gran Meieris nye kjøleanlegg med 460 frysebokser tatt i bruk,"; "Hokksund meieri innvier stort lagerbygg og boksfryseri," Norsk Fryserinæring 3 (1953): 55.
26. Det Norske Arbeiderparti, Valgprogram for Det Norske Arbeiderparti, 16.
27. "Boksfryseanlegg ved Stange," Norsk Fryserinæring 4 (1952): 81.
28. "Nytt fryseri," Norsk Fryserinæring 11 (1949): 11–12.
29. Anderson Jr., Refrigeration in America, 299–301.
30. Pettersen-Hagh, Frysing og fryselagring i USA, 43.
31. Saunes, "Kommersiell Kjøling," 212–30.
32. Pettersen-Hagh, "Refleksjoner omkring stagnasjonen i salget av dypfrosne matvarer i Norge," 1–5; "HJEMME-FRYSERE endelig på det norske marked: Krever lite strøm—motoren nesten lydløs—avbetalingstid helt opp til tre år?" Verdens Gang, July 7, 1956, 8.
33. "HJEMME-FRYSERE endelig på det norske marked."
34. Aanonsen Fabrikker, "De mest moderne hjemmefrysere," Alt om Kaldt (1960): 3; Aanonsen Fabrikker, "Kjøle- og frysedisker – hjemmefrysere og kjøleskap," Alt om Kaldt (1960): 2–3; "Norskamerikansk kjøleskapsamarbeid," Verdens Gang, August 2, 1957, 8.
35. Offergaard, "Lønner det seg å fryse matvarer selv?" 12.
36. Rolf Kirkvaag, "Hjemmefrysere - litt statistikk," Kjøleteknikk og Fryserinæring 5 (1963): 101–2.
37. "Marketing and Consumption of Frozen Fish in OEEC Countries," 34.
38. Kirkvaag, "Hjemmefrysere – litt statistikk," 101–2.
39. Nils W. Pettersen-Hagh, "Norsk Kjøleteknikk 1965," Kjøleteknikk og Fryserinæring 2 (1966): 30–2.
40. Berge Furre, Norsk historie 1914–2000: Industrisamfunnet – frå vokstervisse til framtidstvil, vol. 6, Samlagets Norsk historie 800–2000 (Oslo: Samlaget, 1999); Avdem, Husmorparadise.
41. "Boksanlegg i USA," Norsk Fryserinæring 9 (1952): 169.
42. Statens forsøksvirksomhet i husstell: Gjennom 25 år (Oslo: Statens forsøksvirksomhet i husstell, 1965).
43. "Nå begynner det å gli," Norsk Fryserinæring 9 (1952): 1.
44. "Fremtidens boliger: Husmødre liker ikke det kollektive," Husmorbladet, September 13, 1956, 9.
45. Offergaard, "Lønner det seg å fryse matvarer selv?" 12.
46. Aanonsen Fabrikker, "Les vårt serviceblad," Servicebladet, May 1955, 1.
47. Aanonsen Fabrikker, "Det moderne stabbur," Alt om Kaldt (1957): 4.
48. Aanonsen Fabrikker, "Aanonsen hjemmefryser," Husmorbladet, August 15, 1959.
49. Aanonsen Fabrikker, "Husmorens skattkammer på land og i by," Alt om Kaldt (1959): 1–4.
50. "HJEMME-FRYSERE endelig på det norske marked," 8.
51. Offergaard, "Lønner det seg å fryse matvarer selv?"12; "Frysingen overtar kjellerens oppgave," 4.
52. Converted to the value of the Norwegian kroner in 2008, a freezer cost approx. 21,000 kroner. Statistics Norway, "Consumer Price Index Calculator," accessed April 29, 2009, http://www.ssb.no/vis/kpi/kpiregn.html; Historisk Statistikk 1994, Norges offisielle statistikk (Oslo: SSB, 1995), 262.

53. Statistics Norway: *Statistiske analyser nr. 28. Beholdning og anskaffelse av varige forbruksvarer i private husholdninger* (Oslo: SSB, 1976), 25.
54. "HJEMME-FRYSERE endelig på det norske marked," 8.
55. See Faith Fenton and June Darfler, "Foods from the Freezer: Precooked or Prepared," *Cornell Bulletin for Homemakers* 692 (1946); Karin Fredrikson, *Konserveringsboken: Dypfrysning, hermetisering, saftning og syltning* (Oslo: Cappelen, 1966); Britt-Marie Andersson, *Dypfrysing* (Oslo: Cappelen, 1969).
56. Myrvang, *Forbruksagentene*; Susan Strasser, *Never Done: A History of American Housework* (New York: Pantheon, 1982).
57. "Vedtekter for Dypfrysingskontoret," S-1623 Norsk Produktivitetsinstitutt, Serie: DF-NPI-Prosjekter 1953-1985, Eske L0351, Sak: 010194 Etablering av Dypfrysingskontor i Norge, The National Archives of Norway.
58. Bjørg Eliassen, *Vi dypfryser* (Oslo: Tanum, 1965), 12, 265.
59. Ibid., 266.
60. "Prøver utført for Freia ved direktør Throne Holst," Statens Forsøksvirksomhet i Husstell, November 23, 1950, box 1: oppskrifter på frysevarer 1949–1951, SIFO; "Prøver for A/S Frossenfisk," Statens Forsøksvirksomhet i Husstell, June 17, 1950, box 1: oppskrifter på frysevarer 1949–1951, SIFO.
61. Nils L. S. Jacobsen, "Innlandet," *Norsk Fryserinæring* 6 (1949): 1–2.
62. Pettersen-Hagh, *Frysing og fryselagring i USA*, 43.
63. "Marketing and Consumption of Frozen Fish in OEEC Countries," 32–5.
64. Rolf Kirkvaag, "Dypfrysingen i Norge," *Norsk Fryserinæring* 12 (1960): 3–13.
65. Rolf Kirkvaag, "Dypfrysingens fremtidsmuligheter," *Kjøleteknikk og Fryserinæring* 6 (1962): 150–4.
66. Terje Finstad, "Familiarizing Food: Frozen Food Chains, Technology and Consumer Trust, Norway 1940–1970," *Food and Foodways* 21 (2013): 22–45.

5
Americanization and Authenticity: Italian Food Products and Practices in the 1950s and 1960s

Emanuela Scarpellini

Food Culture

In 1954, the American political scientist Edward Banfield traveled from Chicago to Chiaromonte, a small village in southern Italy. Banfield's goal was to discover why the villagers' lives had been so poor—and so unchanged—for centuries. After nine months of research, Banfield concluded that the family was at the center of life in Chiaromonte—to the detriment of every other institution. It was the family that guaranteed assistance and emotional support, the family that functioned as the economic center of production and consumption. As the only environment in which trust and respect reigned, the family also operated as the starting point for all social relationships, vital to everything from meeting new people to finding a job. But there was a steep downside: this attitude of "Why trust a foreigner?" blocked all external forms of solidarity and cooperation. The singular emphasis on family inhibited the development of a modern society, which Max Weber characterized as anonymous, rationalized, bureaucratic, and capitalistic. In contemporary terms, the family blocked the creation of social capital; the villagers' amoral familism, as Banfield called it, condemned the society to backwardness.[1]

Banfield's analysis was subsequently criticized, above all for its reference to an alleged Mediterranean paradigm of backwardness, implicitly opposed to the civic progress of northern societies. Critics claimed that the situation in Chiaromonte could be either the cause or the effect of a long history of poverty and isolation,[2] and that the centrality of the family could have positive effects in other contexts, such as in northern Italy.[3] Critics also claimed that the family's centrality could disappear in cases of great social tension,[4] and that the family structure could morph and flex, depending on the context.[5]

While the familism of Chiaromonte may have represented an extreme, similar forms of traditional family have long been a keystone of Italian society, as subsequent social and economic research has shown.[6] And family structures have long been acknowledged as a key to understanding the various new challenges to existing consumption regimes. In the 1950s and 1960s, the traditional Italian family structure endured, and with it, a quintessential ritual: the family dinner. Eating together served to strengthen the bonds among family members and to ensure cohesion. Eating together enabled family members to enact various social roles, and the ritual underscored gender differences. Crucially, the family dinner established clearly who belonged—and who did not belong—to the family. According to many studies, these features of traditional Italian family life were so defining that they continued among emigrant communities over time. Donna Gabaccia has shown how the influence of food has been carried on by Italo-Americans, for example.[7]

Historical scholarship has long maintained that understanding the relationship with food is vital to understanding any culture. And beyond this notion of food's universal importance is the idea of food as bearing special importance in selected cultures. Indeed, this chapter emphasizes the special role that food, in all its manifestations, has played in Italian life. To substantiate this, consider how sociologist Norbert Elias related the development of courts to the civilizing process; other scholars have identified further hallmarks of the process, which include centuries-long traditions, an ancient heritage, literary mediators, important trade markets, and historical periods of great affluence. All of these civilizing elements existed in Italy; they have contributed to assigning food a prominent place in Italian culture—if not Italian "high" culture. Food occupies a distinctive place in other European countries, such as France, as well, but food is not equally influential in every European setting.

Analyzing food and its various contexts, from supermarkets to kitchens, is vital to understanding points of cultural continuity as well as points of cultural disruption. In Italian history—and indeed the history of other European countries—one of these significant points was the time of the "economic miracle": the 1950s and 1960s. This was a time of rapid industrialization; internal migration (from south to north and from rural to urban areas); and pronounced urbanization. Like other European countries, Italy experienced a sudden rise in per-capita income as well as profound social and cultural transformations. And the wave of change was, to a large extent, perceived as deriving from the United States. To Italians, the American way of life soon became synonymous with novelty and modernity, progress and practicality. For many Italians during the Cold War era, identifying with America and its private-consumer culture meant distancing themselves from the Soviet model of government. After all, Italy was close to the Iron Curtain and supported a powerful Communist Party of its own. In this context, appropriating American elements signified a political stance that was rife with contradictions. On the one hand, the Christian Democrats, Italy's main political party, was a conservative force, deeply rooted as it was in peasant culture, the lower-middle class, and the Catholic Church. At the same time, the Christian Democrats were tied politically to the United States; the party considered practically every American innovation and trend to be a symbol of modernism—and even civilization. On the other hand, the Italian Communist Party took its cues from the United States' rival, the Soviet Union, and Communists harbored contempt for nearly all things American. The party had its own political base among workers and intellectuals; was less socially conservative (especially regarding the role of women in society); and welcomed innovation.[8] A tension could be felt not only between the two parties, but between the political and the social stances of members within those parties. And, often, it was American innovation that created pressure—and triggered political controversy.

Generally speaking (with the exception of the Communist Party), "American" and "Americanization" had positive connotations in the media and in social discourse. Often, the terms were used to denote facts and products that had no connection with the United States, but happened to be new, modern, advanced, and practical. The way in which Italians imagined America had little to do with actual, contemporary American society and far more to do with Italian ideas about tradition versus modernity, the past versus the future. Songs and movies proclaimed a new, projected-American way of life, as portrayed in the popular film *An American in Rome*, directed by Stefano Vanzina in 1954. Meanwhile, mass-media attention focused relentlessly on American innovations.[9] This reinforced the propagandist effort that followed the Marshall Plan in Italy and elsewhere in Europe (see also Karin Zachmann's chapter in this volume).

Pop culture and mass media notwithstanding, the success of this great transformation to an "Americanized" Italian culture was a grassroots matter. Recent scholarship has emphasized the role of consumers and users along with the role of producers. In addition to consumers, others were active in this process: advertisers and designers, for example, acted as experts and intermediaries who mediated between producers and consumers; this helped to shape a tripartite relationship. Increasingly, scholars' attention is being devoted to daily aspects of domestic life. Accordingly, the history of the kitchen is heuristically fertile ground for gaining insights into new technologies—and understanding ways in which those technologies met with resistance, hybridization, and domestication, for example.[10] In this chapter—and indeed this volume—we compare the dominant narrative with consumers' actual practices. This serves to deconstruct the innovations' symbolic meaning—and allows us to assess the real-world impact of new technologies.

In this chapter, we examine the interactions between American models and Italian food as well as the Italian kitchen—the setting for preparing food. How profound was the American influence? Is it accurate to speak of appropriating American elements in the name of progress—and to resist in the name of maintaining authenticity? Were producers' choices compatible with those of consumers?

To answer these questions, we work from the premise that Italy's political parties paid no direct attention to the domain of the kitchen, yet this was a domain of fierce confrontation. We analyze products as well as their associated cultural practices, which also conveyed their meaning: the food-related consumption regime. Specifically, we study food in its domestic context, analyzing whether or not changes in the kitchen parallel changes in selected technical innovations and new food products. Our thesis here, as in the rest of the volume, is that *process* innovation and *product* innovation must be considered separately.[11] For changes in process, from food-preparation practices to technical devices and technologies, were accepted faster—and to a greater extent—than changes linked to food products themselves.

An "American" Kitchen: Selling the Dream

After the Fascist period and the Second World War, Italian homes lacked most basic appliances; only the water heater and the stove were commonly found. In 1946, only 1 percent of Italians owned a refrigerator, the first appliance to be widely appropriated. By 1958, this had risen to 6 percent, and market studies assumed that "we can rule out Italy developing a strong autonomous refrigerator industry or a broad interesting market in this sector being created."[12] After all, some Italians still believed that the refrigerator served a purpose only in the summer and was thus not really necessary.[13]

In 1966, a survey by the National Bank of Italy showed that the refrigerator was already a common appliance, with 60 percent of Italian families owning one. In 1977, the refrigerator was almost omnipresent: 94 percent.[14] What led to this development in such a short period? The first images of American kitchens—along with tail-finned cars, modern cities, and glamorous actresses—were probably transmitted to Italy through popular Hollywood films. Brand-new, modular kitchens with advanced appliances were an integral part of this future world. American magazines arrived along with the Allies and United Nations Relief and Rehabilitation Administration supplies, which were another vehicle of market penetration. In the 1950s, various popular women's magazines began to introduce this kitchen as an ideal model for the modern woman.

Particular attention was paid to domestic appliances. The heart of the traditional Italian kitchen had always been the stove, which was placed adjacent to the sink. The new appliances, starting with the refrigerator, proposed a novel layout, ideally a triangle of stove, refrigerator, and sink. In June of 1953, the magazine *Italian Cuisine* (*La Cucina Italiana*), the most influential periodical of its kind, published an article presenting the Frigidaire Model OMM 74. Emphasized here were the refrigerator's technical characteristics; its sturdiness; and its reputation as a state-of-the-art appliance. The article concluded that "Frigidaire is the brand name used by General Motors for the production of domestic appliances and, while there are many refrigerator models on the market, there is only one 'Frigidaire.' "[15] This is a significant statement, given that the term Frigidaire had already become synonymous with the word refrigerator and had entered the daily vocabulary. Thus the dream of—and the proposed need for—owning a refrigerator was born even before the possibility of fulfilling the need existed.

The Frigidaire sparked great interest: the prototype for the *Kitchen of Tomorrow* (an exhibit presented by Frigidaire in Paris and elsewhere in February and March of 1957) appeared in all of the Italian newspapers. This was a kitchen whose boldness both frightened and fascinated Italians; it embodied the contradictory identity of the modern kitchen as an efficient workplace on the one hand, and as a pleasant, convivial place on the other. One journalist observed:

> I won't discuss, as the architect Giò Ponti did with me one day, whether the kitchen in a modern house represents food cooked in a rational way or whether it is an instrument of an eternal, delicious song of conviviality and a culinary art. I want to tell you my realistic point of view on this dramatic 'Year 2000' kitchen, which news magazines have latched onto today, after a well-known American

firm launched it in Paris.... By our present standards, a happy life in this bizarre concoction of automatism—which stifles personality; kills all initiative; and worse still, eliminates all personal interpretation—seems pretty absurd. Just to give you an idea of this nevertheless fascinating kitchen concept.[16]

Similar comments were expressed in Milan, at the presentation of a high-tech kitchen on display at fair the following year:

Although they use many names, Americans also call it the 'kitchen of the future' without thinking about the complication of devices hidden behind apparently simple lockers on the floor or wall, and the difficulty of keeping these kitchens efficient, which would require the housekeeper to know as much as an electronics expert. We don't know how far off this tomorrow is, but for sure, each of us hopes that at least one of these wonders will be coming soon.[17]

The American kitchen—the term that quickly came to denote a modern kitchen with cabinet units and domestic appliances—thus produced cultural tension. In the traditional structure, the kitchen was the place of family reunion; love; the shared ritual of meals; and the symbolic strengthening of bonds. Female domestic chores were, of course, part of this structure, but they came second, "dignified" by the woman's devotion to home and family. Again, this traditional structure was not unique to Italian life, though its staying power was remarkable.

In contrast, the American kitchen represented the kitchen as workplace. With its aims of lightening the load and improving results, the kitchen opened the door to new technologies (although women's work was not destined to decline, as studies like Ruth Schwartz Cowan's show).[18] Often, this vision was rejected from a conservative perspective, because it clashed with the prevailing image of women and the family in the 1950s. "Work" outside the home was not comparable to "work" in the kitchen, on behalf of the family; this was not a real job but a mission of sorts, a pleasant occupation (significantly, beyond the commercial, monetary domain). The American kitchen challenged a foundation on which the very idea of modern domesticity was built, as Simon Schama describes: we see the separation of the external, social sphere of work and money from the interior, domestic realm based on feelings such as love, solidarity, and sacrifice.[19] Moreover, this new vision introduced another transgression: the technical world, culturally understood as a masculine domain, was transferred to a female space par excellence:

the kitchen.[20] Unsurprisingly, some consumers and some in the media were perplexed by this new scenario; others rejected it outright. For still others, this bright, new technological kitchen was merely a mirage. At the same time, however, the image of the American kitchen was a seductive one: it planted the desire in women to ease the burden of domestic chores, which was genuinely needed. So, the narratives of the traditional kitchen and the modern one seemed to pull Italians in opposite directions.

Kitchen Producers and Mediators

Some consumers welcomed the idea of particular American innovations—the refrigerator and modern kitchen units, for example. But consumers discovered that these items—which were at least made available for mass-consumption by America if not actually invented in America—actually did not suit the Italian kitchen: they were overpriced; too large and bulky; and did not match the look of Italian homes. Trends changed, however, when Italian industry began its own production of kitchen appliances and fixtures. It is worth noting that large companies did not invest significantly in the new sector: for a few years, Fiat produced refrigerators under a Westinghouse license and then quit, for example. The victors in the Italian market were small artisans and former workers such as Giovanni Borghi, who set up shop in the small town of Comerio, near Milan, in 1946. Borghi designed a refrigerator suitable for all families: it was low-cost; shaped as a simple square, to adapt to every environment; and available in various models, all of which were compact. By 1958, Borghi's company, Ignis, managed to sell refrigerators for 40 percent less than imported products. It was the start of a commercial achievement that introduced the refrigerator throughout Italy and led to increased exports. By 1970, Italy's household-appliance sector had mushroomed into the world's second-largest producer of refrigerators after the United States, with more than 5 million units sold annually.[21]

Interestingly, the "small" Ignis refrigerators incorporated advanced technology, employing a hermetically protected Freon compressor; these compressors were built in Italy by Fiat and Necchi (a former sewing-machine manufacturer) at sharply competitive prices. To ensure economy of scale and the resulting low cost, Ignis built its refrigerators at large factories.

An attractive line and adaptability were important features, and not only for appliances. Remarkably, success in the household-appliance

Figure 5.1 In the case of refrigerators, large companies in Italy did not invest significantly in the new sector. For for several years, Fiat produced refrigerators under the Westinghouse license before ceasing production. The victors in the Italian market were small players.

sector translated to success in the kitchen-furniture market, which was boosted by the technological influence of the American kitchen as well as iconic European experiences, from the famous "Frankfurt Kitchen" to the Italian functionalist tradition. In the 1950s, new processes and technologies emerged; experiments used traditional Italian materials—including walnut, ash, and olive wood—in new ways. In a short time, the relationship between appliance producers and designers became closer. This yielded "Italian style"—a key to the resulting commercial boom.[22]

Designers thus became important mediators in this process. A classic example: one of Italy's foremost manufacturers, Aristide Merloni, commissioned designer Makio Hasuike (born in Japan and living in Milan) to devise an Italian version of the American kitchen. It was to be a close "translation" of the American model, to embrace the characteristic U.S. technology, convenience, and practicality—but suited to the Italian setting in scale and cost. This new kitchen also had to look stylish, befitting the Italian market. The result of this process was "Unibloc" by Ariston, created in 1962, and in production as of 1968. It was a compact kitchen unit, available in a single, small, basic version (one meter) and one larger version (2.7 meters). Both versions contained a refrigerator, stove, sink, water heater, electrical wiring system, and cabinets. The larger version included a dishwasher. Elegant wooden cabinet doors hid some of the appliances; a steel worktop—which appeared to be a single piece—covered everything.[23] The size was compact, the price competitive, and the design simple and linear. The result was a great success for a product designed to "anticipate the kitchen of the future"—yet supremely suited to the present.[24]

Manufacturers, however, needed other mediators in order to reach the end consumer: they relied on advertisers and the media world at large. With television still in its infancy, popular women's magazines were chosen as the perfect vehicle for spreading the message. But what kind of message did producers use to sell their new products? An analysis of the popular magazine *La Cucina Italiana* from 1952 to 1962 reveals the key sales concepts of the era.

The first idea concerned saving money: advertisements always stated the product's sale price and the fact that maintenance costs were low—the main worry in a market with weak purchasing power. So, the refrigerator became "a convenience that pays for itself." The second selling point was technical innovation. All of the appliance's main characteristics were described in minute detail; Fargas used this approach for its kitchens as did Frigidaire for its refrigerators. Another American company, Tappan, presented its AV 668 model ("the Cadillac of the American gas kitchens") in the following way: "Since it is impossible to describe all of the features of this marvelous kitchen here, an illustrated flyer will be sent to the reader, upon request." Other companies insisted on the solidity and safety of their products; in the case of the Ready refrigerator, ads proclaimed the appliance to be hygienic. Many other articles in the 1950s asserted that the new kitchen appliances—from the refrigerator to the electric oven—eliminated servitude, themselves becoming "mechanical servants" or "mechanical assistants."

By the beginning of the 1960s, advertising had changed markedly. Increasingly, print advertisements presented domestic appliances as a means of creating leisure time and providing happiness; attention shifted from technical to aesthetic qualities. Accordingly, the Singer gas kitchen promised a kind of serenity, while the Fiat refrigerator boasted a "modern and sober line" and promised to run silently.

The iconography is also interesting. Most of the time, the early appliances were photographed on their own, with the brand name in full view and copy explaining the item's benefits. Later, however, appliances were displayed with elegant women or in the context of the kitchen, while men were always absent. Advertisers, then, chose these key selling points for the new kitchens and appliances: they were cost-saving, technologically advanced, safe, labor-saving, and aesthetically pleasing.

Italian Kitchens and Consumers

How did Italian consumers themselves respond to the new technologies? In 1958, the magazine *La Cucina Italiana* published various studies of Italian families, including many photos and long excerpts from interviews. The first was with Giovanni C., a worker at a large company in the Lombardian countryside. His life and that of his extended family (a wife, three young daughters, and two additional relatives) revolved around the factory, where he cycled daily: "[H]is situation doesn't allow him the luxury of a motor[ized vehicle], but the factory is only a few kilometers away and a [bike] ride is good for one's health."[25] His wife, Ernesta, had worked in the same factory as her husband until the birth of their daughters; she then devoted herself to the family and the home, helped by her unmarried sister, who was also a worker: "[H]ousework and sewing are her favorite jobs; as with all women accustomed to working in a factory, she devotes less time to cooking," the interviewer remarked.[26] At the time of the interview, the family had lived in their new house for one year, and they economized on everything in order to afford their home. The C. family eked out their meals from their garden's produce, and no domestic appliances appeared in the home, except for an electric water heater that served the kitchen and bathroom.

A remarkably similar case was that of Mario S., an artisan. This master glassworker from the island of Murano earned slightly more than the average income for a member of the working class. Again, there was nothing wasted in the S. family household; no financial cushion; and no domestic appliances—only an ordinary stove. Money was used largely to buy the ingredients to cook "simple, quick fare, based, above all, on good soups" for six days, plus a more substantial lunch on Sundays.[27]

The circumstances of a Sicilian fisherman were hardly better: Sebastiano C., with his boat *Tremagli*, also earned approximately the same amount of money, thanks mostly to his wife, Anna Maria, who sold the fish caught by Sebastiano directly to the market. At home, his wife prepared practically all of the family's food personally or with her mother's help. The photo depicts her in a simple kitchen excluding appliances; when asked whether or not she owned appliances Anna Maria responds, "No, unfortunately. Not for now, at least."[28]

Migrating to the north could improve a worker's economic prospects only partially, as Benito S., a security guard who lived in the outskirts of Milan, well understood. Consumer goods were minimal in the S. family household, where 75 percent of the family income was spent on food. The home lacked most domestic appliances—notably a refrigerator ("I long for one. For now, all I have is an electric floor polisher," said his wife).[29]

Higher on the social ladder, in the middle class, was the example of a public official: Giulio P., an engineer. He lived with his wife and five children outside of Naples, in a beautiful house with antique furniture. The differences were evident: the P. family had household help, and the family also owned a large refrigerator. This was no reason to renege on the moral duty to save: expenditures on entertainment were totally banned, and Signora Giulia strove to save in every way. For example, she hung in her kitchen a chart with the cooking times for various foods—so as not to waste a single extra drop of gas.[30]

For the upper classes, food accounted for no more than 40 percent of the family income. This was the case for one manager at a large Milanese company. Carlo G. lived in downtown Milan, in a four-room apartment with a small but highly functional kitchen. His wife, Mariuccia, pointed out, "I really have everything by way of appliances for the house...from the Frigidaire to the liquidizer, from the washer to the polishing machine and the vacuum cleaner; if they don't invent something atomic, there's nothing left for me to wish for."[31] This family of five had household help, and there was enough money for vacations, a wardrobe of suits, even savings.

Finally, the upper classes were represented in the research by the family of a Turinese professional, Filippo A., a doctor at Fiat. Most likely, Filippo earned three times the wages of the average worker. The doctor's home boasted all manner of modern conveniences. Filippo's wife, Ada, explained: "I have a refrigerator, a floor polisher, a washing machine, and a liquidizer: these are the four pillars on which my domestic economy and my housekeeper's life depend."[32]

Accompanying these interviews was convincing visual evidence. In addition to photos of the husbands in their work environments, the magazine included two symbolic sets of recurring images: photographs of the whole family—usually assembled in the living room—and the requisite scene of the wife in the kitchen. Significantly, in all photos the scenario is almost always the same: the housekeeper is seen either serving food at the table or standing near the stove.

Looking beyond the magazine interviews (which, like all other media, were forms of representations, after all) we find portraits of Italian families in other studies—and the results are consistent. In 1960, for example, Ernest Dichter's Institute for Motivational Research prepared a report for Fargas, the Italian kitchen company. Based on more than a hundred detailed interviews with Italian housewives, the conclusion showed just how widespread the desire was for a modern, luxurious kitchen. For 15 percent of the women surveyed, this kitchen was at the top of the wish list—trumping even a Fiat 600 car and a trip to Spain. The interviews also indicated that the fantasy kitchen was embodied by the American kitchen per se. As one woman interviewee said:

> My ideal would be a complete American kitchen, just like my newly married friend's kitchen, it lacks nothing, do you remember those kitchens you can see in the American movies? Well, something like that, with better taste.[33]

But ambivalences were soon to surface: the perfect kitchen should adapt to Italian tastes and homes; it should be very practical, well designed, and easy to use as well as to clean. It should be totally white, without too many technical devices. (Surprisingly, perhaps, there was no mention of price.) The kitchen emerged in the interviews as a useful vehicle for helping the woman to play her key roles both in the family—

earning praise from her husband as well as older women relatives—and on the social scene, among friends and relatives.[34] The emphasis was more on the woman's social context than on her technical prowess or economic standing.

Many studies of the Italian postwar period have showcased new technologies in shaping new social identities. New technologies symbolized a country in transition. On the one hand were images of extreme poverty and hunger, still alive in the older generation's memory. On the other hand were household appliances, cars, scooters—a higher standard of living in material terms. Adopting these technologies was seen as a sign of integrating into modern society.[35] This belief was especially relevant to women. It also applied to immigrants from southern Italy who were experiencing a new life and new social roles in the industrialized cities of the north.[36]

Thus, manufacturers' fears that the new appliances would fail to meet Italian women's approval were generally unfounded: refrigerators and modern kitchens were every housewife's dream. Women of all social categories longed for these items, although, in 1958, only a few women were actually in a position to buy them. Within the Italian class system, domestic appliances were, first and foremost, a status symbol. Only the richest families owned appliances—and not in place of servants, but in addition to them. The typical advertising rhetoric of "mechanical servants" that would replace human work did not resonate with the spirit of the time: the wealthiest families used both human and mechanical labor. Advertising was not the primary influence; refrigerators and American kitchens first assumed social value. This was confirmed by questionnaires and oral surveys conducted for this chapter: many Italian women remembered that they had seen—and wanted—a domestic appliance for the first time while visiting a friend or neighbor's house. The next most common context was at a shop or exhibit; advertising ranked only third.[37] The first conclusion, then, is that during the 1950s and early 1960s, the shift toward modern kitchens in Italian society did not take place entirely within the confines of the home. Indeed, there was substantial social discourse—and that discourse bristled with symbolic meaning.

In further analyzing women's relationships with technology, a problem arises. Namely, in our interviews, inconsistent answers often emerged; undoubtedly, some women expressed fear regarding appliances as technological artifacts. Usually, these technologies were viewed as part of the masculine cultural world—as the current scientific literature has emphasized strongly.[38] The potential conflict between women and technology was resolved in two ways. First, despite manufacturers' advertising, which insisted on detailed technical descriptions, the woman consumer voiced her need for simplicity and practicality. Second, new appliances entered the traditional kitchen without disturbing the familiar set-up; appliances were added as additional pieces of furniture. Unlike the imposing, curvilinear, highly visible American appliances, the smaller, square, rectilinear Italian products harmonized better with the existing environment and looked more appropriate. Disguised as pieces of furniture to hide their technological nature, appliances blended in with the rest of the home, cushioning their technical impact. In the most luxurious homes, the disguise was literal: wood panels or other forms of decoration covered the exterior. Appliances did not impose a new spatial arrangement; they were brought to the existing setting as an improvement: it was evolution, not revolution.

Italian women may well have greeted with caution the idea of the American kitchen, but some of its features were quickly appropriated. American elements were domesticated and absorbed into the traditional Italian vision of the kitchen; the prevailing aesthetics of the time; as well as social roles and societal structure. The new appliances were introduced in a language that consumers already knew, the language of tradition and authenticity. And so they were appropriated widely in a remarkably short time, exceeding producers' and experts' expectations.

Italian Food, American Influence

In the 1950s and early 1960s, Italian food—one of the country's cultural hallmarks—took on new forms and new meanings; a certain fascination with the American model of food and eating took hold. The first sign was the increased use of English terms: *cocktails*, for example, were often prepared in *shakers*; the familiar slice of meat became a *beefsteak*; a gathering of friends transformed into a *party*; and a meal outdoors was the occasion for a *picnic*. American elements appeared, first and foremost, in the form of a language that punctuated the Italian narrative.

In reality, few made-in-America products reached Italian tables. The most celebrated of products was surely Coca-Cola, whose history is well known: in Italy, as everywhere else in Europe, Coke came to symbolize the young, dynamic lifestyle. Advertisements displayed the famous bottles in the hands of young people who were inevitably enjoying Wrigley's or Brooklyn-brand chewing gum (the latter produced by the Perfetti brothers at a plant outside Milan).[39]

forma un vero e proprio mobiletto per gli utensili da cucina, pur lasciando un certo ripiano scoperto usufruito come scaffale.
La foto n. 9 presenta il mobiletto per la scorta di pasta e farine interamente realizzato in acciaio inossidabile.
La foto n. 10 illustra un'originale sistemazione delle tazze da caffè e da tè le quali occupano solitamente molto prezioso spazio. Con questa soluzione le tazze sono bene in vista, comode a prendersi ed il rischio delle rotture è praticamente scomparso. Per questa installazione sono state adoperate delle viti con gancio ricurvo fissandole al legno del mobile.
Le cucine riprodotte nelle foto nn. 11 e 12 sono di concetto americano: della n. 11 presentiamo l'angolo dedicato ai conteggi e alle fatture del ménage familiare. E' lì che la brava padrona di casa raccoglie, e accuratamente conserva in diverse cartelle, i conti della luce, del gas, del telefono, dell'affitto, del vestiario, del vitto, ecc. collocandole nei tre cassetti del piccolo tavolo scrivania. La macchina da scrivere serve per la sua corrispondenza commerciale e per compilare i menus del giorno. Da notare i diversi blocchetti per le note appesi alla bella parete di masonite i cui fori permettono la facile applicazione degli appositi ganci per sostenere oggetti o scaffalature (in Italia questo tipo di parete è già in vendita in diverse tinte). Non mancano le piantine verdi vicino ai libri di cucina, la piccola radio portatile sullo scaffale, il portariviste, il cestino per la carta straccia e infine la lavagna tanto utile per segnare eventuali acquisti urgenti da fare o per lasciare degli ordini promemoria alla cameriera.

La cucina n. 12 rappresenta il sogno della massaia moderna: qui tutto è stato studiato razionalmente e con intelligenza, dai piani di lavoro alla cappa con apparecchio aspirante, all'armadietto per la scorta dello scatolame, al piccolo piano da lavoro realizzato in pesante legno che, unito alla lampada ed alla parete in legno, segno il particolare « antico » nel bioncore di questa cucina modernissima, alla quale però la padrona di casa ha saputo infondere una sua nota personale.

Figure 5.2 Featured here: one version of the modern "American" kitchen within an ideal home. Italian women approached the American kitchen with caution. In fact, the women of Italy domesticated American elements, absorbing them into the traditional Italian vision of the kitchen.

In many cases, the "new" products were native to other countries and merely disguised as American. It was not easy to win the trust of a market that was habitually so careful with its food; initially, the majority of new products met with suspicion. This was the case for ready-made soups. Among the first to be marketed were Campbell's canned soup and Knorr dehydrated soup packets. Obviously, the latter did not originate in the United States—but that was a trifling detail; both forms of soup were bound to be interpreted as an "American" innovation.

To understand this resistance, it is important to consider the cultural references within the family context. The 1950s and early 1960s were a time in which the trend toward women working outside the home grew rapidly. The traditional housewife's role was to ensure that standards were maintained in the home and money could be saved—thanks to the thrift of home cooking. The prospect of a woman working outside the home was considered positive because it generated additional money, but negative because the woman "neglected" the family and the house. The words of a housewife by the name of Graziella summarize this situation eloquently:

> Well, I did notice I consumed more, going to the factory. When I got home, it was a great rush, sticking things on the stove...and everything...whereas when I stayed at home...I used to cook properly and if there was a little sauce left over, or a bit of pasta, I would use it up in something else. I never tossed anything into the trash bin....
>
> I used to spend less, staying at home, 'cause I had time: if I had some rice or something left over, I'd use it to make a couple of rice balls...not like when you got home from work...one time I tried it on him . . . I was in a hurry, I stopped a moment and said to myself, "Hang on, I'll get some of them Knorr packets," they do bean soup. I came home and said: "I ain't got no time to cook..." (you see, we cook our own beans, I don't go and get food...well, there is a tin in the pantry, but for us cooking is, you know...boiled meats, beans, potatoes, stew. It's none of your old slab of meat rustled up in a hurry, no, then there's polenta...). Anyway, that day, I was worn out so I warmed up some of that Knorr. Then I put it in his thermos and off he went to work. Comes home in the afternoon and says to me, "Here, what kind of soup was that you gave me? What did you do to it?"
>
> "Same as usual," I say.
>
> "Never."
>
> "What d'you mean?"

"I haven't eaten a bloody thing, I threw it away, it turned my stomach. It smelled like a bouillon cube!" Then he says: "This better be the last time; you just watch it, or I'll throw you off that balcony!" That was the last time I bought ready-made stuff.[40]

The Knorr soup here takes on a wider meaning: it symbolized the rejection of the traditional housewife role. And it represented the new circumstances of the working woman, who could not find time for—or did not feel like—cooking as she once did. Her husband, meanwhile, violently opposed all of these changes. Interestingly, a gender-related problem crops up here. Namely, interpretations regarding food and cooking usually refer to women only; women are deemed culturally resistant. In contrast, the previous account reminds us that men were as important as women when it came to food, as noted in Dichter's interviews. In the previous case, it was the man who rejected the innovation. Typically, the new foods tasted "bad" or "different"—and a simple soup could spark a revolution in terms of social roles.

Some canned products sold more successfully: beans and peas (especially when out of season) and, above all, canned meat. In this case the product was not a replacement for the main course. For example, ads recommended serving frozen or canned meat on hot summer days; it was also earmarked for emergency meals, picnics, and TV dinners—a novelty at the time. Apart from the market leaders (Simmenthal, followed by Manzotin), the producer Luigi Cremonini of Modena represents an interesting example in this sector. For his canned-meat product, launched in 1963, Cremonini chose an allusive name: Montana. The product became famous thanks to a particular television commercial shot in an American Western-style setting.[41] In short, canned meat from America was sold to Italians as a novelty food to be consumed on special occasions; it did not challenge the structure of the traditional Italian meal.

Among the new product categories to gain rapid popularity in the 1950s and early 1960s were bouillon cubes and meat extract for broth, as well as margarine and vegetable oil. Maggi cubes and Liebig meat extract were already well known, but a new brand took over as the market leader; it was an Italian company with another symbolic name: Star. A marketing survey in 1961 showed that 60 percent of Italian families—especially those in the urban centers of northern Italy—used this category of product regularly; peak usage was 77 percent.[42] In the same years, vegetable oils were introduced, particularly as a suitable means of frying, a cooking method now considered more modern and pleasant than the old-fashioned boiling or roasting. The margarine Gradina, produced by the British company Unilever, which had bought up Gaslini-Arrigoni in Italy, entered the Italian market in the mid-1950s. The most famous advertisement depicted an average middle-class family eating in their kitchen. The housewife had made *spaghetti*, as usual, one imagines, for her husband and daughter, using the new margarine instead of traditional butter or oil. The husband says: "Well, you were right; we can eat well with Gradina."[43] In this case, the new product was framed as part of a particularly conservative context. Gradina did not threaten tradition; on the contrary, the product was portrayed as bolstering tradition.

Marketing surveys showed that, over a two-year period, Italian families demonstrated a rapid increase in margarine consumption: it jumped from 10 percent in 1957 to 31 percent in 1959. Interestingly, the greatest consumption took place among the upper-middle classes (40 percent in 1959) rather than among the lower-middle classes (29 percent) and lower classes (23 percent); consumption in northern Italy was double that of southern Italy: 38 percent and 19 percent respectively.[44] Given that the price of margarine was lower than the cost of butter and olive oil, this data proves that the symbolic and cultural value of food can be independent of its economic value in the eyes of consumers. In other words, innovative food need not always be expensive to be appreciated by the upper classes, while the more expensive traditional food remained the lower-class choice. These examples also affirm that, despite the efforts of manufacturers and advertisers, consumers reacted in different ways to newfangled American products, welcoming some with immediate interest and curiosity, while mistrusting or completely rejecting others. In the final considerations that follow, we analyze further this gamut of reactions.

Culture, Class, and Forms of Innovation

Our first conclusion is that understanding the phenomena of appropriation hinges on understanding the social and cultural context of the 1950s and 1960s. This is a time in which a delicate transition took place. Italian society entered this period as relatively static, with traditional family values placed firmly at its core, and roles sharply divided along gender lines. Emerging from the 1960s, Italian society was dynamic; characterized by social and geographical mobility; and in the process of redefining family roles.

The new food products and the latest appliances adopted by this society in ferment represented much more than just technical and

Figure 5.3 Despite the efforts of manufacturers and advertisers, consumers responded in different ways to newfangled American products. Italian consumers happened to be enthusiastic about margarine—and adopted it as part of their traditional meals.

qualitative improvements. These foods and devices were an explicit part of the "new world"—modernity represented by speed, practicality, technology, and urbanism. And, for Italians, this new world was the embodiment of America. It is no accident that references to America were pervasive—even for products that were completely unrelated to the United States. America was the world of the future; engaging in that world meant owning modern appliances, sipping *cocktails* and drinking Coca-Cola (rather than the traditional daily wine), as well as eating Knorr soups and the like. Inhabiting this world could place one in cultural conflict with the traditions of the "old" Italy, perceived as backward, rural, and static. The new products came to mean a break with the past and a desire to integrate with the emerging modern, urban society. Factors including social class, geographical location, and gender influenced attitudes toward appropriating food and kitchens—whether enthusiastically for, vociferously against, or any of the nuanced positions in between.

This society in transformation retained strong class features. Kitchens and most foods carried social connotations; practically all products introduced as social-status symbols—whether targeting the established classes or the recently wealthy—were immediately successful. As we have seen, this was true of modern domestic appliances and "luxury" products, such as Coca-Cola, which triumphed over traditional drinks. Even margarine was appropriated, having been introduced as a healthy product in line with modern/American trends. Similarly, innovative products that were not presented as status symbols tended to languish on the Italian market. For example, frozen foods introduced without the backing of prestigious brands, and presented as low-cost products, were tacitly labeled as inferior—and rejected.

Our final conclusion concerns the day-to-day impact of American innovations on food-consumption patterns in Italy. We find that products intended to replace the traditionally prepared Italian meal often met with mistrust: the presence of these products at the table challenged the cultural value of the original creation, as in the case of ready-made meals. In contrast, individual ingredients like bouillon cubes and vegetable oils were more fully appropriated. As an innovation, the bouillon cube facilitated the food-preparation process by eliminating the intermediary step of boiling the meat to make a broth—without noticeably altering the qualities of the final product. The non-invasiveness of these new ingredients was crucial to their success.

Domestic appliances, too, were more readily welcomed. As with time-saving ingredients, these technologies—starting with the refrigerator—had the power to transform food-preparation processes. In economic parlance, we could say that process innovations succeeded much better and faster than product innovations. On the one hand, if the same meal could be prepared in less time, with less work and at lower expense, that was an acceptable improvement. On the other hand, if the final meal were distinctly altered (in appearance, flavor, color, or consistency, for example), that was unacceptable in the eyes of most Italian consumers.

The same pattern of appropriation appears to have been at work in many other contexts throughout Europe: the concept of authenticity, commonly interpreted as proximity to tradition, was the main cultural tool for judging innovative foods. The resulting judgments related mostly to the final food product rather than the intermediary phases or methods leading to that final product.

Throughout the 1950s and early 1960s, producers, mediators, and consumers all experienced ambivalence toward the idea of "American modernity." But, by selectively appropriating new "American" foods, appliances, and kitchens, Italian society emerged from the Cold War period with a dynamic balance of traditional and modern food products and processes.

Notes

1. Edward C. Banfield, *The Moral Basis of a Backward Society* (Glencoe, IL: Free Press, 1958).
2. Sydel F. Silverman, "Agricultural Organization, Social Structure, and Values in Italy: Amoral Familism Reconsidered," *American Anthropologist* 70 (1968): 1–20.
3. John Davis, *Land and Family in Pisticci* (London: Athlone Press, 1973).
4. Thomas Belmonte, *The Broken Fountain* (New York: Columbia University Press, 1979).
5. David I. Kertzer, *Family Life in Central Italy, 1880–1910: Sharecropping, Wage Labor, and Coresidence* (New Brunswick, NJ: Rutgers University Press, 1984); Donald S. Pitkin, *The House That Giacomo Built: History of an Italian Family, 1898–1978* (Cambridge: Cambridge University Press, 1985).
6. Alesina Alberto and Ichino Andrea, *L'Italia fatta in casa: Indagine sulla vera ricchezza degli italiani* (Milan: Mondadori, 2009).
7. Donna R. Gabaccia, *Italy's Many Diasporas* (London: UCL Press, 2000).
8. Stephen Gundle, *Between Hollywood and Moscow: The Italian Communists and the Challenge of Mass Culture, 1943–1991* (Durham, NC: Duke University Press, 2000); Agostino Giovagnoli, *Il partito italiano: La Democrazia Cristiana dal 1942 al 1994* (Rome: Laterza, 1996).
9. David W. Ellwood and Gian Piero Brunetta, eds., *Hollywood in Europa: Industria, politica, pubblico del cinema 1945–1960* (Florence: Ponte alle Grazie, 1991); David Forgacs and Stephen Gundle, *Mass Culture and Italian*

Society from Fascism to the Cold War (Bloomington: Indiana University Press, 2007).
10. Ruth Oldenziel and Karin Zachmann, eds., Cold War Kitchen: Americanization, Technology, and European Users (Cambridge, MA: MIT Press, 2009).
11. James M. Utterback and William J. Abernathy, "A Dynamic Model of Product and Process Innovation," *Omega* 3 (1975): 639–56.
12. Tersilla Faravelli Giacobone, Paola Guidi, and Anty Pansera, *Dalla casa elettrica alla casa elettronica: Storia e significati degli elettrodomestici* (Milan: Arcadia, 1989), 52.
13. Elettrodomestica advertisement, *La Cucina Italiana*, 1957.
14. Banca d'Italia, "Reddito risparmio e struttura della ricchezza delle famiglie italiane nel 1966," *Bollettino* 4 (1967); Banca d'Italia, *Risparmio nel 1975* (Rome: Banca d'Italia, 1976); Carmela D'Apice, *L'arcipelago dei consumi: Consumi e redditi delle famiglie in Italia dal dopoguerra ad oggi* (Bari: De Donato, 1981).
15. Frigidaire advertisement, *La Cucina Italiana*, June 1953.
16. Brunetta Angeletti, "La cucina del '2000,'" *La Cucina Italiana*, May 1957, 400.
17. A.M. Banchieri, "Avremo la cucina elettronica!" *La Cucina Italiana*, May 1958, 459.
18. Ruth Schwartz Cowan, *More Work for Mother: The Ironies of Household Technology from the Open Hearth to the Microwave* (New York: Basic Books, 1983). See also Claudia Goldin, *Understanding the Gender Gap: An Economic History of American Women* (New York: Oxford University Press, 1990); Sarah Stage and Virginia B. Vincenti, eds., *Rethinking Home Economics: Women and the History of a Profession* (Ithaca, NY: Cornell University Press, 1997); Angela Groppi, ed., *Il lavoro delle donne* (Rome and Bari: Laterza, 1996).
19. Simon Schama, *The Embarrassment of Riches: An Interpretation of Dutch Culture in the Golden Age* (New York: Knopf, 1987).
20. Ruth Oldenziel, *Making Technology Masculine: Men, Women and Modern Machines in America, 1870–1945* (Amsterdam: Amsterdam University Press, 1999).
21. Giacobone, Guidi, and Pansera, *Dalla casa elettrica alla casa elettronica*, 52.
22. Stefano Follesa and Anna Nuzzacci, "Storia della cucina componibile in Italia," accessed May 15, 2010, http://divisare.com/lesson/37.
23. Francesco Zurlo, *Makio Hasuike* (Milan: Abitare Segesta, 2003).
24. Luce Historical Archive, cinema clip *Caleidoscopio Ciac C1742*, March 2, 1966; cinema clip *Radar R0107*, March 15, 1967.
25. A. Rocco, "Come vive la famiglia tipo in Italia. La famiglia dell'operaio," *La Cucina Italiana*, August 1958, 705.
26. Ibid.
27. A. Rocco, "La famiglia del vetraio," *La Cucina Italiana*, June 1958, 547.
28. A. Rocco, "Come vive la famiglia tipo in Italia: La famiglia del pescatore," *La Cucina Italiana*, May 1958, 425.
29. A. Rocco, "La famiglia di una 'guardia giurata,'" *La Cucina Italiana*, March 1958, 215.
30. A. Rocco, "La famiglia di un funzionario statale," *La Cucina Italiana*, November 1958.
31. A. Rocco, "La famiglia di un capoufficio," *La Cucina Italiana*, February 1958, 136.
32. A. Rocco, "La famiglia del medico," *La Cucina Italiana*, April 1958, 349.

33. Rapporto finale dell'inchiesta motivazionale sulle cucine in Italia, December 1960, 23, Hagley Museum and Library, Ernest Dichter papers, Accession 2407, box 65.
34. Ibid. See also Adam Arvidsson, "The Therapy of Consumption Motivation Research and the New Italian Housewife, 1958–62," *Journal of Material Culture* 5 (2000): 251–74.
35. Francesco Alberoni, *Consumi e società* (Bologna: Il Mulino, 1964). For the symbolic value of cars, see Federico Paolini, *Storia sociale dell'automobile in Italia* (Rome: Carocci, 2007). For the cultural and social meaning of consumer culture in this period in Italy, see Emanuela Scarpellini, *Material Nation: A Consumer's History of Modern Italy* (Oxford: Oxford University Press, 2011), 125–222. For more on the washing machine, see Enrica Asquer, *La rivoluzione candida: Storia sociale della lavatrice in Italia (1945–1970)* (Rome: Carocci, 2007).
36. Goffredo Fofi, *L'immigrazione meridionale a Torino* (Milan: Aragno, 1964); Franco Alasia and Danilo Montaldi, *Milano Corea: Inchiesta sugli immigrati* (Milan: Feltrinelli, 1960); Alessandro Pizzorno, *Comunità e razionalizzazione* (Turin: Einaudi, 1960). For more information on women in particular, see Anna Badino, *Tutte a casa? Donne tra migrazione e lavoro nella Torino degli anni Sessanta* (Rome: Viella, 2008); Laura Minestroni, *Casa dolce casa: Storia dello spazio domestico tra pubblicità e società* (Milan: Franco Angeli, 1996).
37. These findings come from the interviews on food and food habits that I conducted in Milan from January to May of 2009. This research comprises a total of 250 documents (part semi-structured questionnaires, part audio interviews, and part video interviews).
38. Oldenziel, *Making Technology Masculine*; Nina E. Lerman, Ruth Oldenziel and Arwen Mohun, eds., *Gender and Technology: A Reader* (Baltimore, MD: Johns Hopkins University Press, 2003).
39. Brooklyn Perfetti television clip, 1966.
40. Badino, *Tutte a casa?* 220.
41. Montana television clip, 1966.
42. Pierpaolo Luzzatto Fegiz, *Il volto sconosciuto dell'Italia: Seconda serie, 1956–1965* (Milan: Giuffrè, 1966), 75–6.
43. Gradina advertisement, *La Cucina Italiana*, 1958.
44. Fegiz, *Il volto sconosciuto dell'Italia*, 62–4.

6
Love and Hate in Industrial Design: Europe's Design Professionals and America in the 1950s

Kjetil Fallan

In the postwar landscape of the 1950s, American attitudes gained traction in Europe, prompting ambivalence on the part of Europeans. These mixed feelings can be characterized roundly as a love-hate relationship with American design. Few European intellectuals expressed that ambivalence more poignantly than the young Norwegian writer Jens Bjørneboe in his aptly titled essay, "The Fear of America within Us" ("Frykten for Amerika i oss"): "While Russia bids us the prospects of hell on earth—*here* and *now*, the U.S.A. can serve up paradise on earth. But in this paradise, when one has lived there for a while, one must put makeup on the apples and oranges in order to spot them. Life must be technicolorized."[1] Having traveled to the U.S., Bjørneboe had first-hand experience of the spectacle of abundance that American consumer society represented, but he feared the consequences of American cultural dominance. Similarly, the mythical notion of "America" represented both fears and desires to European design communities.

To some extent, these ambivalent attitudes grew out of ideological currents and broader geopolitical developments, such as the Korean War and the Marshall Plan. But, above all, these mixed feelings came from changes in—and conflicts between—various consumption regimes. Like the consumers they addressed, European designers and design ideologues had scant experience with the mass-consumption society they saw emerging from the U.S. in the 1950s. The massive increase in the consumption of consumer goods and durables throughout Western Europe during this period had a powerful effect on designers and their work. These revved-up consumption regimes were, in turn, shaped by designers and their work. New and more diverse consumer groups wielded their ever-increasing dispensable income and expressed their preferences in the marketplace and on the social scene. Meanwhile, new manufacturing technologies were beginning to surpass traditional ones—even in the smaller European countries. So, the dogmatic "salon-revolutionary" approach that had dominated design reform since the Industrial Revolution transformed into a far more pluralistic discourse. The aim was to revise design ideologies and practices to align with these rapidly changing consumption regimes, which were based on economics, class, politics, and taste, among other factors.

In this chapter, I examine different images of America during the 1950s. My focus is the design communities of postwar Europe: I trace the multitude of modernisms constructed by various mediators of "good design." I examine the relationships between European design communities and American industrial design in the 1950s; this was a period of intense, transatlantic dialogue on design—a formative period for European consumption regimes. This Norwegian case study correlates to other European countries, as well.

First, I outline how the European–American design discourse evolved. Next, I follow a Norwegian husband-and-wife designer team on their pilgrimage to the United States. Then I examine the fevered debates in which America featured prominently. These were heated dialogues among European design communities—discussions about new, unfamiliar, and "American" modes of designing, manufacturing, marketing, and consumption. In the final sections of the chapter, I explore the mediation of design via the official promotional vehicle of exhibits. Here I analyze the American push to sell high-end design in Scandinavia as well as the counterstrike to this offensive: the Scandinavian campaign to promote their design in America.

Industrial design constitutes the crucial mediation point between technology and the marketplace: design is the interface by which consumers find meaning in the artifacts of technology. As such, design is particularly interesting to study in transatlantic perspective: arguably, the profession of industrial design in its current form emerged from the United States in the 1930s. Some European design professionals were deeply fascinated by design developments in the United States; others felt alienated by the corporatization of U.S. design. American films, music, and TV programs—along with the array of American industrial-design products—constituted a pervasive presence of American mass culture in postwar European life. But as American popular culture took hold among European consumers, many European design professionals expressed a pronounced antagonism toward mainstream American design. Meanwhile, in the U.S., Scandinavian design professionals were subtly but effectively promoting a carefully orchestrated version of Scandinavian design. American design professionals—and upper-middle-class elites—appropriated Scandinavian design enthusiastically as a high-end alternative to America's own mass culture. This reality challenges Victoria de Grazia's concept of a one-directional American empire that was irresistible to Europeans.[2] In fact, the popularity of Scandinavian design in the U.S. is testimony to a two-way cultural influence, which contradicts the notion of American hegemony. Artifacts of American popular culture did indeed flood Europe in the aftermath of the Second World War. And, in their eagerness to develop their own lucrative exports, European industrial managers saw the U.S. as the promised land, as did ambitious European engineers who sought the latest technological advances. But for modernist missionaries in Europe—including the broader community of design professionals—U.S. design was anything but a revelation. In fact, American material culture was rarely adopted unconditionally, rarely incorporated wholesale into European cultural practices, including design. More often than not, American elements were selectively appropriated, modified to suit European circumstances.[3] Mediators of "good design" in Europe unanimously considered much of mainstream American design to be monstrous. These arbiters of taste were reacting to the formalist, commercial elements of U.S. design, the aesthetic extravaganza for which Thomas Hine coined the word *populuxe*.[4] This was epitomized by the outsized, voluptuous shapes of American cars.

In contrast, some designers managed to see beyond the "immoral" aesthetics of American design; these European professionals drew inspiration from their U.S. counterparts. The twelve founding members of Norwegian Industrial Designers (Norske Industridesignere)—a professional organization established in 1955—exemplified this point of view. This group was less comfortable with the applied-art (*brukskunst*) focus of the so-called Scandinavian Design movement; instead, the members of Norwegian Industrial Designers resonated more to industrial design. In this setting, small manufacturing companies dominated, and most designers came from an applied-art background—a handicap in winning approval from industrial managers. Envious of their American colleagues, who were taken more seriously in industry, this subset of aspiring industrial designers assumed a more tolerant, less condemning stance toward American design. Some Swedish industrial-design pioneers, in their passion for American design, even went so far as to use a formal visual language that was strongly influenced by streamlining. These designers, while not from an applied-art background, had lived and worked in the United States during the 1920s and 1930s.[5]

These early Scandinavian industrial designers were part of a larger design community that was generally less commercially oriented, less technologically attuned, more elitist in their tastes, and more social democratic in rhetoric; they harbored "Eurocratic" and allegedly anti-American attitudes. The more traditional design community eagerly mediated Scandinavian design as a cultural expression in the United States—most notably through the *Design in Scandinavia* exhibit that toured art museums in North America from 1954 to 1957. The exhibit was met with great critical acclaim by the American design elite, who were no fonder than their European colleagues of excessive applications of streamlining (such as tail-finned cars and stylized household irons). Scandinavian design was thus appropriated as part of America's modernist mission at home. One of America's most influential mediators of "good design" was Edgar Kaufmann, Jr. As director of the Industrial Design department (1946–1948) at New York's Museum of Modern Art (MoMA), and as a research associate there (1948–1955), Kaufmann championed modernist industrial design. His mission was to foster in America a kind of modernist design founded on a prewar European tradition—specifically, Bauhaus and International Style. He became a key mediator between the European and American industrial-design communities.

A Pilgrimage and a Homecoming

In the late 1940s, the Norwegian design community began to rebuild international relations, both officially and privately. Most efforts at rebuilding were directed toward the same regions and cultures that had attracted Norwegian cultural elites before the Second World War: neighboring Nordic countries, Britain, and continental Europe, for the most part. But some found their relationships across the Atlantic to be a greater lure. For example, Arne Korsmo, a well-regarded architect, and Grete Prytz Korsmo, a silversmith and Arne's wife, resided in the United States as Fulbright scholars for a year (1949–1950). The couple collaborated on the design of silver and enameled-steel products; Arne taught at the National College of Art and Design in Oslo. During their year in the United States, the Korsmos lived in Chicago, where Grete attended the Institute of Design at Illinois Institute of Technology (IIT). They traveled throughout the country, visiting people and places associated with high-end American architecture and design. The Norwegian designers crossed paths with many major figures, including Kaufmann—they also befriended Charles and Ray Eames.[6]

This close encounter with American design elites impacted the Korsmos' creative output and, more importantly, Arne's later teaching at the National College of Art and Design; Korsmo applied many principles learned in the United States. In 1952, a summer course in industrial design with visiting lecturers from the Institute of Design in Chicago took place in Oslo.[7] Korsmo recruited five professors from the U.S. institute to teach the aspiring Norwegian industrial designers who would attend the summer course. Students from design schools across the Nordic countries—120 people in all—attended the three-week summer course.[8] Korsmo was becoming a champion of high-end American design in Norway and Scandinavia.

Korsmo was also emerging as a mediator between traditional, craft-based methods of design and the new, industrial methods and practices he had been exposed to at the cutting-edge IIT Institute of Design. After all, Korsmo had evolved his teaching philosophy during his American sojourn. Back in Oslo, presenting a photo exhibit dedicated to the teaching methods of the IIT Institute of Design the preceding year, Korsmo wrote in the design magazine *Bonytt*: "Both through analysis and the shaping ability of Man, the aim must be to unite the craftsman's model-making abilities with industry's method of repetition through the machine."[9] Here, Korsmo reveals a key trope in contemporary design: the challenge of integrating craft and industry in design practice. On the one hand, Korsmo was a progressive modernist who enjoyed an extensive international network—given his Fulbright year in America, he possessed intimate knowledge of design and design education as practiced in the heartland of industrial mass production. On the other hand, he continued to consider craft-based skills essential to design. Ultimately, Korsmo was an idealist and a visionary. He was more interested in the *idea* of American-style, industrial mass production than in its practical applications in Norway, with its vastly different infrastructure, market structure, and economy.

Not everyone shared Korsmo's enthusiasm for the American industrial design process as presented at the photo exhibit. Odd Brochmann—architect, passionate critic, and newly appointed professor at the Norwegian Institute of Technology—was far less positive. He characterized the methods employed at the IIT Institute of Design as abstract and scientific. In Brochmann's view, this obsession with abstract formal analysis would "do more harm than good" and obscure the artistic, creative element he considered to be at the core of every design process: "But the glow, the idea, where do they find that?"[10] Brochmann was no less of a modernist than Korsmo, but Brochmann based his modernist ideals on a paradoxical combination of a commitment to classical European cultural education and radical socialist ideals.[11] Seeking inspiration for his thinking on modernist design, Brochmann traveled not to the United States, but to the Soviet Union.[12] For Brochmann, the connection between American industrial design and capitalism was more troubling than it was to Korsmo.

The knowledge of American industrial design that circulated in the Norwegian design community was by no means embraced uncritically. Rather, Norwegians reacted with ambivalence, which was expressed as everything from reflexive resistance to lingering reluctance to critical appropriation.

Fighting Fordism

When industrialized mass production became a hot topic for them in the 1950s, members of the Norwegian design community inevitably associated it with *American*-style mass production—epitomized by Fordism and Taylorism. The debate revealed deep concerns about the ability to maintain product quality in the context of this industrialized process. Questions about cultural matters also arose, as a genuine fascination with mass production's potential social and democratic ramifications took hold. And designers wondered if industrialization could create new opportunities for designers. Many from the older generation, trained as they were in the craft-based manufacturing tradition, continued to argue against industrialized mass production. Often, design veterans used tradition as a proxy for quality—a tactic also employed in the Italian kitchen debate (see Emanuela Scarpellini's chapter in this volume).

In 1950, Danish architect and furniture designer Finn Juhl launched one of the more curious attacks on Fordism. Juhl argued that the vast financial investment required by mass production rendered it a noncompetitive process. The high cost of manufacturing facilities and equipment, he wrote, "forced [one] to produce a very large number of copies." In order to dispose of these products, one was "forced to...make use of wholesalers and insanely expensive advertising."[13] Industrial factories also required much larger administrative staffs, Juhl contended. The result? Mass-produced goods that would cost as much as products manufactured in a smaller series by means of craft-based production systems. Juhl offered as an example the 1948 *Womb Chair*, designed by Eero Saarinen for Knoll; the chair's high price—$210—proved his point, he said. Juhl tried to discredit this icon of American design still further: he claimed that the molded plastic shell—the chair's key innovation—was a dishonest use of materials, "hidden" as it was by foam-rubber and fabric upholstery. But Juhl failed to appreciate that despite its "industrial" appearance, the *Womb Chair* was not a generic, mass-produced product. It was a high-end luxury item—a fact borne out by its big price tag.[14]

Knut Greve, cultural historian and president of the Norwegian Applied Art Association, also acknowledged the sizeable investments required for advanced industrial mass production. In contrast to Juhl, Greve did not dismiss the system on the basis of cost per se. Greve's concern was one of scale; the Nordic countries' small populations and small-scale industry would not allow for American-style mass production. He wrote, "The most interesting and intriguing experiments in the field of applied art today are related to completely new materials....Such experiments can only be carried out in the laboratories of large-scale industry and subsidized by its mighty economic resources."[15]

Greve's article, entitled "Experiment or Tradition," was written as a reflection on the reactions to MoMA director Edgar Kaufmann, Jr.'s 1948 visit to the Nordic countries. Kaufmann had been invited by

Figure 6.1 Norwegian designers understood both mass production and plastics technology—despite the controversy surrounding them. Pictured here: allegedly the world's first telephone made entirely from thermoplastics. Designed by Arne E. Holm and Johan Christian Bjerknes, manufactured by Elektrisk Bureau (1953).

the four national applied-art associations to visit Denmark, Norway, Sweden, and Finland. The intention was for Kaufmann to assess the countries' production in the field of design. In the best-case scenario, he would return to MoMA with favorable impressions—as well as many Nordic design objects. It was an initiative based on the associations' firm belief that the Nordic countries were among the world leaders in design. The hope was that an exhibit of Nordic design at MoMA would open the doors to the vast and highly lucrative American market. Unfortunately, Kaufmann was not impressed, and the Scandinavians' dream of being showcased in his cathedral of high-end modernism vanished. Remarkably, this particular incident instilled a profound feeling of betrayal and disappointment. The editor of *Form*, the design magazine of the Swedish Applied Art Association, interpreted the incident as a sign that it was "now America's turn to act as a creator of design and culture." The editor painted a bleak picture of the Nordic countries' position in this "brave, new world" of industrial design, which was led by the United States: "We have seen how we have fallen by the wayside and have been regarded as idly picking flowers along the Scandinavian roadside while progress has whizzed past us."[16] One of the co-editors of *Bonytt*—the official voice of the Norwegian Applied Art Association —characterized the event simply as a "defeat."[17]

For members of the Nordic design communities, Kaufmann's unwillingness to champion them in America stirred up deeply emotional reactions, from anger to disbelief and disillusionment. Greve offered a more nuanced—if not opportunistic—interpretation. He argued that Kaufmann and MoMA prized exceptional and experimental work, which was doomed to fail in Scandinavia. This was not due to lack of skill or talent, but to structural considerations: Greve recognized that Scandinavia did not possess the means to compete in the realm of the experimental avant-garde. But, he claimed,

> [there] is still no doubt that the Scandinavian countries lead when it comes to popularizing good design. We have reached the general public. Our exhibits are visited by people who, in any other country in the world, would not set foot in a design exhibit....[G]ood design is manufactured by more companies, sold in more stores, and purchased by a larger percentage of the population than anywhere else in the world.[18]

Greve's defense hinges on social responsibility and democratic values. As he put it: "Two rooms plus a kitchen is the social framework on which we wish to focus our efforts."[19] But engaging in a social mission had its price, he seems to argue; exceptional and experimental design were sacrificed. In order to reach the general public, one had to use forms and colors, for example, that the public would accept: "It must be connected to a known tradition. All extreme experiments seem strange and hostile to this public."[20] Evidently, Greve had little faith in the public's competence, curiosity, and taste. As such, he adheres to a longstanding tradition in the applied-art community: that good taste, social responsibility, and democratic values must be instilled in the ignorant public by the enlightened and philanthropic elite.

In a fascinating chain of associations, Greve links large-scale industry with MoMA's highly elitist, avant-garde design culture. Further, he associates the Nordic applied-art tradition of artisans and craft-based production systems with the principles of democracy and social responsibility. The connection between mass production and avant-garde culture is especially surprising. Within the applied-art community, industrial mass production had been portrayed as a predominantly evil force that vulgarized material culture; Greve's portrayal was the antithesis.

Coping with Commercialism

It was during the late 1940s and the 1950s that the industrial design profession came into its own in Europe, managing to distinguish itself from applied-art traditions. Still, industrial design was commonly identified as an American phenomenon, which evoked ambivalence concerning the profession. Scandinavians respected the Americans' working methods but spurned their mainstream aesthetics. This is consistent with the findings of other case studies in this book, namely, that American process innovations were more readily appropriated by Europeans than were product innovations. For example, in his chapter in this volume, Adri Albert de la Bruhèze shows how Dutch hotels of the same period avoided all references to American design—while adopting American planning, organizational, and management principles. Similarly, Nordic designers were greatly impressed by the sheer size and organization of the industrial-design profession in the United States. Scandinavians envied the profession's strong standing and key role in the manufacturing industry; there was much to learn from the systematic methodology developed in American design practice. But European designers ridiculed the stylistic devices and formal language that dominated mainstream American industrial design—MoMA-sanctioned "good design" notwithstanding. This attitude surfaces in an article in which architect Åke H.

Huldt—director of the Applied Art Association's school in Gothenburg and director of the Swedish Applied Art Association—seeks to introduce industrial design in the Scandinavian context. Under the subheadline "Yank Tanks and Streamlined Refrigerators," Huldt explains Americans' increasing appreciation of industrial design's commercial aspects—and the resulting boom in the profession:

> Design consultants have opened offices with large staffs and [they receive] sizable royalties and [they maintain] practices that lie somewhere between the architectural office and the ad agency.... [The design consultant's] work can easily—and there are many examples of this—become superficial, motivated exclusively by inciting interest in and demand for a product by means of a sensational appearance....[With] American cars...and elsewhere, one has committed a terrible sin against the important commandment that should apply to all modern design: the demand for truth and honesty.[21]

Within the Nordic design communities, mainstream American industrial design had become a Janus-faced figure: alluring and inspirational when showing its organizational side, ridiculous and appalling when showing its aesthetic side.

Mirroring the growing awareness that design belongs to the cultural sphere as well as to the world of commerce, Jens von der Lippe, a *Bonytt* co-editor argued:

> [The designer] must work for the factory, not against it; he must make the factory's products better, more profitable, more appropriate and attractive to the public, more saleable for the retailers; he must sense the public's demands and desires when they are current—and before they are current.[22]

This was a call for a less "artsy" attitude on the part of designers; von der Lippe not only legitimatized but encouraged the commercial and consumerist dimensions of design. Similarly, positive attitudes toward trends, marketing, and consumer behavior were expressed by the editor of *Bonytt*, Arne Remlov, in his report on a panel discussion about the designer's role in Norwegian industry. Making an analogy to the French fashion industry, Remlov suggested that the Norwegian consumer-goods industry "launch" its designers and "brand" their names—all in service to deploying marketing strategies and fulfilling sales potential. Remlov saw such strategies emerging in the neighboring countries; he feared Norway would lose out in the intensifying international competition. Remlov also accused Norwegian industry of withholding designers' names, not as a deliberate strategy, but because of "gaucherie and lack of flair for the subtleties of public relations."[23] Designer Thorbjørn Rygh also petitioned for "a greater interest in the designer behind the furniture," and made a puzzling analogy to the artist's "signature as the reassuring and (or) decisive" factor when purchasing a painting.[24] The irony of Rygh's comparing the designer's role to the artist's role is this: the following year, 1955, Rygh would co-found Norwegian Industrial Designers, an organization whose very existence depended on the perceived need to distance the world of design from the realm of art.[25] Rygh's motivations aside, his statements represent a sharp departure from the rationalistic logic and utilitarian attitudes of the immediate postwar years. Within a decade, the act of analyzing and responding to trends and public taste had been transformed: the dreadful sin of pandering to the public was now normalized; it was a legitimate marketing tool for achieving good design.

Nordic industrial design came of age in concert with new consumption regimes. From the mid-1950s onward, tariff barriers fell like dominoes, and import restrictions were relaxed. For the Norwegian consumer-goods industry, this meant increased foreign competition in the formerly protected domestic market. Norway needed export markets for its rapidly growing production volumes.[26] So, mediating between culture and commerce became crucial in promoting design. And Remlov's suggestion—to turn Norwegian (or Nordic) industrial design into a version of French fashion—was understandable.

Negotiating American Design

The official American design-propaganda machine made landfall in Scandinavia in 1953. An exhibit called *American Design for Home and Decorative Use* portrayed a very different side of U.S. design, indeed. The exhibit toured major Nordic cities before traveling to Belgium and Italy. The exhibit was commissioned by the newly established United States Information Agency (USIA), a government agency set up to influence foreigners by means of cultural propaganda—and thus contribute to the "psychological warfare" against the USSR.[27] The USIA entrusted the task of organizing the show to MoMA and Edgar Kaufmann, Jr., who had experience with similar projects.[28] Anticipating European skepticism of American mass production and its effects on design practice, Kaufmann emphasized the continued importance of tradition and craft; he

Figure 6.2 In 1953, the official U.S. design-propaganda machine made landfall in Scandinavia. Pictured here: the *American Design for Home and Decorative Use* exhibit, on the first leg of its tour, in Oslo.

deliberately downplayed the role of Taylorist and Fordist principles.[29] Kaufmann was determined not to alienate European audiences with what he feared could be interpreted as "inhuman" design objects. This may explain, in part, his choice to exhibit household objects only—about 300 in all. Appropriately enough, it was the America-inspired Arne Korsmo and his students at the National College of Art and Design that organized the exhibition in Oslo.[30]

The show generated great expectations in the Norwegian design community and was indeed met with relative enthusiasm. But an otherwise positive *Bonytt* review of the exhibit made an essential point: in contrast to the show's sweeping title, the exhibit represented anything but average American design. As the review explained, the objects on display were "typical of another America that exists perhaps particularly in and around the Museum of Modern Art in New York....[T]he circle associated with this exclusive museum is an elite one."[31] And it was this MoMA-approved elite design—not mainstream American design—that was applauded in the Norwegian design community. Arguably, the elitism on display was equally evident in Scandinavian design exhibits on tour abroad. As we shall see, these were no more representative of "average" design and production than the MoMA show in Scandinavia. In a more in-depth review of the exhibit, Thorbjørn Rygh expounded on this distinction. He was awed by the experimental furniture on show designed by MoMA protégés. But he did not approve of most mainstream American design, which he characterized as more generic, more popular, and more commercial:

> America gives in to formalism...it does not seem to bother anyone that a household iron appears to be built for high speed. The car has also become a grotesque example of irrelevance. The exterior shape has become a garment that changes according to fashion, independent of developments in the car's engineering.[32]

The ambivalent response to the exhibit in Norway was echoed in other host countries as well, especially Denmark.[33] The Danish response has striking similarities to the general reception to American design elsewhere in Europe—Italy, for example. Here, the editor of the design magazine *Stile Industria* expressed the same contempt for the "dishonesty" and "shallowness" of American styling, but he was also genuinely impressed by the positions designers held in American industry. The scale of the American industrial-design market; the advanced industrial research; and the experiments undertaken also impressed the magazine's editor.[34] Even the design community of Great Britain—a region representing a relatively large market and highly industrialized economy—expressed a similar attitude. The editor of the Council of Industrial Design's house organ, a magazine titled *Design*, wrote: "American mass-production methods are hardly appropriate to the makers of say, Staffordshire bone china, Yorkshire woolen cloth, Walsall leather goods," and claimed that in American society, industry completely lacked the "aristocratic background to set such standards [of] tradition for quality" upon which most "British industries depend for their existence."[35] The deep-seated resistance toward American mass production has been expressed poignantly by historian Patrick Maguire, who observed that "even Ford UK showed very few Fordist tendencies."[36]

European design elites were not the only ones to condemn the American streamlining aesthetic; their American counterparts were equally ardent in their battle against perceived vulgarity.[37] In the United States, the crusaders for "good design" included MoMA; the communities evolving around design schools (Cranbrook Academy of Art and the IIT Institute of Design, for example); and several high-end furniture manufacturers. The U.S. scene featured two extremes: MoMA elitism at one end of the spectrum, and a populist belief in styling, at the other end. A large industrial design profession sought to mediate between the two.[38] Design elites were not the only critics of commercial, mainstream American design—streamlining in particular. For example, historian Joy Parr has shown that, in the 1950s, Canadian women consumers formed broad alliances to boycott streamlined products exported from the United States. These consumers objected to the massive marketing apparatus surrounding these products—and sought to disassociate themselves from the consumer frenzy of their U.S. neighbors.[39]

In Britain in particular, plastics embodied the "menace" and "vulgarization" ushered in by American design and mass production.[40] Meanwhile, the Norwegian plastics industry grew rapidly throughout the 1950s—despite Knut Greve's claim that Norwegian designers were incapable of working with that medium.[41] This resulted in many new manufacturers and innovative products—designed with or without the mediation of art-school-trained designers. Entrepreneurs and engineers in the Norwegian

Figure 6.3 In the 1950s, fiberglass leisure boats emerged as a market for the Norwegian plastics industry. In this photo, a Skibsplast Seamaster 15' (1958), inspired by American boat magazines, skims the waters of a fjord.

plastics industry viewed American material and production technology as a vital source of inspiration and of knowledge—rather than a target of condemnation and disdain.[42]

Counterstrike: Promoting Scandinavian Design in the U.S.

Indeed, Scandinavian design communities debated the merits and misdoings of American design, fretting about the impact of American mass culture. But all the while, Nordic design professionals were orchestrating a counterstrike: widespread campaigns to promote Scandinavian design in the United States. One early—and admittedly unconventional—effort to promote Norwegian design in the U.S. resulted from a private initiative headed by the furnishings retailer and *Bonytt* co-founder Per Tannum in cooperation with the goldsmith Torolf Prytz. In May of 1951, they launched a showroom exhibit, entitled *Norway Designs for Living*, on North Michigan Avenue in Chicago. Despite its origin as a private initiative, the exhibit garnered official support from several sources. First, Prytz was president of the Norwegian Applied Art Association, a fact that signaled endorsement by the Norwegian design community. Second, governmental agencies, including the Norwegian Export Council and the Royal Norwegian Foreign Ministry, also backed the exhibit, conferring strong political support.[43] And the Norwegians vanquished any doubts about their intentions by selecting none other than the social democrat prime minister, Einar Gerhardsen, to open the show.[44]

Ninety manufacturers and craftspeople were represented, all of whom exemplified, according to Tannum, the modern, new Scandinavian design characterized by "light colors, an honest use of material, and simple practical lines."[45] The rhetoric of this show surpassed the usual vocabulary for describing Scandinavian design: honest, natural materials, supreme usability, and elegant forms. The show's organizers also communicated the country's egalitarian values; the objects in the show were meant to convey Scandinavian social-democratic traditions.[46] Arne Remlov had observed instances of Americans trying to reduce Scandinavian design to style; in his opinion, this was equivalent to mannerism.[47] So, the Norwegian mediators deemed it crucial to emphasize that the designs on show were based on ideology, not style. After all, to be credible, Scandinavian design needed an identity that was distinct from the disputed American formalism.

Chicago was chosen for several reasons. It was a strategic commercial center for the Midwest. The region was home to a vast population of Scandinavian descent. And it was an intellectual center, home to the

IIT Institute of Design, among other design schools and universities. With its comparatively high prices and limited production volumes, Scandinavian design in the U.S. targeted primarily upper-middle-class intellectuals. A commercially motivated initiative, the exhibit sought to test the U.S. market's interest in Norwegian design; it was, in a sense, a feasibility study of the market for regularly organized exports.

Arne Korsmo and a former student, designer Birger Dahl, designed the exhibit. In hindsight, Korsmo reported that he had enjoyed the challenge—but that he would rather have seen the objects subjected to jury selection. Korsmo went so far as to quote his new friend and mentor Charles Eames, who said that the large quantity of objects on display obscured the aesthetic quality of the products.[48] Korsmo's wife and sometime collaborator, Grete, was represented at the Chicago exhibit, and their acquaintance, Edgar Kaufmann, Jr., subsequently invited her to exhibit one of her silver platters at a MoMA *Good Design* show.[49] With its reported 10,000 visitors—Eames and Kaufmann among them—*Norway Designs for Living* seems to have made the impression it intended, mediating Norwegian design to an upscale American public.

It was an optimistic venture, and an ambitious one. Rather than risk fading from the public's memory, the exhibit was converted into a permanent business called Norway Designs A/S, with seventy-eight companies as shareholders. In December of 1951, Tannum had accepted an order for 8,000 chairs from a U.S. furniture wholesaler. No Norwegian manufacturer had the capacity—even via inter-company collaboration—to meet such a huge order, and it had to be canceled.[50] Due to financial problems, Tannum was forced to shutter its Chicago shop a few years later. This exemplifies the problem faced by the Norwegian consumer-goods industry throughout the 1950s. In trying to establish viable export schemes, the Norwegians discovered that the most lucrative market of them all, the United States, was simply too big. *Norway Designs for Living* failed to generate substantial Norwegian export revenue. But the initiative represents an interesting early attempt to piggyback on the growing popularity of Swedish and Danish design in the U.S. at the time.[51]

Of the institutions and events that promoted Nordic design internationally in the 1950s, many highlighted the Scandinavian dimension rather than the individual national identities. Unquestionably, the most celebrated of them all was *Design in Scandinavia—An Exhibition of Objects for the Home*, which toured the U.S. and Canada from 1954 to 1957. The exhibit toured approximately thirty venues and attracted more than 650,000 visitors.[52] As we will see, the Norwegian contribution reveals how its creators across Nordic nationalities sought to portray a curated cultural image of Scandinavian design in America.

In the fall of 1953, an article by Torolf Prytz in *Bonytt* announced the forthcoming pan-Nordic campaign in North America. Prytz framed this opportunity in terms of export possibilities—despite the fact that his organization's primary responsibilities were domestic, not international.[53] Given its limited financial resources, the association required full financing for the project by the host museums in America—even before planning could begin with the Nordic governments.[54] The Scandinavian organizing committee was comprised of national subcommittees. The Norwegian committee consisted of Torolf Prytz, Arne Remlov, and Ferdinand Aars, secretary general of the Norwegian Applied Art Association and a member of *Bonytt*'s editorial committee.[55] Remlov was also entrusted with the task of editing the exhibit catalog.[56] The inclusion of these three high-profile representatives signals that the Norwegian contribution to *Design in Scandinavia* expressed the official attitudes and ideology of that country's design community.

The goal was clear: the chieftains of the Norwegian applied-art movement were to present modern Norwegian "craft, industrial art, and industrial design."[57] The catalog's introductory text, which was written by Swedish art historian Gotthard Johansson, was accompanied by three photos from each of the four participating nations—Sweden, Denmark, Norway, and Finland. Of the three photos, one image portrayed a typical national landscape; one depicted an iconic building type; and one image showed an interior meant to convey the country's design culture. For the landscape shot, Norway was represented by a photo of a fjord surrounded by steep, snow-clad mountains. For the building shot, they used a large, traditional, wood-paneled Oslo house. But the interior chosen to represent Norway was of a completely different nature. The seating in the photo consisted of a settee and an easy chair of light, organic forms; bright colors; and unconventional construction, designed by Torbjørn Afdahl and manufactured by Sandvik & Co. These were accompanied by a glass table with steel legs, designed and executed as a prototype by Cato Mansrud.[58] Intriguingly, neither Afdahl nor Sandvik & Co. feature in the catalog's list of exhibitors, while Mansrud does. In other words, the industrially manufactured settee and easy chair were not part of the exhibit, despite having been chosen to represent Norwegian design in the catalog's introduction. Mansrud's name, on the other hand, was on the list—as both designer and manufacturer.[59]

Settee and easy-chair designed by Torbjørn
Afdahl, manufacturer: Sandvik & Co., Håvoll, Norway. Rya-Rug designed by Knut
Rumohr, executed by Anne-Lise Knudtzon,
Oslo. Table designed by Cato Mansrud, Oslo.

Figure 6.4 The Nordic countries promoted their design internationally. Perhaps the most celebrated event: *Design in Scandinavia—An Exhibition of Objects for the Home*, which toured the U.S. and Canada from 1954 to 1957. Featured here: the illustration of a Norwegian interior included in the introduction to the exhibit catalog.

This example underscores the fact that industrial-design and mass-produced objects were sorely underrepresented in the Norwegian committee's selection—despite the stated goal to include "craft, industrial art, and industrial design."[60] A possible key to understanding this bias can be found in a request by Prytz, a request made in connection with the 1953 presentation of the planned exhibit: "All of our designers and companies [must] make an effort to create good things.... [The exhibition] should and must be a stimulus for manufacturers and artists."[61] Notice how Prytz implies that the exhibit would not be a collection of products easily available to the broader public—it would not be "democratic" industrial design, that is. Rather, it was intended to showcase elite objects of supreme artistic quality. So, in addition to the large proportion of craft objects in the selection, the industrial manufacturers' products were, for the most part, commercially insignificant. They were interesting mainly artistically—and likely to garner attention for the company from that perspective. Prytz's justification for the association's involvement in the project—that it would promote exports—seems rather dubious. Judging by the products on show, the selection criteria had very little to do with the products' export potential. But, in mediating Norwegian design abroad, Prytz and his cohorts invoked commercial arguments as a pretext for creating good will toward Scandinavian design abroad.

Indeed, the Norwegian committee's selection criteria for *Design in Scandinavia* reveal an ideology that prizes art over commerce. But, importantly, this elitism was neither practiced nor preached rigorously on the domestic scene. Far from it: Prytz proclaimed his concern that "[m]any applied artists [*brukskunstnere*] throw around the word art [*kunst*] to describe their profession." This was unhealthy, he said, because the applied-art community needed "the collaboration with both industry and with studio craft, perhaps especially with industry."[62] His insistence on the growing importance of the industrial production of consumer goods indicates a marginally increased acceptance of industrial manufacturing. But Prytz was far from romantic in his embrace of mass production. The notion still prevails of the designer as domesticator, the cultivator of uncivilized, savage machines: "Machines are, after all, severely limited creatures, even when a creative, imaginative mind knows how to exploit them." Prytz ended his manifesto with a tellingly visionary appeal: "In time, [industry must] allow the leading designers to have a place in its organization alongside research directors, production managers, and sales managers."[63] "Just as they do in the United States," he might well have added.

Conclusion

This chapter has explored how European and American design cultures engaged each other in the 1950s. We have seen how, in this most American of decades, American industrial design was both loved and hated by Europeans. Using Norway and Scandinavia as case studies, we have observed how both personal and institutional bonds were forged, facilitating a rich but challenging transatlantic design dialogue. For European design communities, the early postwar period offered a close encounter with American material culture in all its many forms.

American design, from the pedestrian to the pretentious, was met with both keen interest and ambivalence. At the same time, Scandinavian design was engaged in a counterstrike. Proponents of "good design" mediated a deliberately constructed version of Scandinavian design culture in the United States. Through this exchange, new design cultures and consumption regimes emerged in Europe. Design elites in the U.S. were eager to prove that American material culture had more to offer than just Juicy Fruit chewing gum and Rock-Ola jukeboxes. Meanwhile, the Nordic applied-art associations were struggling to adjust to new developments in the practice of design and in consumer culture. Europe's pioneering industrial design professionals were striving to prove their worth as masters of a design culture that often resonated more in America than in Europe—technologically and sociologically.

The young Bjørneboe's ambivalence toward the United States, cited in the introduction to this chapter, eventually became a political crusade. This is best expressed in his 1966 essay, "We Who Loved America" ("Vi som elsket Amerika"):

> The title of this article is not ironic. I myself belong to those who have truly loved America, and I know how it feels....America was the land of dreams, freedom, opportunities, and adventure....I cannot say exactly when it was, but one day I realized I no longer loved the U.S.A. It must have been at the beginning of the 1950s. America had become dangerous, frightening, scary. It represented conformity, corruption, violence, the world's strongest military, and it aspired to become the world ruler.[64]

Bjørneboe's shift in attitude toward the United States in the 1960s may indicate a broader development. To cultural radicals in Europe, the United States and the military power and hedonistic consumption it represented became a projection screen for all that was wrong with contemporary society. Design discourse was deeply affected by this change of heart. Diminished were the fears of American mass production; disdain for the U.S. styling extravaganza; and desires for American consumer goods and lifestyles. All of this yielded to a growing concern with issues such as ecology, sustainability, and social responsibility. The 1950s represented a period in which transatlantic design dialogue was at a high point. These were conversations rife with contrasts and contradictions, ambivalences, ambiguities—tensions that, arguably, have since been mitigated. As design critic Arthur Hald wrote in 1953, reflecting on his own mixed feelings toward American design: "But in the confrontation between one's own prejudices and ideals and those one encounters lies perhaps the beginning of an understanding."[65]

Notes

1. Jens Bjørneboe, "Frykten for Amerika i oss," *Spektrum* 5–6 (1952): 373. Reprinted in Jens Bjørneboe, *Norge, mitt Norge: Essays om formyndermennesket* (Oslo: Pax, 1968), 213–22.
2. Victoria de Grazia, *Irresistible Empire: America's Advance through Twentieth-Century Europe* (Cambridge, MA: Belknap Press of Harvard University Press, 2005).
3. Adrian Horn, *Juke Box Britain: Americanisation and Youth Culture, 1945–60* (Manchester: Manchester University Press, 2009); Siv Ringdal, *Det amerikanske Lista: Med 110 volt i huset* (Oslo: Pax, 2002).
4. Thomas Hine, *Populuxe* (New York: Alfred A. Knopf, 1986).
5. Hugo Lindström, "Min tid med Ralph Lysell og Alvar Lenning," in *Svensk industridesign: En 1900-talshistoria*, ed. Lasse Brunnström (Stockholm: Prisma, 1997), 86–103.
6. They also met, for example, Frank Lloyd Wright, Louis Kahn, Alexander Girard, Ludwig Mies van der Rohe, and Walter Gropius. Grete Prytz Kittelsen interviewed in Karianne Bjellås Gilje, ed., *Grete Prytz Kittelsen: Emalje og design* (Oslo: Gyldendal, 2007), 57.
7. Åke H. Huldt, "Industrial Design," in *Nordenfjeldske kunstindustrimuseum— Årbok 1951*, ed. Thorvald Krohn-Hansen (Trondheim: Nordenfjeldske kunstindustrimuseum, 1952), 51.
8. Nina Berre, "Fysiske idealer i norsk arkitekturutdanning 1945–1970" (PhD diss., Norwegian University of Science and Technology, 2002), 154.
9. Arne Korsmo, "Formgivningens A.B.C.," *Bonytt*, January 1951, 16.
10. Odd Brochmann, "Form—filologi," *Bonytt*, January 1951, 17.
11. Odd Brochmann , *Rent Bord: En historie om funksjonalismen og funksjonalistene i Norge* (Oslo: Arkitektnytt, 1987), 41–7.
12. Odd Brochmann, "Brukskunst for folket," *Bonytt* 20 (1960): 41–3.
13. Finn Juhl, "Den 'riktige' form," *Bonytt*, January 1950, 5.
14. Ibid., 4–7.
15. Knut Greve, "Eksperiment eller tradisjon," *Bonytt*, January 1950, 17.
16. Arthur Hald, "Om Amerikansk Form," *Form* 10 (1953), 221.
17. Håkon Stenstadvold, "Nederlag," *Bonytt*, March 1949, 55.
18. Greve, "Eksperiment eller tradisjon," 16.
19. Ibid., 17.
20. Ibid.
21. Huldt, "Industrial Design," 54–6.
22. Jens von der Lippe, "Wilhelm Kåge: Kunstner og håndverker i en storbedrift," *Bonytt*, April 1954, 70.
23. Arne Remlov, "Blir designeren hørt?" *Bonytt*, June 1954, 102.
24. Torbjørn Rygh, "En møbeltegners syn," *Bonytt*, September 1954, 154.
25. Kjetil Fallan, "How an Excavator Got Aesthetic Pretensions: Negotiating Design in 1960s' Norway," *Journal of Design History* 20 (2007): 44.

26. For a case study exploring this issue, see Kjetil Fallan, "The *Realpolitik* of the Artificial: Strategic Design at Figgjo Fajanse Facing International Free Trade in the 1960s," *Enterprise and Society* 10 (2009): 559–89.
27. Richard Pells, *Not Like Us: How Europeans Have Loved, Hated, and Transformed American Culture since World War II* (New York: Basic Books, 1997), 84; Greg Castillo, *Cold War on the Home Front: The Soft Power of Midcentury Design* (Minneapolis: University of Minnesota Press, 2010), 118.
28. During the 1950s, at the request of various U.S. government agencies, MoMA organized several design exhibits that would tour Europe. For more information on some of these examples, see Gay McDonald, "Selling the American Dream: MoMA, Industrial Design and Post-War France," *Journal of Design History* 17 (2004): 397–412; Gay McDonald, "The 'Advance' of American Postwar Design in Europe: MoMA and the *Design for Use, USA* Exhibition 1951–1953," *Design Issues* 24 (2008): 15–27.
29. Edgar Kaufmann, Jr., "Moderne formgivning i De Forenede Stater," in *Amerikansk form: En samling håndverks- og industrivarer sammenstillet av Museum of Modern Art, New York* (Oslo: Foreningen brukskunst, 1954), 5–8.
30. Jens von der Lippe, "Amerikansk virksomhet," *Bonytt*, April 1954, 66.
31. Ibid., 65.
32. Thorbjørn Rygh, "'Amerikansk Form,'" in *Nordenfjeldske kunstindustrimuseum—Årbok 1953*, ed. Thorvald Krohn-Hansen (Trondheim: Nordenfjeldske kunstindustrimuseum, 1954), 14. The same denunciation of streamlining was later made by Ferdinand Aars in an English-language booklet promoting Norwegian design published by the Royal Norwegian Ministry of Foreign Affairs' Office of Cultural Relations. Ferdinand Aars, *Arts and Crafts—Industrial Design in Norway* (Oslo: The Royal Norwegian Ministry of Foreign Affairs, 1957), 7.
33. Gay McDonald, "The Modern American Home as Soft Power: Finland, MoMA and the 'American Home 1953' Exhibition," *Journal of Design History* 23 (2010): 387–408.
34. Alberto Rosselli, "Incontro alla realtá," *Stile Industria* 3 (March 1955): 1–2. See also Kjetil Fallan, "Heresy and Heroics: The Debate on the Alleged 'Crisis' in Italian Design around 1960," *Modern Italy* 14 (2009): 261.
35. Alec Davies, "Editorial," *Design* 42 (December 1952): 2.
36. Patrick Maguire, "Craft Capitalism and the Projection of British Industry in the 1950s and 1960s," *Journal of Design History* 6 (1993): 101.
37. Edgar Kaufmann, Jr., "Borax, or the Chromium-Plated Calf," *Architectural Review*, August 1948, 88–92.
38. Jeffrey L. Meikle, *Design in the USA* (Oxford: Oxford University Press, 2005), 138–73.
39. Joy Parr, *Domestic Goods: The Material, the Moral, and the Economic in the Postwar Years* (Toronto: University of Toronto Press, 1999).
40. Claire Catterall, "Perceptions of Plastics: A Study of Plastics in Britain, 1945–1956," in *The Plastics Age: From Bakelite to Beanbags and Beyond*, ed. Penny Sparke (Woodstock, NY: Overlook Press, 1993), 67–73.
41. Greve, "Eksperiment eller tradisjon," 17.
42. Liv Ramskjær, "Users and Producers of Plastics in Post-World War II Norway: Building a New Industry Through Transfer of Technology," *Comparative Technology Transfer and Society* 3 (2005): 76–102; Liv Ramskjær, "Plast i det

moderne Norge: Introduksjon, gjennombrudd og spredning av plastprodukter i Norge 1930-1974," in *Volund 1999-2000: Plast i det moderne Norge*, ed. Frode Weium (Oslo: NTM, 2001), 162-80.
43. Per Tannum, "Norway Designs for Living," *Bonytt*, April-May 1951, 64.
44. Widar Halén, "Korpusdesigneren," in *Grete Prytz Kittelsen*, 78.
45. Tannum, "Norway Designs for Living," 64.
46. Bernt Heiberg, "The Norwegian Public and Industrial Design," *Bonytt*, April-May 1951, 73.
47. Arne Remlov, "Norwegian Modern," *Bonytt*, April-May 1951, 77.
48. Arne Korsmo, "Norsk brukskunst i Chicago," *Bonytt*, December 1951, 210.
49. Halén, "Korpusdesigneren," 80.
50. Wenche Anette Johannessen, "Brukskunst-senteret PLUS: Per Tannums ønske om å etablere et designsentrum" (MPhil thesis, University of Oslo, 2000), 13-4.
51. An engaging account of the success of Danish furniture in the U.S. during this period can be found in: Per H. Hansen, "Networks, Narratives, and New Markets: The Rise and Decline of Danish Modern Furniture Design, 1930-1970," *Business History Review* 80 (2006): 449-83.
52. Ingeborg Glambek, *Det Nordiske i arkitektur og design—sett utenfra* (Oslo: Arkitektens forlag & Norsk arkitekturforlag, 1997), 117-35.
53. Torolf Prytz, "Brukskunsts under utstilling," *Bonytt*, April 1953, 78.
54. Arne Remlov, "'Design in Scandinavia,'" *Bonytt*, February 1954, 29.
55 Arne Remlov, ed., *Design in Scandinavia: An Exhibition of Objects for the Home* (Oslo: Kirstes, 1954), 5.
56. Remlov, "'Design in Scandinavia,'" 31.
57. Ibid., 29.
58. Remlov, ed., *Design in Scandinavia*, 27.
59. Ibid., 116-19.
60. Idem, "'Design in Scandinavia,'" 29.
61. Prytz, "Brukskunsts under utstilling," 78.
62. Ibid.
63. Ibid.
64. Jens Bjørneboe, "Vi som elsket Amerika," *Orientering*, 1966. Reprinted in Jens Bjørneboe, *Vi som elsket Amerika: Essays om stormaktsgalskap, straffelyst, kunst og moral* (Oslo: Pax, 1970), 22-3.
65. Hald, "Om Amerikansk Form," 217.

7
Confronting the Lure of American Tourism: Modern Accommodation in the Netherlands

Adri A. Albert de la Bruhèze

After the Second World War, the United States played an active, direct role in Europe's recovery and integration. The effort to modernize the European tourism industry—including its physical infrastructures—became a cornerstone of U.S. postwar foreign policy. The American goal was to create a single, open European market and a "modern consumer society." This was to counter the perceived communist and socialist threats. The plan was for European leisure patterns to resemble—if not mimic—the "American way of leisure." By the late 1940s, this American consumption regime was clearly defined, characterized by individual freedom; car mobility; national and transnational highways; roadside hotels and restaurants; open borders; and open skies.

As part of the plan, U.S. officials targeted American tourism to Europe; this was one way to help close the "dollar gap" between the United States and European countries. In the words of one high-ranking U.S. official, American tourism provided "a speedy, direct, supplementary means of injecting dollars into the economy of Western Europe."[1] Using the framework of the Marshall Plan (European Recovery Program), U.S. officials made it a priority to modernize the European hotel industry.[2] The European reaction was ambivalent. On one hand, European officials welcomed aid—financial assistance in particular—from the U.S. On the other hand, Western European countries resisted U.S. policy in favor of finding their own way of managing consumption. Both sides were invested in the transition from the bourgeois tourism of the prewar period to the changed consumption patterns of the postwar time. In Europe, reconstruction included the process of creating national welfare states.[3] And, according to European official thinking, an inevitable outcome of this modern welfare society would be mass tourism—a future social problem that required state-led guidance and control.[4]

U.S. and European tourism policies may have shared a focus on middle-class mass tourism, but their overall approaches differed widely. The U.S. policies emphasized individual consumption, and private enterprise took center stage; this was free-market-driven production and consumption of leisure products and services. State policies actively promoted and supported this approach, as did popular-culture industries as well as U.S. travel and tourism industries, notably the American Express Company, Hilton Hotels International, and Trans World Airlines. Together, private market interests and U.S. foreign-policy goals constituted a powerful package deal.[5] In contrast to the American way, European countries focused on collective and individual consumption that was guided and controlled by the nation-state. It was the nation-state that would speak and act on behalf of consumers and producers, the nation-state that would arrange "responsible" leisure for all citizens.

In analyzing the divergent attitudes toward consumption, Victoria de Grazia describes the American consumption regime as Fordist.[6] In the context of this volume, a Fordist tourism regime is defined by four features. First, it requires large, open markets. Second, it is a standardized, tradable commodity—with highly standardized services designed for a standardized, middle-class tourist. Third, the regime is produced efficiently via uniform methods by a network of private corporations. And fourth, the state as well as non-governmental organizations support the regime with their policies.

According to de Grazia, the prospect of U.S. tourism bridging the dollar gap between the United States and Europe accelerated the "Americanization" of Europe. De Grazia argues that the United States, as a postwar world power, imposed its Fordist consumption regime on Europe.[7] In this chapter, using the Netherlands as a case study in European tourism, I refute de Grazia's claim. Here, I reframe how the Dutch reinterpreted the promises and challenges of the American tourism regime. I argue that, by focusing on the design of new, "modern" tourist accommodation, the Dutch reinterpretation was a complex, dynamic process that involved many actors, many variables. Far from reproducing the American approach to tourism in the Netherlands, Dutch actors reworked, redesigned, and selectively appropriated elements—including management principles—of "the American way of leisure."

Tourist Accommodation for the Working Class: Camping Centers and Holiday Villages

The history of Dutch consumption and leisure is a history of patronage. The role of the patron materialized in cultural and social relationships. From 1850 to 1945, patrons emerged from civil society; from 1945 to 1990, patrons were embodied by state actors. Given that cultural and political elites defined leisure as a social problem, this top-down guidance was considered a necessity. Specifically, elites viewed "the masses" as unable to cope with their increasing leisure time; the fear was that "the masses" would develop immoral, disorderly behavior.[8] To prevent this, patrons linked leisure activities to education, culture, and nature. Initially, both religious and secular civil-society organizations—the secular Royal Dutch Touring Club (Algemene Nederlandse Wielrijdersbond or ANWB) among them—managed this moral responsibility.

At first, the mediation of Dutch leisure and tourism was an open-ended affair. Neither the state nor the marketplace took particular interest; no party intervened systematically. Leisure and tourism were unregulated and negotiations informal. These circumstances provided civil-society organizations (religious and secular) with a social mandate and an area of expertise to claim their own. In speaking and acting on behalf of the leisure sector and leisure consumers, the self-appointed spokespeople articulated social and cultural values—and aligned those values with user requirements. It was these spokespeople in civil-society organizations who negotiated the form and function of Dutch leisure and tourism. They based their model of leisure and tourism on principles that were at once moralistic, patronizing, and elitist. Elevating the lower classes—educating and protecting them: these were the goals. Interactions and power relationships between the national state, the market, and civil society contributed to shaping Dutch tourism.[9]

After the Second World War, this became clear with the emergence of the powerful state, which gradually took over from civil-society organizations. This harmonized with the postwar mentality of mass tourism as a crucial feature of the modern social welfare state. A new, academically trained professional elite within the government emerged as the new intermediaries. These elites became the keepers of this modern social problem. For example, the Government Planning Service (Rijksdienst voor het Nationale Plan) was charged with the spatial planning of Dutch mass tourism. The task fell to them as planners of the Netherlands' limited available space (most of which was already designated for future housing, industry, and agriculture).[10] In this postwar context, the Dutch acted like many other European welfare states, using social planning as the guiding principle in construction projects. And it was state institutions like the Government Planning Service—alongside technical experts and other professionals—that acted as the newly self-appointed spokespeople for consumers; it was primarily the state that negotiated the design of Dutch tourism.[11] And these new spokespeople adopted the existing tourism regime that condescended to "the masses"—although these new actors used more technocratic, neutral- and objective-sounding language and different methods to achieve their aims.[12]

Almost all of the planners agreed on the projected shortage of appropriate accommodation for Dutch mass tourism; the design and construction of new tourist accommodation became the priority.[13] To determine needs, planners divided consumers and their accommodation requirement into two main categories: working-class tourists and middle-class tourists. The working-class subcategories were: families with young children, childless couples, and couples with married or older children. The middle-class subcategories were: "tourists with more money to spend" and "car owners traveling with a tent, caravan, or tent trailer." Working-class tourists were the focus, given the attitude that they were most in need of guided, "responsible leisure." Middle-class tourists who owned cars and traveled with tents, caravans, or tent-trailers received little attention. This was due, in part, to the absence of policy on private-car mobility. From 1945 to 1965, planners postponed building car infrastructure, giving priority instead to industrial reconstruction and social-housing programs.[14] It was accommodation for the working class—who traveled by bicycle, motorcycle, train, or bus—that generated concern. Working-class families with young children received particular attention, labeled, as they were, the "most difficult category." For this group, the ANWB and the Government Planning Service proposed to build camping centers and holiday villages consisting of simple sleeping huts or small summerhouses. Communal dining and relaxation facilities would enable collective, organized, "responsible leisure activities."[15]

While Dutch-tourism policymakers focused on working-class tourists who traveled mainly by bicycle and public transportation, the U.S. Marshall Aid emphasized car-dominated middle-class tourism.[16] But, the Marshall Plan made a provision for tourism that averted this potential policy clash. In 1948, European countries were informed that the U.S. Marshall Aid would also be used for the modernization of European tourism; this was to increase U.S. leisure travel to Europe.

The American funding would be available to build and reconstruct hotels that met "U.S. standards."[17] European nations responded to the promise of hotels as a way to attract growing numbers of U.S. tourists, who would, indeed, increase the dollar revenues of Europe's dollar-hungry nations. According to estimates made by the Economic Cooperation Agency (ECA)—the U.S. government's administration center for the Marshall Plan in Europe—by 1952, 500,000 Americans were expected to visit Europe annually; they would spend between $200 million and $250 million annually.[18]

Dutch policymakers interpreted this promise of a U.S.-dollar bonanza in different ways; controversy erupted over the accurate definition of modern leisure and the concept of "Dutch" leisure. Policymakers also debated the parameters of appropriate tourist accommodation; who the tourist really was; and what that tourist really wanted. Civil-society actors like the tourist organization ANWB discussed American influences in cultural and moral terms. Meanwhile, state actors discussed Marshall Plan policies in mostly economic terms. Corporate actors, like the Dutch hotel and catering industry, began to assess the possible ramifications for their trade. Large travel and tourism companies with international interests, including the Holland America Line and Royal Dutch Airlines (KLM), saw Marshall Plan policies primarily as opportunities to expand their markets.

For the Dutch government, the influx of foreign currency—the closing of the dollar gap—was a key issue. One opportunity to boost dollar revenues arose in the late 1940s, when the Dutch Ministry of Reconstruction and Housing approved construction of a British "Butlins" holiday camp—initially for British "lower-class" tourists—in the coastal town of Zandvoort, the Netherlands. This announcement fuelled fierce reactions: Dutch tourist organizations associated Butlins camps with commercial, large-scale, organized amusement, which was considered "irresponsible" and an expression of "bad taste." Further, almost all of these negative features were deemed "American." For example, the ANWB painted the Butlins holiday camps as "American forms of amusement," dismissing them as "massive and passive" and as the result of "shameless exploitation"—in short, as "un-Dutch." According to one ANWB official, the Butlins company even resembled the German National Socialist Strength-Through-Joy movement (*Kraft durch Freude*) in its methods.[19] The Dutch hotel and catering industry viewed the Butlins concept of commercial, commodified leisure as a form of "Americanism" that would "promote a mechanization of free time," and that would "destroy every individual initiative, every free activity, and every creative ability in man."[20]

Figure 7.1 Dutch tourist organizations frowned on the "American leisure activities" sponsored by British-run Butlins holiday camps, featured in this photo. The Dutch feared these activities would encourage "irresponsible and disorderly behavior" on the part of working-class tourists.

The Butlins plans stirred social controversy in virtually every imaginable context—from women's organizations to youth organizations to tourist organizations; and from the hotel and catering industry to clerical organizations and the press. To end the controversy—and to conform to the social-housing priority that dominated postwar reconstruction—the plans were canceled.[21] Moreover, U.S. Marshall Plan officials voiced another important reason to cancel the project: it represented organized "massive working-class tourism" which, they argued, did not meet the standards of American middle-class tourism.

In the late 1940s, the Dutch tourism actors concurred that working-class tourism should not be "Americanized." In their view, Dutch working-class tourists should not be exposed to negative—large-scale, commercial, and hedonistic—forms of tourism stamped "U.S. culture." This consensus dovetailed with the traditionally patronizing stance toward Dutch consumption and leisure: the lower classes could not cope with their increasing leisure time, vulnerable as they were to "stimuli" that sparked hedonistic, immoral, and disorderly behavior.

The U.S.-funded "Marshall hotels"—built for middle-class American and European tourists—would also be contested in the late 1940s and early 1950s. This controversy would make for fraught interactions, at times, between state organizations; the traditionally small-scale hotel and catering industry; and large travel and tourism companies with transnational interests.

Tourist Accommodation for the Middle Class: Marshall Hotels

In the Netherlands, the Marshall Plan's "tourism aid" message spread quickly via the American Business Club, the U.S. embassy, and the American Express Company.[22] In March of 1949, the Dutch government considered spending 15 million guilders (approximately $5.6 million) of its "counter-value" Marshall Plan budget on the reconstruction and building of "modern" hotels. This was expected to generate approximately 700 new "international" hotel beds.[23] Reactions came from the Dutch hotel and catering industry—notably, its trade organization, HORECAF (referred to here as the Dutch Hotel Association), comprised mainly of small and medium-sized family-owned Dutch hotels. The Dutch Hotel Association asserted that Marshall Plan money should be spent on reconstructing and modernizing existing hotels—instead of building large-scale new ones.[24]

In June of 1949, the Dutch government announced that it would be spending 7 million guilders (approximately $2.6 million) of Marshall Plan money to modernize the Dutch hotel industry.[25] Upon hearing this news, the Dutch Hotel Association voiced its fear of the government investing in large-scale "dollar-earning hotels." Their concern was that the accommodations would serve only American tourists and large, international travel and tourism corporations. Dutch tourists and the entire Dutch hotel industry would be left out, they feared. This concern was justified. Indeed, the government evaluated the planned hotels based on what they added to existing tourist accommodations; on how appropriately they addressed the demands of American mass tourism; and on how they proposed to increase the volume of U.S. tourists and dollar revenues for the national economy.[26] The Dutch Hotel Association's fears materialized in the form of a list: the preliminary group of Dutch "Marshall hotels" consisted mainly of large international hotels located in cities, like Amsterdam, that attracted the most foreign tourists.[27] The large Dutch travel and tourism companies applauded this policy. According to W.H. De Monchy, managing director of the Holland America Line, immediate measures were required if American tourists were to be guaranteed appropriate accommodation. This was vital to making the Netherlands more attractive to American tourists.[28]

Who were these American tourists, and what were their demands? In the summer of 1949, an American official voiced the answers at a press conference in the Hague. Theo J. Pozzy was head of the U.S. Travel Development Section at the ECA; he defined the American tourist as a middle-class American looking for non-luxurious, middle-class accommodation furnished with "appropriate sanitary equipment" and providing "appropriate services." To illustrate his point, Pozzy recommended the Statler and Hilton hotels as American examples to follow. These hotels had been successfully standardized—from their planning to their construction and layout to their room design and general interior design. This created economies of scale—including sustainably low room prices. It was these hotels that set the standard for modern American hotel architecture, however contested. The design was functional, with unadorned façades, rectilinear interiors, and a great deal of

Figure 7.2 The American hotel represented a decidedly modernist blueprint, which became controversial in Europe: each country had its own hotel traditions, standards, and architecture. Pictured here: a quintessentially American Statler Hotel room of the 1930s, complete with studio bed.

glass.²⁹ Pozzy's examples and recommendations betrayed his—and the ECA's—modernist bias. The image of America he offered was a decidedly modernist blueprint—a blueprint for a future European consumer and tourism society. In Europe, this image was to become controversial: European countries had developed their own hotel traditions, hotel standards, and hotel architecture.

During a meeting in July of 1949, Pozzy discussed the hotel issue with the Dutch Secretary of Economic Affairs, Van den Brink. Pozzy offered U.S. technical assistance in modernizing the Dutch hotel industry—to catch up with American developments. Minister Van den Brink appreciated the offer, claiming it would be "nonsensical if we did not benefit from technical progress realized elsewhere."³⁰ Well-acquainted with modern yet controversial American hotel architecture, Van den Brink challenged the alleged Dutch backwardness. Reacting against the standardized, contemporary U.S. hotel architecture, Van den Brink emphasized the importance of "Dutchness," defined as the "Dutch character" of hotels, evident in their exterior appearance and interior furnishings.³¹ On the matter of Dutchness, Van den Brink found an ally in Dr. Hirschfeld, the government commissioner for the European Recovery Plan at the Dutch Ministry of Foreign Affairs. Hirschfeld saw American hotels as substantially more practical and modern than Dutch accommodations—especially regarding sanitary equipment and service; despite this view, he did not advocate that the Dutch copy all American developments. Similarly, Hirschfeld believed that the Dutch hotel industry could benefit from U.S. technical assistance in many areas. At the same time, he preached preservation of the domestic architecture's "Dutch character"—a modern, world-renowned architectural heritage. In order to explore the possibilities of combining modern Dutch and American hotel features, Hirschfeld advised Minister Van den Brink to send a study group to the United States—and to draft a Dutch hotel plan as soon as possible.³²

The ECA representatives considered Van den Brink and Hirschfeld's remarks. In July 1949, Clarence Hunter, the chief of the ECA Mission to the Netherlands wrote to Hirschfeld. Hunter stated that he and Pozzy had not intended to convey "that the American designer is superior to all others," but that "the opportunity is here to benefit by our latest experience in this field and it was sincerely with this in mind that technical assistance was suggested." Hunter added that he wanted to "concur with Mr. Pozzy that we do not wish to force the 'American way' on interior decorations, but from the view of modern comfort, to which the traveling world has become accustomed, we can, I feel, make a valuable contribution in layout planning." According to Hunter, this and other U.S. assistance could "speed the Netherlands in securing their greatest possible share in the rapidly increasing dollar tourism anticipated for Europe."[33]

To his own staff, Minister Van den Brink admitted that Dutch hotels indeed fell short quantitatively and qualitatively of meeting American tourists' needs—and in securing substantial dollar revenues, as a result. And he continued to oppose the idea of equating the modernization of Dutch hotels with meeting American demands. The minister predicted that the Dutch hotel industry, still comparatively small, would fear and resist unfair competition from the large-scale, modern "Marshall hotels."[34]

Van den Brink's prediction materialized; the promised bonanza of American tourists and dollar revenues became a contested issue. Some parties promoted the idea of building new, modern hotels to attract American tourists. These promoters included the Dutch government, large Dutch travel and tourism companies, and the Netherlands National Tourist Office (Algemene Nederlandse Vereniging voor Vreemdelingen Verkeer). But the Dutch Hotel Association was skeptical about the "American promise." Members of the association claimed that to rely on U.S. tourism was to make the Dutch hotel and catering industry dependent and vulnerable. The association members suggested domestic tourism as an alternative. This implied their agreement with the ANWB and the Government Planning Service: all preferred to see more accommodations that catered to Dutch tourists. This meant adding more of the medium-sized hotels that were less expensive and relatively simple, though providing "complete Dutch care."[35] To support their argument, the association underscored the idea that American tourists would visit the Netherlands only during a few weeks in summer; this would cause room vacancies as well as other operational and commercial problems. So, building new *American*-style hotels would not be a profitable investment, the Dutch Hotel Association claimed.[36]

In June of 1950, the Dutch Hotel Association's chairman, J.G. Meyer, publicly stated that the Dutch hotel sector did not need "big American-style hotel palaces" and that the unique, "cozy" character of small-scale Dutch hotels must be preserved. According to Meyer, every hotel should provide the highest-level service possible—without allowing themselves to be dictated to by the (impossible) demands of "the spoiled Americans."[37]

Powerful Dutch stakeholders with transnational interests challenged this position. The Holland America Line and KLM, for example, had vested interests in providing transatlantic transportation to American tourists. These companies pressured the government constantly to build new, large-scale modern hotels. This was to attract and accommodate increasing numbers of foreign tourists, Americans in particular. In 1951 and 1952, the Holland America Line launched two new passenger ships: the *Rijndam* and the *Maasdam*. According to the company's managing director, De Monchy, the vessels were specially designed to "serve mass tourism that will determine the future." Further, KLM's general director, Albert Plesman, opined that the Dutch hotel and catering industry should be grateful to the Holland America Line and KLM for providing so many foreign customers. During a Dutch Hotel Association conference in November of 1950, Plesman openly criticized the association's "conservative" attitude. For the offense of opposing the construction of modern, U.S.-inspired hotels, Plesman told association members, "You should get your ears boxed. You do not see the importance of the future that I have an interest in."[38]

Dutch and European Hotel Developments

In December of 1949, the U.S. technical-assistance program was well under way; the Tourism Committee of the Organisation for European Economic Cooperation (OEEC) decided to send several study groups to the United States to learn more about American hotel equipment, construction, and administration as well as hotel management, and services.[39] The Dutch government had a specific request of the committee members, all of whom represented the Dutch hotel and catering industry.[40] They were to study the construction and the organization of medium-sized hotels. This translated to accommodations of no more than 300 beds, therefore comparable to large Dutch hotels. All of the American cities selected featured the same climate as the Netherlands: rainy, but temperate.[41]

In its July 1950 report, the Dutch delegation expressed particular enthusiasm for U.S. hotel practices and methods concerning operations and management. Members of the delegation concluded that the Dutch hotel industry could benefit from Americans' travel-agency expertise. The Dutch wanted to know more about a range of activities, from organizing sightseeing trips to doing market research and public relations; from vocational training to standardized billing methods; from the "scientific" hotel construction to the vital issue of professional hotel management to improve efficiency. In comparing operational practices on both sides of the Atlantic, the study group declared Dutch hotels smaller, more disorderly, and less efficiently run than their American counterparts. Other comparisons produced different outcomes, however. When it came to hotel architecture and layout, the design of hotel rooms and interiors, the study group deemed the Dutch hotels more authentic and personal, warmer and cozier than their American cousins. Significantly, the report also specified that American authorities expected the European "reception structure" to be adapted to the demands of U.S. middle-class tourists who visited Europe. To clarify these expectations, Pozzy drafted a "helpful" document entitled "Suggestions to European Hotel-Keepers as to How to Please their American Clientele." Pozzy explained that "American customers, particularly the new postwar types, differ fundamentally from Europeans in their way of living and their taste of [sic] food."[42] The twenty-five suggestions stressed the need to introduce modern services and conveniences. For example, serving ice water and installing ice-making facilities were now priorities. Service was to be quick, with no waiting time between courses at meals and a high standard of efficiency overall. Each room was to have a working telephone. Hotels needed laundry, dry-cleaning, and elevator services. Hot water was to be available around the clock; a free English-language newspaper given to guests each morning; sanitary facilities kept clean. When it came to new hotels, Pozzy proposed to build "Statler-type" living room-bathroom arrangements. He also lobbied for installing cold- and hot-water facilities as well as air-conditioning in each room; ice machines and modern, high-speed elevators should grace the hotel corridors.[43] Pozzy pointed to every single state-of-the-art feature found in American hotels, using the Statler and Hilton hotels as exemplars for European hotel modernization.

In the Netherlands, the report's publication did not go unnoticed. The modernistic blueprint for Dutch hotel design and management made an impact. In November of 1950, for example, the ANWB's house organ, *Tourists' Champion* (*Toeristen Kampioen*), began a series of articles called "A Guest at the Marshall Hotel for Two Days" ("Twee dagen te gast in het Marshall hotel"). The pieces focused on the facilities and services that "modern" hotels required; the articles meant "to provide a mirror to hotel keepers." Set in the future, the series followed an imaginary middle-class American family's stay at a newly "modern" Dutch hotel; the reports sketched out future Dutch hotel life and management. Described on these pages were furnishings, gadgets, and appliances, all of which were unknown in Dutch hotels at the time; the personal and technical services described, like ice machines, showers, and air-conditioning, were especially unfamiliar.[44] In publishing this series, the ANWB contributed to the image—and the anticipation—of a modern, America-inspired future.

At roughly the same time, U.S. ECA officials began to acknowledge the realities of bridging the dollar gap by targeting U.S. tourists: few if any Dutch hotels could survive on American tourists alone, who comprised 15 percent of all foreign visitors who stayed at Dutch hotels.[45] Dutch and American policymakers agreed: the Dutch government would merely consult the ECA on how to distribute Marshall Plan money; final decisions were up to the Dutch government.[46] As a result, in 1951, the Dutch government selected—from 200 applications—the twenty hotels to receive U.S. Marshall Aid. Predictably, these hotels served foreign *and* Dutch visitors who were middle-class and traveled primarily via airplane.[47]

In July of 1951, Dutch parliament ratified the law on construction and modernization of the hotel sector. Two key officials emphasized that modern hotels (those meeting U.S. standards) would attract foreign revenues and tourists—particularly Americans. One exemplary recipient of Marshall Plan funding collected 1.1 million guilders (approximately $418,000). Amsterdam's Grand Hotel Krasnapolsky was renowned for its "cosmopolitan character": two-thirds of its guests were foreign. "Kras" was also valued "for its Dutch character of cleanliness and geniality."

The Krasnapolsky's management projected Amsterdam as a future tourism center and foresaw a room shortage. They decided to modernize by forming an alliance with KLM. The airline flew in potential middle-class guests: tourists, businesspeople, and conference participants. Krasnapolsky made special arrangements with KLM; increased its size; added rooms; and expanded its conference facilities. As important, all new rooms contained a bath, shower, toilet, and radio; some new rooms were "Statler proof."[48]

After the Dutch hotel law passed, the Dutch Hotel Association acquiesced to the construction of "Marshall hotels." After all, the nation's transnational tourism policy had shifted definitively from rationing to modernistic refurbishment.[49] In 1952, the association announced that it would abstain from participating in the "Invasion of Europe" debates. This European controversy challenged U.S. hotel firms (like Hilton) that were supported by the new Eisenhower administration.[50] That same year, budget cuts following the Korean War had abolished the U.S. Travel Development Section of the ECA. Members of the Dutch Hotel association realized that key hotel developments on both sides of the Atlantic would be discussed mainly at a transnational level—not in Europe, per se.

The OEEC and its Tourism Committee emerged as the crucial transnational European actor. In the 1950s, the organization's core task remained to "concentrate on the European hotel situation in order to see whether this was sufficient to cater for an ever-increasing number of tourists from overseas and particularly from America"—despite the fact that the policy context had changed.[51] In the United States, the policy shift from a Democratic to a Republican administration implied a farewell to New Deal policies. In 1952, the U.S. representative on the OEEC council stated America's new European policy: create a single European market by liberalizing trade. To this end, the U.S. fostered European productivity, their effort embodied by creating the European Productivity Agency in 1953. "Social tourism"—working-class tourism—was now seen as crucial to productivity.[52] And, stimulating European tourism meant charting and comparing national developments, coordinating and standardizing them. The OEEC Tourism Committee made it a priority to develop a standard European tourism-accommodation classification. This was to create alignment with transport companies, travel agencies, and car-centric infrastructure policies.

Hotels were now urged to focus on economies of scale (their "self-financing capacity"); on rationalizing all phases of hotel management; on standardizing hotel management and services; as well as on improving marketing research and public relations. Actors in the Dutch hotel sector also sought greater transnational standardization in other areas. In the name of uniformity, they weighed the merits of adopting the U.S. accounting system, for example.[53] And in the late 1940s, inspired by the American Hotel Association's standardizing of vocational training, the Dutch hotel sector launched a similar four-year "practical" vocational program in national schools.[54] To gain the considerable "capacity" and expertise these initiatives required, hotels relied closely on non-governmental organizations. Called into service were the International Hotel Association, the European Travel Commission, and the European Branch of the Union of Official Travel Organizations, among other groups.

Conclusion

After the Second World War, Europeans contested the very definition of "the American way of life." In this Cold War context, Europeans debated whether American products and processes should be adopted, reworked, or rejected. The controversy encompassed many social domains, including tourism. Confronted with the modernistic image of America—conjured, in part, by the ECA's U.S. Travel Development Section—Dutch actors in the hotel sector constructed their own images of America.

These interpretations of America—and the prospect of a modernistic, U.S.-guided future for the Dutch hotel sector—evoked feelings of national identity. Dutch actors rediscovered and reconstructed the Dutch identity, the "Dutch character" of their tourism industry. In the Netherlands, the identity issue centered on postwar reconstruction debates in which the management of social-class issues was crucial; the Butlins camp controversy of the late 1940s and the "Marshall hotel" issue of the 1950s demonstrate this. The spokespeople for Dutch tourism agreed on the meaning of Americanization: it was commercial, individualistic, and hedonistic. They also agreed that American-style working-class tourism should be avoided, as it led to irresponsible, immoral behavior. Middle-class tourism was the way forward—with a mix of modern American and Dutch features. The Dutch interpretation of "modern tourist" accommodation was a top-down process; fear of American homogenization and standardization were recurring themes. The spokespeople for tourism also differentiated the old system of patronage from its new, "modern" elements. Social-class distinctions were seen as playing an important role.

By no means did Dutch tourism's spokespeople fully adopt the image of America projected by modernistic Marshall planners. In fact, actors in the Dutch tourism sector re-purposed U.S. examples and developments, reinterpreted American challenges and pressures. The results could be characterized as neither "American" nor "Dutch." This was a hybrid tourism regime comprised of collective, individual, commercial, and state-led initiatives. In its 1955 review of the Marshall Plan years, the Dutch Ministry of Economic Affairs acknowledged the hybrid nature of it accommodations. The ministry noted that, initially, the ECA had pushed the model of U.S. tourism: building American-style hotels with hundreds of rooms, shopping malls, and adjacent conference facilities. The review stated the negotiated consensus among Dutch tourism actors: that modernization of European hotels should fit local markets, contexts, and traditions—while meeting American standards of hygiene, management, and service.

This outcome was also evident in other European countries. In France, for example, transatlantic contact only reinforced the need for defining the French national character. The pattern of selective appropriation—with variations, of course—was also visible in other European countries. In all cases, European actors focused on American processes rather than on American technologies and tourism "products." Actors in European tourism were more inclined to accept U.S. models and standards for process innovation; these actors rejected the aesthetics and the scale of U.S. products, from hotel architecture to interior design, ice machines to air-conditioning. European actors actively co-constructed the new transnational tourism regime. U.S. policies and challenges, American dollars and management models served as strong influences. Marshall Plan policies successfully portrayed American management methods, if not technologies, as efficient, promising, modern—and inevitable. Ultimately, actors in Dutch tourism believed they could benefit from U.S. models, standards, and methods. After all, everything from information campaigns to education programs, study tours to technical assistance, helped confirm this. If any doubt remained, transnational tourism companies like Holland America Line and KLM stepped in to assert their stake in the tourism sector. These power relationships, too, were part of the Dutch process of inventing modern tourism accommodation.

Notes

1. Neal Moses Rosendorf, "Be El Caudillo's Guest: The Franco Regime's Quest for Rehabilitation and Dollars after World War II via the Promotion of U.S. Tourism to Spain," *Diplomatic History* 30 (2006): 380. U.S. official citation in: OEEC Executive Committee, "Executive Committee: Supplementary Report on Tourism," OEEC/1020, CE (49)024, February 25, 1949, 9, Historical Archives of the EU, European University Institute (EUI), Florence, Italy (hereafter cited as Historical Archives of the EU). The OEEC, established to administer Marshall Aid, bluntly stated in 1951 that from the onset it had "been concerned with the question of American tourism in Europe, for it was realized that this invisible export in the fullest sense of the word could make an important contribution towards solving the dollar shortage. It is for this reason that the Council has, from time to time, taken a number of decisions for the purpose of promoting the development of the tourist industry." See OEEC, *Tourism and European Recovery* (Paris: OEEC, 1951), 5.
2. Christopher Endy, *Cold War Holidays: American Tourism in France* (Chapel Hill: University of North Caolina Press, 2004), 9, 12, 81–2; Brian A. McKenzie, "Creating a Tourist's Paradise: The Marshall Plan and France, 1948 to 1952," *French Politics, Culture and Society* 21 (2003): 35–54.
3. Mark Mazower, *Dark Continent: Europe's Twentieth Century* (London: Penguin Books, 1999), 290–331.
4. See also the contribution of Thomas Kaiserfeld (chapter 8) in this volume.
5. Ruth Oldenziel, "Is Globalization a Code Word for Americanization?" *Tijdschrift voor Sociale en Economische Geschiedenis* 4 (2007): 84–106; Rosendorf, "Be El Caudillo's Guest," 367–407.
6. In focusing on the differences between European and U.S. distribution systems, and how the U.S. system changed European systems, De Grazia

introduced the concept of the consumption regime. Because tourism, like distribution, both embodies and links production and consumption, I use the term "tourism regime." See Victoria de Grazia, "Changing Consumption Regimes in Europe, 1930–1970: Comparative Perspectives on the Distribution Problem," in *Getting and Spending: European and American Consumer Societies in the Twentieth Century*, ed. Susan Strasser, Charles McGovern, and Matthias Judt (Cambridge: Cambridge University Press, 1998), 78. De Grazia's regime argument is also central but less pronounced in her *Irresistible Empire: America's Advance through 20th-Century Europe* (Cambridge, MA: The Belknap of Harvard University Press, 2005).

7. De Grazia, "Changing Consumption Regimes in Europe, 1930–1970," 61.
8. Ruth Oldenziel and Adri A. Albert de la Bruhèze, "Theorizing the Mediation Junction for Technology and Consumption," in *Manufacturing Technology, Manufacturing Consumers: The Making of Dutch Consumer Society*, ed. Adri A. Albert de la Bruhèze and Ruth Oldenziel (Amsterdam: Amsterdam University Press, 2009), 9–40; Theo Beckers and Hans Mommaas, "Onderzoek van de vrijetijd," in *Het Vraagstuk van den Vrijen Tijd: 60 jaar onderzoek naar vrijetijd*, ed. Theo Beckers and Hans Mommaas (Leiden: Stenfert Kroese, 1991), 2–10.
9. A narrative on the mediation of Dutch consumer society in the twentieth century can be found in *Manufacturing Technology, Manufacturing Consumers: The Making of Dutch Consumer Society*, ed. Adri A. Albert de Bruhèze and Ruth Oldenziel (Amsterdam: Amsterdam University Press, 2009).
10. Although mass tourism was predicted, in the period from 1945 to 1970 more than half of the Dutch population did not take a summer vacation. See Matea F. A. Linders-Rooijendijk, *Gebaande wegen voor mobiliteit en vrijetijdsbesteding II: De ANWB van Vereniging naar Instituut, 1937–1983* (The Hague: ANWB, 1992), 732; Aaltje Hessels, *Vakantie en Vakantiebesteding sinds de Eeuwwisseling* (Assen: Van Gorcum, 1973), 225, 233. In the 1950s, the Dutch Central Statistics Agency (Centraal Bureau voor de Statistiek) defined a vacation as "a stay of two or more days outside of one's own domicile." Recreation was defined as "less than a two-day stay outside of one's own domicile." See Linders-Rooijendijk, *Gebaande wegen voor mobiliteit en vrijetijdsbesteding II*, 622. In 1955, a one-week paid holiday for all employees was regulated by law. In 1961, the five-day work week was introduced; in 1963 the government ended its controlled wage policy; and in 1966 a two-week paid vacation was mandated by law. This included a vacation allowance of 4 percent of the annual salary. See Gijs Mom and Ruud Filarski, *Van Transport naar Mobiliteit: De mobiliteitsexplosie, 1895–2005* (Zutphen: Walburg Pers, 2008), 249.
11. Wiardi Beckman Stichting, *De Consument in de Maatschappij: De organisatorische behartiging van het consumentenbelang* (Amsterdam: Wiardi Beckman Stichting, 1956); Elisabeth Boissevain and Ton de Joode, *Tussen Koop en Miskoop: De Consument en zijn belangen in Nederland* (Amsterdam: Ideeboek, 1976), 61–3; Nederlandse Katholieke Middenstandsbond, *Middenstand en Consument: Verslagboek Studiedagen N.R.K.M. 1964, Scheveningen* (The Hague: Nederlandse Katholieke Middenstandsbond, 1964), 18–23; Oldenziel and Albert de la Bruhèze, "Theorizing the Mediation Junction for Technology and Consumption," 9–40.
12. Beckers and Mommaas, "Onderzoek van de vrijetijd," 132; Liesbeth Bervoets and Ruth Oldenziel, "Speaking for Consumers, Standing Up as Citizens: The

174 Adri A. Albert de la Bruhèze

Politics of Dutch Women's Organizations and the Shaping of Technology, 1880–1980," in *Manufacturing Technology, Manufacturing Consumers*, 41–71.
13. Elisabeth G. Boissevain, member of the Dutch Physical Planning Service, "Vacantiemogelijkheden in de toekomst," *Toeristen Kampioen* 9 (1946): 7–9; Centraal Werkcomité Vacantie, *Verslag van het Congres inzake de toekomstige ontwikkeling van de vacantie-accommodatie in Nederland, belegd op 10 december 1949 te Utrecht* (The Hague: Centraal Werkcomité, 1949); Theo Beckers, "Planning voor Vrijheid: Een historisch-sociologische studie van de overheidsinterventie in rekreatie en vrije tijd" (PhD diss., Landbouwhogeschool Wageningen, 1983); Beckers and Mommaas, *Het Vraagstuk van den Vrijen Tijd*.
14. Theo Siraa, *Een Miljoen Woningen: De rol van de Rijksoverheid bij wederopbouw, volkshuisvesting, bouwnijverheid en ruimtelijke ordening 1940–1963* (The Hague: SDU, 1989), 53; Mom and Filarski, *Van Transport naar Mobiliteit*; Johan Schot, Gijs Mom, Ruud Filarski, and Peter Eloy Staal, "Concurrentie en Afstemming: Water, Rails, Weg en Lucht," in *Transport en Communicatie*, vol. 5, *Techniek in Nederland in de Twintigste Eeuw*, ed. Johan Schot et al. (Zutphen: Walburg Pers, 2002), 38.
15. Boissevain, "Vacantiemogelijkheden in de Toekomst," 7–9.
16. Frank Schipper, *Driving Europe: Building Europe on Roads in the Twentieth Century* (Amsterdam: Aksant, 2008), 172–86.
17. W. Boreel, "Vergadering 'Commission Européenne de Tourisme' te Parijs," Netherlands National Archive (hereafter cited as NNA), Archive Ministry of Economic Affairs (hereafter cited as Archive MEA): Central Archive, 1944–1965 (2.06.087), Inv. no. 1371.
18. Executive Committee OEEC, "Executive Committee: Supplementary Report on Tourism," OEEC/1020, CE (49)024, February 25, 1949, 1–22, quote on p. 19, Historical Archives of the EU; Executive Committee OEEC, "Executive Committee: Urgent Matters for the Development of Tourism in Europe," OEEC/1020, CE (49)035, March 2, 1949, 1–9, Historical Archives of the EU.
19. Archive ANWB, Management Archive, Meetings and Reports from the Daily Board, 1947–1948, D18; Archive ANWB, Management Archive, Filing Cabinet 55, Box K06-Camp Tourism; "Een Butlinkamp in Zandvoort." *De Kampioen* 8 (1947); J. Veeninga, "Vacantie met z'n duizenden," Archive ANWB, Management Archive, Meetings and Reports from the Daily Board, 1947–1948, D18.
20. Archive ANWB, Management Archive, Meetings and Reports from the Daily Board, 1947–1948, D18.
21. Beckers, "Planning voor Vrijheid," 162–9; Jos Berendsen, Peter Saal, and Flip Spangenberg, *Met Zicht op Zee: Tweehonderd jaar bouwen aan badplaatsen in Nederland, België en Duitsland* (The Hague: Staatsuitgeverij, 1985), 81–6.
22. "Twee Amerikaanse Stemmen," *Hotelwereld* 3, no. 3 (1948); "Om de Amerikaanse reisdollar," *Hotelwereld* 3, no. 3 (1948).
23. From 1948 to 1952, Marshall Aid to the Netherlands totaled 3.5 billion guilders in the form of gifts and credits. See Siraa, *Een Miljoen Woningen*, 69; The Minister of Economic Affairs to the Minister of Financial Affairs, March 8, 1949, NNA, Archive MEA: Central Archive, 1944–1965 (2.06.087), Inv. no. 1371. In the bilateral tourism agreements between the ECA and European governments, the latter promised to "facilitate and encourage the promotion and

development of travel by citizens of the United States to and within participating countries." This clause also implied the modernization of transportation structures. See "Goedkope vacantieoorden zijn nodig," *Toeristen Kampioen* 13 (1950): 12.
24. "Onze taak tot een nieuwe welvaart," *Hotelwereld* 3 (1949): 439–41; "Bouwt Hotels," *Hotelwereld* 4, no. 2 (1949): 19–20.
25. This was a substantial amount of money: it equaled the amount of corresponding funds spent by the French government on French tourism projects in 1950. See McKenzie, "Creating a Tourist's Paradise," 39.
26. "De ondernemers van morgen," *Hotelwereld* 4, no. 4 (1949): 47–8; "De Stand van Zaken in de Marshall-hulp voor de Nederlandse Hotellerie," *Hotelwereld* 5, no. 3 (1950): 33–4.
27. Groeneveld Meyer, Government Commissioner for Tourism, Ministry of Economic Affairs, to Dr. Hirschfeld, Government Commissioner for the European Recovery Program, Ministry of Foreign Affairs, March 17, 1949, NNA, Archive MEA: Central Archive, 1944–1965 (2.06.087), Inv. no. 1372. The first list contained the following hotels: the Carlton Hotel in Amsterdam, Hotel Paulez in The Hague, Hotel Atlanta in Rotterdam, Captains Hotel in Rotterdam, Hotel Sonsbeek in Arnhem, and Hotel Den Burg in Middelburg.
28. W.H. De Monchy, Managing Director of Holland America Line, to Dr. Hirschfeld, Government Commissioner for the European Recovery Program, Ministry of Foreign Affairs, June 28, 1949, NNA, Archive Ministry of Foreign Affairs (hereafter cited as Archive MFA), 1945–1954 (2.05.117), Inv. no. 10512.
29. "Mr. Pozzy adviseert en suggereert: Miljoenendans om dollars en toeristen," *Hotelwereld* 4, no. 6 (1949): 77–9; Andrew K. Sandoval-Strausz, *Hotel: An American History* (New Haven, CT: Yale University Press, 2007), 111, 129–33; Annabel Jane Wharton, *Building the Cold War: Hilton International Hotels and Modern Architecture* (Chicago: University of Chicago Press, 2001), 1–11, 159–93. In 1954, the Hilton Hotel Corporation took over the Statler Hotel Company.
30. The Minister of Economic Affairs, Prof. Van den Brink, to Dr. Hirschfeld, Government Commissioner for the European Recovery Program, Ministry of Foreign Affairs, July 19, 1949, NNA, Archive MFA, 1945–1954 (2.05.117), Inv. no. 10512.
31. Ibid.
32. Dr. Hirschfeld to the Minister of Economic Affairs, July 20, 1949, NNA, Archive MEA: Central Archive, 1944–1965 (2.06.087), Inv. no. 1372.
33. Clarence E. Hunter, Chief of the ECA Mission to the Netherlands, to Dr. H.M. Hirschfeld, Government Commissioner for the European Recovery Program, Ministry of Foreign Affairs, July 25, 1949, NNA, Archive MEA: Central Archive, 1944–1965 (2.06.087), Inv. no. 1372.
34. The Minister of Economic Affairs, Prof. Van den Brink, to Dr. Hirschfeld, Government Commissioner for the European Recovery Program, Ministry of Foreign Affairs, August 23, 1949, first draft letter, NNA, Archive MEA: Central Archive, 1944–1965 (2.06.087), Inv. no. 1372.
35. Rijksdienst voor het Nationale Plan, *Beschouwingen Betreffende de Wederopbouw der Noordzeeplaatsen* (The Hague: Rijksdienst voor het Nationale Plan, 1947); "Vreemdelingenverkeer in de Benelux," *Toeristen Kampioen* 12 (1949): 376; "Niet kortzichtig maar voorzichtig," *Hotelwereld* 4, no. 10 (1949): 131–3; "De

nieuwbouw van hotels," *Hotelwereld* 4, no. 11 (1949); "Electorale show van ondernemingsgeest en doorzettingsvermogen," *Hotelwereld* 5, no. 10 (1950): 128–9.

36. "De Hotellerie in de onzichtbare export," *Hotelwereld* 4, no. 9 (1949): 118–21. How the Netherlands would benefit from U.S. tourism dollars—and who would benefit most—became highly contested issues. In 1948, U.S. tourists spent $4 million in the Netherlands. In 1949, 48,200 U.S. tourists spent $6 million, and in 1950 the same amount was spent by 56,000 U.S. tourists. In 1949 and 1950, only Austria ($2.5 and $3 million), Belgium ($5.5 and $4.5 million), and Denmark ($3.5 and $4 million) received fewer U.S. tourism dollars. See "Aantekening: Amerikaans toerisme in Europa," *Economisch-Statistische Berichten* 36, no. 1785 (1951): 580–1; OEEC, *Tourism and European Recovery*, 22.
37. "Het vreemdelingenverkeer groeit," *Toeristen Kampioen* 13 (1950): 392.
38. "Scheepvaart stelt een voorbeeld," *Hotelwereld* 5, no. 13 (1950): 181–3; *Conference Issue Hotelwereld* (1950): 64; "Nogmaals: Nieuwbouw van Hotels," *Hotelwereld* 5, no. 13 (1950): 186–8.
39. Dr. Hirschfeld, Government Commissioner for the European Recovery Program, Ministry of Foreign Affairs, to the Minister of Economic Affairs, Van den Brink, August 1, 1949, NNA, Archive MFA (6010–31), Inv. no. 10512 (hotel plan). The Dutch Hotel Union openly questioned the usefulness of sending a study group because the "funder wants to make sure that the funds will be spent in the way in which they were intended." See "Hoteldeskundigen naar Amerika," *Hotelwereld* 4, no. 15 (1949): 230–1.
40. F.A. Pfeifer, chairman, secretary of the corporate hotel and catering industry; H. van Beelen, director of the Hotel Noordzee in Noordwijk; W. Bergmans, director of the Hotel Pomona in The Hague; J.W.C. Boks, architect of the Bouwcentrum in Rotterdam; and J.J. Poutsma, head of the hotel, café, and restaurant building of N.V. Heinekens Bierbrouwerij Maatschappij.
41. OEEC Tourism Committee, "Tourism Committee: Technical Assistance in the Field of Tourism," OEEC/1300, TOU (50)2, April 18, 1950, 1–10, Historical Archives of the EU; Groeneveld Meyer, Government Commissioner for Tourism, Ministry of Economic Affairs, "Nota 373," to the Minister of Economic Affairs, August 8, 1950, NNA, Archive MEA: Central Archive, 1944–1965 (2.06.087), Inv. no. 1372.
42. "Beknopte samenvatting van het verslag der Hotelcommissie Pfeifer van de onder auspiciën van de E.C.A/O.E.E.C. in de Verenigde Staten van Amerika ontvangen Technical Assistance," NNA, Archive MEA: Central Archive, 1944–1965 (2.06.087), Inv. no. 1372. Quotes on p. 4 and p. 6.
43. OEEC Working Papers, OEEC/1300, TOU (50)6, August 30, 1950, 1–23, quote on p. 17, Historical Archives of the EU.
44. "Twee dagen te gast in het Marshall Hotel," *Toeristen Kampioen* 13 (1950): 690–3; "Twee dagen te gast in het Marshall Hotel," *Toeristen Kampioen* 13 (1950): 711–13; "Twee dagen te gast in het Marshall Hotel," *Toeristen Kampioen* 13 (1950): 756–8.
45. Contemporary data on the dollar amount spent by U.S. tourists in the Netherlands are rather ambiguous. According to a publication of the Krasnapolsky Hotel in Amsterdam, 27,000 Americans visited the Netherlands in 1948, spending $1,677,000 (approximately 4.5 million guilders). In 1949,

34,000 visiting Americans spent $2,763,000 (7.5 million guilders), and in 1950, 44,000 visiting Americans spent $4,571,000 (12.3 million guilders). When the total revenues from foreign tourism in the Netherlands are tabulated, the dollar amount spent by U.S. tourists in 1948–1950 illustrates that Dutch hotels could not survive on American tourists alone. The total revenues from foreign tourism in the Netherlands in 1948 was 26 million guilders; in 1949 it was 35 million guilders; in 1950 it was 63 million guilders; and in 1951 it was 107 million guilders *"Kras" Commercieel, cultureel en zakelijk middelpunt: De financiering van haar modernisering en uitbreiding in een moeilijke tijd* (Amsterdam: Grand Hotel Krasnapolsky, 1952), 7, 10; Albertus B. A. Van Ketel, "Het voorbeeld van Marshall-steun voor de hotel-industrie in Nederland," *Maandschrift Economie: Tijdschrift voor algemeen economische, bedrijfseconomische en sociale vraagstukken* 16 (1952): 410.
46. "Nota inzake het vreemdelingenverkeer en de logiesaccomodatie," second draft, June 15, 1955, NNA, Archive MEA: Central Archive, 1944–1965 (2.06.087), Inv. no. 1372.
47. The selected hotels were Wapen van Giethoorn, Giethoorn; Grand Hotel, Scheveningen; Krasnapolsky, Amsterdam; Bellevue, Arnhem; 's Koonings Jaght, Arnhem; Haarhuis, Arnhem; Bosch, Arnhem; De Pauw, Arnhem; Regina, Rotterdam; West-Ende, Helmond; Oud St. Jan, Haarlem; Den Burg, Middelburg; Van Diepen, Volendam; Stadsherberg, Kampen; Bouwes, Zandvoort; Zeezicht, West-Terschelling; Marie-Rose, Noordwijk; Hof Gelria, Doesburg; Kasteel Oud-Wassenaar, Wassenaar; Smits, Utrecht; Wageningse Berg, Wageningen; Hotel Kissels, Roermond; Hotel Hoornwijk, Rijswijk. See "Nota inzake het vreemdelingenverkeer en de logiesaccommodatie," July 5, 1955, NNA, Archive MEA: Central Archive, 1944–1965 (2.06.087), Inv. no. 1372.
48. With a total number of 300 beds, Krasnapolsky became the biggest hotel in Amsterdam. Gerard Werkman, *Kras = 100: 100 = Kras* (Amsterdam: Grand Hotel Krasnapolsky, 1966), 162–5, 184; Van Ketel, "Een voorbeeld van Marshall-steun voor de hotel-industrie in Nederland," quote on p. 413; Krasnapolsky archive (1140), City Archive Amsterdam, Boxes 691, 692, and 1507; "Het financieringsproject voor de hotel uitbreiding van de Grand Hotel Krasnapolsky N.V.," 8, 12. Krasnapolsky Archive (1140), City Archive Amsterdam, Box 401.
49. "Zon en regen," *Hotelwereld* 5, no. 24 (1951): 337–9; "Tweede Kamer over Marshall-Hulp aan Hotellerie," *Hotelwereld* 5, no. 26 (1951): 371–2.
50. See Wharton, *Building the Cold War*.
51. Citation by the German representative during the OEEC Executive Committee meeting on April 30, 1953, Executive Committee, OEEC/139, CE/M(53) 1–8, Historical Archives of the EU.
52. In the Mutual Security Program of 1952, $100 million was allocated for the support of European productivity programs. 195th OEEC Council Meeting, October 20, 1952, OEEC Council Minutes, OEEC/35, C/M (52) 32-35, Historical Archives of the EU.
53. OEEC Tourism Committee, OEEC/OECD 129, TD/TOU/52/-/53, Historical Archives of the EU.
54. These practical schools for lower-level personnel co-existed with the higher-level hotel school that had existed since 1930. See "Research," *Hotelwereld* 4, no. 7 (1949): 89–90; *De Zakenwereld* 29, no. 3 (1951): 39.

8
Exploring European Travel: The Swedish Package Tour

Thomas Kaiserfeld

In March of 1963, one of Sweden's largest newspapers broke the story of "scandalous tours" (*skandalresor*)—a pernicious trend affecting leisure travelers.[1] The article described how Sweden's booming leisure-travel industry—especially package tours by air—failed to deliver the experiences depicted in travel companies' advertising. "Travel and get rich," one brochure of the time proclaimed.[2] The travel experience, within Sweden and abroad, would provide all things glorious, memories to enrich and last a lifetime. Ads and brochures extolled the virtues of everything from the luxurious hotels to the accessible beaches and ease of transportation.

The reality was starkly different, however. Hotels, the article asserted, were anything but luxurious, beaches anything but close by, and transportation was neither quick nor convenient.[3] The newspaper cited international statistics showing chartered tours by air to be significantly more dangerous than regular flights. In 1962, for example, chartered tours accounted for only 10 percent of all passenger flights, yet 36 percent of all flight deaths occurred on chartered aircraft.[4] This reported that fatal flight accidents were five times more common on chartered flights than on standard runs. Further analysis proved that safety was on the rise for regular flights, while safety was decreasing on chartered flights. Beside the life-threatening dimension of travel, tourists were also subject to severe disappointments: pre-paid packages of several-months' salary that led to being stranded in dreadful destination points—and ruined vacations.

It was in the late 1950s and early 1960s that new patterns of leisure-travel consumption emerged in Europe. The trend was most pronounced in the small, wealthy countries on Europe's periphery—regions like Scandinavia that were relatively unscathed by the Second World War. Package-tour vacations became more popular during this period, when travel technologies were shifting from the bus to the airplane; the transformation of package-tour practices was under way.[5]

But the shift toward air travel proved problematic. Virtually every component of air travel was more complicated than busing tourists around Europe on the ground. In flux during this period was everything from tour companies' practices to consumers' expectations, the industry's rules to countries' regulations. The mid-1960s brought changes to the entire package-tour consumption regime: package tours by air started to replace bus travel; travel was faster; and the processes—from air-traffic control to purchasing aircraft—were more complex logistically as well as more regulated.

By the mid-1960s, consumers were accustomed to pre-paying for all forms of entertainment, including opera performances and sports events, for example, as well as travel and tourism experiences. Trips by bus, train, and air—no matter how short—relied on such pre-payments, which were confirmed with a ticket. In this context, pre-payment of package tours by air represented a departure from the normal expenditure on entertainment: air package tours were significantly more costly. Justifiably, middle-class families perceived air-package tours as a major investment. After all, the tours included flights, hotels, selected meals—sometimes for several weeks at a time. Never had the stakes been this high in a consumer entertainment market—only the highest-ticket items, like homes and cars, could compare. Accordingly, the air-package-tour supplier's failure to deliver on the promises advertised could create a financial and personal disaster for the consumer: a "scandalous tour."

Resolving Sweden's "Scandalous Tours": An Iconic European Process

The focus of this chapter is the Swedish scandalous package-tour phenomenon, specifically, the resolution of this conflict as an iconic European process. As we will see, the Swedish package tour as a product alone was influenced by the U.S. in a limited, contained, and often indirect way. As we will also see, American infrastructure afforded Swedes mass-scale tourism, starting in the 1950s. But the development of Swedish tours—the way in which the consumption regime evolved—retained a resolutely Swedish, if not European, character. Specifically, in order to resolve the problems of "scandalous tours" reported by the press, a host of intermediary actors were introduced. These included the public authority of the Swedish National Consumer Council (Statens konsumentråd); various government commissions; and journalists, among others. The political action that ensued often involved negotiations between interest groups such as branch organizations or consumer cooperatives. The outcome was a transformation of the package-tour consumption regime: a government commission investigated the existing package-tour regime and, subsequently, the government passed a law in 1967 to provide a guarantee for consumers' purchases of package tours.

The argument in this chapter revolves around the concept of the mediation junction, in particular the mediation junction that emerged around the "scandalous tours," as the defining Swedish—if not European—phenomenon. In this chapter and, indeed, in this book, a mediation junction is defined as an institutional and organizational space in which different stakeholders negotiate technological developments. Representatives of the state, the market, and civil society may all participate in a mediation junction; exploring the interactions between these actors sheds light on the processes involved in creating and forming consumption regimes.[6] Successful negotiations between these intermediary actors depend on the existence of a recognized mediation junction. This, in turn, carries weight when scripts for consumer behavior are created. The existence of functioning mediation junctions is thus a necessary but not sufficient condition for the influence of intermediary actors on the establishment of a consumption regime.

The existence of mediation junctions can be linked to neo-corporatism, the political system in which society is seen as a corporate based on voluntary agreement between government and labor and business interests where societal needs are generally satisfied by tripartite negotiations. In Sweden, for example, a lack of housing during the 1920s was dealt with by creating housing cooperatives and various housing programs: national, regional, and local. This can be characterized as a neo-corporative solution. Frequently, neo-corporatism has been associated with social democracy. This was the case in Sweden: from the post-Second World War period until the mid-1970s, the Swedish Social Democratic Labor Party, which dominated government. Accordingly, it was this arguably neo-corporative government that prevailed in Sweden during the period examined in this chapter.[7] The same model of tripartite negotiations—between capital, labor, and the state—has been observed in many other political settings, especially in smaller European countries.[8]

The Swedish Package Tour as a Product: 1950s and 1960s

As a product, the package tour was widely known in Sweden and in Europe at large. It comprised a means of transport (such as train; bus; and, later, airplane); accommodation with fixed departure and arrival dates; and sometimes meals as well as a sightseeing itinerary—all included for a set price. Travel agents sold the package tours to individual consumers and aggregated them to form tourist groups that followed the same itinerary. This cut costs and facilitated planning for travelers. In addition, the security of a largely homogenous group of companions emboldened less-experienced tourists.[9] Non-profit organizations, such as the Workers' Travel Association, a union-run group in Great Britain, also organized package tours for their members during the 1950s and 1960s. Their aim was to facilitate holidays for union members and their families. Other non-profit organizations were organized specifically to promote tourism, including the Swedish Tourist Association (Svenska turistföreningen), for example, which had a different, more ideological goal in mind: to spread knowledge about Sweden.[10]

The huge growth in the Northern European package-tour industry during the 1960s involved a growing middle-class eager to appropriate the "exclusive" leisure practices previously reserved for the wealthy. This trend gained momentum on both sides of the Atlantic. From the second half of the nineteenth century, paving the way for this trend, American and European aristocracy had bought mansions and created artist colonies in Mediterranean fishing villages and walled, medieval towns such as Cannes and St. Tropez. It was the aristocracy that pioneered tourism in these places. By the 1960s, mass air tourism introduced Northern Europe's middle- and lower-class travelers to these chic destinations. Now, for example, the middle classes—and even a small number of working-class families—could afford to visit European cities and seaside resorts previously dominated by the wealthy.[11] Leisure trips to the Mediterranean—and the whole "sun, sea, and sand" experience—were now common: it was tourism on an industrial scale, mass tourism along the lines of Fordist consumption regimes. Now, trips to the Mediterranean matched consumption patterns for cars and restaurant visits, for example.[12]

The paid vacation comprised one important prerequisite for the "mass" phenomenon of package tours by airplane. New labor laws, passed in 1938, introduced a minimum of two weeks of vacation for all of the Scandinavian countries—as well as for many other European countries. In 1951, standard vacations were increased to three weeks; by 1963, four weeks were the norm. This made package tours more accessible to lower- and middle-class Swedes in the early 1950s—and even more widely accessible in the early 1960s.[13] And, through agreements with companies rather than through legislation, many groups of employees managed to secure much longer vacations. As the economies of Northern Europe grew after the Second World War, Europeans' vacation time increased. Workers in Sweden benefited in particular; the country's successful, some say treacherous, foreign policy toward Nazi Germany had spared Sweden from becoming embroiled in the Second World War—and from German occupation.[14] During the five years following the end of the Second World War, wages in the Swedish industrial sector increased by 30 percent. Five years later, wages had jumped by another 30 percent. After a period of slower expansion, wages again rose by 58 percent during the 1960s. This fueled tourism in Sweden, creating a contrast between that country and the war-stricken European nations, of which there were many.[15]

Another contributing factor was the affordability of travel: between 1945 and 1975, Swedish tourism prices fell by an annual average of 6 percent.[16] This was due to reduced costs in every form of transport, especially air travel. Planes were now cheaper to purchase and more cost-efficient to operate. In fact, it was the introduction of American passenger jet airliners that helped drive down the cost of air travel.[17] The combination of lower transport costs and higher wages led to an increase in Swedish travel consumption more than any other consumption sector between 1950 and 1964.[18]

American Influences on European Tourist Regimes

When it came to European tourist destinations, in the early 1960s, Spain was the most popular vacation spot, followed by Italy and Greece.[19] The interest in Spain emerged from Spanish officials' efforts to establish the country as a primary tourist destination for Americans. The Spaniards competed directly with established contenders for American tourism dollars: France, Italy, and Switzerland, among others.[20] Experts in the Spanish tourism sector formed alliances with their American counterparts and corporations, such as American Express, Hilton Hotels, and Trans World Airlines. Travel professionals on both sides of the Atlantic marketed Spain as a travel destination in advertisements; through travel guides; via promotional film productions in Spain; and through other means of cultural expression. In any case, the efforts to sell vacations to this travel destination succeeded: from 1950 to 1951, the number of American tourists in Spain rose from 25,000 in 1950 to approximately 60,000 the next year. By 1964, tourism had increased tenfold to 600,000 tourists. So, from 1950 to 1964, the number of tourists from all countries traveling to Spain rose from 1 million to 11 million.[21] Apparently, campaigns to attract Americans to Spain also influenced the European market.

In addition, American interests influenced the formation of transport and housing infrastructure so important to the tourist industry. In the previous chapter, Albert de la Bruhèze shows how Americanization processes influenced powerfully the construction of resorts and hotels. A companion case of American influence on European travel infrastructure was the effort to create a European network of bus lines in the early 1950s. At this time, American organizations promoting U.S. tourism in Western Europe served to support European economic growth in this postwar period; to expand the European market for American goods and services; and to close the so-called dollar gap.[22]

The European network of civil-air transport developed along the same lines. Civil jet aviation was introduced and expanded rapidly in the 1950s. But the work to regulate international passenger traffic had already started in the fall of 1944, when the International Civil Aviation Organization (ICAO) was formed to coordinate safety and technical aspects of civil aviation. Different solutions were presented, such as multilateral agreements, to secure the right to fly over—and land on—the territory of other nations. Other issues were settled through bilateral agreements.[23] Just over a year later, the International Air Transport Association (IATA) was formed to promote cooperation between airlines.[24]

Equally important were agreements made in order to coordinate civil and military air traffic. In the mid-1950s, military and civil air traffic control in Europe were managed by two parallel systems. But the introduction and rapid expansion of civil jet aviation led to the idea of merging civil with military air traffic control in both space and time.[25] Coordination seemed to make sense, given that it promised cost-efficiency for both systems as well as a way to avoid accidents. In order to achieve this, the ICAO and NATO organized a committee in 1955, with the IATA represented. By this time, an overhaul of European air traffic control systems had begun. This was to accommodate new technologies, including radar, advanced control systems, and faster jets. At the same time, new routines were introduced for communications between the civil and military aviation authorities. For example, civilian air traffic controllers were alerted to the schedule of military air exercises. American influence on European air traffic control systems was considerable, in line with America's profound military interests in Europe.[26]

Starting in 1958, a new generation of jet airliners made mass-produced package tours to Europe more affordable and time-efficient for Americans.[27] For example, the duration of flights for trips within Europe were nearly halved. Early on in the development of European tourism,

American airplanes were popular among Scandinavian airlines, which were engaging in charter tourism during the 1950s.[28] During the Second World War, to secure air assistance, the Allied forces had built airports in the Mediterranean. After the war, some of these airports were repurposed for tourism. So, the earlier deployment of American military technology in Europe promoted civil passenger aviation throughout the 1950s and 1960s. Another example: the widespread use of the American-made Douglas DC-6, a piston-engine airplane with a pressurized cabin originally developed for military transport, led to dramatically lower priced package tours by air from Scandinavia to the Mediterranean. The DC-6 made it possible to cruise at an altitude of 30,000 feet and to fly over—rather than around—the Alps, without having to refuel.[29] The DC-6 and other types of airplanes were comparatively inexpensive and readily available after the Second World War. Scandinavian air-package tours—and indeed the European tourism industry—relied on the American military's ability to make trans-European civil aviation possible. Efforts by NATO and the IATA pioneered secure trans-European civil aviation. This allowed the expansion of middle-class air tourism.

The leisure consumption regime of air package tours brought with it a transformation of travel practices. Before air tourism became widespread, transportation by bus was more the norm. Bus package tours included everything from city sightseeing and visits to cultural landmarks to sunbathing on beaches and salt-water swimming.[30] But cultural sightseeing largely disappeared with buses. An air package tour to Majorca or the Canary Islands, for example, often included hotel accommodation and meals at the destination. No longer were there visits along the way to cultural landmarks on the European continent.[31] In this way, package tours by air transformed the European continent into a so-called space of denial: now, Scandinavian tourists traveling by air merely flew over these areas, en route to Southern Europe. This was a complete turnaround from the previous practice of making cultural visits on bus tours.[32]

In Scandinavia, mass tourism—especially package tours—grew explosively after the Second World War. In fact, in the mid-1960s, the Scandinavian package-tour markets were the largest per capita in Europe, with Denmark and Sweden in the lead.[33] French figures show that, in 1965, the country with the largest share of chartered flights in Europe was Great Britain, with 36.5 percent. This was followed by Scandinavia, with 26.7 percent; and West Germany, with 23 percent. In terms of consumption per capita, it is clear that chartered flights were 2.5 times more common among the Danes, Norwegians, and Swedes

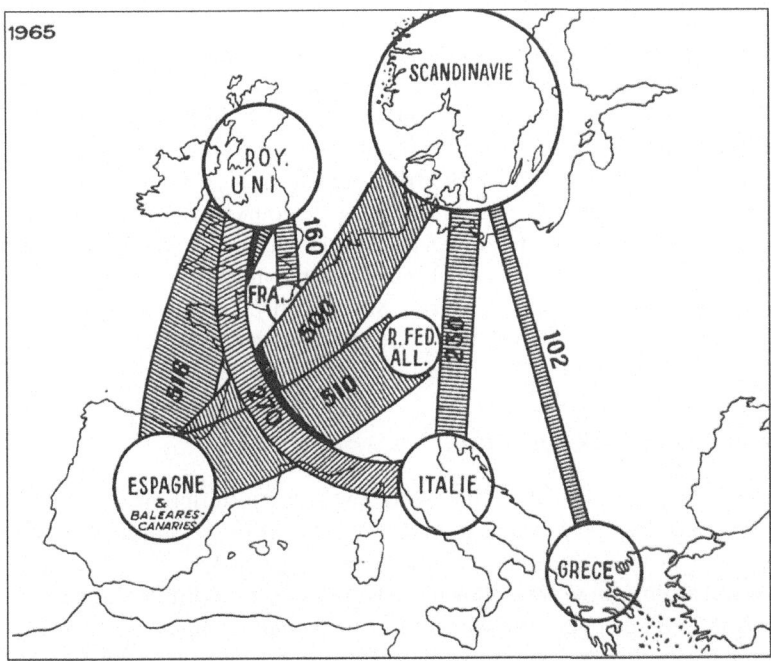

Figure 8.1 This graph shows the flow of non-scheduled civil air traffic between European countries in 1965. The numbers relate to units of 100,000 passengers; only volumes of 100,000 passengers appear on the chart.

than among the British. And chartered flights were easily four times more common for Scandinavians than for West Germans.[34] Having avoided much of the devastation wrought by the Second World War, Scandinavia was more prosperous economically than Britain and West Germany at this time. But another component contributed to the postwar popularity of package tours: the geography and climate of the Nordic countries. Given the darkness (in winter months) and cold of the Scandinavian regions, package tours represented an escape route to the south—an escape route that has become part of the Nordic identity.[35] In this context, it is understandable that Denmark, Norway, Sweden, and Finland (to a lesser extent) have particularly high numbers of package-tour charter flights per capita.[36]

Thus, the Nordic countries, despite their relatively small populations, provided charter-tour passengers for Southern Europe's nascent tourist markets. Sweden and Denmark led the trend. In Sweden, tourism abroad took off in the decade after the Second World War: 75,000 Swedish tourists traveled outside Scandinavia in 1947, compared to 373,000 travelers in 1950. By 1954, more than 1 million Swedes were traveling abroad each year.[37] Most of the tourists chose bus-package tours, which dominated tourist trips outside of Scandinavia throughout the 1950s. Many fewer chose package tours that included nonscheduled flights—charter-air package tours.[38] Later, the trend reversed: from the mid-1960s, this form of travel became much more popular and package tours by air (departing from Sweden only) grew exponentially.[39] In 1965, 86 percent of Swedish package tours were charter-*air* package tours. Of these, about 90 percent flew to the Mediterranean.

Regulating Package Tours

Indeed, in the first half of the 1960s, Swedish consumption of package tours grew massively—and converted from bus travel to air travel. Many different factors contributed to the new regime, although some forces worked against these developments. For example, the airline Scandinavian Airlines System (SAS) attempted to restrict charter flights, which were more competitively priced than the airline's standard flights. In 1954, SAS reframed their business concern about being undersold in the air-travel market as a scheduling concern: SAS officials told Scandinavian transportation ministers that increased charter traffic threatened to infringe on scheduled SAS traffic. The airline demanded that aviation authorities issue regulations to limit charter flights. And SAS prevailed: transportation ministers authorized the aviation authorities of Denmark, Norway, and Sweden to draw up a set of shared rules for charter traffic.[40]

In this way, the Royal Swedish Board of Civil Aviation (Luftfartsverket) was pressured into introducing flight restrictions in 1957. By 1964, all airlines in all of the Scandinavian countries were subject to flight restrictions. One rule effectively reduced the charter-air business' threat of infringement by increasing the charter tourist's minimum length of stay to one week. Another rule contributed to keeping the price of charter-air tours in line with non-charter tours by requiring that hotel accommodation as well as breakfasts be included in the total price. Yet another regulation buffered the competition from charter flights by requiring a minimum of fifteen charter passengers per group (this was later lowered to ten).[41] This made it hard for air-charter companies to arrange tours for longer periods, given that most charter passengers favored trips no longer than a week or two.[42]

The Swedish Package Tour 187

These regulations helped to shape the consumption regime of air-package tours.[43] It was primarily the collaboration between the state-controlled SAS and the aviation authorities of the various Scandinavian countries that enabled the regulation to be created. Such close collaboration was indeed a pan-European phenomenon. During this period, most non-charter airlines were state owned—a clear advantage when it came to securing permits from the air traffic control authorities.[44] In its attempts to curb the competition from the charter industry, the state-controlled SAS was clearly in a position to influence aviation authorities directly; no intermediary was necessary.

Other forms of regulation were introduced to protect consumers from being defrauded by corrupt travel agents. The kind of regulation used in this case was authorization: designating some tour operators as having the official approval of the travel industry. Starting in the late 1930s, various authorization measures were put in place. The goal was to create an efficient system that could be approved by travel agents, consumers, as well as by bus companies (and, later, airlines). Authorization emerged as a way to avoid sub-standard tour experiences, as well. For example, immediately after the Second World War, tours were occasionally arranged randomly, by self-proclaimed, ad-hoc travel agents who had managed to get their hands on a bus and rounded up customers. Accommodation and activities were more or less improvised.

In an early attempt to regulate the worst con artists in the trade, a branch organization of the Association of Swedish Travel Agents (Svenska Resebyråföreningen) was formed in 1937. At the same time, the Travel and Holiday Organization of the Cooperative Movements in Sweden (Reso) began to organize vacations for the masses. Significantly, both organizations were established the year before the two-weeks-minimum-vacation plan was introduced. Both organizations also requested that the government regulate the travel industry. In 1949, yet another intermediary organization arose. A council of passenger-transportation companies, this group's task was to agree on rules and regulations for travel agents and organizers.[45]

Requests for the Swedish government to regulate the travel industry were largely denied: freedom of trade should prevail in the industry, the government argued. In 1951, a government commission upheld this judgment.[46] But one member of this commission, a Reso representative, disagreed. He stressed the importance of regulating travel agents at a time when "the clientele of travel life was broadened" to include the masses. For the wealthier traveler, a disastrous vacation was experienced merely as a lesson to be learned, he claimed. For the less-wealthy traveler, however, a botched vacation could amount to a personal catastrophe.[47] After all, some vacationers "saved up" for what promised to be the trip of a lifetime.

Starting in 1953, the Swedish Council for Passenger Transport Companies (Svenska Trafikföretagens Råd) became responsible for authorizing travel agents as well as package-tour organizers. (Notably, during this period, authorization was optional.) This was an unsatisfactory solution, given that the Association of Swedish Travel Agents was itself a member of the council: this placed travel agents in the untenably self-referential position of having the authority to authorizing themselves! To rectify this situation, the process was reorganized in 1960. Now, travel companies were subject to the approval of the Authorization Council of Swedish Carriers and Travel Agencies (Svenska Trafik- och Resebranschens Auktorisationsnämnd). This group's eight independent members were appointed by the Stockholm Chamber of Commerce (Stockholms Handelskammare)—yet another actor involved in regulating Swedish package tours.[48]

The various attempts to tighten charter-travel regulations via authorization reflect the different interpretations of how intermediary actors could be effective. Interestingly, negotiations that took place within government commissions and within local chambers of commerce often resulted in creating still more intermediary organizations that provided mediation junctions. For example, the Authorization Council of Swedish Carriers and Travel Agencies was an intermediary actor: it presented a viewpoint that had been negotiated among various stakeholders. The council was also a mediation junction: an organizational space in which different stakeholders could meet and hold discussions.

In December of 1963, the authorization council established new regulations. To secure authorization, travel agents and organizers were now required to demonstrate financial stability, reliability, as well as knowledge of the trade.[49] The proof-of-financial-stability requirement was now more explicit: every organizer and travel agent was obliged to pay a deposit equivalent to €50,000 and €100,000, respectively. These were funds to be used if and when travel operators were unable to fulfill their commitments to customers.

Ironically, having such funds on hand did not remedy the situation, given that most of those travel agents involved in "scandalous tours" had means available. But, insisting on deposits was at least a way of preventing bankrupt travel agencies from flying air-charter passengers abroad and leaving them there, bereft of tickets home. With package tours by air, the stakes were higher than with tours conducted by bus.

Consider the contrast between the air- and bus-travel regimes. With bus travel, the practice was for customers holding pre-paid hotel vouchers to travel via the chartered vehicle with the driver and a guide, both of whom stayed with the group of passengers throughout the trip. With air travel, on the other hand, the industry practice was for tour operators to collect payments from consumers *before* the trip—and to pay airlines and hotels only *after* the trip. This practice made it possible to start up a travel agency without financial means.[50] Given these circumstances, travel agents in financial trouble were indeed tempted to cancel the payments to airlines—and leave customers stranded. This loophole was another powerful motivation to reform the existing package-tour consumption regime. In May of 1964, yet another government commission was appointed. This group was tasked with analyzing the market conditions for package tours, especially tours that included chartered flights. The commission was also to survey the possibilities and demand for consumer guidance in this area.[51]

To recap, in the early 1960s, the bus-travel regime had begun to change, now embracing air transport. Government commissions and other travel-industry related organizations emerged, including the Swedish Council for Passenger Transport Companies. Various intermediary actors also emerged, such as the Authorization Council of Swedish Carriers and Travel Agencies. Still absent among these groups, however, were package-tour consumers: the travelers themselves.

Protecting Package-Tour Consumers: Swedish-Style

This was the context in which Sweden's "scandalous tours" first made headlines in March of 1963. Implicit in the press reports of "scandalous tours" was a demand for action, although it was unclear by whom and to what end. Behind the alarming news of package-tour consumers duped by travel agents was an even darker reality: no one before had spoken on behalf of package-tour consumers. The press had now assumed this role of defending consumers. As such, instead of using traditional channels such as government commissions or trade organizations, the press conducted its defense on its own territory: the pages of newspapers and magazines.

In the first half of the 1960s, the Swedish press and other media publicized "scandalous tours" so proactively that, eventually, these tours-gone-wrong received political attention. In response to press reports, the government agency for consumer issues—the Swedish National Consumer Council (Statens konsumentråd)—launched an investigation.

This may be interpreted as a sign of the agency's willingness to act on behalf of consumers. In any case, this willingness harmonized with the spirit of the era: on both sides of the Atlantic, consumer awareness came of age in the mid-1960s. Economic growth after the Second World War had stoked private consumption. In Sweden, this led to the creation in 1962 and 1963 of three distinct government commissions, all committed to "consumer enlightenment." One result of these commissions' efforts: the consumer council broadened its view of consumer issues to include package tours.[52]

In fact, the investigation initiated by the consumer council resulted in a report on Swedish package tours. The primary focus was air tours conducted between July and October of 1964. The typical traveler analyzed in the report was urban (from larger cities, like Stockholm), middle-class, white-collar, and earned an above-average income.[53] Given that many package-tour travelers had experienced earlier trips abroad, the package-tour-market expansion was attributed to the growing group of travelers making repeated trips.

In 1964, the new government commission coordinated the efforts of the press and the Swedish National Consumer Council in analyzing "scandalous tours" and the market conditions surrounding them. At last, package-tour consumers had an intermediary acting on their behalf in a formally organized mediation junction. The government commission of 1964 included more than the "usual suspects"—politicians, industry representatives, as well as experts on consumer issues. To some extent, the government commission defined which interest groups and intermediary actors would have a voice in the debate about consumers' "scandalous tours"—a term coined by the press.

The government commission of 1964 soon established that "scandalous tours" included those canceled at the last minute. Also deemed "scandalous" were those tours that had taken place only after extraordinary efforts on the part of the organizer, as well as tours that resumed only after extended delays. A third category considered "scandalous" was the tour in which travelers experienced far-lower-than-advertised levels of service. Tours for which there was no return flight—or a substantial delay before the return flight—were also branded as "scandalous."[54] These were serious shortcomings on the part of travel agents and tour organizers that propelled tours into the "scandalous" category. A bumpy flight or missed meals did not qualify.

Having worked for close to two years on the problem, the commission of 1964 noted that at least fifteen "scandalous tours" had been reported in the media over the course of twenty-seven months: January of 1964 to April of 1966. Almost all of these debacles had involved canceled outward-bound or return flights. The reasons for the canceled flights were either non-payments to airlines or the airline having had its landing rights in Sweden revoked. In several cases, tour operators' outstanding debts to hotels had resulted in tourists being threatened with eviction.[55] One of the commission's major conclusions was that "scandalous tour" applied only to package tours that included chartered flights. This conclusion supported the notion that air transport led to inefficiencies in the package-tour consumption regime—inefficiencies that had been less salient when dominated by bus transport. Apparently, package tours by other means of transport, such as bus or train, did not entail the same risk of cancellation.

In one case, the commission managed to interview sixty-eight out of seventy-six adult tourists involved in a failed package tour. In August of 1965, several newspapers had exposed this "scandalous tour," in which the return trip from Palma de Majorca had been delayed for three days. The reason: the airline had not received the agreed-upon payments from the tour operator. Interestingly, many of the consumers interviewed protested the image portrayed by the press: they did not regard their tour experience as "scandalous." The commission of 1964 also demonstrated that the press had grossly exaggerated the plight of the stranded tourists; press reports had contained inaccuracies.[56] Another investigation had shown that almost two-thirds of package-tour tourists were totally satisfied with their vacations, while approximately 30 percent had minor complaints. Only in exceptional cases did consumers have major complaints—and almost all these cases involved one particular travel agent.[57] Thus, the notion of defective air-package tours as widespread became discredited. The press reports that, three years earlier, had prompted the government inquiry were also now cast into doubt.

Intermediaries confirmed that a problem existed, although they maintained that the press had exaggerated. So, in 1966, the commission of 1964 concluded that "scandalous tours" were limited in scope, relevant only to some travelers in the package-tour market. Most of the currently available tours were organized and sold by authorized companies; smaller, unauthorized agents only accounted for a tiny fraction of the market. Even these fringe agents rarely failed to such an extent that the resulting tour could correctly be termed "scandalous." The problem was contained to a mere 1 percent of all package tours. But given the approximately 400,000 travelers per year, the problem was still noteworthy.[58] Finally, the matter was resolved: despite the media spotlight on "scandalous tours," the 1964 commission rejected the idea of imposing new legislation on travel agents to control the package-tour market, citing as sufficient the existing Norwegian legislation of 1948. The main argument against new legislation however, was politically driven: it was the fear of restricting competition. To resolve the matter while not restricting travel agencies, the 1964 commission proposed to create a new board for handling complaints between consumers and travel companies. Actually, such an organization had existed since 1960: the Association of Swedish Travel Agents had set up the Committee on Charter Trips (Sällskapsresekommittén). This was to address cases in which consumers and travel agents had been unable to negotiate mutually satisfactory deals. But, according to the 1964 commission, the existing committee was problematic: the Association of Swedish Travel Agents appointed the members, and there were signs of prejudice among the committee's practices.[59] Further, the Committee on Charter Trips was seen more as an intermediary actor representing travel agents—and less as a mediation junction in which consumers and travel agents could negotiate seemingly neutrally.

Another problem plagued the committee: few package-tour consumers knew of its existence, and the committee had few cases. In its little more than five-year existence (1960 to 1964), it had handled only forty-six cases, most of them regarding complaints about accommodation. In thirty-four of those cases, the committee had ruled in favor of the travel agent. These figures contrast sharply with the estimated one thousand annual complaints, written and verbal, received by the industry, though many of these grievances turned out to be minor.

In order to overcome the problems with the Association of Swedish Travel Agents' Committee on Charter Trips, the commission now proposed a new agency: the Swedish Travel Agents' Consumer Complaints Board (Resebranschens reklamationsnämnd) would handle package-tour consumer complaints. The new organization would be co-founded by the Swedish National Consumer Council, the Authorization Council of Swedish Carriers and Travel Agencies, and the Association of Swedish Travel Agents. This was a typically Swedish neo-corporative solution: an agency with representatives of both industry and consumers would be the mediation junction substituting for an intermediary actor. And this agency would handle complaints from consumers.

Some tourism-industry representatives disagreed with this solution. These representatives argued that, rather than form a whole new agency, it would be more efficient to make the authorization of travel agencies and organizers obligatory by law. They also observed that almost all

The Swedish Package Tour 193

of the problematic package tours had been organized by unauthorized agencies.[60] These were not the only reasons that representatives promoted obligatory legal authorization: it was also a way for the organizers and agencies to maintain control of the package-tour market. The majority of the 1964 commission, however, opted for the creation of a new organization, a new mediation junction for negotiations. After all, the decision-making power was with the government commission, which maintained close ties to the Swedish Parliament—and its power to establish new agencies.

The 1964 commission specified another important way to regulate the problems in the package-tour consumption regime: boost consumer education. Accordingly, the commission recommended that the Swedish National Consumer Council publish a text with basic information for package-tour consumers.[61] The suggestion was soon realized in the form of a magazine published by the consumer council; years of informative articles followed.[62] In addition to the proposed new agency, the commission suggested making minor changes to the existing institutional frameworks. Most notably, an increased guaranteed sum was to be put at the disposal of the board appointed by the Stockholm Chamber of Commerce.[63] The guarantee was to be obligatory by law for all package-tour agencies and organizers.

After it was published, the commission's report was submitted for comments to more than thirty agencies and interest groups, all of which largely agreed with the conclusions. (Some organizations believed the whole idea of "scandalous tours" had been exaggerated in the press—and that a legal framework was unnecessary.)[64] This round of comments can be understood as yet another mediation junction for intermediary actors without representation elsewhere. Most of the official commentators who responded to the report approved of the proposal to establish yet another committee for handling complaints. But the Social Democratic government finally rejected the idea: the Swedish National Consumer Council had only recently formed the Public Complaints Board (Allmänna reklamationsnämnden), and it included the travel industry.[65]

This rejection did not go unnoticed by the Swedish Parliament. Seven members of the Liberal Party introduced private members' bills seeking a specific department for package tours within the Public Complaints Board.[66] Other bills, seeking to eliminate the requirement for mandatory guarantees, were also introduced.[67] These initiatives signaled that the negotiations on package-tour consumption had reached the ultimate mediation junction in a democratic society: the negotiations had reached parliament. These proposed bills were discussed—and rejected. On its own initiative, the Public Complaints Board nevertheless formed a specific department for travel and accommodation within its own organization.

In May of 1967, the new law requiring monetary guarantees was debated in the Swedish Parliament: Were "scandalous tours" a significant enough social problem to merit obligatory monetary guarantees of such large sums, namely the equivalent of €200,000? Many parliamentarians cited the commission's report, which showed that "scandalous tours" were rare. Politicians also referred to the opinion on large financial guarantees articulated in the report: that this could hinder smaller-scale package-tour players. Many believed that the solution was disproportional to the problem. Worse, it threatened the existence of many innocent companies.[68] The press had created a problem that did not exist—or was small enough to be contained by less-dramatic measures. Despite this reasoning, the Social Democratic majority passed a new law requiring financial guarantees from every package-tour agency and organizer.

Conclusion

The Swedish package-tour industry actively promoted tourism consumption, which led to greater European interconnectedness. As the plane came to replace the bus as the preferred means of transportation, the package-tour consumption regime transformed. Having started in the 1960s, air-package tours to the Mediterranean came to represent an important part of Swedish consumer culture, symbolizing a middle-class—even an emerging working-class—pursuit of happiness and leisure. Package tours constituted a service requiring substantial pre-payments by consumers, making them vulnerable when agencies and organizers failed to meet their commitments. The result, initiated by press reports and negotiated by representatives of different interest groups, was an institutional solution. This was introduced to protect consumers from travel agents and organizers who took advantage of customers' pre-payments, threatening the notion of a perfect holiday in the sun.

When "scandalous tours" became a well-known term in the early 1960s, mediation junctions, such as government commissions, were established to protect consumers. In turn, consumers came to see themselves as represented by an intermediary actor in the form of a government agency: the Swedish National Consumer Council. Within five years of the appearance of the first press article mentioning "scandalous tours," the social democratic government also passed a new law requiring travel agencies and package-tour organizers to provide a deposit equivalent to €200,000. This would serve as a guarantee to be paid out in case of tour arrangements falling short. Eventually, the Public Complaints Board established a specific department for travel and accommodation.

All of these efforts reflected more than just the "scandalous tours" phenomenon and the associated press campaign. More important was exposing the dysfunctional package-tour consumption regime that had emerged when bus transportation yielded to air travel: consumers were left in need of representation. The reaction to this perceived imbalance was swift and thorough. Barely one year after the first press report, a mediation junction was created in the form of a government commission. Two years after that, the commission's report was published; various intermediary actors voiced their responses. The following year, the problem was resolved in parliament.

This process proceeded relatively swiftly, despite the complexity of involving practically every category of actor associated with the package-tour market: from SAS to government agencies, travel agents to tourists. All of these actors had a say in the decision-making process leading to the new law and the complaints board. On closer investigation, some portrayed by the press as victims of "scandalous tours" proved to be unscathed. But the "scandalous tours" scenario still provided a platform for setting up institutions to protect consumers from unscrupulous travel agents and organizers. The press informed the public and set the political process in motion: commissions, investigations, and debates eventually brought about new regulations for package-tour consumption.

During the postwar period, Sweden was a neo-corporative state. Accordingly, the resolution of the "scandalous tours" debate represents a prototypically neo-corporative solution: organizations were set up to facilitate tripartite negotiations. Consider the various sets of actors involved: the department of travel and accommodation included three representatives of consumer interests on one side, appointed, for example, by the Swedish National Consumer Council, and three representatives from different branch organizations on the other side. Chairing the group was a legal expert with experience as a judge. In processing complaints, written statements from the parties involved were used, but the parties themselves were not allowed to participate in the negotiations.[69] This was a mediation junction populated by intermediary actors alone.

The state intervention that took place in Sweden was of a particular kind: this intervention affected the country's package-tour consumption regime; often, the intervention was close at hand when it came to regulating markets; and this kind of intervention took place in the Scandinavian countries at large, as well. American interests had a limited influence indeed. The U.S. supplied infrastructure in the form of airplanes, airfields, and international agreements on military and civil aviation. Arguably, American promotion and advertising—to Americans—of certain Mediterranean tourist destinations also may have triggered greater numbers of Europeans to visit those destinations. But the scale of Swedish package-tour consumption during the 1960s and 1970s was, if anything, a European way of life in its own right, with its own institutional solutions and prerequisites.

Notes

1. *Svenska Dagbladet* (A edition), March 24, 1963 (No. 82), 5.
2. The Swedish Royal Library, Stockholm, Okat., Utländska resor, Program och prospekt, 1956:1, Kvalitetsresor 1956.
3. *Svenska Dagbladet* (A edition), March 24, 1963 (No. 82), 5.
4. "Alarmerande olyckskurva för växande charterflyg," in ibid.
5. Thomas Kaiserfeld, "From Sightseeing to Sunbathing: Changing Traditions in Swedish Package Tours: From Edification by Bus to Relaxation by Airplane in the 1950s and 60s," *Journal of Tourism History* 2 (2010): 149–63.
6. Ruth Oldenziel, Adri A. Albert de la Bruhèze and Onno de Wit, "Europe's Mediation Junction: Technology and Consumer Society in the 20th Century," *History and Technology* 21 (2005): 107–39. See also Ruth Schwartz Cowan, "The Consumption Junction: A Proposal for Research Strategies in the Sociology of Technology," in *The Social Construction of Technological Systems*, ed. Wiebe E. Bijker, Thomas P. Hughes, and Trevor Pinch (Cambridge, MA: MIT Press, 1989), 261–80; Karin Zachmann, "A Socialist Consumption Junction: Debating the Mechanization of Housework in East Germany, 1956-1957," *Technology & Culture* 43 (2002): 73–99.
7. A discussion on the Swedish welfare state and consumption can be found in Helena Mattsson and Sven-Olov Wallenstein, "Introduction," in *Swedish Modernism: Architecture, Consumption and the Welfare State*, ed. Helena Mattsson and Sven-Olov Wallenstein (London: Black Dog Publishing, 2010), 6–33; Mattias Tydén and Urban Lundberg, "In Search of the Swedish Model: Contested Historiography," in *Swedish Modernism*, 36–49.
8. Peter J. Katzenstein, *Small Countries in World Markets: Industrial Policy in Europe* (Ithaca, NY: Cornell University Press, 1985); Bo Rothstein, *Den korporativa staten: Intresseorganisationer och statsförvaltning i svensk politik* (Stockholm: Norstedts, 1992); Bo Rothstein, "State Structure and Variations in Corporatism: The Swedish Case," *Scandinavian Political Studies* 14 (1991): 149–71.

9. Orvar Löfgren, "Längtan till landet Annorlunda," in *Längtan till landet Annorlunda: Om turism i historia och nutid* (Hedemora: Gidlund, 1990), 9–49.
10. Lena Eskilsson, "Svenska turistföreningen från fjäll till friluftsliv: Från den vetenskaplige vildmannen till den cyklande husmodern," *Historisk tidskrift* 116 (1996): 257–82; Lena Lötmarker and Bo-A Wendt, *Resmål till salu: Svenska turistbroschyrers textuella och språkliga utveckling under hundra år* (Lund: Sekel, 2009).
11. Mary Blume, *Côte d'Azur: Inventing the French Riviera* (London: Thames & Hudson, 1992); Paolo Capuzzo, "Spectacles of Sociability: European Cities as Sites of Consumption," in *Urban Machinery: Inside Modern European Cities*, ed. Mikael Hård and Thomas J. Misa (Cambridge, MA: MIT Press, 2008), 99–120. For an analysis of Americanization and Swedish everyday life, the conclusion of which is that Sweden was Americanized in a very Swedish way, see Tom O'Dell, *Culture Unbound: Americanization and Everyday Life in Sweden*, new ed. (Lund: Nordic Academic Press, 2012).
12. Adrian Franklin and Mike Crang, "The Trouble with Tourism and Travel Theory?" *Tourist Studies* 1 (2001): 5–22; Pau Obrador Pons, Mike Crang, and Penny Travlou, eds., *Cultures of Mass Tourism: Doing the Mediterranean in the Age of Banal Mobilities* (London: Ashgate, 2009).
13. The reason that no major changes were made in the 1940s to the labor laws has been attributed to the fact that unions as well as employers gave priority to economic growth. Later, vacationing was promoted as a cheaper way to cut working time, compared to shorter workdays or workweeks. See Carina Gråbacke, *När folket tog semester: Studier av Reso 1937–1977* (Lund: Sekel, 2008), 43; Hans Hellström, *Struktur, aktör eller kultur? Arbetstidspolitik i det industrialiserade Sverige* (Stockholm: Almqvist & Wiksell International, 1992), 103–85.
14. Regarding the debate on Sweden's relations with Nazi Germany, see Ingela Karlsson, "Sig själv närmast," in *En (o)moralisk hållning? Sveriges ekonomiska relationer med Nazityskland*, ed. Charlotte Haider (Stockholm: Forum för levande historia, 2006), 7–39.
15. Gråbacke, *När folket tog semester*, 45.
16. Ibid., 46.
17. Gustav Endrédi, *Resekonsumtionen 1950–1975* (Stockholm: Industrins utredningsinstitut, 1967), 83–4, 86.
18. Ibid., 19.
19. Roger Marjavaara, "Mot Fjärran land—svensk flygcharterturism 1962–1993" (Master's thesis, Umeå University, 1998).
20. Neal Moses Rosendorf, "Be El Caudillo's Guest: The Franco Regime's Quest for Rehabilitation and Dollars after World War II via the Promotion of U.S. Tourism to Spain," *Diplomatic History* 30 (2006), 367–407.
21. Ibid., 385, 405.
22. Frank Schipper, *Driving Europe: Building Europe on Roads in the Twentieth Century* (Eindhoven: Aksant, 2008), 231–40.
23. Göte Rosén, *Vägen till Palma. 25 års "luftaffärer": en memoarbok om charterflygets utveckling* (Malmö: CEGE, 1970), 63–4.
24. Rosenberg, *Air Travel within Europe*, 26–97.
25. NATO Archives, DES(98)1, Part XIV, CEAC, 1, accessed October 22, 2010, http://www.nato.int/archives/tool2.htm.

26. NATO Archives, DES(94)2, Part XIV, Miscellaneous Documents, 1955–1958, 4–5, accessed October 22, 2010, http://www.nato.int/archives/tool2.htm; Leif Klette, "The European Air Traffic Crisis: NATO's Search for Civil and Military Cooperation," *NATO Review* 39 (1991), 24–9.
27. Richard Pells, *Not Like Us: How Europeans Have Loved, Hated, and Transformed American Culture since World War II* (New York: Basic Books, 1997), 137.
28. Rosén, *Vägen till Palma*, 88, 124–6.
29. Ibid., 88.
30. Klas Grinell, *Att sälja världen: Omvärldsbilder i svensk utlandsturism* (Gothenburg: Acta Univesitatis Gothenburgensis, 2004), 164.
31. Kaiserfeld, "From Sightseeing to Sunbathing." Trips by plane became even faster with jet airliners, which reduced the flight time between Copenhagen and Athens from eleven to six hours, for example. See Östen Johansson, "Börja i god tid med att förverkliga semesterdrömmen," *Råd och rön* 10, no. 2 (1967): 26–8.
32. This is a theme that has been overlooked in tourism research. See Armando Montanari and Allan M. Williams, eds., *European Tourism: Regions, Spaces and Restructuring* (Chichester: Wiley, 1995).
33. Arne Rosenberg, *Air Travel within Europe* (Stockholm: The National Swedish Consumer Council and Norstedts, 1970), 22. The number of Swedish airplane charter tourists multiplied seventeen times between 1955 and 1962: "133 000 svenskar reste förra året med charterflyg," *Svenska Dagbladet* (A edition), March 24, 1963 (No. 82), 5.
34. In 1965, the populations of Great Britain; the Scandinavian countries (Sweden, Denmark, and Norway); and West Germany were 54, 16, and 60 million, respectively.
35. Ole Wæver, "Nordic Nostalgia: Northern Europe after the Cold War," *International Affairs* 68 (1992): 77–102.
36. Douglas C. Pearce, "Mediterranean Charters: A Comparative Geographic Perspective," *Tourism Management* 8 (1987): 291–305.
37. Göran Andolf, *Sverige och utlandet 1930–1975: Indikatorer för mätning av Sveriges kulturella beroende* (Lund: Lund University, 1977), 32–3.
38. For information on the difference between scheduled and non-scheduled flights, see Rosenberg, *Air Travel within Europe*, 68–70, 134–50.
39. Endrédi, *Resekonsumtionen*, 85; *Sällskapsresor: Betänkande avgivet av Statens konsumentråds sällskapsreseutredning*, Statens offentliga utredningar 1966:25 (Stockholm: Handelsdepartementet, 1966), 16–17.
40. Rosenberg, *Air Travel within Europe*, 70–3.
41. Ibid., 71; Göte Rosén, *Orädd att flyga* (Uppsala: Nybloms, 1976), 79.
42. Thomas von Seth, *Charterhistoria* (Lidingö: Vivlio Förlag, 2008), 57–8.
43. Rosén, *Vägen till Palma*, 64–5.
44. Ibid.
45. *Sällskapsresor*, 17, 26–7.
46. *Turisttrafiken från utlandet: Betänkande avgivet av 1948 års utredning angående turisttrafiken från utlandet*, Statens offentliga utredningar 1951:49 (Stockholm: Handelsdepartementet, 1951); Gråbacke, *När folket tog semester*, 196–200.
47. *Sällskapsresor*, 27.
48. Ibid., 21–3.
49. Ibid., 49.

50. "Utredningsförslag: Lagstifta mot skandalresor. Inrätta reklamationsnämd," *Råd och rön* 9, no. 7 (1966): 14–15.
51. *Sällskapsresor*, 12. No further information on the government commission or its background has been found in relevant archives, including those of the Swedish National Consumer Council in the Swedish National Archives.
52. Sophie Elsässer, *Att skapa en konsument: Råd och Rön och den statliga konsumentupplysningen* (Gothenburg: Makadam, 2012), 79–81, 126–35.
53. "Välbetald storstadsbo sällskapsreser mest," *Råd och rön* 8 (May–June 1965): 2.
54. *Sällskapsresor*, 51.
55. Ibid., 52–5.
56. Ibid., 195–202.
57. "Välbetald storstadsbo sällskapsreser mest."
58. "Utredningsförslag."
59. *Sällskapsresor*, 96–9.
60. Ibid., 126–7; Gråbacke, *När folket tog semester*, 203–4.
61. *Sällskapsresor*, 115.
62. Johansson, "Börja i god tid med att förverkliga semesterdrömmen"; Östen Johansson, "Planerar ni för sällskapsresa?" *Råd och rön* 11, no. 3 (1968): 16–23.
63. *Sällskapsresor*, 37–8, 60–7; Gråbacke, *När folket tog semester*, 203.
64. The Swedish National Archives, Cabinet Records, Ministry of Trade and Industry, March 17, 1967, No. 20; *Bihang till riksdagens protokoll 1967*, Saml. 1, Proposition 106, 4–5.
65. *Bihang till riksdagens protokoll 1967*, Saml. 1, Proposition 106, 29.
66. *Bihang till riksdagens protokoll 1967*, Saml. 3, Motioner i första kammaren 829, 9; *Bihang till riksdagens protokoll 1967*, Saml. 4, Band 3, Motioner i andra kammaren 1032, 9–10.
67. *Bihang till riksdagens protokoll 1967*, Saml. 3, Motioner i första kammaren 826–28; *Bihang till riksdagens protokoll 1967*, Saml. 4, Band 3, Motioner i andra kammaren 1030–1 och 1033.
68. *Riksdagens protokoll 1967*, Första kammaren, Band 3, N:r 32, May 25, 44–57; *Riksdagens protokoll 1967*, Andra kammaren, Band 5, N:r 32, May 25, 72–92.
69. *Rese-reklamationer: En genomgång av reklamationer rörande charterresor* (Stockholm: Allmänna reklamationsnämnden and Liber/Allmänna förlaget, 1985), 9–10.

9
Coping with Cars, Families, and Foreigners: Swedish Postwar Tourism

Per Lundin

In January of 1950, the chairman of the Swedish Tourist Association wrote a manifesto-like letter to an industrialist. The tourist association chairman was Arthur Lindhagen, who was also a justice of Sweden's Supreme Court. The industrialist in question was Erland Waldenström, CEO of the large, state-owned mining company, LKAB. In the letter, Lindhagen invited Waldenström to join the tourist association's board. Lindhagen also expressed a concern: in the minds of the Swedish public, he wrote, tourism had become "synonymous with the efforts to attract foreign tourists to the country for economic reasons, especially from countries with hard currency." For his part, Lindhagen viewed this development with "suspicion"—even "animosity." He assured Waldenström, however, that the Swedish Tourist Association—the country's oldest, largest tourist organization—transcended all forms of "dollar tourism."[1]

The Swedish Tourist Association had been founded in 1885 by a group of upper-middle-class male academics; the organization became the key intermediary in the Swedish tourism arena. "Know Your Country!" ("Känn ditt land!")—the Swedish Tourist Association's motto—echoed an ambition to shape national identity through tourism. As Lindhagen had voiced in earlier writings, the association worked "exclusively in the interest of the fatherland" with "the touring of Swedes in Sweden" as its aim.[2] This was clearly a paternalistic and romantic nationalistic ideology—and it was part of a broader European pattern. During the second half of the nineteenth century, the industrializing nations established alpine clubs and tourist associations as a part of the nation-building processes that took place throughout Europe.

The Swedish Tourist Association targeted youth and eventually workers: by discovering their country, its unique cultural heritage and national landscapes, tourists would ostensibly discover themselves.

With the advent of the railway, the mountain regions in northern Sweden had become accessible; hiking trails and mountain cabins were soon built under the auspices of the association.[3] The association's brand of tourism embodied a longing for authenticity and the simple life, an antidote to the fast-paced though comfortable life led by the bourgeois middle classes in Sweden's modern, industrializing cities. This version of tourism posited that the experience of nature in its pure form could be attained by stripping away the culture's layer of varnish.[4] A physically active, even strenuous regime, the tourism promoted by the association represented a bourgeois form of masculinity in which the family was strangely absent, and sexuality was suppressed by the disciplining of the body.[5] For example, the association organized daylong hikes—and often separated men and women in lodgings. In the 1930s, the association established a network of hostels (*vandrarhem*, literally translated as "wanderers' homes"). A collective form of accommodation, the hostels were simple affairs in which men and women indeed stayed in different dormitories. Swedish hostels were designed with the bicycle in mind. Often, hostels were situated in old farmhouses, manor houses, monasteries, and schools in the Swedish heartland—buildings and landscapes that the association considered to be culturally and historically significant. By the end of the decade, the original twenty-nine hostels had increased to a nation-wide network consisting of nearly 300 such structures; in the early 1950s, the association claimed to have a monopoly on roadside lodging in Sweden.[6] The hostel movement became the most enduring physical manifestation of the association's ideology. In fact, the hostel itself still flourishes in Sweden, albeit in a thoroughly updated form. And it is the Swedish Tourist Association that indirectly retains control of Swedish hostels today.

In his letter to Waldenström, Lindhagen argued that the Swedish Tourist Association, with its ambition to foster national integration through tourism, presented an alternative to the commercial forms of mass tourism. With its focus on an individual, physically active, outdoor form of tourism that was "preferably hard and very demanding," Lindhagen claimed that the association stood for a "vintage bourgeois idealism."[7] As such, Lindhagen practically spelled it out: the Swedish Tourist Association embraced a bourgeois form of tourism. This originated in the mid-nineteenth century. Subsequently bourgeois tourism acquired a hegemonic position that lasted well into the 1930s, if not longer. In the words of the American historian Ellen Furlough, tourism was mainly a "practice of privilege" during this period. It was limited to the social groups that enjoyed the privilege of paid vacations and had the financial means to travel for leisure. Bourgeois tourism entailed a social hierarchy of taste and expenditure that reflected steep income inequalities. A significant marker of class boundaries, bourgeois tourism enforced social distinctions and signaled prestige.[8] Bourgeois tourism took various forms—the Swedish Tourist Association represented one version only—but there were common traits. Specifically, most elites valued quality and personal interaction when they traveled; they regarded tourism as a project that promoted individualism and forged national identity.[9] A coalition of powerful civil-society organizations shaped the ideologies, institutions, and technologies of tourism. These organizations were populated—and frequently controlled—by the educated middle classes, the so-called *Bildungsbürgertum*. And, according to the German historian Jürgen Kocka, the culture of the educated middle classes tended

Figure 9.1 The hostel offered low-cost, communal accommodation with minimal amenities. Originally, hostels served biking tourists, especially youth. Often, these simple accommodations were located in rural settings—in this case, a farm building.

to permeate society at large. An essential feature of this culture was the *embourgeoisement* of society's non-middle-class strata.[10] The Swedish Tourist Association exemplifies this feature: after all, the association labored to make the working classes "middle-classier" by exposing them to bourgeois norms and values.

The American Challenge

As the 1950s approached, bourgeois tourism met with more and more challenges. And the main source of these challenges—as Lindhagen had implied in his letter to Waldenström—was America, at least in the eyes of most Europeans. These were the years in which the United States was at its most powerful, the years of the Marshall Plan (1948–1952). As Adri A. Albert de la Bruhèze discusses in Chapter 7, part of the plan was to attract American tourists to Europe so they could spend U.S. dollars to help reduce the foreign-currency deficit (hence Lindhagen's disparaging remark about "dollar tourism"). Although Sweden had maintained neutrality in the Second World War, the country did participate in the Marshall Plan. Compared with other European countries, however, Sweden received limited economic aid.[11] But the U.S. influence was not only economic, nor was it limited to the workings and to the time frame of the Marshall Plan.[12] Above all, America presented itself as the key cultural power of the twentieth century—as the model of modernity. Indeed, the United States has meant many different things to Europeans, the British historian David W. Ellwood asserts, but common among these representations "has always been an impression of the future, or at least one powerful version of it."[13]

In the case of tourism, it was the car-centered American way of life, above all, that represented the U.S. to Europeans. Some would argue that the car served as the ultimate symbol of American modernity. As the distinguished economist W.W. Rostow pointed out in his seminal book, *The Stages of Economic Growth* (1960), the social and economic effects of the affordable, mass-produced automobile were quite revolutionary. America had invented the age of mass consumption with Fordism; America had embraced it as a way of life in the 1920s; and America had taken it to its logical conclusion in the postwar decade.[14] When it came to the car, European commentators were convinced that the European countries would follow in the footsteps of America. For example, after visiting the United States, one Swedish architect and urban planner declared: "The motor car is not a pastime of the better off, but *an inescapable factor in the progress of society*. Our whole way of life is sliding towards Americanization."[15] As this quotation implies—and, indeed, as this book illustrates—Europeans did not interpret American ways of life altogether approvingly: to many, the car-centered American way of life was seen as promising and desirable; to others, it was viewed as threatening and frightening. For virtually all Europeans, however, the car-centered way of life was perceived as inevitable.

Arguably, the first Swedish hotel with automobile facilities was Gyllene Uttern (The Golden Otter), which, early on, elicited ambivalent attitudes on the part of Swedes. It was in 1933 that a private entrepreneur established Gyllene Uttern close to the town of Gränna, midway between Stockholm and Malmö. The hotel's founder had made multiple trips to the U.S. and had been inspired by the country's nascent car culture. Modeled on American "tourist cabins"—a forerunner to the motel—the hotel consisted of five small cottages organized around a restaurant, a coffee shop, and a gas station. Guests parked their cars just outside the cottages. A display of national flags signaled to international guests that—contrary to traditional Swedish lodging—the facility offered a modern (as in international) standard of accommodation. Some commentators depicted Gyllene Uttern as a "Hollywood milieu," and questioned whether or not Swedes were ready for the wave of "Americanization unfolding over their old country." Others hailed Gyllene Uttern as the first Swedish hotel that was adapted to the car. Reactions ranged from dismay to enthusiastic approval.[16]

Admittedly, Gyllene Uttern appeared on the scene nearly two decades before the breakthrough of mass motorization. But the example illustrates that, from early on, visionaries in the Swedish hotel and tourism industry—from architects to contractors and developers, hotel managers to automobile associations—were paying close attention to American service infrastructure, which had already adapted to mass motorization. This attention to America intensified in the early 1950s: using the U.S. example as the basis for their argument, these visionaries claimed that the "nature of the car" would revolutionize Swedish tourism. In the case of accommodation—a critical component of tourism—attention turned to an American invention: the motel.[17]

The world's first motel had been established in San Luis Obispo, California, in 1926; the construction of motels in the U.S. had exploded during the succeeding decades. Forward thinkers in Sweden anticipated how a network of motels along the nation's trunk roads would replace the railway-based—and apparently obsolete—structure of commercial hotels and resort hotels. If these bourgeois, European forms of accommodation mirrored the hierarchical "old" society, the democratically inspired, American motel model reflected the "new" society. The American version of the motel comprised standardized rooms of equal size. Room layouts were identical, as if produced on a Fordist assembly line. Management procedures were also codified: guests paid in advance at reception (no tipping required), received the room key, drove up to their unit, and parked in their designated spot. Thus, the motel was more than a new form of accommodation for the "modern auto tourist": the motel also symbolized a new way of life. Specifically, the Swedish tourism visionaries depicted the modern auto tourist as a "car vagabond" who valued freedom, independence, and mobility. But the car vagabond shared few characteristics with the traditional vagabond. In fact, this newfangled vagabond—usually a man traveling with his family—was neither a hobo nor a tramp: the newly car-mobile tourist required comfort and efficiency, modern amenities and service. The motel promised all of this without restricting freedom and independence. As an idea, the motel embodied key elements of the American model of modernity. It was these that apparently proved irresistible to Europeans during the twentieth century—especially, perhaps, during the immediate postwar decades.[18]

In Sweden, this interest in—and selective enthusiasm for—the American way of life coincided with the transition from a bourgeois mode of tourism to a mass-scale mode. Two structural changes helped to catalyze this transition: the democratization of leisure time and motorization. These changes took place against a background of economic transformation: during the 1950s, the average salary for a male worker rose by 116 percent, while prices rose by only 50 percent. This was the context in which spare time became democratized.[19]

With the introduction of statutory two weeks' paid vacation in 1938, new social groups became tourists. The impact was dramatic. In less than two decades, the total number of vacation days more than tripled. The lion's share of this vacation time was spent in Sweden rather than abroad. An official report estimated that, in 1949, an astounding 80 percent of Swedish Trade Union Confederation members, all of whom were working class, had spent their vacation time away from home. For members of the Swedish Confederation of Professional Employees, all of whom were lower-middle class, 91 percent vacationed away from home—mostly in Sweden.[20]

Leaving work—and leaving home—for a couple of weeks during the summer had now become a reality for the broader social strata of Swedish society; routinely, time was reserved for leisure activities, pleasure, and travel. In 1951, paid vacation was extended to three weeks, and in 1963, to four. Together with the breakthrough of mass motorization—the second structural change—the gradual increase in vacation time created opportunities for new vacation patterns. In the 1950s, the number of cars almost quintupled from 252,000 to 1,193,900 (and the population grew from 7,041,000 to 7,497,000), with the result that Sweden attained the highest level of car ownership per capita in Europe.[21] Increased travel followed the increased car ownership. Between 1950 and 1964, travel consumption rose by 6 percent annually. This represented a greater increase than in any other category of consumption: by 1964, the car accounted for almost three-quarters of total travel consumption. During the initial postwar decades, motoring was primarily a leisure activity, and traffic peaked during weekends and summer holidays.[22]

The democratization of tourism by car challenged the Swedish hostel movement, which had been designed around the bicycle and walking as primary means of transportation. The American-style motel, rather than the established Swedish hostel, seemed better suited to accommodating the growing numbers of Sweden's automobile tourists. In fact, the bourgeois mode of tourism that sustained the hostel movement was about to lose its hegemony. The bourgeois middle classes had witnessed the disintegration of their exclusive economic and social privileges, while the lower classes were enjoying greater-than-ever economic and social mobility. Almost as an omen, one of the staunchest defenders of bourgeois tourism died at this liminal moment in the transition toward mass tourism: Arthur Lindhagen passed away in 1950, just a few weeks after having written to Waldenström.[23]

In this chapter, I consider how, as an iconic promoter of Sweden's bourgeois tourism regime, the Swedish Tourist Association encompassed the American challenge. More specifically, I examine how the hostel movement—the key embodiment of the association's ideology—coped with the exponentially increasing auto tourism and the motel as the promising new form of accommodation that followed in its wake.

I claim that the bourgeois-tourism ideology did not oppose modernization per se, but that it promoted a different version of modernity— and "modernized" according to its principles. For those who espoused bourgeois tourism, America had a rhetorical meaning: the U.S. projected a contrasting image of modernity that, in turn, prompted the Swedish Tourist Association to modernize. The argument here is that the Swedish Tourist Association modernized the hostel movement by selectively appropriating component processes of the American model of modernity: the car-centered way of life; the family-centered way of life; and the highly mobile way of life—without appropriating the American concept of comfort. Contrary to the gadget-filled, standardized, and efficient, but anonymous and mass-produced motel, the modernized hostel continued to manifest austerity and simplicity, outdoor life, and pastoral romanticism. The hostel remained popular to Swedes, presumably because it expressed one of modern tourism's more indispensable qualities: authenticity. The motel, by contrast, never became more than a fad, and, as I have discussed elsewhere, it remained a marginal phenomenon in Swedish—not to mention European—tourism.[24]

Building a Bourgeois Tourism Regime

Given its central position in Sweden's tourism regime—and, indeed, in Swedish society at large—the Swedish Tourist Association managed to modernize the hostel movement successfully. But how did the association gain prominence as a prime promoter of bourgeois tourism? And how do we interpret the association's ideology, aims, and actions?

During the interwar period, the Swedish Tourist Association entered its most expansive and dynamic decades. It had grown rapidly from fewer than one hundred members in its first year to about approximately 25,000 at the turn of the century. In 1924, it boasted 100,000 members, and the figure continued to increase during the following decades; by 1951, membership had reached 165,000. Originally, the association's members had hailed from the Swedish bourgeoisie. By the interwar period, in contrast, the membership reflected a considerably broader social spectrum. Clerks, elementary school teachers, and nurses; policemen, and shopkeepers joined the association. Even factory workers, for example, joined, though admittedly in small numbers.[25] Rather than developing into a broad and democratic popular movement—like the labor movement, the temperance movement, or the Free Churches, for example—the association maintained a strictly centralized, top-down-controlled organization whose board members belonged to the bourgeoisie exclusively. Typically, they were high-ranking academics, jurists, military officers, and politicians who occupied key positions in the expanding public administration of the modern new nation-state.[26] Often, board members held key positions in other civil-society organizations, as well. Personal acquaintanceships and friendships contributed to forging strong, lasting bonds between the various organizations.

Close scrutiny reveals the small network of individuals that controlled the key organizations in Swedish leisure and tourism. This network, which expanded over time, included the key government organizations within railway transportation (the Swedish State Railways and the Swedish Railway Board) and public education (the Swedish Board of Education), for example. Also included in the network were civil-society organizations for cultural heritage and local history (the Swedish Homestead Society); as well as nature preservation, outdoor life, and tourism (the Swedish Society for Nature Conservation, the pro-military Swedish Ski Association, and the more commercially oriented Swedish Association for Tourist Traffic). Thus, a host of government and civil-society organizations coalesced around the Swedish Tourist Association's views on tourism. Accordingly, when the association undertook initiatives, it could count on broad economic, institutional, and even political support.[27]

In fact, the Swedish Tourist Association became embedded in Swedish society; the association functioned as a government organization. Predictably, the association and its fellow bourgeois-tourism organizations argued against state initiatives in tourism. This contingent maintained that the nation's civil-society institutions were perfectly capable of organizing the tourism sector. But, when the Social Democratic Party came to power in the early 1930s, the pressure to institute state-led social reforms increased. In 1937, the social democratic Minister for Health and Social Affairs inaugurated a government commission whose task it was to suggest state initiatives to improve leisure and outdoor life. Interestingly, the arbiters of the existing bourgeois-tourist regime managed to wrest control of the commission. The Swedish Tourist Association's vice chairman (1929–1950) and former executive (1914–1919), Hilding Kjellman, was appointed as the commission's chairman; representatives of the Swedish State Railways, the Swedish Railway Board, and the Swedish Ski Association became delegates.[28] Among other outcomes, the committee helped to found a government body for leisure and tourism in 1939. One significant task of the new organization, named the Swedish State Board for Leisure, was to fund domestic infrastructure for leisure and outdoor life. Intriguingly, a large portion of the funding was channeled to the Swedish Tourist Association as well as the Swedish Ski Association. And so the bourgeois regime of tourism was able to shape the Swedish state's initiatives in leisure and tourism, with the government funding the association's activities and supporting its goals.[29]

The governmental arm of the bourgeois regime shared the Swedish Tourist Association's ideology, which, as we have seen, was inflected by paternalism, puritanism, and romantic nationalism. These traits became even more clearly defined during the interwar years, fueled, in part, by the political turmoil in the wake of the First World War.

At the turn of the century, the notion of the "Russian Menace" had already begun to loom large in leading Swedish circles. When the Bolsheviks seized power in Russia, fears of a *morbus Asiaticus* threatening the Western world reached new heights. The Swedish bourgeoisie were petrified that the Russian Revolution and the upheavals on the continent would spread. The Swedish labor movement's revolutionary rhetoric escalated—and remained pronounced throughout the 1920s. The bourgeois middle classes mobilized against this "[socialist] threat to the [bourgeois] system."[30] The Swedish Tourist Association took part in a loosely knit effort to curb the working classes' internationalist and socialist tendencies: the strategy was to include the working classes in the nation-building process.

Somewhat paradoxically, the Swedish Tourist Association began to view commercial tourism with suspicion, believing that it, too, fostered internationalism. As such, commercial interests threatened the association's ambition of shaping the Swedish national identity by promoting domestic tourism. Arthur Lindhagen's appointment as the Swedish Tourist Association's new chairman in 1929 exemplified this shift towards a heightened, even aggressive nationalism. In his inaugural address, Lindhagen echoed the xenophobia and racism that pervaded many debates of the interwar years, when the potential influx of immigrants was often seen as a threat to employment; order and security; and the "purity" of the Nordic race.[31] Verbally, he violently attacked the massive Swedish influx of foreign tourists, which he found utterly "useless" and, even worse, "dangerous to our beautiful country." Lindhagen feared that the foreign mass tourism would lead to a banalization, commercialization, industrialization, and over-exploitation of Sweden's pristine natural environment—and the "disappearance of the Swedishness." Admitting that domestic tourism might also do harm as well, he maintained that Swedish tourism was a sacrifice duly counterbalanced by a purely idealistic motive: "the strengthening of the feelings for the fatherland."[32] Lindhagen defined and legitimated the association's ideology vis-à-vis the commercial, industrialized, and standardized mass tourism, which aimed at comfort and pleasure—as represented by an imagined America. I maintain that Lindhagen's beliefs were reflected in the top-down-controlled association.[33] Lindhagen was a close friend of the geographer Carl-Julius Anrick, the association's dynamic and forceful managing director from 1919 to 1958, and his wife, Calla Anrick, who edited the association's journal. This troika shared an ideology; their views largely defined the content, direction, and pace of change of the association's activities for the following two decades.

Figure 9.2 The Swedish Tourist Association's chairman, Arthur Lindhagen (in the middle), with the association's managing director, Carl-Julius Anrick, and his wife, Calla Anrick. Taken at the inauguration of the first Swedish hostel in the town of Gränna: May, 1933.

Since its inception, the Swedish Tourist Association had organized trips to the mountains for secondary-school students and, later, for elementary-school students, as well. The explicit aim was to help youth from the bourgeois middle classes "to feel at home in the nation."[34] After the First World War, the association decided to target a considerably broader social spectrum. The association collaborated with the Swedish Board of Education, Swedish State Railways, the Swedish Railway Board, and the Swedish Ski Association. Together, they organized school trips for working-class youth, as well as domestic package tours for working-class adults. Allied with the railway authorities, the association was able to offer discounted fares.[35] In contrast with the labor movement, which gave priority to the class struggle and promoted internationalism, the association strove to downplay differences between the classes by emphasizing solidarity with the nation. In effect, the Swedish Tourist Association made the conservative proclamation that the rift between classes should be bridged by strengthening the Swedish national identity.[36]

The association managed to reach only a small fraction of the working class with these school trips and package tours to the mountain regions in the far north. By the end of 1920s, civil-society groups and school authorities began to lobby for a network of low-price roadside youth hostels in the more densely populated regions to be built for Swedish youth involved in biking and hiking. The association adopted the idea and drafted a proposal, which it submitted to a range of civil-society organizations.[37] The purpose was two-fold: to solicit comments and suggestions, and to secure organizations' support. It is noteworthy that, in this process, the association was perceived as—and acted as—a government body.

The Hostel as a European Phenomenon

In 1933, the Swedish Tourist Association established twenty-nine hostels with a total of 750 beds. During this first year, students comprised 40 percent of the visitors. The remaining guests were from the lower-middle classes—they were elementary-school teachers, in particular—as well as from the working classes. A mere six years later, in 1939, the number of hostels had jumped to 284 with a total of 7,300 beds.[38] From 1939 onwards, the Swedish Tourist Association received government support from the Swedish State Board for Leisure, the government body controlled by the bourgeois tourist regime. This additional funding consolidated the movement: the hostel system was firmly in place.

Originally a German idea, the youth hostel was called the *Jugendherberge*. It was the product of a youth movement rooted in the bourgeois middle classes; established in the 1890s, the movement was a reaction against industrialization and modernization. The *Wandervögel*, as the movement was called, promoted the simple life. The German Youth Hostel Association launched its first youth hostels in the years before the outbreak of the First World War. According to the movement's ideals, the hostels were to be close to nature and remote from industry. Everyday activities and living conditions were organized around cleanliness, orderliness, and rational simplicity. The German Youth Hostel Association developed into a radical organization that promoted

212

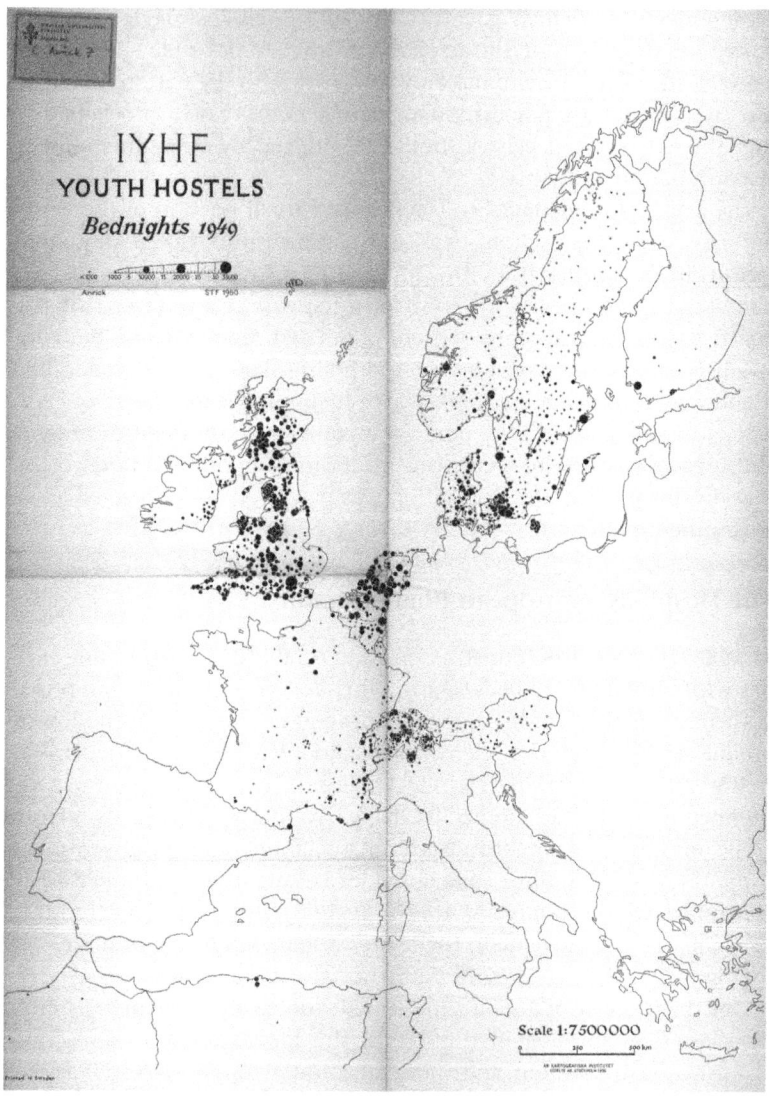

Figure 9.3 These two maps compare the number of "bed nights"—occupancies—at hostels in Europe and the U.S. in 1949. The figures reinforce the idea of the hostel as a primarily European phenomenon.

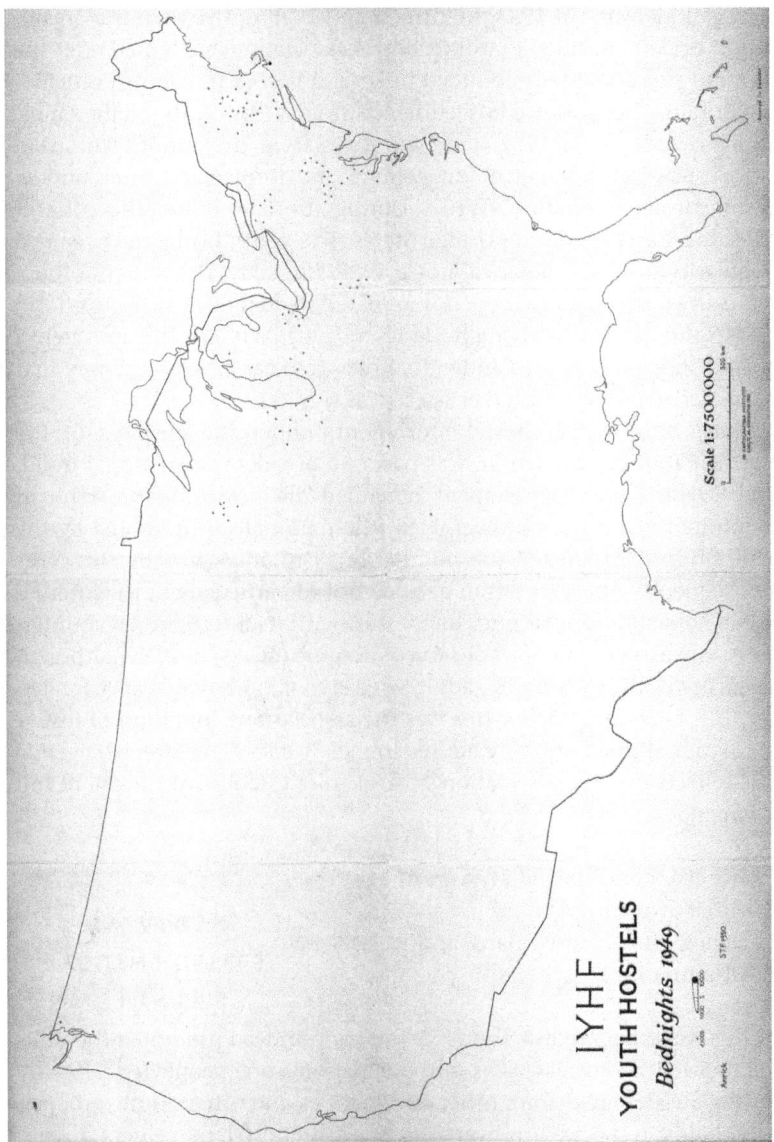

Figure 9.3 Continued.

internationalism. (In 1933, that trend ended abruptly when the organization became nazified.)[39] Youth hostel associations patterned after the German prototype were founded in several European countries including Britain, Czechoslovakia, Denmark, Estonia, France, the Netherlands, and Switzerland. In 1932, representatives from the various European branch associations met in Amsterdam and formed the International Youth Hostel Federation (IYHF). During the late 1930s, the concept spread to Canada and the United States. The youth hostel never gained popularity in North America, however. Presumably, the hostel's proponents in North America were not prepared to adapt this collective form of accommodation—originally designed for hikers—to the continent's great distances and to the individualized—and car-based—mobility that characterized American travel as early as the 1930s.[40]

Thus, the Swedish hostel movement, under the auspices of the Swedish Tourist Association, was part of a broader transnational trend. The Swedish hostel movement remained distinct from the trend in two important ways, however. First, the nationalism promoted by the association contradicted the internationalism advocated by the IYHF. Consequently, the association decided not to participate in the international collaboration. Second, in contrast with its international counterparts, the association did not serve young people exclusively: although Swedish youth had priority, adult Swedes took precedence over foreign youth.[41] One rationale for this was the association's ambition of fostering national integration by addressing all Swedes. The Swedish agenda was reflected in the association's list of rules established in case of full occupancy:

1. Swedish youth below 21 years of age
2. Other Swedes
3. Danes, Finns, Norwegians, and Icelanders
4. Other national subjects.[42]

In this way, the Swedish Tourist Association indeed promoted the uniting of Sweden's social classes into one nation—one people (*ett folk*)—by setting Swedes apart from other nationalities and other ethnic groups.

In many respects, however, the Swedish hostel movement resembled its German role model. The hostel movement featured a carefully thought-out aesthetic that, above all, served to express closeness to allegedly Swedish traditions. School buildings had often served as temporary hostels during the early years of the hostel movement, but, from the outset, the association aimed to situate their facilities in national-heritage buildings. For example, a preserved fourteenth-century monastery in the Swedish town of Vadstena became a hostel in 1938. Notably, it was the task of an art historian and archaeologist employed by the association to identify potential buildings and sites for the hostels.[43]

Austerity and simplicity pervaded the hostels' physical set-up. The hostels' collective lodgings were divided into women's and men's dormitories (children under 6 years of age were banned), which were lined with bunk beds. Mattresses and pillowcases were stuffed with straw; common washing facilities featured little more than washbowls and cold water. In addition, a strict regimen applied to lodging at the hostels. Smoking and drinking were strictly forbidden; meals were served at regular times; eating in the dormitories was discouraged; and the curfew was ten o'clock in the evening. From ten-thirty on, visitors were obliged to be silent. Order and cleanliness were to be maintained; beds were to be made.[44] Although the hostels maintained no dress code, hostel staff and indeed the association's staff frequently remarked if clothing was "improper." They disparaged the "modern tendencies" and "uninhibited emancipation" displayed by some visitors, in particular the "half-naked" female guests.[45] All in all, the Swedish hostel movement conveyed the paternalistic, puritanical, and romantic nationalistic ideology of the bourgeois tourist regime.

Although its leadership denounced the commercial American model of mass tourism, the Swedish Tourist Association nevertheless deployed American franchising methods in organizing the hostel movement. In fact, the association's managing director and his wife, the Anricks, had traveled to the U.S. to study the American tourism industry and had been duly impressed by its efficiency and considerable scale. Once back home, the managing director reported that Swedish tourism had a lot to learn from America. While it was impossible to "copy" the American ideas, U.S. concepts could well "be adapted" to Swedish circumstances.[46] As we shall see, the Swedish Tourist Association used the franchising methods not to pursue a commercial agenda, but to fulfill its ideological agenda.

The majority of hostels were owned by private innkeepers, landlords, or municipalities; only a few facilities were owned by the association. Contracts with the franchisees were negotiated annually. Franchisees were provided with standardized signage indicating that the hostel operated under the association's auspices. The managers of participating hostels agreed to display the association's plaque at the entrance; to fly the association's flag; and to display the association's books, journals, and leaflets. Franchisees were strictly forbidden to display commercial brochures or political pamphlets. They received detailed instructions concerning the mandatory equipment they were to provide—and they were furnished with much of the necessary equipment. The franchising agreement also required hostels to serve breakfast, lunch, and dinner at fixed prices; minimum requirements defined what each meal should include. To help enforce the rules and regulations it set for hostel visitors, the association retained hostel inspectors to tour facilities every summer. The inspectors encouraged compliance and reported infractions on the part of guests and hostel management, including substandard hostel conditions. In cases where inspectors' findings were grim, the hostel in question was forced to shut down.[47]

Tightly controlled and longstanding though it was, this bourgeois tourism regime would be confronted by three broader, closely interrelated trends. The internationalization, motorization, and familization of tourism would challenge the bourgeois virtues upon which the Swedish Tourist Association had been founded.

Confronting Next-Stage Tourism

By the mid-1940s, the isolation of the interwar and war years had come to an end. It was no longer possible nor was it desirable for the Swedish Tourist Association to shun international cooperation: in 1946, the association joined the IYHF. This meant that every member of a national hostel association belonging to the IYHF was entitled to stay at Swedish hostels.[48] The number of foreign guests at the Swedish hostels began to increase accordingly: in 1949, non-Swedes accounted for roughly 20 percent of all hostel visitors, most of them youth.[49]

This sudden influx of foreigners challenged the overtly nationalist ideology of the association, and tensions arose. Especially during the first postwar decade, the association's leadership and hostel inspectors debated the "foreigner problem." Some innkeepers expressed discontent, animosity, even sheer xenophobia. Many foreigners—Danish, German, and French visitors, in particular—were considered noisy and disrespectful of the hostels' rules and regulations. One innkeeper displayed deep resentment toward Eastern European refugees, accusing Latvians, Poles, and Romanians of a "carelessness and thievishness" that had "no limits."[50]

The association was particularly disturbed by foreign youths who hitchhiked. When the Second World War ended, car- and traffic-related restrictions (on gasoline, oil, and tires) were gradually lifted, and the number of automobiles and trucks on Swedish roads began to increase. An unanticipated consequence was hitchhiking, which had developed in tandem with the increasing automobility in the United States during the interwar period. The originally American practice of hitchhiking spread to Europe, gaining popularity after the end of the Second World War.[51] Many European youth hostel associations condemned the practice of hitchhiking, which they placed on a par with begging. Taking a particularly harsh position, the Swedish Tourist Association regarded hitchhiking as an international practice and accused foreign youth for having introduced the practice in Sweden. Association members believed that hitchhiking encouraged pushy, bold, impulsive behavior—behavior that could lead to theft or rape. To members of the association, hitchhiking foreigners threatened the image of the hostel movement as a nurturing haven for Swedish youth.[52]

But the emerging car-based mobility would challenge the ideology of the hostel movement in yet another way. In the autumn of 1952, after the summer holiday season had ended, the respected Swedish journalist Nils Horney highlighted changing tourism patterns in a feature article published in the leading social democratic newspaper, *Morgon-Tidningen* (The Morning Paper). In his article, Horney described the biking youths—replete with sleeping bags and tents—who had been so abundant in the 1930s; the writer observed that this category of tourist was on the cusp of disappearing from the roads. Bicycle tourists' predominance in rural Swedish tourism had yielded to "motorized families." Auto tourism, once an exclusively bourgeois domain, was now a pastime of the working class as well.[53]

In addition to maintaining a decades-long career as a prolific writer for the labor press, Horney was a key figure in Swedish tourism. All along, Horney had commuted easily between civil-society organizations, government agencies, and the media. As a former board member of the Swedish Tourist Association (1929–1940), he had played a key role in launching the hostel concept. He had also been a member of the government commission that founded the Swedish State Board for Leisure, on whose board he sat from 1940 until 1967.[54] Horney used his authority to assert that the Swedish Tourist Association should incrementally adapt to the labor movement's ideology of inclusiveness. In his feature article, Horney showed concern for the new, less-than-prosperous auto tourists. Coming from the rank and file, many working-class families had spent all of their savings on buying a car for family vacations. Consequently, they led a truly Spartan life along the roads. He sympathized that the lack of money forced many families to stay at campgrounds—a particular hardship given the cold, rainy summer—that were "so unpleasant and littered that decent people tried to avoid them at any cost." Wasn't it possible to provide inexpensive accommodation for the new tourists and their families? Horney foresaw a choice between hostels and motels.[55]

Horney felt ambivalent about the choice. Hostels indeed provided low-cost lodging. Currently, however, hostels did not offer a solution for the family car phenomenon, given that they banned children younger than 6 years of age and prevented families from staying together in rooms of their own. Horney also felt skeptical about wholesale appropriation of the motel model, this most American solution to the accommodation problem; the journalist remained convinced that "vacationing families probably would prefer a more idyllic, peaceful, and pleasant surrounding than a gas station as their lodging."[56]

Within the context of doubting the development of Swedish tourism along U.S. lines, Horney did identify an urgent need to modernize Sweden's hostel movement. The Swedish Tourist Association heeded Horney's concerns: the association's administrative director, Halvar Sehlin, was dispatched to the U.S. to study the role of the automobile in the American tourism industry. The Sweden-America Foundation funded the trip, dedicated as it was to helping Swedes learn from the American example.[57] In the late autumn of 1952, Sehlin traveled from New York to San Francisco. Above all, Sehlin was struck by the great mobility of the American tourist and the rapidly increasing auto tourism. The trend towards "car-minded" tourism was unmistakable. More than 80 percent of Americans on vacation traveled by car. Further, Sehlin reported that, to satisfy demand, an astounding 4,000 motels per year were being built in the U.S.

It was not only the number of cars and motels that struck Sehlin as different from the realities of Swedish tourism. The nature of American motels was entirely different, equipped, as they were, with all the comfort technologies one could imagine, from private bathrooms replete with tubs and showers, to radios and, in some cases, TVs. American motels were also conveniently situated on the outskirts of cities and towns. The luxe American motel, Sehlin concluded, could not be compared with the cheap Swedish hostel.[58]

Believing that it maintained a monopoly on roadside lodging in Sweden, the Swedish Tourist Association was alarmed by Sehlin's report—particularly by his unflattering comparison. In Sweden, competition from motels built by the motoring associations would not merely challenge this monopoly but would effectively end the hostel movement.[59] Sehlin's American experiences and related observations catalyzed members of the Swedish Tourist Association to act: they would modernize the country's hostel movement.

The Swedish Tourist Association established a working group to research how to attract the increasing number of families that vacationed by car. Members of the working group considered three alternatives: creating accommodations for families at the association's hostels—"families" being defined as families with children; expanding existing hostels to function as a combination of hostel and motel; or constructing and operating motels under the auspices of the association. The second and third alternatives would require, as the association put it, "a number of deviations from the rules and regulations of the hostel movement." Rooms would need to be larger and more comfortable. Curfews would need to be extended beyond the stipulated 10 o'clock in the evening; hostels might even be required to remain accessible to guests all night. What's more, innkeepers would be obliged to spend more time cleaning and preparing the rooms, given that guests traveling by car most likely would not bring their own bed and bath linens—or make their own beds. The list went on: guests would require parking spaces as well as service and gas stations close to their lodgings. And the association would need to charge increased rates to cover higher maintenance costs. After lengthy discussions, the association decided to pursue family rooms at their existing hostels.[60]

In a memo, working-group members considered the pros and cons of creating family rooms at hostels. Above all, the group cited the greater comfort and well-being that would be afforded to families lodging together rather than in gender-separated dormitories. Moreover, if family rooms were introduced, children under 6 years of age would be welcome. On the other hand, refusing family room rights to married couples without children would likely prove difficult. The working group anticipated that it would be particularly difficult to enforce such a rule during the end of the season, when visitors were sparse and available rooms plentiful. The group also identified a far more serious concern: creating family rooms would clearly violate one of the international hostel movement's basic principles: the strict separation of men and women in different dormitories. Further, the group feared the repercussions of Swedish participation in the international hostel movement would be "very serious" indeed.[61] After all, The Swedish Tourist Association could be expelled from the IYHF for accepting tourists who traveled by car and for implementing family rooms—both of which were controversial practices.[62]

Ultimately, the working group judged family rooms as the most plausible way to modernize the hostel movement, yet the group advised the Swedish Tourist Association to proceed with caution. One suggestion was to raise the issue of auto-tourist accommodation with other Swedish stakeholders in tourism.[63] In line with the working group's recommendations, the Swedish Tourist Association invited the key civil-society organizations in tourism to an "informal meeting" in the spring of 1953. These included the association's long-time fellow partners: the Swedish Ski Association and the Swedish Association for Tourist Traffic. They also included the Royal Automobile Club, the Swedish Automobile Association, the Travel and Holiday Organization of the Cooperative Movements as well as the Swedish Resort Hotel Association.[64] Gathering broad support for their plans constituted one main goal; another motive was to ensure that fellow stakeholders did not see the association's plans as a threat to their own businesses.

The Swedish Tourist Association asked for—and received—carte blanche from their tourism colleagues. It then decided to provide family rooms on a trial basis for the summer of 1954, organizing the new form of accommodation in about a hundred of its nearly 300 hostels. The rooms were intended primarily for families with children aged between 2 and 12. Married couples without children were "under no circumstances" allowed to make use of the family rooms.[65]

Family rooms became a great success. Innkeepers reported to the association that family rooms were sometimes fully booked, and numerous families with children that were on the vacation trail had to be turned away. The new plan's popularity convinced the association to make the change a permanent one. Gradually, another change was introduced in the spirit of modernization: the association relocated hostels closer to the country's trunk roads. Originally, accommodations in the hostel network were spaced an average of 50–75 kilometers—the distance that a bicyclist could comfortably travel in one day. Given that the majority of guests now arrived by car, however, this distribution of hostels no longer made sense logistically. So, when poor-quality hostels were forced to close, they were replaced with new facilities located along the trunk roads. Gradually, the hostel network was re-purposed for the motorist, with a day's trip estimated at 300–400 kilometers. In order to garner more family rooms, many innkeepers moved to new properties; in 1958, more than 60 percent of hostels featured family rooms.

Other countries soon followed the Swedish example. In 1955, Finnish and Norwegian hostels introduced family rooms. In 1957, the British hostel movement followed, and, in 1959, the Danish movement featured family rooms as well. In 1973, the German Youth Hostel Association—the most ardent defender of the movement's original practices—finally, began to allow car-based families at its hostels, admittedly on a limited scale.[66]

The hostel movement's adaptation to the car made it better prepared to meet the motel challenge. During the late 1950s, it became evident that the new tourists—families vacationing by car—had largely replaced youths traveling by bike. In 1933, nearly all tourists had reached hostels either via bicycle or on foot. In 1948, bicycle tourists still comprised 54 percent of visitors. By 1954, the summer when the family rooms were introduced, their share had decreased to 12 percent, and four years later it had dropped to a mere 7 percent. The share of auto tourists rose in inverse proportion: 12 percent in 1948, 54 percent in 1954, and 61 percent in 1958.[67] The association had managed to retain its central position in Swedish tourism and attract auto tourists to its hostels, despite initial fears.

Figure 9.4 In the postwar period, the hostel's "family room" replaced the hostel dormitory, which had accommodated men and women in separate rooms. Aside from being updated in various ways, hostels remained simple accommodations.

Rethinking the Bourgeois Tourism Ideology

Family rooms were far from the Swedish Tourist Association's only adaptation to changing tourism patterns; the process that led to family rooms' introduction, I contend, however, was the decisive modernization process. The association used the American experience to explore how another path to modernity could be forged. The process of adaptation was a painful one nonetheless. Several of the policy changes defied the hostel movement's core values, and the association's directors felt compelled to rethink the organization's ideology: "We must learn to understand that it is a wholly 'new humanity' that travels along the roads, and if we want to continue to promote tourism, we must carefully imagine how this new form of humanity perceives travel." This "new humanity," one of the association's board members observed, considered it essential to have a car of one's own. Indeed, car ownership boosted owners' self-esteem, proffered individual independence, and introduced unprecedented travel possibilities. Eventually, he was to write that the car provided a "wonderful sensation of independence and supremacy."[68] Freedom and ownership, comfort and pleasure were about to replace paternalism and romantic nationalism, austerity and simplicity.

The ideological U-turn the association had made was symbolized by a change in leadership. When longstanding managing director Anrick retired in the late 1950s, he was replaced by Halvar Sehlin, who, having visited the U.S. at the start of the decade, was well versed in car-friendly American mass tourism. With the departure of Anrick and the death of Lindhagen, "vintage bourgeois idealism" lost its vice-like hold on the Swedish Tourist Association.

In fact, within a ten-year period, the Swedish hostel movement had been transformed almost completely. Inspections conducted during the summer of 1959 highlight the deep and rapid changes that had taken place. One of the association's hostel inspectors observed that the visitors consisted of two general groups: Swedish families and foreign youth. The Swedes who visited hostels were almost exclusively families with children—and they arrived by car. The fraction of foreigners (primarily German) who visited hostels had increased to one-quarter. Although the association did not present statistical information on how the foreigners arrived, the hostel inspector depicted them as the "foreign hitch-hiking clientele." This slur notwithstanding, the inspector's general impression was that the hostel clientele—foreigners included—had become much nicer and middle-classier (*borgerligare*). Other observations included that innkeepers had become far more service minded and commercially oriented; many had begun to sell coffee and soda, postcards and other souvenirs. The flipside was that innkeepers no longer respected the hostel movement's rules and regulations: curfews were disregarded, and the male–female division of dormitories was transgressed. Innkeepers no longer enforced the age limits for children: the maximum age of 16 was often infringed, for example. Frequently, extended families were packed into family rooms.[69]

The hostel inspector remarked that "old-school" innkeepers who demanded compliance often ran into trouble with visitors—and lost guests as a result. The large numbers of families apparently sparked a demand for self-catering: the hostels' regimented mealtimes were a mismatch for families with children. Many guests also called for more comforts, services, and amenities. The biking clientele had simply crashed into bed, exhausted after a day of cycling; the car clientele, by contrast, dressed more elegantly and required the facilities for washing up before going out in the evening.[70]

Conclusion

The processes of adapting Swedish hostels to changing tourism patterns comprised three interconnected processes: internationalization, familization, and motorization. As I have shown in this chapter, the changes were comprehensive and rapid, the results dramatic.

The Swedish Tourist Association played a crucial part in this process. For decades, the association had been the key intermediary in national tourism. The association collaborated closely with a list of other civil-society and government organizations in the tourism industry. As Arthur Lindhagen himself had maintained, the association stood for an undeniably "vintage bourgeois idealism." However, Lindhagen also emphasized its non-partisan status: indeed, over the years, the association represented the public interest. Deeply embedded as it was in Swedish society, the association enjoyed broad, if not unanimous, support for both its ideology and its actions.

Initially, the American-style motel seemed to be a perfect fit for the highly mobile car- and family-based tourism that was about to emerge in Sweden. To some Swedes, the motel embodied an attractive version of modernity. As such, some met this new form of accommodation with enthusiasm. Others were less approving. Adapting the American-style motel to the Swedish cultural and social setting turned out to be an intricate task. And, in contrast to the hostel, the motel lacked a powerful advocate.

The car-minded American tourism—especially the American-style motel—served as a catalyst for the modernization of the Swedish hostel movement. In essence, the Swedish Tourist Association rejected the standardized, comfort-oriented motel room, but it adapted to a highly mobile car- and family-based tourism. The modernized hostel can best be described as a hybrid solution. The hostel continued to be a simple affair, and to represent outdoor life. Although it no longer celebrated romantic nationalism, it certainly continued to express pastoral romanticism. To Swedes, the hostel retained its aura of authenticity in the age of the automobile.

Notes

1. Albert Lindhagen quoted in Halvar Sehlin, *Känn ditt land: STF:s roll i den svenska turismens historia* (Stockholm: Svenska turistföreningen, 1998), 118.
2. Lindhagen quoted in Sehlin, *Känn ditt land*, 117. See also Orvar Löfgren, "Know Your Country: A Comparative Perspective on Tourism and Nation Building in Sweden," in *Being Elsewhere: Tourism, Consumer Culture, and Identity in Modern Europe and North America*, ed. Shelley Baranowski and Ellen Furlough (Ann Arbor: University of Michigan Press, 2001), 137–54.
3. Lena Eskilsson, "Svenska turistföreningen från fjäll till friluftsliv: Från den vetenskaplige vildmannen till den cyklande husmodern," *Historisk tidskrift* 116 (1996): 257–82; Svenbjörn Kilander, *"En nationalrikedom av hälsoskatter": Om Jämtland och industrisamhället 1882–1910* (Hedemora: Gidlund, 2008).
4. Niels Kayser Nielsen, "The Cult of the Nordic Superman – between the Pre-modern and the Modern," *The Sports Historian* 19 (1999): 61–80.
5. Henrik Meinander, *Towards a Bourgeois Manhood: Boys' Physical Education in Nordic Secondary Schools 1880–1940* (Helsinki: Societas scientiarum Fennica, 1994); David Tjeder, *The Power of Character: Middle-class Masculinities, 1800–1900* (Stockholm: Stockholms universitet, 2003).
6. Letter from Arne Freese to the board of the Swedish Tourist Association, "Angående vandrarhemmen," September 15, 1952, National Archives of Sweden, Swedish Tourist Association's Archive, F18:2.
7. Sehlin, *Känn ditt land*, 118–19.
8. Ellen Furlough, "Making Mass Vacations: Tourism and Consumer Culture in France, 1930s to 1970s," *Comparative Studies in Society and History* 40 (1998): 259.
9. See the essays in Shelley Baranowski and Ellen Furlough, eds., *Being Elsewhere: Tourism, Consumer Culture, and Identity in Modern Europe and North America* (Ann Arbor: University of Michigan Press, 2001); Rudy Koshar, ed., *Histories of Leisure* (Oxford: Berg, 2002).
10. Jürgen Kocka, "'Bürgertum' and Two Professions in the Nineteenth Century: Two Alternative Approaches," in *Professions in Theory and History: Rethinking the Study of the Professions*, ed. Michael Burrage and Rolf Torstendahl (London: Sage, 1990), 66.

11. For a discussion of the Marshall Plan's impact on Sweden's economic and political life, see Birgit Karlsson, "Sweden and the Marshall Plan," in *The Marshall Plan*, Fredrik Erixon et al. (Stockholm: Timbro, 2008), 36–50.
12. Philipp Gassert, "The Spectre of Americanization: Western Europe in the American Century," in *The Oxford Handbook of Postwar European History*, ed. Dan Stone (Oxford: Oxford University Press, 2012), 182–200.
13. David W. Ellwood, *The Shock of America: Europe and the Challenge of the Century* (Oxford: Oxford University Press, 2012), 1.
14. Ellwood, *The Shock of America*, 392.
15. Sven Tynelius quoted in Per Lundin, "Mediators of Modernity: Planning Experts and the Making of the 'Car-Friendly' City in Europe," in *Urban Machinery: Inside Modern European Cities*, ed. Mikael Hård and Thomas J. Misa (Cambridge, MA: MIT Press, 2008), 271.
16. Mari Lundberg, *I bilismens barndom: Om bilturism och Gyllene Uttern* (Gränna: Gränna hembygdsförening, 1990), 15–26.
17. Per Lundin, "Confronting Class: The American Motel in Early Post-war Sweden," *Journal of Tourism History* 5 (2013): 305–24.
18. Ibid. For further reading on the American motel, see Warren James Belasco, *Americans on the Road: From Autocamp to Motel, 1910–1945*, new ed. (Baltimore, MD: Johns Hopkins University Press, 1997); John A. Jakle, Keith A. Sculle, and Jefferson S. Rogers, *The Motel in America* (Baltimore, MD: Johns Hopkins University Press, 1996).
19. For an overview, see Lena Eskilsson, "Fritid som idé, struktur och praktik: Rätten till lättja eller friluftsliv i folkhemmet," *Historisk tidskrift* 120 (2000): 29–52.
20. *Utredning med förslag angående behovet av åtgärder för främjande av verksamheten inom turisthotellnäringen* (Stockholm: Handelsdepartementet and Svenska Turisttrafikförbundet, 1954), 6–7.
21. Per Lundin, *Bilsamhället: Ideologi, expertis och regelskapande i efterkrigstidens Sverige* (Stockholm: Stockholmia, 2008).
22. Gustav Endrédi, *Resekonsumtionen 1950–1975* (Stockholm: Industrins utredningsinstitut, 1967), 19, 97; *Trafiksäkerhet II: Betänkande avgivet av 1953 års trafiksäkerhetsutredning*, Statens offentliga utredningar 1957:18 (Stockholm: Kommunikationsdepartementet, 1957), 12–13.
23. Sehlin, *Känn ditt land*, 117.
24. Lundin, "Confronting Class."
25. Sehlin, *Känn ditt land*, 68–91.
26. "Svenska Turistföreningens styrelse 1885–1944" (Stockholm, 1944), Uppsala University Library's Manuscript Collections, Calla Anrick's Archive, box 6.
27. Martin Emanuel and Per Lundin, "Fostering Youth, Curbing Revolution: The Development of a Swedish Bourgeois Tourism Regime, 1885–1939" (paper presented at 6th Plenary Conference of Tensions of Europe, Paris, September 19–21, 2013); Sehlin, *Känn ditt land*, 68–91.
28. Kjellman would eventually succeed the late Lindhagen as the association's chairman, a position he held until his death in 1953. Emanuel and Lundin, "Fostering Youth, Curbing Revolution."
29. Ibid.
30. Gunnar Åselius, *The "Russian Menace" to Sweden: The Belief System of a Small Power Security Elite in the Age of Imperialism* (Stockholm: Stockholms

universitet, 1994), 7; Håkan Blomqvist, "Inledning," in *Kommunismen – hot och löfte: Arbetarrörelsen i skuggan av Sovjetunionen 1917–1991*, ed. Håkan Blomqvist and Lars Ekdahl (Stockholm: Carlssons, 2002), 8–9; Francis Sejersted, *The Age of Social Democracy: Norway and Sweden in the Twentieth Century*, trans. Richard Daly (Princeton, NJ: Princeton University Press, 2011), 73–4.
31. Thomas Hammar, *Sverige åt svenskarna: Invandringspolitik, utlänningskontroll och asylrätt 1900–1932* (Stockholm: Stockholms universitet, 1964).
32. See the clippings "Turistföreningen till storms mot turisttrafiken," *Stockholms Dagblad*, February 26, 1929, and "Liten men vald krets av utländska turister," *Svenska Dagbladet*, February 26, 1929, in Calla Anrick's Archive, box 4.
33. For instance, the theme of the association's fifty-year anniversary in 1935 was "Swedes and Sweden." "Svenskarna och Sverige," *UNT*, February 15, 1935, Calla Anrick's Archive, box 7.
34. Petra Rantatalo, *Den resande eleven: Folkskolans skolreserörelse 1890–1940* (Umeå: Umeå universitet, 2001), 86.
35. Emanuel and Lundin, "Fostering Youth, Curbing Revolution."
36. Cf. Klas Sandell and Sverker Sörlin, "Naturen som fostrare: Friluftsliv och ideologi i svenskt 1900-tal," *Historisk tidskrift* 114 (1994): 13–18.
37. Minutes, "STF:s konferens angående vandrarhem," December 12, 1932, Swedish Tourist Association's Archive, F3A:1.
38. "Antalet vandrarhem 1933–1948," Swedish Tourist Association's Archive, F3A:2; Sehlin, *Känn ditt land*, 231–3.
39. For more information on the German youth movement, see Peter D. Stachura, *The German Youth Movement 1900–1945: An Interpretative and Documentary History* (London: Macmillan, 1981); Walter Laqueur, *Young Germany: A History of the German Youth Movement*, new ed. (London: Transaction Books, 1984). For further reading on the German youth hostel, see the essays in Jürgen Reulecke and Barbara Stambolis, eds., *100 Jahre Jugendherbergen 1909–2009: Anfänge – Wandlungen – Rück- und Ausblicke* (Essen: Klartext, 2009).
40. Anton Grassl and Graham Heath, *The Magic Triangle: A Short History of the World Youth Hostel Movement* (London: International Youth Hostel Federation, 1982), chaps 4 and 5.
41. Minutes, January 30, 1933, Swedish Tourist Association's Archive, F3A:1.
42. "STF:s vandrarhemsverksamhet: Översikt 1933–1953," January 1954, Swedish Tourist Association's Archive, F3A:2.
43. Carl Falkman, "En bädd för natten," *Svenska Turistföreningens årsskrift* (1986): 172.
44. See the leaflet "STF:s vandrarhem för svensk ungdom" (Stockholm, 1933) in the Swedish Tourist Association's Archive, B6b:27, as well as the following memos in F3A:2: "P.M. angående anordnande av vandrarhemmen," June 20, 1944; "Svenska vandrarhem," n.d.; "Till STF:s vandrarhemsföreståndare 1945," April 15, 1945; "P.M. för STF:s vandrarhemsinspektörer," n.d.; "P.M. angående gruppförläggningar på STF:s vandrarhem," April 1, 1954.
45. "Ordningsföreskrifter för STF:s vandrarhem," n.d., Swedish Tourist Association's Archive, F3A:1. Carl Falkman, "Vandrarhemsvärden och hans gäster," Svenska Turistföreningens vandrarhemskonferens i Vadstena 22–24 maj 1943, Swedish Tourist Association's Archive, F10:17.

46. See numerous clippings in Calla Anrick's Archive, box 5.
47. See memos and contracts in the Swedish Tourist Association's Archive, F3A:2.
48. By the mid-1950s, IYHF included thirty countries with a total of 3,000 hostels with a total of more than 12 million guest nights per year. Memo, "Vandrarhemmet på Omberg," September 5, 1956, Swedish Tourist Association's Archive, F3A:2.
49. "Svenska turistföreningens vandrarhemsrörelse under 1949," Swedish Tourist Association's Archive, F3A:2.
50. Carl-Julius Anrick, "Anteckningar från inspektionsresa till 53 STF:s vandrarhem juli 1939," n.d., and "Anteckningar från inspektionsresa till 25 STF:s vandrarhem 1946," June 20, 1946, Calla Anrick's Archive, box 8; Birigit Lundin, "Utlänningar på vandrarhemmen," in "Svenska Turistföreningens vandrarhemskonferens i Stockholm 24–26 april 1949," in the Swedish Tourist Association's Archive, F10:17, and "P.M. beträffande utlänningarna på vandrarhemmen 1957," August 16, 1957, in F3A:2.
51. John T. Schlebeker, "An Informal History of Hitchhiking," *The Historian* 20 (1958): 305–27.
52. "Är liftning opassande?" *STF* 16 (1948): 24; "Lift, hitch-hiking, auto-stop, blaff – det är danska – à pied, by foot och vandrande," *STF* 17 (1949): 141; "En vädjan till bilisterna," *STF* 18 (1950): 82–3; Greta Öhrn, "Ingen liftning i år," *STF* 21 (1953): 53.
53. Nils Horney, "Familjen turistar i bil, färre cykelungdomar," *Morgon-Tidningen*, September 7, 1952.
54. Nils Horney, *Stora män och tidningsmän: En reporters minnen från fem decennier* (Stockholm: Natur och kultur, 1969), 142–8.
55. Horney, "Familjen turistar i bil, färre cykelungdomar."
56. Ibid.
57. See Dag Blanck, "Scholars across the Seas: The American-Scandinavian Foundation and the Sweden-America Foundation in the Transatlantic Exchange of Knowledge," *American Studies in Scandinavia* 40 (2008): 110–25.
58. Halvar Sehlin, "STF i USA," *STF* 20 (1952): 172; "Intervju med Amerikastipendiat," *Bilekonomi*, 1953, no. 3: 13.
59. "Angående vandrarhemmen."
60. Draft Memo, "Några synpunkter på," n.d., Swedish Tourist Association's Archive, F18:2.
61. Ibid.
62. Grassl and Heath, *The Magic Triangle*, 95, 151–3.
63. "Några synpunkter på"; Memo, "Preliminär P.M. angående möjligheterna att ordna familjeinkvartering på vissa vandrarhem," February 2, 1953, Swedish Tourist Association's Archive, F18:2.
64. Copy of outgoing letter, May 29, 1953, Swedish Tourist Association's Archive, F18:2.
65. See the memo "Meddelande angående familjeinkvartering på STF:s vandrarhem," April 20, 1954, Swedish Tourist Association's Archive, F3A:2.
66. See the memo "Vandrarhem utmed de större riksvägarna," 1956, in the Swedish Tourist Association's Archive, F3A:2, as well as the memos

"Konferensen på Omberg 7–9 oktober 1958," and "Sammanfattning av intryck från inspektionsresan sommaren 1959", July 31, 1959, in F3A:3; Grassl and Heath, *The Magic Triangle*, 155–6.
67. Memo, "P.M. angående STF:s vandrarhem," November 9, 1955, Swedish Tourist Association's Archive, F3A:2, as well as the memos "Vandrarhemmen rustas för bilturisterna," Summer 1958, and "Vandrarhemsverksamhet," December 12, 1958, in F3A:3. "Vandrarhemmen ger billig men trivsam bilsemester," *Motor* 17, no. 17 (1959): 18.
68. Memo, "Några synpunkter på och tankar om vandrarhem," October 1, 1957, Swedish Tourist Association's Archive, F3A:2.
69. "Sammanfattning av intryck från inspektionsresan sommaren 1959."
70. Ibid.

Select Bibliography

Aars, Ferdinand. *Arts and Crafts—Industrial Design in Norway*. Oslo: The Royal Norwegian Ministry of Foreign Affairs, 1957.

Agriculture and Food: Summary Report on Activities Undertaken by EPA since Its Establishment in 1953. Paris: EPA, 1960.

Akcan, Esra. "Civilizing Housewives versus Participatory Users: Margarete Schütte-Lihotzky in the Employ of the Turkish Nation State." In *Cold War Kitchen: Americanization, Technology, and European Users*, ed. Ruth Oldenziel and Karin Zachmann. Cambridge, MA: MIT Press, 2009.

Alasia, Franco, and Danilo Montaldi. *Milano Corea: Inchiesta sugli immigrati*. Milan: Feltrinelli, 1960.

Alberoni, Francesco. *Consumi e società*. Bologna: Il Mulino, 1964.

Albert de Bruhèze, Adri A., and Ruth Oldenziel, eds. *Manufacturing Technology, Manufacturing Consumers: The Making of Dutch Consumer Society*. Amsterdam: Amsterdam University Press, 2009.

Alberto, Alesina, and Ichino Andrea. *L'Italia fatta in casa: Indagine sulla vera ricchezza degli italiani*. Milan: Mondadori, 2009.

Aly, Götz. *Hitler's Beneficiaries: Plunder, Racial War, and the Nazi Welfare State*. Trans. Jefferson Chase. New York: Metropolitan Books, 2007.

Andersen, Arne. "Das 50er-Jahre-Syndrom: Umweltfragen in der Demokratisierung des Technikkonsums." *Technikgeschichte* 65 (1998): 329–44.

Anderson Jr., Oscar Edward. *Refrigeration in America: A History of a New Technology and Its Impact*. Princeton, NJ: Princeton University Press, 1953.

Andolf, Göran. *Sverige och utlandet 1930–1975: Indikatorer för mätning av Sveriges kulturella beroende*. Lund: Lund University, 1977.

Application of Atomic Science in Agriculture and Food: Report of Mission to the United States Sponsored by the European Productivity Agency under Project No. 396. Paris: EPA, 1958.

Arvidsson, Adam. "The Therapy of Consumption Motivation Research and the New Italian Housewife, 1958–62." *Journal of Material Culture* 5 (2000): 251–74.

Åselius, Gunnar. *The "Russian Menace" to Sweden: The Belief System of a Small Power Security Elite in the Age of Imperialism*. Stockholm: Stockholms universitet, 1994.

Asquer, Enrica. *La rivoluzione candida: Storia sociale della lavatrice in Italia (1945–1970)*. Rome: Carocci, 2007.

Austigard, Bjørn. "Frå stabbur til frysar: omkring konservering og lagring av mat i Romsdal." In *Årbok Romsdalsmuseet*. Molde: Romsdalsmuseet, 2006.

Avdem, Anna Jorunn. *Husmorparadiset*. Oslo: Samlaget, 2001.

Avdem, Anna Jorunn, and Kari Melby. *Oppe først og sist i seng: Husarbeid i Norge fra 1850 til i dag*. Oslo: Universitetsforlaget, 1985.

Bacevich, Andrew J., ed. *The Short American Century: A Postmortem*. Cambridge, MA: Harvard University Press, 2012.

Badino, Anna. *Tutte a casa? Donne tra migrazione e lavoro nella Torino degli anni Sessanta*. Rome: Viella, 2008.

Banfield, Edward C. *The Moral Basis of a Backward Society*. Glencoe, IL: Free Press, 1958.
Baranowski, Shelley, and Ellen Furlough, eds. *Being Elsewhere: Tourism, Consumer Culture, and Identity in Modern Europe and North America*. Ann Arbor: University of Michigan Press, 2001.
Barraclough, Geoffrey. *Introduction to Contemporary History*. Baltimore, MD: Penguin, 1967.
Baudrillard, Jean. *The Consumer Society: Myths and Structures*. Thousand Oaks, CA: Sage, 1998.
Beckers, Theo. "Planning voor Vrijheid: Een historisch-sociologische studie van de overheidsinterventie in rekreatie en vrije tijd." PhD diss., Landbouwhogeschool Wageningen, 1983.
Beckers, Theo, and Hans Mommaas, "Onderzoek van de vrijetijd." In *Het Vraagstuk van den Vrijen Tijd: 60 jaar onderzoek naar vrijetijd*, ed. Theo Beckers and Hans Mommaas. Leiden: Stenfert Kroese, 1991.
Beckman Stichting, Wiardi. *De Consument in de Maatschappij: De organisatorische behartiging van het consumentenbelang*. Amsterdam: Wiardi Beckman Stichting, 1956.
Belasco, Warren James. *Americans on the Road: From Autocamp to Motel, 1910–1945*. New ed. Baltimore, MD: Johns Hopkins University Press, 1997.
Belasco, Warren James. *Meals to Come: A History of the Future of Food*. Berkeley: University of California Press, 2006.
Belmonte, Thomas. *The Broken Fountain*. New York: Columbia University Press, 1979.
Benjamin, Walter. "The Work of Art in the Age of Mechanical Reproduction." In *Illuminations: Essays and Reflections*, ed. Hannah Arendt, trans. Harry Zohn. New York: Schocken Books, 1969.
Bercovitch, Sacvan. *The American Jeremiad*. Madison: University of Wisconsin Press, 1980.
Berendsen, Jos, Peter Saal, and Flip Spangenberg. *Met Zicht op Zee: Tweehonderd jaar bouwen aan badplaatsen in Nederland, België en Duitsland*. The Hague: Staatsuitgeverij, 1985.
Berman, Sheri. *The Primacy of Politics: Social Democracy and the Making of Europe's Twentieth Century*. Cambridge: Cambridge University Press, 2006.
Berre, Nina. "Fysiske idealer i norsk arkitekturutdanning 1945–1970." PhD diss., Norwegian University of Science and Technology, 2002.
Bervoets, Liesbeth. "'Consultation Required!' Women Coproducing the Modern Kitchen in the Netherlands, 1920–1970." In *Cold War Kitchen: Americanization, Technology, and European Users*, ed. Ruth Oldenziel and Karin Zachmann. Cambridge, MA: MIT Press, 2009.
Bervoets, Liesbeth. "The Marshall Plan and the Promise of Industrial Housing: The Appropriation of a 'Failed' Revolution in Post-War Holland." Paper presented at the European Ways of Living in the American Century Conference, Stockholm, January 16–17, 2010.
Bervoets, Liesbeth, and Ruth Oldenziel. "Speaking for Consumers, Standing Up as Citizens: The Politics of Dutch Women's Organizations and the Shaping of Technology, 1880–1980." In *Manufacturing Technology, Manufacturing Consumers*, ed. Adri A. Albert de la Bruhèze and Ruth Oldenziel. Amsterdam, 2009.
Beschouwingen Betreffende de Wederopbouw der Noordzeeplaatsen. The Hague: Rijksdienst voor het Nationale Plan, 1947.

Betts, Paul. "Building Socialism at Home: The Case of East German Interiors." In *Socialist Modern: East German Everyday Culture and Politics*, ed. Katherine Pence and Paul Betts. Ann Arbor: University of Michigan Press, 2008.
Betts, Paul, and David Crowley. "Introduction." In "Domestic Dreamworlds: Notions of Home in Post-1945 Europe," special issue. *Journal of Contemporary History* 40 (2005): 213–35.
Bigazzi, Duccio. "Gli operai della catena di montaggio: la Fiat 1922–1943." In *Annali della Fondazione Giangiacomo Feltrinelli* (1979–1980). Milan: Feltrinelli, 1981.
Bijker, Wiebe, and John Law, eds. *Shaping Technology/Building Society: Studies in Sociotechnical Change*. Cambridge, MA: MIT Press, 1992.
Bjellås Gilje, Karianne, ed. *Grete Prytz Kittelsen: Emalje og design*. Oslo: Gyldendal, 2007.
Bjørneboe, Jens. *Norge, mitt Norge: Essays om formyndermennesket*. Oslo: Pax, 1968.
Bjørneboe, Jens. *Vi som elsket Amerika: Essays om stormaktsgalskap, straffelyst, kunst og moral*. Oslo: Pax, 1970.
Blanck, Dag. "Scholars across the Seas: The American-Scandinavian Foundation and the Sweden-America Foundation in the Transatlantic Exchange of Knowledge." *American Studies in Scandinavia* 40 (2008): 110–25.
Blomqvist, Håkan. "Inledning." In *Kommunismen – hot och löfte: Arbetarrörelsen i skuggan av Sovjetunionen 1917–1991*, ed. Håkan Blomqvist and Lars Ekdahl. Stockholm: Carlssons, 2002.
Bluche, Lorraine, and Kiran Klaus Patel. "Der Europäer als Bauer: Das Motiv des bäuerlichen Familienbetriebes in Westeuropa nach 1945." In *Der Europäer – Ein Konstrukt: Wissensbestände, Diskurse, Praktiken*, ed. Lorraine Bluche, Veronika Lipphardt, and Kiran Klaus Patel. Göttingen: Wallstein, 2009.
Blume, Mary. *Côte d'Azur: Inventing the French Riviera*. London: Thames & Hudson, 1992.
Boehling, Rebecca. "U.S. Cultural Policy and German Culture during the American Occupation." In *The United States and Germany in the Era of the Cold War, 1945–1968: A Handbook*, ed. Detlef Junker. New York: Cambridge University Press, 2004.
Boel, Bent. "The European Productivity Agency: A Faithful Prophet of the American Model?" In *The Americanisation of European Business: The Marshall Plan and the Transfer of US Management Models*, ed. Matthias Kipping and Ove Bjarnar. London: Routledge, 1998.
Boel, Bent. *European Productivity Agency and Transatlantic Relations, 1953–1961*. Copenhagen: Museum Tusculanum Press, 2003.
Boissevain, Elisabeth, and Ton de Joode. *Tussen Koop en Miskoop: De Consument en zijn belangen in Nederland*. Amsterdam: Ideeboek, 1976.
Bowden, Sue, and Avner Offer. "Household Appliances and the Use of Time: The United States and Britain since the 1920s." *Economic History Review* 47 (1994): 725–48.
Brinkley, Alan. "The Concept of an American Century." In *The American Century in Europe*, ed. R. Laurence Moore and Maurizio Vaudagna. Ithaca, NY: Cornell University Press, 2003.
Brochmann, Odd. *Rent Bord: En historie om funksjonalismen og funksjonalistene i Norge*. Oslo: Arkitektnytt, 1987.
Buchli, Victor. "Khrushchev, Modernism, and the Fight against *Petit-bourgeois* Consciousness in the Soviet Home." *Journal of Design History* 10 (1997): 161–76.

232 Select Bibliography

Buck-Morss, Susan. *Dreamworld and Catastrophe: The Passing of Mass Utopia in East and West*. Cambridge, MA: MIT Press, 2000.
Capuzzo, Paolo. "Spectacles of Sociability: European Cities as Sites of Consumption." In *Urban Machinery: Inside Modern European Cities*, ed. Mikael Hård and Thomas J. Misa. Cambridge, MA: MIT Press, 2008.
Carbone, Cristina. "Staging the Kitchen Debate: How Splitnik Got Normalized in the United States." In *Cold War Kitchen: Americanization, Technology, and European Users*, ed. Ruth Oldenziel and Karin Zachmann. Cambridge, MA: MIT Press, 2009.
Carter, Erica. *How German Is She? Postwar German Reconstruction and the Consuming Woman*. Ann Arbor: University of Michigan Press, 1996.
Castillo, Greg. "Domesticating the Cold War: Household Consumption as Propaganda in Marshall Plan Germany." *Journal of Contemporary History* 40 (2005): 261–88.
Castillo, Greg. "The American 'Fat Kitchen' in Europe: Postwar Domestic Modernity and Marshall Plan Strategies of Enhancement." In *Cold War Kitchen: Americanization, Technology, and European Users*, ed. Ruth Oldenziel and Karin Zachmann. Cambridge, MA: MIT Press, 2009.
Castillo, Greg. *Cold War on the Home Front: The Soft Power of Midcentury Design*. Minneapolis: University of Minnesota Press, 2010.
Catterall, Claire. "Perceptions of Plastics: A Study of Plastics in Britain, 1945–1956." In *The Plastics Age: From Bakelite to Beanbags and Beyond*, ed. Penny Sparke. Woodstock, NY: Overlook Press, 1993.
Cohen, Jean-Louis. *Scenes of the World to Come: European Architecture and the American Challenge, 1893–1960*. Paris: Flammarion, 1995.
Cohen, Lizabeth. *A Consumers' Republic: The Politics of Mass Consumption in Postwar America*. New York: Knopf, 2003.
Conekin, Becky E. "'Here Is the Modern World Itself': The Festival of Britain's Representations of the Future." In *Moments of Modernity: Reconstructing Britain, 1945–1964*, ed. Becky Conekin, Frank Mort, and Chris Waters. London: Rivers Oram Press, 1999.
Conekin, Becky E. *"The Autobiography of a Nation": The 1951 Festival of Britain*. Manchester: Manchester University Press, 2003.
Corni, Gustavo, and Horst Gies. *Brot – Butter – Kanonen: Die Ernährungswirtschaft in Deutschland unter der Diktatur Hitlers*. Berlin: Akademie-Verlag, 1997.
Cowan, Ruth Schwartz. *More Work for Mother: The Ironies of Household Technology from the Open Hearth to the Microwave*. New York: Basic Books, 1983.
Cross, Gary. *An All-Consuming Century: Why Commercialism Won in Modern America*. New York: Columbia University Press, 2000.
Crossick, Geoffrey, and Serge Jaumain, eds. *Cathedrals of Consumption: The European Department Store, 1850–1939*. Aldershot: Ashgate, 1999.
Crowley, David. "Europe Reconstructed, Europe Divided." In *Cold War Modern: Design, 1945–1970*, ed. David Crowley and Jane Pavitt. London: V&A Publishing, 2008.
Crowley, David. "Paris or Moscow: Warsaw Architects and the Image of the Modern City in the 1950s." *Kritika* 9 (2008): 769–98.
Crowley, David. "Thaw Modern: Design in Eastern Europe after 1956." In *Cold War Modern: Design, 1945–1970*, ed. David Crowley and Jane Pavitt. London: V&A Publishing, 2008.

D'Apice, Carmela. *L'arcipelago dei consumi: Consumi e redditi delle famiglie in Italia dal dopoguerra ad oggi*. Bari: De Donato, 1981.

Dauvergne, Peter. *The Shadows of Consumption: Consequences for the Global Environment*. Cambridge, MA: MIT Press, 2008.

Davis, John. *Land and Family in Pisticci*. London: Athlone Press, 1973.

de Grazia, Victoria. "Changing Consumption Regimes in Europe, 1930–1970: Comparative Perspectives on the Distribution Problem." In *Getting and Spending: European and American Consumer Societies in the Twentieth Century*, ed. Susan Strasser, Charles McGovern, and Matthias Judt. Cambridge: Cambridge University Press, 1998.

de Grazia, Victoria. *Irresistible Empire: America's Advance through Twentieth-Century Europe*. Cambridge, MA: Belknap Press of Harvard University Press, 2005.

de Grazia, Victoria, and Ellen Furlough, eds. *The Sex of Things: Gender and Consumption in Historical Perspective*. Berkeley: University of California Press, 1996.

De Vos, Els. "The American Kitchen in Belgium: A Story of Countering, Reversing, Selective Appropriation and Sidelining." Paper presented at the European Ways of Living in the American Century Conference, Stockholm, January 16–17, 2010.

Der ideale Haushalt: ein Sonderheft der Constanze-Verlag. Hamburg: Constanze-Verlag, 1958.

Domosh, Mona. *American Commodities in an Age of Empire*. New York: Routledge, 2006.

Douglas, Mary, and Baron C. Isherwood. *The World of Goods*. New York: Basic Books, 1979.

Durth, Werner. "Architecture as a Political Medium." In *The United States and Germany in the Era of the Cold War, 1945–1968: A Handbook*, ed. Detlef Junker. New York: Cambridge University Press, 2004.

Eco, Umberto. *Travels in Hyperreality: Essays*. New York: Harcourt Brace Jovanovich, 1986.

Eisenstadt, Shmuel N. "Multiple Modernities." In *Multiple Modernities*, ed. Shmuel N. Eisenstadt. New Brunswick: Transaction Publishers, 2002.

Eliassen, Bjørg, *Vi dypfryser*. Oslo: Tanum, 1965.

Ellwood, David W. *The Shock of America: Europe and the Challenge of the Century*. Oxford: Oxford University Press, 2012.

Ellwood, David W., and Gian Piero Brunetta, eds. *Hollywood in Europa: Industria, politica, pubblico del cinema 1945–1960*. Florence: Ponte alle Grazie, 1991.

Elsässer, Sophie. *Att skapa en konsument: Råd och Rön och den statliga konsumentupplysningen*. Gothenburg: Makadam, 2012.

Emanuel, Martin, and Per Lundin. "Fostering Youth, Curbing Revolution: The Development of a Swedish Bourgeois Tourism Regime, 1885–1939." Paper presented at 6th Plenary Conference of Tensions of Europe, Paris, September 19–21, 2013.

Endrédi, Gustav. *Resekonsumtionen 1950–1975*. Stockholm: Industrins utredningsinstitut, 1967.

Endy, Christopher. *Cold War Holidays: American Tourism in France*. Chapel Hill: University of North Carolina Press, 2004.

Eskilsson, Lena. "Svenska turistföreningen från fjäll till friluftsliv: Från den vetenskapliga vildmannen till den cyklande husmodern." *Historisk tidskrift* 116 (1996): 257–82.

Eskilsson, Lena. "Fritid som idé, struktur och praktik: Rätten till lättja eller friluftsliv i folkhemmet." *Historisk tidskrift* 120 (2000): 29–52.

European Refrigeration Research and Its Practical Applications: Project No. 239. Paris: EPA, 1959.

Fallan, Kjetil. "How an Excavator Got Aesthetic Pretensions: Negotiating Design in 1960s' Norway." *Journal of Design History* 20 (2007): 43–59.

Fallan, Kjetil. "Heresy and Heroics: The Debate on the Alleged 'Crisis' in Italian Design around 1960." *Modern Italy* 14 (2009): 257–74.

Fallan, Kjetil. "The *Realpolitik* of the Artificial: Strategic Design at Figgjo Fajanse Facing International Free Trade in the 1960s." *Enterprise and Society* 10 (2009): 559–89.

Fegiz, Pierpaolo Luzzatto. *Il volto sconosciuto dell'Italia: Seconda serie, 1956–1965*. Milan: Giuffrè, 1966.

Finstad, Terje. "Varme visjoner og frosne fremskritt: Om fryseteknologi i Norge, ca. 1920–1965." PhD diss., Norwegian University of Science and Technology, 2011.

Finstad, Terje. "Familiarizing Food: Frozen Food Chains, Technology and Consumer Trust, Norway 1940–1970." *Food and Foodways* 21 (2013): 22–45.

Fofi, Goffredo. *L'immigrazione meridionale a Torino*. Milan: Aragno, 1964.

Food Consumption Levels in OEEC Countries: Report of the Working Group on Food Consumption Levels. Paris: OEEC, 1950.

Food for Europe after Victory. Washington: National Planning Association, 1944.

Food Marketing and Economic Growth. Paris: OECD, 1970.

Forgacs, David, and Stephen Gundle. *Mass Culture and Italian Society from Fascism to the Cold War*. Bloomington: Indiana University Press, 2007.

Franklin, Adrian, and Mike Crang. "The Trouble with Tourism and Travel Theory?" *Tourist Studies* 1 (2001): 5–22.

Fridenson, Patrick. "Ford as a Model for French Car Makers, 1911–1939." In *Ford: The European History, 1903–2003*, ed. Hubert Bonin, Jannick Lung, and Steven Tolliday. Paris: Éditions P.L.A.G.E., 2003.

Friedmann, Harriet. "The Political Economy of Food: The Rise and the Fall of the Postwar International Food Order." In "Marxist Inquiries: Studies of Labor, Class, and States," supplement, *American Journal of Sociology* 88 (1982): 248–86.

Furlough, Ellen. "Making Mass Vacations: Tourism and Consumer Culture in France, 1930s to 1970s." *Comparative Studies in Society and History* 40 (1998): 247–86.

Furre, Berge. *Norsk historie 1914–2000: Industrisamfunnet – frå vokstervisse til framtidstvil*. Vol. 6 of *Samlagets Norsk historie 800–2000*. Oslo: Samlaget, 1999.

Gabaccia, Donna R. *Italy's Many Diasporas*. London: UCL Press, 2000.

Garcia, Rosanna, and Roger Calantone. "A Critical Look at Technological Innovation Typology and Innovativeness Terminology: A Literature Review." *The Journal of Product Innovation Management* 19 (2002): 110–32.

Gassert, Philipp. "The Spectre of Americanization: Western Europe in the American Century." In *The Oxford Handbook of Postwar European History*, ed. Dan Stone. Oxford: Oxford University Press, 2012.

Giacobone, Tersilla Faravelli, Paola Guidi, and Anty Pansera. *Dalla casa elettrica alla casa elettronica: Storia e significati degli elettrodomestici*. Milan: Arcadia, 1989.

Gifft, Helen H., Marjorie B. Washbon, and Gail G. Harrison. *Nutrition, Behavior, and Change*. Englewood Cliffs, NJ: Prentice-Hall, 1972.

Select Bibliography 235

Giovagnoli, Agostino. *Il partito italiano: La Democrazia Cristiana dal 1942 al 1994*. Rome: Laterza, 1996.
Glambek, Ingeborg. *Det Nordiske i arkitektur og design—sett utenfra*. Oslo: Arkitektens forlag & Norsk arkitekturforlag, 1997.
Goldin, Claudia. *Understanding the Gender Gap: An Economic History of American Women*. New York: Oxford University Press, 1990.
Gråbacke, Carina. *När folket tog semester: Studier av Reso 1937–1977*. Lund: Sekel, 2008.
Grassl, Anton, and Graham Heath. *The Magic Triangle: A Short History of the World Youth Hostel Movement*. London: International Youth Hostel Federation, 1982.
Grinell, Klas. *Att sälja världen: Omvärldsbilder i svensk utlandsturism*. Gothenburg: Acta Universitatis Gothoburgensis, 2004.
Gronow, Jukka. *Caviar with Champagne: Common Luxury and the Ideals of the Good Life in Stalin's Russia*. Oxford: Berg, 2003.
Groppi, Angela, ed. *Il lavoro delle donne*. Rome and Bari: Laterza, 1996.
Grosman, Robert. "Ford not Freud." *New Yorker*, December 9, 1974.
Gruber, Helmut. *Red Vienna: Experiment in Working-Class Culture, 1918–1934*. New York: Oxford University Press, 1991.
Grumet, Michael. *Images of Liberty*. New York: Arbor House, 1986.
Gundle, Stephen. *Between Hollywood and Moscow: The Italian Communists and the Challenge of Mass Culture, 1943–1991*. Durham, NC: Duke University Press, 2000.
Haddow, Robert H. *Pavilions of Plenty: Exhibiting American Culture Abroad in the 1950s*. Washington, DC: Smithsonian Institution Press, 1997.
Halén, Widar. "Korpusdesigneren." In *Grete Prytz Kittelsen*, ed. Karianne Bjellås Gilje. Oslo: Gyldendal, 2007.
Hamilton, Shane, *Trucking Country: The Road to America's Wal-Mart Economy*. Princeton, NJ: Princeton University Press, 2008.
Hamilton, Shane. "Supermarket USA Confronts State Socialism: Airlifting the Technopolitics of Industrial Food Distribution into Cold War Yugoslavia." In *Cold War Kitchen: Americanization, Technology, and European Users*, ed. Ruth Oldenziel and Karin Zachmann. Cambridge, MA: MIT Press, 2009.
Hammar, Thomas. *Sverige åt svenskarna: Invandringspolitik, utlänningskontroll och asylrätt 1900–1932*. Stockholm: Stockholms universitet, 1964.
Hansen, Per H. "Networks, Narratives, and New Markets: The Rise and Decline of Danish Modern Furniture Design, 1930–1970." *Business History Review* 80 (2006): 449–83.
Hård, Mikael. "The Good Apartment: The Social (Democratic) Construction of Swedish Homes." *Home Cultures* 7 (2010): 117–34.
Harris, Steven E. "In Search of 'Ordinary' Russia: Everyday Life in the NEP, the Thaw and the Communal Apartment." *Kritika* 6 (2005): 583–614.
Harsch, Donna. *Revenge of the Domestic: Women, the Family, and Communism in the German Democratic Republic*. Princeton, NJ: Princeton University Press, 2007.
Heathcote, David. *Barbican Penthouse Over the City*. Chichester: Wiley, 2004.
Heineman, Elisabeth. *What Difference Does a Husband Make? Women and Marital Status in Nazi and Postwar Germany*. Berkeley: University of California Press, 1999.
Hellström, Hans. *Struktur, aktör eller kultur? Arbetstidspolitik i det industrialiserade Sverige*. Stockholm: Almqvist & Wiksell International, 1992.
Hessels, Aaltje. *Vakantie en Vakantiebesteding sinds de Eeuwwisseling*. Assen: Van Gorcum, 1973.

Hessler, Martina. "Die Einführung elektrischer Haushaltsgeräte in der Zwischenkriegszeit: Der Angebotspush der Produzenten und die Reaktion der Konsumentinnen." *Technikgeschichte* 65 (1998): 297–312.

Hessler, Martina. "The Frankfurt Kitchen: The Model of Modernity and the 'Madness' of Traditional Users, 1926–1933." In *Cold War Kitchen: Americanization, Technology, and European Users*, ed. Ruth Oldenziel and Karin Zachmann. Cambridge, MA: MIT Press, 2009.

Higham, John. *Send These to Me: Jews and Other Immigrants in Urban America*. New York: Atheneum, 1975.

Hilck, Erwin, and Rudolf Hövel. *Jenseits von minus Null: Die Geschichte der deutschen Tiefkühlwirtschaft*. Cologne: Deutsches Tiefkühlinstitut, 1979.

Hill, Stephen. *Europe's Promise: Why the European Way Is the Best Hope in an Insecure Age*. Berkeley: University of California Press, 2010.

Hine, Thomas. *Populuxe*. New York: Alfred A. Knopf, 1986.

Hixson, Walter L. *Parting the Curtain: Propaganda, Culture, and the Cold War, 1945–1961*. New York: St. Martin's Press, 1998.

Hobsbawm, Eric. *The Age of Empire, 1875–1914*. New York: Vintage, 1989.

Hodgson, Godfrey. *The Myth of American Exceptionalism*. New Haven, CT: Yale University Press, 2009.

Hoganson, Kristin. "Stuff It: Domestic Consumption and the Americanization of the World Paradigm." *Diplomatic History* 30 (2006): 571–94.

Hoganson, Kristin. *Consumers' Imperium: The Global Production of American Domesticity, 1865–1920*. Chapel Hill: University of North Carolina Press, 2007.

Holder, Julien. "The Nation State or the United States? The Irresistible Kitchen of the British Ministry of Works, 1944–1951." In *Cold War Kitchen: Americanization, Technology, and European Users*, ed. Ruth Oldenziel and Karin Zachmann. Cambridge, MA: MIT Press, 2009.

Horn, Adrian. *Juke Box Britain: Americanisation and Youth Culture, 1945–60*. Manchester: Manchester University Press, 2009.

Horney, Nils. *Stora män och tidningsmän: En reporters minnen från fem decennier*. Stockholm: Natur och kultur, 1969.

Huldt, Åke H. "Industrial Design." In *Nordenfjeldske kunstindustrimuseum—Årbok 1951*, ed. Thorvald Krohn-Hansen. Trondheim: Nordenfjeldske kunstindustrimuseum, 1952.

Ibelings, Hans. *Americanism: Nederlandse architectuur en het transatlantische voorbeeld: Dutch Architecture and the Transatlantic Model*. Rotterdam: NAi, 1997.

Jakle, John A., Keith A. Sculle, and Jefferson S. Rogers. *The Motel in America*. Baltimore, MD: Johns Hopkins University Press, 1996.

Jarausch, Konrad H., and Michael Geyer. *Shattered Past: Reconstructing German Histories*. Princeton, NJ: Princeton University Press, 2002.

Jefferson, Thomas. *Notes on the State of Virginia*. London: J. Stockdale, 1787.

Johannessen, Wenche Anette. "Brukskunst-senteret PLUS: Per Tannums ønske om å etablere et designsentrum." MPhil thesis, University of Oslo, 2000.

Judt, Tony. *Postwar: A History of Europe since 1945*. New York: Penguin, 2005.

Judt, Tony. *Ill Fares the Land*. New York: Penguin, 2010.

Kaiserfeld, Thomas. "From Sightseeing to Sunbathing: Changing Traditions in Swedish Package Tours: From Edification by Bus to Relaxation by Airplane in the 1950s and 60s." *Journal of Tourism History* 2 (2010): 149–63.

Kaplan, Stephen S. "United States Aid to Poland, 1957–1964: Concerns, Objectives and Obstacles." *The Western Political Quarterly* 28 (1975): 147–66.

Karlsson, Birgit. "Sweden and the Marshall Plan." In *The Marshall Plan*, Fredrik Erixon et al. Stockholm: Timbro, 2008.

Karlsson, Ingela. "Sig själv närmast." In *En (o)moralisk hållning? Sveriges ekonomiska relationer med Nazityskland*, ed. Charlotte Haider. Stockholm: Forum för levande historia, 2006.

Katzenstein, Peter J. *Small Countries in World Markets: Industrial Policy in Europe*. Ithaca, NY: Cornell University Press, 1985.

Kaufmann, Jr., Edgar. "Moderne formgivning i De Forenede Stater." In *Amerikansk form: En samling håndverks- og industrivarer sammenstillet av Museum of Modern Art, New York*. Oslo: Foreningen brukskunst, 1954.

Kertzer, David I. *Family Life in Central Italy, 1880–1910: Sharecropping, Wage Labor, and Coresidence*. New Brunswick, NJ: Rutgers University Press, 1984.

Kilander, Svenbjörn. *"En nationalrikedom av hälsoskatter": Om Jämtland och industrisamhället 1882–1910*. Hedemora: Gidlund, 2008.

Kilgannon, Corey. "Cameras to Seek Faces of Terror In Visitors to the Statue of Liberty." *New York Times*, May 25, 2002.

Kinsey, Jean D. "The New Food Economy: Consumers, Farms, Pharms, and Science." *American Journal of Agricultural Economics* 83 (2001): 1113–30.

Kipping, Matthias, and Ove Bjarnar, eds. *The Americanisation of European Business: The Marshall Plan and the Transfer of US Management Models*. London: Routledge, 1998.

Kipping,Matthias and Nick Tiratsoo, eds. *Americanisation in 20th Century Europe: Business, Culture, Politics*, vol. 2. Lille: Centre d'Histoire de l'Europe du Nord-Ouest, 2001.

Knudsen, Ann-Christina L. "Ideas, Welfare, and Values: Framing the Common Agricultural Policy in the 1960s." In *Fertile Ground for Europe? The History of European Integration and the Common Agricultural Policy since 1945*, ed. Patel Kiran Klaus. Baden-Baden: Nomos, 2009.

Kocka, Jürgen. "'Bürgertum' and Two Professions in the Nineteenth Century: Two Alternative Approaches." In *Professions in Theory and History: Rethinking the Study of the Professions*, ed. Michael Burrage and Rolf Torstendahl. London: Sage, 1990.

Koshar, Rudy, ed. *Histories of Leisure*. Oxford: Berg, 2002.

Kotkin, Stephen. *Magnetic Mountain: Stalinism as Civilization*. Berkeley: University of California Press, 1995.

Kras = 100: 100 = Kras. Amsterdam: Grand Hotel Krasnapolsky, 1966.

"Kras" Commercieel, cultureel en zakelijk middelpunt: De financiering van haar modernisering en uitbreiding in een moeilijke tijd. Amsterdam: Grand Hotel Krasnapolsky, 1952.

Krige, John. *American Hegemony and the Postwar Reconstruction of Science in Europe*. Cambridge, MA: MIT Press, 2006.

Kroes, Rob. *If You've Seen One, You've Seen the Mall: Europeans and American Mass Culture*. Urbana: University of Illinois Press, 1996.

Kroes, Rob. *Photographic Memories: Private Pictures, Public Images, and American History*. Lebanon, NH: University Press of New England, 2007.

Kuisel, Richard F. *The French Way: How France Embraced and Rejected American Values and Power*. Princeton, NJ: Princeton University Press, 2012.

Kvaal, Stig. "Janus med tre ansikter: Om organiseringen av den industrielt rettede forskningen i spennet mellom stat, vitenskap og industri i Norge, 1916–1956." PhD diss., Norwegian University of Science and Technology, 1997.
Kvaal, Stig, and Astrid Wale. *En spenningshistorie: Trondheim Energiverk gjennom et århundre*. Trondheim: Trondheim Energiverk, 2000.
Lamartine Yates, Paul. *Food, Land and Manpower in Western Europe*. London: Macmillan, 1960.
Laqueur, Walter.*Young Germany: A History of the German Youth Movement*. New ed. London: Transaction Books, 1984.
Lerman, Nina E., Ruth Oldenziel, and Arwen Mohun, eds. *Gender and Technology: A Reader*. Baltimore, MD: Johns Hopkins University Press, 2003.
Lévi-Strauss, Claude. "Das kulinarische Dreieck." In *Strukturalismus als interpretatives Verfahren*, ed. Helga Gallas. Darmstadt: Luchterhand, 1972.
Lewchuk, Wayne. "Fordist Technology and Britain: The Diffusion of Labour Speed-up." In *The Transfer of International Technology: Europe, Japan and the USA in the Twentieth Century*, ed. David J. Jeremy. Aldershot: Edward Elgar, 1992.
Linders-Rooijendijk, Matea F. A. *Gebaande wegen voor mobiliteit en vrijetijdsbesteding II: De ANWB van Vereniging naar Instituut, 1937–1983*. The Hague: ANWB, 1992.
Lindström, Hugo. "Min tid med Ralph Lysell og Alvar Lenning." In *Svensk industridesign: En 1900-talshistoria*, ed. Lasse Brunnström. Stockholm: Prisma, 1997.
Loehlin, Jennifer Ann. *From Rugs to Riches: Housework, Consumption and Modernity in Germany*. Oxford: Berg, 1999.
Löfgren, Orvar. "Consuming Interests." *Culture and History* 7 (1990): 5–25.
Löfgren, Orvar. "Längtan till landet Annorlunda." In *Längtan till landet Annorlunda: Om turism i historia och nutid*. Hedemora: Gidlund, 1990.
Löfgren, Orvar."Materializing the Nation in Sweden and America." *Ethnos* 58 (1993): 161–95.
Löfgren, Orvar. "Know Your Country: A Comparative Perspective on Tourism and Nation Building in Sweden." In *Being Elsewhere: Tourism, Consumer Culture, and Identity in Modern Europe and North America*, ed. Shelley Baranowski and Ellen Furlough. Ann Arbor: University of Michigan Press, 2001.
Logemann, Jan. *Trams or Tailfins? Public and Private Property in Postwar West Germany and the United States*. Chicago: University of Chicago Press, 2012.
Lötmarker, Lena, and Bo-A Wendt. *Resmål till salu: Svenska turistbroschyrers textuella och språkliga utveckling under hundra år*. Lund: Sekel, 2009.
Lundberg, Mari, *I bilismens barndom: Om bilturism och Gyllene Uttern*. Gränna: Gränna hembygdsförening, 1990.
Lundestad, Geir. "Empire by Invitation? The United States and Western Europe, 1945–1952." *Journal of Peace Research* 23 (1986): 263–77.
Lundestad, Geir. "'Empire by Invitation' in the American Century." *Diplomatic History* 23 (1999): 189–217.
Lundin, Per. *Bilsamhället: Ideologi, expertis och regelskapande i efterkrigstidens Sverige*. Stockholm: Stockholmia, 2008.
Lundin, Per. "Mediators of Modernity: Planning Experts and the Making of the 'Car-Friendly' City in Europe." In *Urban Machinery: Inside Modern European Cities*, ed. Mikael Hård and Thomas J. Misa. Cambridge, MA: MIT Press, 2008.
Lundin, Per. "Confronting Class: The American Motel in Early Post-war Sweden," *Journal of Tourism History* 5 (2013): 305–24.

Maddison, Angus. *Monitoring the World Economy, 1829–1992*. Paris: OECD, 1995.
Maguire, Patrick. "Craft Capitalism and the Projection of British Industry in the 1950s and 1960s." *Journal of Design History* 6 (1993): 97–113.
Maier, Charles S. *In Search of Stability: Explorations in Historical Political Economy*. Cambridge: Cambridge University Press, 1987.
Malchow, Howard Le Roy. *Special Relations: The Americanization of Britain?* Stanford, CA: Stanford University Press, 2011.
Marchand, Roland. *Advertising the American Dream: Making Way for Modernity, 1920–1940*. Berkeley: University of California Press, 1985.
Marcus, George H. *Design in the Fifties: When Everyone Went Modern*. Munich: Prestel Verlag, 1998.
Marjavaara, Roger. "Mot Fjärran land—svensk flygcharterturism 1962–1993." Master's thesis, Umeå University, 1998.
Marling, Karel Ann. *As Seen on TV: The Visual Culture of Everyday Life in the 1950s*. Cambridge, MA: Harvard University Press, 1994.
Mattsson, Helena, and Sven-Olov Wallenstein. "Introduction." In *Swedish Modernism: Architecture, Consumption and the Welfare State*, ed. Helena Mattsson and Sven-Olov Wallenstein. London: Black Dog Publishing, 2010.
May, Elaine Tyler. *Homeward Bound: American Families in the Cold War Era*. New York: Basic Books, 1988.
Mazower, Mark. *Dark Continent: Europe's Twentieth Century*. London: Penguin Books, 1999.
McDonald, Gay. "Selling the American Dream: MoMA, Industrial Design and Post-War France." *Journal of Design History* 17 (2004): 397–412.
McDonald, Gay. "The 'Advance' of American Postwar Design in Europe: MoMA and the *Design for Use, USA* Exhibition 1951–1953." *Design Issues* 24 (2008): 15–27.
McDonald, Gay. "The Modern American Home as Soft Power: Finland, MoMA and the 'American Home 1953' Exhibition." *Journal of Design History* 23 (2010): 387–408.
McGlade, Jacqueline. "Americanization: Ideology or Process? The Case of the United States Technical Assistance and Productivity Programme." In *Americanization and Its Limits: Reworking US Technology and Management in Post-War Europe and Japan*, ed. Jonathan Zeitlin and Gary Herrigel. Oxford: Oxford University Press, 2000.
McGovern, Charles F. *Sold American: Consumption and Citizenship, 1890–1945*. Chapel Hill: University of North Carolina Press, 2006.
McGovern, George S. *War against Want: America's Food for Peace Program*. New York: Walker, 1964.
McKenzie, Brian A. "Creating a Tourist's Paradise: The Marshall Plan and France, 1948 to 1952." *French Politics, Culture and Society* 21 (2003): 35–54.
McKenzie, Fred. *The American Invaders*. New York: Arno Press, 1976.
Meikle, Jeffrey L. *Design in the USA*. Oxford: Oxford University Press, 2005.
Meinander, Henrik. *Towards a Bourgeois Manhood: Boys' Physical Education in Nordic Secondary Schools 1880–1940*. Helsinki: Societas scientiarum Fennica, 1994.
Merkel, Ina. *Utopie und Bedürfnis: Die Geschichte der Konsumkultur in der DDR*. Cologne: Böhlau, 1999.
Meyerowitz, Joanne, ed. *Not June Cleaver: Women and Gender in Postwar America, 1945–1960*. Philadelphia: Temple University Press, 1994.

240 Select Bibliography

Middenstand en Consument: Verslagboek Studiedagen N.R.K.M. The Hague: Nederlandse Katholieke Middenstandsbond, 1964.
Milward, Alan S. *The Reconstruction of Western Europe, 1945–51*. London: Routledge, 1992.
Minestroni, Laura. *Casa dolce casa: Storia dello spazio domestico tra pubblicità e società*. Milan: Franco Angeli, 1996.
Mom, Gijs, and Ruud Filarski. *Van Transport naar Mobiliteit: De mobiliteitsexplosie, 1895–2005*. Zutphen: Walburg Pers, 2008.
Montanari, Armando, and Allan M. Williams, eds. *European Tourism: Regions, Spaces and Restructuring*. Chichester: Wiley, 1995.
Morton, Henry W. "What Have Soviet Leaders Done about the Housing Crisis?" In *Soviet Politics and Society in the 1970s*, ed. Henry Morton and Rudolf L. Tökés. New York: Free Press, 1974.
Myrvang, Christine. *Forbruksagentene: Slik vekket de kjøpelysten*. Oslo: Pax, 2009.
Myrvang, Christine, Sissel Mykleburst, and Brita Brenna, *Temmet eller uhemmet: Historiske perspektiver på konsum, kultur og dannelse*. Oslo: Pax, 2004.
Nathaus, Klaus, ed. "Europop: The Production of Popular Culture in Twentieth Century Western Europe," special issue. *European Review of History: Revue europeenne d'histoire* 20, no. 5 (2013).
Nielsen, Niels Kayser. "The Cult of the Nordic Superman – between the Premodern and the Modern." *The Sports Historian* 19 (1999): 61–80.
Nolan, Mary. "'Housework Made Easy': The Taylorized Housewife in Weimar Germany's Rationalized Economy." *Feminist Studies* 16 (1990): 549–78.
Nolan, Mary. *Visions of Modernity: American Business and the Modernization of Germany*. Oxford: Oxford University Press, 1994.
Nolan, Mary. "Consuming America, Producing Gender." In *The American Century in Europe*, ed. Laurence Moore and Maurizio Vaudagna. Ithaca, NY: Cornell University Press, 2003.
Nolan, Mary. *The Transatlantic Century: Europe and America, 1890–2010*. Cambridge: Cambridge University Press, 2012.
Nye, David E. *America's Assembly Line*. Cambridge, MA: MIT Press, 2013.
Nye, David E., and Mick Gidley, eds. *American Photographs in Europe*. Amsterdam: VU University Press, 1994.
O'Dell, Tom. *Culture Unbound: Americanization and Everyday Life in Sweden*. New ed. Lund: Nordic Academic Press, 2012.
Obrador Pons, Pau, Mike Crang, and Penny Travlou, eds. *Cultures of Mass Tourism: Doing the Mediterranean in the Age of Banal Mobilities*. London: Ashgate, 2009.
Ogburn, William Fielding. *Social Change with Respect to Culture and Original Nature*. New York: B.W. Huebsch, 1922.
Oldenziel, Ruth. *Making Technology Masculine: Men, Women and Modern Machines in America, 1870–1945*. Amsterdam: Amsterdam University Press, 1999.
Oldenziel, Ruth. "Is Globalization a Code Word for Americanization?" *Tijdschrift voor Sociale en Economische Geschiedenis* 4 (2007): 84–106.
Oldenziel, Ruth, and Adri Albert de la Bruhèze. "Theorizing the Mediation Junction for Technology and Consumption." In *Manufacturing Technology, Manufacturing Consumers: The Making of Dutch Consumer Society*, ed. Adri Albert de la Bruhèze and Ruth Oldenziel. Amsterdam: Aksant, 2009.
Oldenziel, Ruth, Adri A. Albert de la Bruhèze, and Onno de Wit. "Europe's Mediation Junction: Technology and Consumer Society in the 20th Century." *History and Technology* 21 (2005): 107–39.

Oldenziel, Ruth, and Karin Zachmann, eds. *Cold War Kitchen: Americanization, Technology, and European Users*. Cambridge, MA: MIT Press, 2009.

Oldenziel, Ruth, and Karin Zachmann. "Kitchens as Technology and Politics: An Introduction." In *Cold War Kitchen: Americanization, Technology, and European Users*, ed. Ruth Oldenziel and Karin Zachmann. Cambridge, MA: MIT Press, 2009.

Oudshoorn, Nelly, and Trevor Pinch, eds. *How Users Matter: The Co-Construction of Users and Technology*. Cambridge, MA: MIT Press, 2003.

Our Dumb Century: The Onion Presents 100 Years of Headlines from America's Finest News Source. New York: Three Rivers Press, 1999.

Page, Max. *The City's End: Two Centuries of Fantasies, Fears, and Premonitions of New York's Destruction*. New Haven, CT: Yale University Press, 2008.

Paolini, Federico. *Storia sociale dell'automobile in Italia*. Rome: Carocci, 2007.

Parr, Joy. *Domestic Goods: The Material, the Moral, and the Economic in the Postwar Years*. Toronto: University of Toronto Press, 1999.

Pearce, Douglas C. "Mediterranean Charters: A Comparative Geographic Perspective." *Tourism Management* 8 (1987): 291–305.

Pells, Richard. *Not Like Us: How Europeans Have Loved, Hated, and Transformed American Culture since World War II*. New York: Basic Books, 1997.

Pence, Katherine. "Domestic Consumption in the Two New German States." In *Gender Relations in German History: Power, Agency, and Experience from the Sixteenth to the Twentieth Century*, ed. Lynn Abrams and Elizabeth Harvey. Durham, NC: Duke University Press, 1997.

Petrick, Gabriella. "The Arbiters of Taste: Producers, Consumers, and the Industrialization of Taste in America, 1900–1960." PhD diss., University of Delaware, 2006.

Pettersen-Hagh, Nils W., and Sæbjørn Røsvik, eds. *Glimt fra norsk kjøleteknisk historie*. Oslo: Norsk kjøleteknisk forening, 1986.

Pitkin, Donald S. *The House That Giacomo Built: History of an Italian Family, 1898–1978*. Cambridge: Cambridge University Press, 1985.

Pizzorno, Alessandro. *Comunità e razionalizzazione*. Turin: Einaudi, 1960.

Pleydell-Bouverie, M. *Daily Mail Book of Post-War Homes*. London: Daily Mail, 1944.

Poiger, Uta. "The Modern Girl Around the World: Cosmetics Advertising and the Politics of Race and Style." In *The Modern Girl Around the World: Consumption, Modernity, and Globalization*, ed. Alys Eve Weinbaum et al. Durham, NC: Duke University Press, 2008.

Project No. 396: Report of Working Conference. Paris: EPA, 1959.

Provoyeur, Pierre, and June Hargrove. *Liberty: The French-American Statue in Art and History*. New York: Perennial Library, 1986.

Ramskjær, Liv. "Plast i det moderne Norge: Introduksjon, gjennombrudd og spredning av plastprodukter i Norge 1930–1974." In *Volund 1999–2000: Plast i det moderne Norge*, ed. Frode Weium. Oslo: NTM, 2001.

Ramskjær, Liv. "Users and Producers of Plastics in Post–World War II Norway: Building a New Industry Through Transfer of Technology." *Comparative Technology Transfer and Society* 3 (2005): 76–102.

Randall, Amy E. *The Soviet Dream World of Retail Trade and Consumption in the 1930s*. Basingstoke: Palgrave Macmillan, 2008.

Rantatalo, Petra. *Den resande eleven: Folkskolans skolreserörelse 1890–1940*. Umeå: Umeå universitet, 2001.

Rasmussen, Wayne D. "The Impact of Technological Change on American Agriculture, 1862–1962." *The Journal of Economic History* 22 (1962): 578–91.
Rasmussen, Wayne D., and Jane M. Porter. "Strategies for Dealing with World Hunger: Post-World War II Policies." *American Journal of Agricultural Economics* 63 (1981): 810–18.
Reagin, Nancy. *Sweeping the German Nation: Domesticity and National Identity, 1870–1945*. New York: Cambridge University Press, 2008.
Reid, Susan E. "Destalinization and Taste, 1953–1963." *Journal of Design History* 10 (1997): 177–201.
Reid, Susan E. "The Khrushchev Kitchen: Domesticating the Scientific-Technological Revolution." *Journal of Contemporary History* 40 (2005): 289–316.
Reid, Susan E. "'Our Kitchen Is Just as Good': Soviet Responses to the American Kitchen." In *Cold War Kitchen: Americanization, Technology, and European Users*, ed. Ruth Oldenziel and Karin Zachmann. Cambridge, MA: MIT Press, 2009.
Remlov, Arne, ed. *Design in Scandinavia: An Exhibition of Objects for the Home*. Oslo: Kirstes, 1954.
Rese-reklamationer: En genomgång av reklamationer rörande charterresor. Stockholm: Allmänna reklamationsnämnden and Liber/Allmänna förlaget, 1985.
Reulecke, Jürgen, and Barbara Stambolis, eds. *100 Jahre Jugendherbergen 1909–2009: Anfänge – Wandlungen – Rück- und Ausblicke*. Essen: Klartext, 2009.
Ringdal, Siv. *Det amerikanske Lista: Med 110 volt i huset*. Oslo: Pax, 2002.
Risparmio nel 1975. Rome: Banca d'Italia, 1976.
Ritzer, George. *The McDonaldization of Society: An Investigation into the Changing Character of Contemporary Social Life*. Thousand Oaks, CA: Pine Forge, 1993.
Rodgers, Daniel T. *Atlantic Crossings: Social Politics in a Progressive Age*. Cambridge, MA: Belknap Press of Harvard University Press, 2000.
Rome, Adam. *Bulldozer in the Countryside: Suburban Sprawl and the Rise of American Environmentalism*. New York: Cambridge University Press, 2001.
Rosén, Göte. *Vägen till Palma: 25 års "luftaffärer": en memoarbok om charterflygets utveckling*. Malmö: CEGE, 1970.
Rosén, Göte. *Orädd att flyga*. Uppsala: Nybloms, 1976.
Rosén, Ulla. "'A Rational Solution to the Laundry Issue': Policy and Research for Day-to-Day Life in the Welfare State." In *Science for Welfare and Warfare: Technology and State Initiative in Cold War Sweden*, ed. Per Lundin, Niklas Stenlås, and Johan Gribbe. Sagamore Beach, MA: Science History Publications, 2010.
Rosenberg, Arne. *Air Travel within Europe*. Stockholm: The Swedish National Consumer Council and Norstedts, 1970.
Rosenberg, Emily S. "Consuming Women: Images of Americanization in the 'American Century.'" *Diplomatic History* 23 (1999): 479–97.
Rosendorf, Neal Moses. "Be El Caudillo's Guest: The Franco Regime's Quest for Rehabilitation and Dollars after World War II via the Promotion of U.S. Tourism to Spain." *Diplomatic History* 30 (2006): 367–407.
Ross, Kristin. *Fast Cars, Clean Bodies: Decolonization and Reordering of French Culture*. Cambridge, MA: MIT Press, 1996.
Rothstein, Bo. "State Structure and Variations in Corporatism: The Swedish Case." *Scandinavian Political Studies* 14 (1991): 149–71.
Rothstein, Bo. *Den korporativa staten: Intresseorganisationer och statsförvaltning i svensk politik*. Stockholm: Norstedts, 1992.

Ruble, Blair A. "From khrushcheby to korobki." In *Russian Housing in the Modern Age: Design and Social History*, ed. William Craft Brumfield and Blair A. Ruble. Cambridge: Cambridge University Press, 1993.

Rudolph, Nicole. "Domestic Politics: The Cité expérimentale at Noisy-le-See in Greater Pairs." *Modern and Contemporary France* 12 (2004): 483–95.

Rudolph, Nicole. "At Home in Postwar France: The Design and Construction of Domestic Space, 1945–1975." PhD diss., New York University, 2005.

Rudolph, Nicole. "Who Should Be the Author of a Dwelling: Architects versus Housewives in 1950s France." *Gender and History* 21 (2009): 541–59.

Rydell, Robert W., and Rob Kroes. *Buffalo Bill in Bologna: The Americanization of the World, 1869–1922*. Chicago: University of Chicago Press, 2005.

Rygh, Thorbjørn. "'Amerikansk Form.'" In *Nordenfjeldske kunstindustrimuseum—Årbok 1953*, ed. Thorvald Krohn-Hansen. Trondheim: Nordenfjeldske kunstindustrimuseum, 1954.

Saarikangas, Kirsi. "What's New? Women Pioneers and the Finnish State Meet the American Kitchen." In *Cold War Kitchen: Americanization, Technology, and European Users*, ed. Ruth Oldenziel and Karin Zachmann. Cambridge, MA: MIT Press, 2009.

Sachse, Carola. *Siemens, der Nationalsozialismus und die moderne Familie: Eine Untersuchung zur sozialen Rationalisierung in Deutschland im 20. Jahrhundert*. Hamburg: Rasch und Röhring, 1990.

Sahlins, Marshall. *Kultur und praktische Vernunft*. Frankfurt am Main: Suhrkamp, 1999.

Sällskapsresor: Betänkande avgivet av Statens konsumentråds sällskapsreseutredning. Statens offentliga utredningar 1966:25. Stockholm: Handelsdepartementet, 1966.

Sandeen, Eric J. "The Family of Man on the Road to Moscow." In *American Photographs in Europe*, ed. David E. Nye and Mick Gidley. Amsterdam: VU University Press, 1994.

Sandell, Klas, and Sverker Sörlin. "Naturen som fostrare: Friluftsliv och ideologi i svenskt 1900-tal." *Historisk tidskrift* 114 (1994): 4–43.

Sandoval-Strausz, Andrew K., *Hotel: An American History*. New Haven, CT: Yale University Press, 2007.

Saunes, Arthur. "Kommersiell Kjøling." In *Glimt fra norsk kjøleteknisk historie*, ed. Nils W. Pettersen-Hagh and Sæbjørn Røsvik. Oslo: Norsk kjøleteknisk forening, 1986.

Saur-Jaumann, Eleonore. *Hausfrau: mach dir die Arbeit leicht*. Heft 1. Munich: Rationalisierungs-Kuratorium der Deutschen Wirtschaft, 1951.

Scarpellini, Emanuela. *Material Nation: A Consumer's History of Modern Italy*. Oxford: Oxford University Press, 2011.

Schama, Simon. *The Embarrassment of Riches: An Interpretation of Dutch Culture in the Golden Age*. New York: Knopf, 1987.

Schipper, Frank. *Driving Europe: Building Europe on Roads in the Twentieth Century*. Eindhoven: Aksant, 2008.

Schlebeker, John T. "An Informal History of Hitchhiking." *The Historian* 20 (1958): 305–27.

Schot, Johan, and Adri Albert de la Bruhèze. "The Mediated Design of Products, Consumption, and Consumers in the Twentieth Century." In *How Users Matter: The Co-Construction of Users and Technology*, ed. Nelly Oudshoorn and Trevor Pinch. Cambridge, MA: MIT Press, 2003.

Schot, Johan, Gijs Mom, Ruud Filarski, and Peter Eloy Staal. "Concurrentie en Afstemming: Water, Rails, Weg en Lucht." In *Transport en Communicatie*. Vol. 5, *Techniek in Nederland in de Twintigste Eeuw*. Zutphen: Walburg Pers, 2002.

Schröter, Harm G. "Economic Culture and Its Transfer: An Overview of the Americanisation of the European Economy, 1900–2005." *European Review of History* 15 (2008): 331–44.

Schumpeter, Joseph A. *The Theory of Economic Development: An Inquiry into Profits, Capital, Credit, Interest, and the Business Cycle*. Cambridge, MA: Transaction Publishers, 1934.

Schwartz Cowan, Ruth. "The Consumption Junction: A Proposal for Research Strategies in the Sociology of Technology." In *The Social Construction of Technological Systems*, ed. Wiebe E. Bijker, Thomas P. Hughes, and Trevor Pinch. Cambridge, MA: MIT Press, 1989.

Sehlin, Halvar. *Känn ditt land: STF:s roll i den svenska turismens historia*. Stockholm: Svenska turistföreningen, 1998.

Sejersted, Francis. *The Age of Social Democracy: Norway and Sweden in the Twentieth Century*, trans. Richard Daly. Princeton, NJ: Princeton University Press, 2011.

Seth, Thomas von. *Charterhistoria*. Lidingö: Vivlio Förlag, 2008.

Shearer, J. Ronald. "The Reichskuratorium für Wirtschaftlichkeit: Fordism and Organized Capitalism in Germany, 1918–1945." *The Business History Review* 71 (1997): 569–602.

Sigfried, Giedion. *Mechanization Takes Command: A Contribution to Anonymous History*. New York: Oxford University Press, 1948.

Silverman, Sydel F. "Agricultural Organization, Social Structure, and Values in Italy: Amoral Familism Reconsidered." *American Anthropologist* 70 (1968): 1–20.

Siraa, H. Theo. *Een Miljoen Woningen: De rol van de Rijksoverheid bij wederopbouw, volkshuisvesting, bouwnijverheid en ruimtelijke ordening 1940–1963*. The Hague: SDU, 1989.

Smil, Vaclav. *Transforming the Twentieth Century: Technical Innovations and Their Consequences*. Oxford: Oxford University Press, 2006.

Smith, Mark B. "Khrushchev's Promise to Eliminate the Urban Housing Shortage: Rights, Rationality and the Communist Future." In *Soviet State and Society under Nikita Khrushchev*, ed. Melanie Ilic and Jeremy Smith. London: Routledge, 2009.

Sollors, Werner. "Of Plymouth Rock and Jamestown and Ellis Island – Or Ethnic Literature and Some Redefinitions of 'America.'" In *Multiculturalism and the Canon of American Culture*, ed. Hans Bak. Amsterdam: VU University Press, 1993.

Spang, Rebecca L. "The Cultural Habits of a Food Committee," *Food and Foodways* 2 (1988): 359–91.

Stachura, Peter D. *The German Youth Movement 1900–1945: An Interpretative and Documentary History*. London: Macmillan, 1981.

Stage, Sarah, and Virginia B. Vincenti, eds. *Rethinking Home Economics: Women and the History of a Profession*. Ithaca, NY: Cornell University Press, 1997.

Stead, W.T. *The Americanization of the World*. New York: Horace Markley, 1901.

Stephan, Alexander, ed. *The Americanization of Europe: Culture, Diplomacy, and Anti-Americanism after 1945*. New York: Berghahn Books, 2006.

Stokes, Raymond G. "Plastics and the New Society: The German Democratic Republic in the 1950s and 1960s." In *Style and Socialism: Modernity and Material*

Culture in Post-War Eastern Europe, ed. Susan E. Reid and David Crowley. Oxford: Berg, 2000.

Strasser, Susan. *Never Done: A History of American Housework.* New York: Pantheon, 1982.

Teuteberg, Hans Jürgen. "Zur Geschichte der Kühlkost und des Tiefgefrierens." *Zeitschrift für Unternehmensgeschichte* 36 (1991): 139–55.

Strasser, Susan, Charles McGovern, and Matthias Judt, eds. *Getting and Spending: European and American Consumer Societies in the Twentieth Century.* Cambridge: Cambridge University Press, 1998.

The Cold Chain in the U. S. A.: Report of a Group of European Experts. Paris: OEEC, 1951.

The Small Family Farm: A European Problem: Methods for Creating Economically Viable Units: Project No. 199/2. Paris: EPA, 1959.

Thévenot, Roger. *A History of Refrigeration throughout the World.* Paris: International Institute of Refrigeration, 1979.

Thiemeyer, Guido. *Vom "Pool Vert" zur Europäischen Wirtschaftsgemeinschaft: Europäische Integration, Kalter Krieg und die Anfänge der Gemeinsamen Europäischen Agrarpolitik, 1950–1957.* Munich: Oldenbourg, 1999.

Tjeder, David. *The Power of Character: Middle-class Masculinities, 1800–1900.* Stockholm: Stockholms universitet, 2003.

Tooze, Adam. *The Wages of Destruction: The Making and Breaking of the Nazi Economy.* New York: Penguin, 2007.

Tourism and European Recovery. Paris: OEEC, 1951.

Trafiksäkerhet II: Betänkande avgivet av 1953 års trafiksäkerhetsutredning. Statens offentliga utredningar 1957:18. Stockholm: Kommunikationsdepartementet, 1957.

Translating Science into Living Habits: Liaison Session of the Committee, May 19, 1945. Washington, DC: National Research Council, 1945.

Trentmann, Frank. "Bread, Milk and Democracy: Consumption and Citizenship in Twentieth-Century Britain." In *The Politics of Consumption: Material Culture and Citizenship in Europe and America,* ed. Martin Daunton and Matthew Hilton. Oxford: Berg, 2001.

Turisttrafiken från utlandet: Betänkande avgivet av 1948 års utredning angående turisttrafiken från utlandet. Statens offentliga utredningar 1951:49. Stockholm: Handelsdepartementet, 1951.

Tydén, Mattias, and Urban Lundberg. "In Search of the Swedish Model: Contested Historiography." In *Swedish Modernism: Architecture, Consumption and the Welfare State,* ed. Helena Mattsson and Sven-Olov Wallenstein. London: Black Dog Publishing, 2010.

Utredning med förslag angående behovet av åtgärder för främjande av verksamheten inom turisthotellnäringen. Stockholm: Handelsdepartementet and Svenska Turisttrafikförbundet, 1954.

Utterback, James M., and William J. Abernathy. "A Dynamic Model of Product and Process Innovation." *Omega* 3 (1975): 639–56.

van Elteren, Mel. *Americanism and Americanization: A Critical History of Domestic and Global Influence.* Jefferson, NC: McFarland & Co, 2006.

Varga-Harris, Christine. "Homemaking and the Aesthetic and Moral Perimeters of the Soviet Home during the Khrushchev Era." *Journal of Social History* 41 (2008): 561–89.

Verslag van het Congres inzake de toekomstige ontwikkeling van de vacantie-accommodatie in Nederland belegd op 10 december 1949 te Utrecht. The Hague: Centraal Werkcomité, 1949.

Volti, Rudi. "William F. Ogburn, Social Change with Respect to Culture and Original Nature." *Technology and Culture* 45 (2004): 396–405.

Wæver, Ole. "Nordic Nostalgia: Northern Europe after the Cold War." *International Affairs* 68 (1992): 77–102.

Wertheimer, Robert G. "The Miracle of German Housing in the Postwar Period." *Land Economics* 34 (1958): 338–45.

Wharton, Annabel Jane. *Building the Cold War: Hilton International Hotels and Modern Architecture.* Chicago: University of Chicago Press, 2001.

Wilde, Mark W. "Industrialization of Food Processing in the United States, 1860–1960." PhD diss., University of Delaware, 1988.

Wildt, Michael. *Am Beginn der 'Konsumgesellschaft': Mangelerfahrung, Lebenshaltung, Wohlstandshoffnung in Westdeutschland in den fünfziger Jahren.* Hamburg: Ergebnisse-Verlag, 1994.

Willard, Barbara E. "The American Story of Meat: Discursive Influences on Cultural Eating Practice." *Journal of Popular Culture* 36 (2002): 105–18.

Wittrock, Björn. "Modernity: One, None, or Many? European Origins and Modernity as a Global Condition." In *Multiple Modernities*, ed. Shmuel N. Eisenstadt. New Brunswick: Transaction Publishers, 2002.

Wolfe, Richard A. "Organizational Innovation: Review, Critique and Suggested Research Directions." *Journal of Management Studies* 31 (1994): 405–31.

Wright, Gwendolyn. "Good Design and 'The Good Life': Cultural Exchange in Post-World War II American Domestic Architecture." In *Across the Atlantic: Cultural Exchanges between Europe and the United States*, ed. Luisa Passerini. Brussels: P.I.E.-Peter Lang, 2000.

Zachmann, Karin. "A Socialist Consumption Junction: Debating the Mechanization of Housework in East Germany, 1956–1957." *Technology and Culture* 43 (2002): 73–99.

Zachmann, Karin. "Managing Choice: Constructing the Socialist Consumption Junction in the German Democratic Republic." In *Cold War Kitchen: Americanization, Technology, and European Users*, ed. Ruth Oldenziel and Karin Zachmann. Cambridge, MA: MIT Press, 2009.

Zachmann, Karin. "Atoms for Peace and Radiation for Safety – How to Build Trust in Irradiated Foods in Cold War Europe and Beyond." *History and Technology* 27 (2011): 65–90.

Zachmann, Karin. *Risky Rays for an Improved Food Supply? Transnational Food Irradiation Research as a Cold War Recipe.* Preprint 7. München: Deutsches Museum, 2013.

Zachmann, Karin, and Per Østby. "Food, Technology, and Trust: An Introduction." In "Food, Technology, and Trust," special issue. *History and Technology* 27 (2011): 1–10.

Zeitlin, Jonathan, and Gary Herrigel, eds. *Americanization and Its Limits: Reworking US Technology and Management in Post-War Europe and Japan.* Oxford: Oxford University Press, 2000.

Zurlo, Francesco. *Makio Hasuike.* Milan: Abitare Segesta, 2003.

Zweiniger-Bargielowska, Ina. *Austerity in Britain: Rationing, Controls, and Consumption, 1939–1955.* Oxford: Oxford University Press, 2000.

Index

Aanonsen Company 96, 98, 99, 100 Fig. 4.2, 101
Aars, Ferdinand 150
Abernathy, William J. 14, 132
advertising
  home freezing 98–9, 100 Fig. 4.2
  imagery in 47–8
Afdahl, Torbjørn 150
Agricultural Trade Development and Assistance Act 71
agriculture 76
  atomic science 79–80, 81 Fig. 3.3, 82
  farm income support programs 83
  fertilizers 10, 66, 71, 74, 78
  industrialized farming 68
  pesticides 74
air conditioners 31
air travel 179, 183–4
Akcan, Esra 40
Alasia, Franco 133
Alberoni, Francesco 133
Albert de la Bruhèze, Adri 9, 14, 107, 142, 157–77, 183, 196, 203
Alberto, Alesina 131
Aldrich, Thomas Bailey 54
Aly, Götz 40
American Century 18, 66
American design 5, 9–10, 11–12, 141, 142, 144, 145 Fig. 6.2, 146, 147 Fig. 6.3, 148
American kitchens 6, 19, 29–31
  appliances 30, 117–18
  kitchen debates 6, 34–5
  marketing 114–17
  as workplace 116–17
American New Woman 25
American-style tourism 158, 182–4, 185 Fig. 8.1, 186, 203–7
Americanization 1–2, 10, 17–19, 20, 113
  as creolized imaginary 45–64
  role of tourism 158
Andersen, Arne 42

Anderson, Oscar Edward 108
Andolf, Göran 198
Andrea, Ichino 131
Angeletti, Brunetta 132
Anrick, Calla 209, 210 Fig. 9.2
Anrick, Carl-Julius 209, 210 Fig. 9.2, 222, 227
appliances 19–20, 30
  kitchen 30, 117–18
Ariston 119
Arvidsson, Adam 133
Åselius, Gunnar 225–6
Associated Press 46
Association of Swedish Travel Agents 187, 188, 192
atomic science, in food and agriculture 79–80, 81 Fig. 3.3, 82
Atoms for Peace 70, 80, 82
Austigard, Bjørn 108
Authorization Council of Swedish Carriers and Travel Agencies 188
automobiles *see* motor cars
Avdem, Anna Jorunn 108
Avedon, Richard 47

Badino, Anna 133
Banfield, Edward 111, 131
Baranowski, Shelley 224
Barthes, Roland 47
Baudrillard, Jean 61, 64
Bauhaus 137
Beckers, Theo 174
Belasco, Warren James 15, 85
Belgium 144
  food irradiation research 80, 81 Fig. 3.3
  home ownership 28
  supermarkets 30
  tourism 176
Benjamin, Walter 63
Bercovitch, Sacvan 63

247

Berre, Nina 154
Betts, Paul 39, 43
Biacobone, Tersilla Faravelli 132
bicycle tourism 217
Bigazzi, Duccio 62
Bijker, Wiebe 107
Bjarnar, Ove 16
Bjerknes, Johan Christian 140 Fig. 6.1
Bjørnboe, Jens 134, 153, 154, 156
Blanck, Dag 227
Bluche, Lorraine 86
Blume, Mary 197
Boehling, Rebecca 41
Boel, Bent 86
Boissevain, Elisabeth 173, 174
Boks, J.W.C. 176
Bon Marché 22
Borghi, Giovanni 117
bourgeois tourism 201, 202 Fig. 9.1
  American challenge 203–7
  development of 207–9, 210 Fig. 9.2, 211
  modernization of 222–3
  see also hostel movement
Bowden, Sue 42
Brenna, Britta 107
Bretton Woods 37
Brinkley, Alan 15
Brochmann, Odd 138–9, 154
Brunetta, Gian Piero 131
Buck-Morss, Susan 40
Butlins holiday camps 161, 162 Fig. 7.1, 171

Calantone, Roger 14
camping centers 159–61, 162 Fig. 7.1, 163
canned goods 21, 126–7
Carbone, Cristina 42
cars *see* motor cars
Cartier-Bresson, Henri 46
Castillo, Greg 40, 42
Catterall, Claire 155
clothes dryers 31
Coca-Cola 17, 124, 130
Cohen, Jean-Louis 40
Cohen, Lizabeth 43
Cold War 4, 7, 28–9, 34, 45–64, 92, 113
  centrality of image 45–8

commercialism 142–4
Committee on Food Habits 69, 70
Conekin, Becky E. 40
consumer citizenship 36–8
consumer durables 30–1, 35
consumerism 11–12
  domestic 19–23, 30, 36–8
  Eastern Europe 34–6
  European response to 23–5
  Italy 120–4
  mass consumption 1–3, 8, 13, 17, 24, 25, 36, 37, 47–8, 60–1, 117, 134, 203
  consumption regimes 2–3, 8, 9–13, 14, 17, 18, 20, 21, 26, 32, 35, 37, 38, 47, 61, 66–7, 74, 78, 83, 84, 89, 90, 95, 105, 107, 112, 114, 134–5, 144, 153, 157–8, 173, 179–81, 184, 187, 189, 191, 193, 194–6
cosmopolitan domesticity 22
Cowan, Ruth Schwartz 89, 107, 116, 132
Crang, Mike 197
Cremonini, Luigi 127
creolization 45–64
  anti-American 57–8
  context of 51–2
  Statue of Liberty 52, 53 Fig. 2.1, 54–5, 56 Fig. 2.2, 57–8, 59 Fig. 2.3, 60–2
Cross, Gary 19, 39
Crossick, Geoffrey 39
Crowley, David 39, 40, 41
cuisine 21, 22, 67, 68, 69, 84
  Italian 124, 126–8, 129 Fig. 5.3
cultural lag 14, 69

Dahl, Birger 149
Darfler, June 110
Dauvergne, Peter 44
Davies, Alec 155
Davis, John 131
de Grazia, Victoria 1, 2, 13, 14, 22, 38, 42, 44, 49, 50, 62, 63, 107, 136, 154, 158, 173
de Joode, Ton 173
De Monchy, W.H. 163–4, 175
De Ruvo, Pascual 63
department stores 22

Index   249

Desrosier, Norman W.   80–1
dishonesty in American design   9, 146
dollar gap   157, 158, 161, 169, 183
dollar tourism   166, 200, 203
domestic consumerism   19–20, 30, 36–8
   pre-First World War   20–3
Domosh, Mona   21, 39
Douglas, Mary   84
Durth, Werner   41
Dutch Hotel Association   7, 163, 166, 169

Eames, Charles   137, 149
Eames, Ray   137
Eastern European consumerism   34–6
Eco, Umberto   61, 64
Economic Cooperation Agency (ECA)   161
Eisenhower, Dwight   70, 79, 82
Eisenstadt, Shmuel   14
Eliassen, Bjørg   101–2, 110
Ellwood, David   38, 131, 203, 225
Elsässer, Sophie   199
Emanuel, Martin   225, 226
Endrédi, Gustav   225
Endy, Christopher   172
Eskilsson, Lena   197, 224, 225
Europe
   alternative models   26–34
   response to American consumerism   23–5
   see also individual countries
European Nuclear Energy Agency   80
European Productivity Agency   74–6, 77 Fig. 3.2, 78–80, 87
European Recovery Program *see* Marshall Plan
European Society of Nuclear Agriculture   82

Falkman, Carl   226
Fallan, Kjetil   5, 9, 134–56
family values   111–12, 128
   hostel accommodation   219–20, 221 Fig. 9.4
   nuclear family   29
FAO *see* Food and Agriculture Organization
Fargas   122

Fegiz, Pierpaolo Luzzatto   133
Fenton, Faith   110
fertilizers   10, 66, 71, 74, 78
Filarski, Ruud   174
Findus   101
Finstad, Terje   12, 89–110
First World War   20–3, 67, 208
Fofi, Goffredo   133
Follesa, Stefano   132
food and agricultural technical information service (FATIS)   78
Food and Agriculture Organization (FAO)   82, 92
food chains
   cooperation and conflict   82–4
   Europe   68–9
   industrialization   68
   modernization   74
   regionality   67
food culture   111–14
Food for Peace Program   70–2, 73 Fig. 3.1, 83–4
foods   22, 29, 65–88
   atomic science   79–80, 81 Fig. 3.3, 82
   Fordist consumption   69–70
   frozen   12, 13, 89–110
   irradiation   80, 81 Fig. 3.3
   Italian   124, 126–8
   marketing   76–8
   nutrition technologies   92–3
   supermarkets   31–2
   see also cuisine
foodways   10, 65–88, 90
   European   74–8
Ford, Henry   25
Fordism   2, 17, 18, 22, 24, 37, 90, 145, 203
   in food consumption   69–70
   revolt against   139, 140 Fig. 6.1, 141–2, 146
   tourism   158
Forgacs, David   131–2
France
   Ministry of Reconstruction and Urbanism   26–7
   motor cars   21
Franklin, Adrian   197
Frederick, Christine   23
Freese, Arne   224
freezer-lockers   90, 91 Fig. 4.1, 92–4, 97

250 Index

freezing *see* home freezing
Freia 102
Fridenson, Patrick 62
Friedan, Betty 31
Friedmann, Harriet 85
Frigidaire 115, 119
Furlough, Ellen 107, 201, 224
Furre, Berge 109

Gabaccia, Donna 112, 131
Galbraith, John Kenneth 31
Garcia, Rosanna 14
Gardner, Alexander 47
Gassert, Philipp 16, 225
General Mills 4
Germany
  domestic consumerism 24, 33–4
  hostel movement 211, 214
  housing 28
  motor cars 21
  Nazi regime 25, 68
  Rationalization Curatorium for the German Economy 33
  Strength-Through-Joy movement 161
Geyer, Michael 16
Gidley, Mick 45, 62
Gifft, Helen H. 85
Giovagnoli, Agostino 131
Girard, Alexander 154
Glambek, Ingeborg 156
Gradina margarine 127–8, 129 Fig. 5.3
Grand Hotel Krasnapolsky 169, 176, 177
Grassl, Anton 226, 227
Greve, Knut 140–2, 147, 154
Grinell, Klas 198
Gronow, Jukka 40
Gropius, Walter 154
Guidi, Paola 132
Gundle, Stephen 131
Guthe, Carl 70
Gyllene Uttern Hotel 204

Haddow, Robert H. 15
Hald, Arthur 153–4, 156
Halén, Widar 156
Hamilton, Shane 16
Hammar, Thomas 226

Hanssen, Otto 103
Hargrove, June 63
Harris, Steven E. 41
Harsch, Donna 43
Hasuike, Makio 119
Heath, Graham 226
hegemony 49–51, 136
Heiberg, Bernt 156
Heineman, Elisabeth 43
Heinz ketchup 20
Hermansen, R.F. 96
Herrigel, Gary 14, 86
Hessler, Martina 39
Higham, John 54, 63
Hilck, Erwin 86
Hill, Stephen 44
Hine, Lewis 47
Hine, Thomas 136, 154
hitchhiking 217
Hitler, Adolf 25
Hixson, Walter L. 42
Hobsbawm, Eric 39
Hodgson, Godfrey 44
Hoganson, Kristin 39
Holder, Julien 42
holiday villages 159–61, 162
  Fig. 7.1, 163
Holland America Line 161, 167
Holm, Arne E. 140 Fig. 6.1
home freezing 12, 13
  advertising 98–9, 100 Fig. 4.2
  American influences 105–6
  effect on consumption 99, 101–2
  freezer as storehouse 100 Fig. 4.2, 106
  Italy 114–15
  Norway 89–110
  promotion of 102–3, 104 Fig. 4.3, 105
home-making and housewifery 22, 23, 24, 32–3, 40, 92, 93, 97, 98, 101, 103, 122
Horn, Adrian 13, 154
Horney, Nils 217–18, 227
hostel movement 201, 202 Fig. 9.1, 206, 211, 212–13 Fig. 9.3, 214–16, 218
  family accommodation 219–20, 221 Fig. 9.4

Index 251

hotels
 Dutch 167–70
 European 167–70
 Marshall hotels 162–3, 164
  Fig. 7.2, 165–7, 171
 motels 6–7, 204–5, 218
 see also individual hotels
household technology 30–1
housing 9–10, 23–4, 26–9
 design of 29
Hövel, Rudolf 86
Hufeisensiedlung 24
Huldt, Åke H. 142–3, 154
Hunter, Clarence E. 175
Hyrvang, Christine 107

IBM 4
Ignis 117
imagery
 Cold War 45–8
 European context 48–9
 Statue of Liberty 52–62
industrial design 134–56
 American 5, 9–10, 11–12, 141, 142, 144, 145 Fig. 6.2, 146, 147 Fig. 6.3, 148
 commercialism 142–4
 international relations 137–42
 Scandinavian 135–9, 148–50, 151 Fig. 6.4, 152
Industrial Revolution 67
industrialization 21
industrialized farming 68
infrastructure 12–13
intermediary actors 3, 7, 188
International Air Transport Association (IATA) 183
International Civil Aviation Organization (ICAO) 183
International Youth Hostel Federation (IYHF) 214
Iron Curtain 18
irradiated foods 80, 81 Fig. 3.3
irrelevance of American design 9
Isherwood, Baron C. 84
Italy 111–33
 Christian Democrats 113
 consumerism 120–4
 cultural context 128, 130–1

family values 111–12
food culture 111–14
foods 124, 126–8
 bouillon cubes and oils 127–8, 129 Fig. 5.3
 canned goods 126–7
kitchen design 113–17, 118 Fig., 119–24, 125 Fig. 5.2
motor cars 21

Jacobsen, Nils L.S. 103, 110
Jarausch, Konrad H. 16
Jaumain, Serge 39
Jefferson, Thomas 72, 86
Joehlin, Jennifer Ann 43
Johannessen, Wenche Anette 156
Johansson, Gotthard 150, 199
Judt, Tony 42, 44
Juhl, Finn 139–40, 154

Kahn, Louis 154
Kaiserfeld, Thomas 13, 178–98
Karl Marx Hof 24
Karlsson, Birgit 225
Karlsson, Ingela 197
Katzenstein, Peter J. 196
Kaufmann, Edgar Jr. 137, 140–1, 144–5, 149, 155
Kertzer, David I. 131
Keynesianism 37
Khrushchev, Nikita S. 6, 27, 34
Kilgannon, Corey 64
Kinsey, Jean D. 84
Kipping, Matthias 13, 16
Kirkvaag, Rolf 101, 105, 109, 110
kitchen appliances 30, 117–18
 see also home freezing; refrigerators
kitchen debates 6, 34–5
kitchens
 American see American kitchens
 Italian 113–17, 118 Fig. 5.1, 119–24, 125 Fig. 5.2
Kjellman, Hilding 208, 225
Klette, Leif 198
Knudsen, Ann-Christina L. 88
Kocka, Jürgen 202–3, 224
Kodak 20, 47
Korsmo, Arne 137–8, 145, 149, 154, 156

Korsmo, Grete Prytz 137–8, 149
Kotkin, Stephen 40
Krige, John 1, 13, 14
Kroes, Rob 14, 38, 45, 48, 51, 60, 62, 63
Kuisel, Richard F. 13–14
Kvaal, Stig 12, 89–110

language 50
Law, John 107
Lazarus, Emma 54
Le Corbusier 27
Lehmkuhl 101
leisure 6–7
Lévi-Strauss, Claude 85
Lewchuk, Wayne 62
Linders-Rooijendijk, Matea F.A. 173
Lindhagen, Arthur 200, 201–2, 206, 209, 210 Fig. 9.2, 222, 224
Lindström, Hugo 154
Löfgren, Orvar 43, 196
Logemann, Jan 14, 40
Lund, Oddvar 94
Lundberg, Mari 225
Lundestad, Geir 38, 50, 63
Lundin, Per 15, 16, 200–28

McDonald, Gay 155
McDonald's 17, 51
McGlade, Jacqueline 16, 86
McGovern, Charles 39
McGovern, George S. 71–2, 85, 86
McKenzie, Fred 20, 39
Maddison, Angus 39
Magnitogorsk 25
Maguire, Patrick 146, 155
Maier, Charles S. 86
mail order selling 22
Mansrud, Cato 150
Mapplethorpe, Robert 47
Marchand, Roland 62
Marjavaara, Roger 197
Market Empire 1
marketing 31–2
Marshall hotels 162–3, 164 Fig. 7.2, 165–7, 171
Marshall Plan 1, 4, 7, 10, 26, 27, 73, 92, 113, 134, 157, 160–1, 203

European foodways 74–8
mass consumption 1–3, 8, 13, 17, 24, 25, 36, 37, 47–8, 60–1, 117, 134, 203
mass production 17–19, 21, 24, 26, 37, 47, 50, 67–8, 138–40, 142, 144, 146–7, 152, 153
see also Fordism
Mattsson, Helena 196
May, Elaine Tyler 32
May, Ernst 23
Mazower, Mark 172
Mead, Margaret 70
Meikle, Jeffrey 15, 155
Meinander, Henrik 224
Melby, Kari 108
Merkel, Ina 43
Merloni, Aristide 119
Meyer, J.G. 166, 175
Meyerowitz, Joanne 43
middle-class tourism 162–3, 164 Fig. 7.2, 165–7, 171
Middleboe, Victor 87
Mies van der Rohe, Ludwig 154
Minestroni, Laura 133
modernity 7–8, 11, 13, 17–44
pre-First World War 20–3
Mom, Gijs 174
Monroe, Marilyn 52
Montaldi, Danilo 133
Morton, Henry W. 41
motels 6–7, 204–5, 218
see also hotels
motor cars 11, 21, 203–4, 216–17
car vagabonds 205
hitchhiking 217
hotel facilities 204
mass motorization 206
Muir and Mirrielees 22
Museum of Modern Art (MoMA) 46, 137, 141, 144, 146–7
Mykleburst, Sissel 107

neo-corporatism 180
neo-liberalism 37
Netherlands 30
Dutch Hotel Association 7, 163, 166, 169

Dutch hotels 167–70
Government Planning
 Service 159–60
Grand Hotel Krasnapolsky 169,
 176, 177
Marshall hotels 162–3, 164
 Fig. 7.2, 165–7, 171
Royal Dutch Airlines (KLM) 161
Royal Dutch Touring Club 8, 159
tourism 157–77
Netherlands National Tourist Office 166
New Deal 37
Nielsen, Niels Kayser 224
Nixon, Richard M. 6, 34–5
Nolan, Mary 2, 4–5, 14, 17–44
Norway
 collective ways of life 94–5
 Deep Freezing Office 101–2
 freezer-lockers 90, 91 Fig. 4.1,
  92–4, 97
 home freezing 95–105
 Mot Dag movement 92
 nutrition technologies 92–3
 State Research Institute of Home
  Economics (SRIHE) 92, 93,
  96, 101
 technology and knowledge
  imports 90, 91 Fig. 4.1, 92
Norwegian Dairy Cooperative 94
Norwegian Dream 106
Norwegian Frozen Fish 101, 102, 103
Norwegian Industrial Designers 136
Norwegian National Nutritional
 Council 93
nuclear family 29
nutrition technologies 92–3
Nuzzacci, Anna 132
Nye, David 5, 45–64

O'Dell, Tom 16
Offer, Avner 42
Offergaard, Ellen 108
Ogburn, William 14, 85
Oldenziel, Ruth 15, 39, 42, 132, 133,
 172, 173, 196
Organisation for European Economic
 Cooperation (OEEC) 73, 92,
 167, 170
Østby, Per 12, 88, 89–110

package tours 178–99
Packard, Vance 31
Page, Max 63
Pansera, Anty 132
Parks, Gordon 46
Parr, Joy 147, 155
Patel, Kiran Klaus 86
Pearce, Douglas C. 198
Pells, Richard 15, 155
Pence, Katherine 43
Pennell, Joseph 59 Fig. 2.3,
 60, 63
People's Capitalism 29
pesticides 74
Pettersen-Hagh, Niels W. 103,
 108, 109
Pfeifer, F.A. 176
Philadelphia Centennial
 Exposition 52, 53 Fig. 2.1
photography 45–64
 as art form 46
 Cold War 45–8
Pitkin, Donald S. 131
Pizzorno, Allesandro 133
plastics 147 Fig. 6.3
Poiger, Uta 40
Poland 72
popular music 51–2
populuxe 136
Porter, Jane M. 84
post-Fordism 2
postwar tourism 200–28
Poutsma, J.J. 176
poverty 30
Pozzy, Theo J. 164–6, 168, 175
process innovations 8–13
product innovations 8–13
productivity missions 92
Provoyeur, Pierre 63
Prytz, Toroff 148, 150, 151–2, 156

racism 25, 209
Ramskjær, Liv 155–6
Randall, Amy E. 40
Rantatalo, Petra 226
Rasmussen, Wayne D. 84
Reagan, Ronald 52
refrigerators 114–15
Reid, Susan E. 41, 43

254 Index

Remlov, Arne 143–4, 148, 150, 154, 156
Rice, Condoleezza 58
Ritzer, George 49, 63
Rocco, A. 132–3
Rodgers, Daniel T. 14, 38
Rome, Adam 42
Rosén, Göte 197
Rosén, Ulla 16
Rosenberg, Arne 198
Rosendorf, Neal Moses 172, 197
Rosselli, Alberto 155
Rostow, W.W. 203
Royal Dutch Airlines (KLM) 161
Royal Dutch Touring Club 8, 159
Royal Swedish Board of Civil Aviation 186
Ruble, Blair A. 41
Rudolph, Nicole 40, 41–2
Rydell, Robert W. 14, 51, 63
Rygh, Thorbjørn 144, 146, 154, 155

Saarinen, Eero 139
Sachse, Carola 40
Sahlins, Marshall 66, 84
Sandell, Klas 226
Saunes, Arthur 108
Saur-Jaumann, Eleonore 43
"scandalous tours" see Swedish package tours
Scandinavian Airlines System (SAS) 186
Scandinavian design 135–9
 promotion in USA 148–50, 151 Fig. 6.4, 152
Scarpellini, Emanuela 6, 43, 111–33
Schama, Simon 116, 132
Schipper, Frank 174, 197
Schlebeker, John T. 227
Schot, Johan 14, 107, 174
Schröter, Harm G. 14
Schumpeter, Joseph A. 14
Schütte-Lihotzky, Margarete 24, 25
Sears and Roebuck 22
Second World War 1, 13, 17, 50, 65, 159
Sehlin, Halvar 218, 222, 224, 227
self-sufficiency 68, 93, 98, 102
shallowness of American design 9
Shearer, J. Ronald 62

Sigfried, Giedion 85
Silverman, Sydel F. 131
Sinclair, Upton 68
Singer sewing machines 20, 21–2
Siraa, Theo 174
Smil, Vaclav 85
Smith, Eugene 46
social policy 36–8
socialism and consumerism 34–6
Sollers, Werner 54, 63
Sörlin, Sverker 226
Soviet Union see USSR
Spang, Rebecca L. 85
Spanish tourism 182
Staal, Peter Eloy 174
Stachura, Peter D. 226
Statue of Liberty 5
 creolization 52, 53 Fig. 2.1, 54–5, 56 Fig. 2.2, 57–8, 59 Fig. 2.3, 60–2
 images 54–5
 symbolism of 54
Stead, William 20
Steichen, Edward 46
Stenstadvold, Håkon 154
Stephan, Alexander 14, 38
Stichting, Wiardi Beckman 173
Stieglitz, Alfred 47
Stockholm Chamber of Commerce 188, 193
Strømmen Værksted 101
supermarkets 31–2
Sweden
 Association of Swedish Travel Agents 187, 188, 192
 Authorization Council of Swedish Carriers and Travel Agencies 188
 Royal Swedish Board of Civil Aviation 186
 Stockholm Chamber of Commerce 188, 193
 Travel and Holiday Organization of the Cooperative Movements in Sweden (Reso) 187
 Swedish Council for Passenger Transport Companies 188
 Swedish National Consumer Council 179, 189–90, 193, 194, 195

Swedish package tours 178–99
  1950s and 1960s 180–2
  consumer protection 189–94
  regulation of 186–9
Swedish postwar tourism 200–28
  development of 216–21
  hostel movement *see* hostel movement
  internationalization 216–17
  motor cars 219–20
  xenophobia 209, 216
Swedish Ski Association 208, 210, 220
Swedish Tourist Association 7, 11, 181, 200–28

Tannum, Per 148, 149, 156
Tappan 120
Taut, Bruno 23
Taylorism 25, 139, 145
  see also Fordism
Thévenot, Roger 108
Tiratsoo, Nick 13
Tjeder, David 224
Tooze, Adam 40
tourism
  air travel 179, 183–4
  American influences 158, 182–4, 185 Fig. 8.1, 186, 203–7
  bourgeois *see* bourgeois tourism
  camping centers and holiday villages 159–61, 162 Fig. 7.1, 163
  hostel movement *see* hostel movement
  hotels *see* hotels
  middle-class 162–3, 164 Fig. 7.2, 165–7, 171
  motor cars *see* motor cars
  Netherlands 157–77
  package tours 178–99
  postwar 200–28
  Sweden 178–99, 200–28
  working-class 162, 170
  tradition 139
Travel and Holiday Organization of the Cooperative Movements in Sweden (Reso) 187
Trentmann, Frank 43
Tynelius, Sven 225

UK, motor cars 21
United Nations 92
  FAO 82, 92
United Press International 46
United States Information Agency (USIA) 4, 26, 29, 46, 49, 144
urbanization 21, 67, 93, 112
USA
  images of 4–7
  kitchen debates 6, 34–5
  Market Empire 1
  motor cars 21
  Museum of Modern Art (MoMA) 46, 137, 141, 144, 146–7
  Philadelphia Centennial Exposition 52, 53 Fig. 2.1
  promotion of Scandinavian design 148–50, 151 Fig. 6.4, 152
  Statue of Liberty *see* Statue of Liberty
  Technical Assistance and Productivity Program 74
  see also entries under American
USSR
  consumerism 34–6
  domestic consumption 25
  food shortages 82
  housing 27
  kitchen debates 6, 34–5
  see also Cold War
Utterback, James M. 14, 132

Vachon, John 46
van Beelen, H. 176
van Elteren, Mel 38
Vanzina, Stefano 113
Varga-Harris, Christine 41
Vietnam War 57
Volkswagen 25
Volti, Rudi 85
von der Lippe, Jens 143, 154, 155

Wæver, Ole 198
Wagner, Martin 23
Waldenström, Erland 200, 201
Wallenstein, Sven-Olov 196
Walt Disney Company 4

Weber, Max 111
Werenskiold, Bergliot Qviller 92
Werkman, Gerard 177
Wertheimer, Robert G. 41
White, Margaret Bourke 46
Wilde, Mark W. 85
Wildt, Michael 42
Willard, Barbara E. 85
Wilson, M.L. 69
Wittrock, Björn 14
Wolfe, Richard A. 14
women 3, 19
  as consumers 25, 30, 32, 147
  cultural resistance of 127
  as home-makers 22–5, 32–3, 40, 92, 93, 97, 98, 101, 103, 116, 122–3
  image of 6, 32–3, 116
  middle-class 21, 22, 35
  societal role 113
  working 21, 120, 126
Workers' Travel Association 181
working-class tourism 159–61, 162
  Fig. 7.1, 163, 170
Wright, Frank Lloyd 154
Wright, Gwendolyn 42

xenophobia 209, 216

Yates, Paul Lamartine 82, 83, 85, 87, 88
youth hostels *see* hostel movement
Yugoslavia 72

Zachmann, Karin 10, 15, 39, 42, 65–88, 132
Zeitlin, Jonathan 14, 16, 86
Zweiniger-Bargielowska, Ina 16

The manufacturer's authorised representative in the EU is Springer Nature Customer Service Centre GmbH, Europaplatz 3, 69115 Heidelberg, Germany. If you have any concerns regarding our products, please contact ProductSafety@springernature.com

Printed and bound by CPI Group (UK) Ltd, Croydon, CR0 4YY

25/03/2026

02078232-0006